HAN...
and the Boys

HANSIE
and the Boys

The Making of the
South African Cricket Team

RODNEY HARTMAN

ZEBRA

ZEBRA

Published by Zebra Press
a division of Struik Publishers (Pty) Ltd
(a member of the Struik Publishing Group (Pty) Ltd)
32 Thora Crescent, Wynberg, Sandton

Reg. No.: 54/00965/07

First published in October 1997
Second impression December 1997
Third impression January 1998
Fourth impression February 1998

Editor Sandra Coelho
DTP Denise Meredith
Cover design Neels Bezuidenhout

Reproduction by Disc Express cc, Johannesburg
Printed and bound by National Book Printers, Drukkery Street, Goodwood, Western Cape

ISBN 1 86872 071 3

FOR EWIE CRONJÉ

Contents

'It is customary for the new boy, or at any rate the youth returning after a long absence, to tread warily upon his return, for the world may have changed, may have left its temporary exiles far behind...

'Yet, everywhere, the team was cheered.'

— PETER ROEBUCK, FORMER SOMERSET COUNTY CRICKETER AND CRICKET WRITER

Foreword

F AR FROM PRETENDING to be a definitive account of the most important decade in the history of South African cricket, this book merely sets out to trace the progress of a group of cricketers from their humble origins to their respective levels of distinction. It is a period that also happily coincides with the emergence and rise to prominence of the current South African captain, Hansie Cronjé.

The idea of a book came from Cronjé. He wanted one to mark his benefit season in 1997/98 but he did not want it to be just about himself. The result of our collaboration is *Hansie and the Boys*, a tribute to a fine band of cricketers and their captain in particular. It is also the story of a stirring transformation in the socio-political history of their country.

I am deeply indebted to Hansie for his co-operation during an especially hectic period in his life. Sincere thanks also go to the many players, officials and friends whose names appear in the text, and for the encouragement, patience and expertise of the excellent people of Zebra Press.

Of those who were willing to offer their advice and assistance, I am particularly grateful to Krish Mackerdhuj, Ali Bacher, Peter Pollock, Bob Woolmer, Mike Procter, Clive Rice, Jimmy Cook, Ewie Cronjé, Basil D'Oliveira, Jackie McGlew, Chris Day, Alan Jordaan, Edward Griffiths, Clifford Green, Fanie de Villiers, Andrew Hudson, Pat Symcox, Gary Kirsten, Jonty Rhodes, Corrie van Zyl, Marga Collings, Sandra Coelho and Tamsin Shelton. Also Andy Capostagno for inventing the now-famous 'frog-in-the-blender' analogy.

I also acknowledge with thanks the numerous sources of information that I drew on to research this book, chief among which were the *Wisden Cricketers' Almanack* under the editorship of Matthew Engel; the *Protea SA Cricket Annual* under the editorship of Colin Bryden; the Internet's cricket pages on the World Wide Web; *SA Cricket Action, SA Cricketer* and *SA Sports Illustrated* magazines; the major South African newspaper groups – Times Media Limited, Independent Newspapers and Nasionale Pers – and the television and radio stations that allowed me to follow those cricket matches that I could not attend in person.

To my wife, Carine, and my boys, Justin, Oliver and Scott, my love and affection for allowing me to spend many hours at those cricket matches I could attend ... and many more hours in the isolation of my work.

Rodney Hartman — *September 1997*

Prologue:
The Ultimate Healing

THE TELEPHONE WAS ringing. It was 6.30 am. Hansie Cronjé was in his hotel room, quietly planning ahead. The next day he was due to lead his country in a limited-overs international against England at Kingsmead. South Africa were already 3–1 up in the best-of-seven series, and the captain knew that one more win would give them an unassailable lead. They could not afford to allow England back into contention.

The intrusive ring of the telephone rudely interrupted the young man's thoughts as he sat silently in his hotel room high above the slumbering beachfront.

The caller was Ali Bacher.

The managing director of the United Cricket Board of South Africa (UCBSA) regularly began his working day at the crack of dawn. It was not unusual for him to make early morning telephone calls. Cronjé listened carefully to what Bacher had to say. He realised that all his diligent planning for the day ahead would come to nought. In the life of a modern-day international cricket captain there was no predicting what might happen next. He had quickly learned that the responsibilities of a captain neither began nor ended on the field of play. It was a busy and sometimes burdensome life not easily appreciated or even understood by the rank and file.

Bacher's instructions were simple but they would complicate his plans. Cronjé was to catch the 10 am plane to Johannesburg. In the arrivals hall he was to look out for a man he had never met before. He would recognise him by the tell-tale blazer he was wearing, the one bearing the badge of the Worcestershire County Cricket Club.

Cronjé had seen many photos of the man before, so it was not as if he were entirely in the dark. He felt confident he would recognise Basil D'Oliveira.

It probably did not cross Cronjé's mind that D'Oliveira would have no difficulty in recognising him either. The young man's face turned heads wherever he went, photographs of him were constantly in the papers and, in the midst of an international series, he was on television for days at a time. D'Oliveira had been in South Africa for several weeks now. Shortly before Cronjé's flight touched down from Durban, D'Oliveira's had come from Cape Town where he had been visiting family and old friends, and watching the cricket.

Once the mutual recognition had taken place and the introductions been made, Cronjé continued to follow Bacher's instructions. Through the bustling arrivals hall of Johannesburg International Airport he led his silver-haired companion to the car-hire ranks. From there they headed to the offices of the United Cricket Board at the Wanderers Club in the northern suburbs of Johannesburg to rendezvous with Bacher and the UCBSA president, Krish Mackerdhuj, before continuing on their journey.

On the morning of 16 January 1996, the hired car proceeded down the M1 motorway, on to the Ben Schoeman highway and northwards to Pretoria. Cronjé was driving, D'Oliveira was in the passenger seat, and the two high-ranking cricket officials were seated behind them. They were going to lunch with the president of the Republic of South Africa.

TALK IN THE CAR was nothing more than idle chatter about the cricket; it bore no testimony to the important assignment of that summer's day.

It had no bearing on an event that had taken place some 27 years before – an episode so well documented, so lamented, so confusing and hurtful as to make it the single most damaging event in the history of South African sport. As the four men headed towards Pretoria, and the president's residence, there was no reference at all to the so-called 'D'Oliveira Affair' of 1968. It was as if it had never happened, a mere mirage.

THE ROUTE TOOK them past a small and modern dormitory town. It had recently changed its name from Verwoerdburg to Centurion, but it had not yet shed all its original trappings. The main arterial route off the highway was clearly marked 'John Vorster Drive', and the name 'Verwoerdburg' could still be seen on the signposts flashing by.

Behind the steering wheel, Cronjé had a sudden urge to push the car harder, even if it meant breaking the speed limit. The young man appreciated the irony of the names that were boldly emblazoned on the highway direction boards. By his own admission, he felt a little uncomfortable.

Hendrik Verwoerd, the first prime minister of the Republic of South Africa, is widely acknowledged as the architect of grand apartheid. His successor, John Vorster, was the man who, in 1968, publicly declared that Basil D'Oliveira, a Cape coloured who had relocated to England, would not be welcome as a member of the MCC team that was due to play in South Africa later that year. It was the likes of Dr Verwoerd that had driven D'Oliveira away from the land of his birth to seek cricketing fame in a foreign country. It was Mr Vorster who had made it plain that he was not welcome to come back and play against South Africa's all-white team.

A car bearing D'Oliveira was now heading past bold monuments to the memory of these politicians *en route* to an official meeting with the republic's new head of state, a man who had been imprisoned for his illegal political activities and held for 27 years by the regimes of Verwoerd and Vorster.

The irony escaped the attention of none of the occupants of the car; for Hansie Cronjé, it meant even more.

HIS HANDS FIRMLY set on the steering wheel and his eyes focused on the road ahead, Cronjé was thinking back to his primary school days in Bloemfontein and his best friend, John Vorster Kolver, a grandson of the then prime minister. Cronjé recalled how he had once asked the premier for his autograph when Vorster attended a school prize-giving function. This was many years after the D'Oliveira Affair; in fact, Cronjé had not even been born when the infamous event took place.

In those primary school days in Bloemfontein, the young Hansie was carelessly naïve of the intricate designs of National Party politics. He would not have known the rights or wrongs of the system; he would have had no inkling of the cause and effects of apartheid and of the international outcry it gave rise to. He had never heard of Basil D'Oliveira and, neither for that matter, of Nelson Mandela. He was just another fun-loving Free State kid with an aptitude for playing sport.

As they drove past Verwoerdburg and John Vorster Drive Cronjé consciously tried to divert the attention of his distinguished passenger. He felt an irritating embarrassment about events over which he had had no control and for which he most certainly was not accountable.

In drawing D'Oliveira into conversation on more mundane subjects, he hoped the old cricketer would not notice the signposts of the past or the awkwardness in the car. At the same time, Cronjé could only wonder at the bizarre chain of events that had driven men from their homeland and sent others to jail; how this had finally been broken and miraculously recast to signal a fresh start. Cronjé's philosophy was that life's journeys always came full circle, and recent events in South Africa, including the one he was now experiencing, clearly illustrated this belief.

In the unfinished business of South African cricket, therefore, the ultimate healing was about to take place.

IT WAS IN 1955 that English journalist, author and broadcaster John Arlott first heard of Basil D'Oliveira. Word came to him in a letter from Bennie Bansda, a barman and freelance journalist in Cape Town, who explained how this coloured cricketer was fast making a name for himself and was anxious to further his career in England. He had first played for the non-white Western Province team at the age of 16 and, aged 23, had scored 45 centuries, including one innings of 225 out of his team's total of 236. As a bowler, he had once taken nine wickets for two runs. Could Mr Arlott perhaps help?

Arlott tried, but in vain. As he later confessed, 'What chance could there be for a young coloured South African without the price of his passage; who had played only in minor cricket; had never faced anyone of known quality and who would have no backing – rather the reverse – from the cricket authority of his own country which was recognised by Lord's?'[†]

D'Oliveira himself started writing to Arlott, but still the great man could not help. 'Mentions in a newspaper column and in broadcasts provoked no response. Direct questions on the fringe of official circles – a grant or scholarship? – produced only sad smiles; of course these people did not play real cricket...'

D'Oliveira's letters did not stop, always polite, always enquiring, always hopeful. Year after year they arrived. Arlott continued trying. There was nothing doing.

Back in South Africa, D'Oliveira continued to impress. Under his captaincy in 1958, a non-white South African team toured Kenya where he achieved a batting average of 46 and a bowling average of under 12 runs for each of his 25 wickets. A year later a team of English professionals played a series of matches in South Africa and, when they returned home, they spoke highly of a Cape coloured cricketer named D'Oliveira. They said he was a fine and gifted all-rounder.

Armed with this information, Arlott tried again. It was 1960. He returned to a man he had been pestering without success for several years, an agent who signed up cricketers for clubs in the Lancashire leagues. Back came the response.

It was no different than before. There was still no chance of D'Oliveira securing a contract. Arlott knew he would have to bring himself to write to D'Oliveira one final time. He would have to tell him that he should give up all hope of ever playing cricket in England. Then it happened.

[†] John Arlott, *John Arlott's Book of Cricketers: 25 Favourites — Past and Present*, Sphere Books Limited, London 1982.

The Middleton Club in the Central Lancashire League had a problem. They had been negotiating with the West Indian fast bowler Wesley Hall, but at the eleventh hour the deal fell through. They were suddenly without a professional and the 1960 season was about to begin. If Basil D'Oliveira were still available, they would be happy to have him. The salary would be £450 for the season.

So Arlott did write his final letter, but its message was far different to the one he had originally intended. It said simply, 'If you ever want to come, you must come now.'

BASIL D'OLIVEIRA MADE a nightmarish start to his new career in England. He was far from home in a strange environment: the cold and wet of Lancashire meant that conditions for playing cricket were totally foreign to him and, at the age of 28, he was mixing with white people on an equal footing for the first time. 'After just a few days in the nets, I realised I knew nothing about this game. I had been used to hitting the ball as far as possible and expecting a fast bowler to try to knock my block off. I had never seen the ball swing through the air before and didn't have a clue how to play from the back foot on slow, wet wickets. I was through with my shot far too early with the ball going straight up in the air. I was a novice, and everyone knew it.'[†]

In his first five matches for Middleton D'Oliveira scored a total of 25 runs. Utterly dejected, embarrassed and homesick, he was on the point of signalling a meek surrender and returning to the Cape and his pregnant wife, Naomi, when suddenly his cricketing fortunes turned. Eric Price, an old pro at Middleton and a former Lancashire and Essex county bowler, took him aside. 'Wait and relax,' he advised, 'the weather will get better and the wickets harder. Till then you've got to wait for the ball to come to you and work it away off the back foot. Also your bowling is far too short. Pitch it up. If you keep dropping it short, they'll murder you.'

Receiving such unsolicited counsel from a hardened veteran made a big impression on D'Oliveira. Until then he had felt alone in his plight and decidedly inferior in the company of more established cricketers in this strange white man's world. It inspired him to concentrate much harder in the nets and to work out ways, based on Price's advice, to adjust his technique to the tricky demands of English cricket. In his next match he scored 78, and by the end of the season he was top of the batting averages for the Central Lancashire League. In second place was Garfield

---

[†] D'Oliviera, Basil, *Time to Declare*, Macmillan, London 1980

Sobers, who two years before had hit the world record Test score of 365 not out for West Indies against Pakistan at Kingston, Jamaica.

Five years later D'Oliveira played his first County Championship match for Worcestershire.

It was against Essex, and he scored 106 and 47. He was now into his thirty-fourth year, although he had disguised his birth date to give the impression he was several years younger. Despite the fact that he had never believed himself capable of playing first-class cricket in the County Championship, he had been persuaded to join Worcestershire by one of England's finest Test batsmen, Tom Graveney, who had become a great admirer of his. They had played together in a number of exhibition matches for star-studded Invitation XIs that sought out D'Oliveira's services after his early successes with Middleton. It was Graveney who first suggested that D'Oliveira might one day play for England. The humble man from the Cape merely laughed at the thought.

In 1966, having become a naturalised British citizen, Basil D'Oliveira was selected by England to play the West Indies. In his second and third Tests he made consecutive scores of 76, 54 and 88 against the world's most feared fast-bowling attack of Wesley Hall and Charlie Griffith. His 88 at Leeds included eight fours and four sixes. A fairy tale had come true in one of cricket's most remarkable rags-to-riches stories. In the words of John Arlott, 'the impossible' had been achieved.

By August 1968, 'Dolly' had played 16 Tests for England, scored two centuries and seven half-centuries for an average of around 50, and had taken 18 wickets with his medium-paced bowling. His game, however, had fallen away sharply during the previous winter season when he played a poor series in the West Indies and could total only 137 runs in eight innings. Still, when the Australians arrived in England in 1968, he was unlucky to be dropped after the first Test at Old Trafford in which he scored an undefeated 87 in the second innings of a beaten cause.

For the final Test at The Oval, however, he made the most of his eleventh hour recall when Roger Prideaux fell ill. He scored 158 and took a vital wicket late on the final afternoon, allowing England to win with six minutes to spare and tie the series.

It could not have come at a better time for him because the MCC (England) team was about to be selected for a tour of South Africa later that year.[†]

[†] At the time England cricket teams toured abroad as the Marylebone Cricket Club (MCC).

THE DAY AFTER the Oval triumph, Basil D'Oliveira was back playing for his county against Sussex at Worcester. Having completed a carefree century, he deliberately surrendered his wicket so that he could be in the dressing room in time to hear the BBC's 6 pm radio news. In the meantime, Graveney had gathered the county's players in the pavilion to listen to the announcement of England's touring party.

The Worcestershire skipper was preparing the celebrations for his friend and team-mate. He was certain that Dolly would get a tour to South Africa and thus become a greater inspiration for his fellow non-white countrymen. A hush fell over the gathering as the radio was turned up in anticipation of the announcement. The names were duly read out by Brian Johnston, the BBC's cricket correspondent. Basil D'Oliveira's was not among them.

The gathering was dumbfounded. Graveney turned to Dolly. He could see the pain and disbelief in the man's eyes. The big captain put his arm around his friend and led him into a private room.

D'Oliveira broke down and sobbed. 'The stomach has been kicked out of me,' was all he could say.

As the embarrassed Worcestershire players stood around speechless and angry, they probably remembered that in January 1967, anticipating D'Oliveira's likely selection for the 1968 tour, South Africa's Minister of the Interior, Piet le Roux, had objected to the cricketer being sent to play in the republic. In a leading article, *The Guardian* responded: 'The secretary of the MCC has said that the matter will be dealt with "when it arises". He evades the issue. The matter has arisen already and should be dealt with now. The MCC should tell Mr Le Roux that England will not tour South Africa in 1968 unless he withdraws his ban on D'Oliveira...'

Now, of course, there was no such matter to be dealt with. D'Oliveira had been omitted from the 16-man MCC party on what the selectors swore were purely cricketing grounds. They reasoned that they had considered him only as a specialist batsman because his bowling was not penetrative enough; as such, they could find no place for him in the side.

The secretary of the MCC, S.C. Griffiths, announced that 'nothing else was discussed at the selectors' meeting other than cricketing considerations'.

There were many well-documented cases of 'certainties' being left out of MCC touring teams before, but D'Oliveira's omission created an uproar that went far beyond the bounds of the game. As Arlott wrote in *The Guardian,* 'For the other cricketers eligible for selection, this was simply another tour. For D'Oliveira it was the peak of ambition for himself and his people ... people to whom this must seem the ultimate betrayal.'

Yet the matter was far from over. In fact, it had only just begun.

A FORTNIGHT AFTER the selection controversy, one of the England fast bowlers, Tom Cartwright, broke down through injury and informed the selectors that he would not be available to tour South Africa. The committee met again. They announced that D'Oliveira would go after all; that a 'specialist batsman' was now being named to replace a fast bowler did not go unnoticed. The irony was soon pointed out to those in political power in South Africa.

A day later Prime Minister John Vorster arrived in Bloemfontein to address a National Party congress. He used the platform that September night in 1968 to announce to a cheering throng that his government would not accept the new MCC team which was being 'thrust upon South Africa by the anti-apartheid movement'. D'Oliveira, he said, was 'a political football'.

The announcement spelled the end of the tour, the end of Dolly's dream to play Test cricket in South Africa and, in a short space of time, the total isolation of South African cricket.

D'Oliveira handled the most agonising period of his life with the utmost dignity. At the time he was totally confused by it all – a cricketer, after all, who had only tried his best – but later he said, 'I understand that Vorster was facing a revolt within his National Party from the rightwing anti-liberal element and he clearly felt he had to clamp down to assert his authority. The game of cricket gave him that opportunity.'

It also gave the world the *cause célèbre* to seek the total expulsion of South Africa from international cricket. This would take a little longer to achieve, and in the meantime D'Oliveira would continue to represent England in the Test arena. There were further centuries: against Pakistan in Dacca, Australia in Melbourne, and New Zealand in Christchurch. When his Test career finally ended in 1972, the man who ousted him from the England side was another South African-born all-rounder named Tony Greig. All in all D'Oliviera had played 44 Tests for England, scoring 2 484 runs and taking 47 wickets.

AS THE HIRED car drew closer to the president's residence, the two men sitting side by side in the back seat chatted amiably about this and that.

At the time of the D'Oliveira Affair the captain-elect of South Africa was a 26-year-old medical doctor named Aron Bacher. He was a fine top-order batsman, fieldsman and tactician who had been appointed captain of Transvaal at the age of 21. He was known as Ali, and was a member of a Jewish family who lived in the middle-class Johannesburg suburb of Yeoville. He had completed his schooling at King Edward VII School, renowned as a nursery of top sportsmen, before going on to the University of the Witwatersrand to study medicine. In the context of South African society at the time, he was a privileged young man.

In 1968, Krish Mackerdhuj was a 29-year-old analytical chemist at the petroleum refineries in Durban. Highly educated, he held a B.Sc. in Zoology and Chemistry, and for a time had taught Maths, Physics and Biology at high school. In the overall setting of South African cricket, he was a virtual unknown outside his segregated Asiatic community. He lived in a township near Durban called Overton, and played for the Crimson Cricket Club. This club fell under the Natal Cricket Board, whose national parent body, the South African Cricket Board of Control (SACBOC), represented the interests of mainly coloured and Asiatic cricketers in South Africa. Between 1958 and 1963 he studied at the University College of Fort Hare in the town of Alice in the Eastern Cape. It was there that he became highly politicised. Fort Hare had long been the spiritual home, academically speaking, of the African National Congress. In the eyes of its detractors, it was a hotbed of black political fervour.

In the context of South African society, Mackerdhuj might also have been described as a privileged young man but, in reality, he was classified as a second-class citizen who did not have the vote.

The outrage of the D'Oliveira Affair had the effect of galvanising political opinion against South Africa. Yet, before the ever-tightening grip of international sanctions could become complete, Ali Bacher would realise his dream of captaining the Springboks. Against an Australian team under Bill Lawry that toured the republic in the summer of 1969/70, Bacher led a team that might well have been the finest white South Africa had ever put into the cricket field. This was the side of Barlow and Goddard, of Barry Richards, and Graeme and Peter Pollock, of Mike Procter, Lee Irvine, Denis Lindsay and Tiger Lance. They crushed Australia in all four Test matches but, although they might have sensed it, none could have known for sure that this was the last official series any of them would play. Scheduled tours to England in 1970 and to Australia in 1971/72 were subsequently cancelled, and the ostracism of South African cricket was complete.

On 25 September 1969, just more than three months before the arrival of Lawry's Australians in South Africa, a second son was born to Ewie and San-Marie Cronjé in Bloemfontein. They christened him Wessel Johannes, but he was always known as Hansie.

IN THE YEARS ahead, the cricket establishment would lament the fact that the Test careers of so many wonderful young cricketers had been cut short so cruelly. Sadly, however, the plight of the non-white cricketers of South Africa who were denied the chance of even attempting to play Test cricket was often overlooked. Was D'Oliveira the only coloured good enough to make his mark in the international game, and why did he have to leave the country of his birth and travel halfway round the world to prove it? Perhaps he too was a privileged young man, although his friends, led by Cape Town barman Benny Bansda, had to pass the hat around in order to collect his airfare to England. Fund-raising matches were organised on his behalf in 1960, and a number of white cricketers also rallied to the cause. Krish Mackerdhuj himself featured in special benefit matches organised by SACBOC on behalf of a man who, they felt, could convey the plight of non-white sportsmen to the world at large.

As time went by, D'Oliveira concentrated his efforts on becoming a good professional cricketer, while Bacher and Mackerdhuj, in the role of administrators, took up diametrically opposed positions across the flawed chessboard of cricket's administration.

IN SEPTEMBER 1977 the world of cricket was abuzz with news of the Kerry Packer revolution in the international game. South Africa found itself on the outside looking in as dozens of the world's top cricketers defected from the establishment to throw in their lot with Packer's rebel World Series Cricket (WSC) operation in Australia. Top South African players seized the offer of lucrative Packer contracts. Among those who saw this as a means to play a kind of international cricket again were Graeme Pollock, Eddie Barlow, Barry Richards, Mike Procter, Clive Rice, Garth le Roux and Denys Hobson. South Africa had nothing better to offer them, so they went. Two of them, Pollock and the wrist spinner Hobson, were subsequently ruled out because, unlike the other South Africans, they did not play county cricket in England. This was used against them by the governments of the black cricketing nations West Indies, India and Pakistan, who forbade their WSC professionals from playing against cricketers based only in South Africa.

Amid this bewildering logic, another convoluted series of developments was taking place in South Africa. It involved the disbanding of certain long-standing cricket bodies and the establishment of others in their place. It signalled hope for some, despair for others and further polarisation in the ranks of the game.

Up until September 1977, the white cricketers of South Africa were represented by the South African Cricket Association (SACA), and black, coloured and Asiatic cricketers by SACBOC and the lesser publicised South African African Cricket Board (SAACB). The president of the hardline and high-profile SACBOC was a prominent Johannesburg businessman named Rashid Varachia. It became apparent, however, that he was a conciliatory man with a devoted following and, after protracted and delicate talks with the white SACA, it was agreed that the two bodies would merge. The SAACB was also persuaded to come to the party, and the multi-racial South African Cricket Union (SACU) was born on 18 September 1977, with Varachia as its first president. His steering committee included another former SACBOC 'dove' named Frank Brache. He was Basil D'Oliveira's brother-in-law.

Under the heading 'One Body at Last', the *SA Cricket Annual* of that year hailed the formation of the new, unified body, suggesting that 'with the cricket administration in South Africa now sorted out, those who rule the game overseas must surely start thinking seriously about South Africa's re-entry into Test cricket. After all, the official calendar of events calls for a tour of England by South Africa in 1980...'

Furthermore, said the *Annual,* the new body would carry with it the best wishes of all sincere cricket lovers, 'even though it goes into action in the knowledge that there are still some dissidents who apparently would be satisfied only if certain conditions were met which are beyond the powers of any cricket administrative body to arrange.'

These unnamed dissidents, so lightly dismissed, included one Krish Mackerdhuj. The president of the Natal Cricket Board, he was one of the SACBOC 'hawks' who refused to follow Varachia and the other 'sellouts' across the floor. In November 1977, the SACBOC hardliners formed a new body called the South African Cricket Board (SACB) in defiant opposition to Varachia's SACU. The president of the new SACB, Hassan Howa, was also in charge of the South African Council on Sport (SACOS) that preached total non-co-operation until apartheid had been completely dismantled.

While this was all going on, Ali Bacher became vice-chairman of the new SACU-aligned Transvaal Cricket Council. He and Mackerdhuj were therefore as far apart as the North and South Poles, and the squares of the chessboard on which they were positioned were, in the overall context of their divided country, clearly demarcated as white and black.

The multi-racial SACU was adamant it was no longer playing on the white squares; it believed the September merger had coloured the entire board grey. The SACB was angered by critics who insisted it was only playing on the black squares. Its view was that, as a non-racial body in defiance of the apartheid system, it was already playing grey.

Claiming to be the single official controlling body for cricket in South Africa, the SACU embarked on annual pilgrimages to the International Cricket Council (ICC) at Lord's in London to advance a case for re-entry into international cricket. It argued with justification that it could not change the laws of the country but that it was playing and administering the game on a non-discriminatory basis. It pointed out that black cricketers could now become qualified on merit and were already playing for some provincial teams under its banner.

The SACB presented a forceful counter-argument. With equal justification it asked how a black cricketer could be allowed to play alongside white cricketers one minute and then be forced to bow to the apartheid laws the next. What kind of society required cricketers to carry permits to allow them to play on whites-only grounds, but could not guarantee them the right to mix freely with their team-mates in whites-only pubs after the close of play?

On moral grounds such questions could not be faulted, but the majority of South African sportswriters could not be persuaded that the SACB was anything but a political organisation that did not care for sport. They might have done well to heed the words of Arlott when he wrote at the time of the D'Oliveira Affair, 'The final argument of those who live within the boundaries of the cricket field is that politics should not be allowed to intrude upon cricket. They must, however, recognise that the totalitarian countries have employed sport for prestige purposes and that racial problems, in cricket or elsewhere, are political problems which must be faced politically.'

The SACB continued to declare its commitment to non-racialism, and steadfastly refused to join any multi-racial alliance. It was at the forefront of a campaign to force the ICC not to accept the SACU as the representative body of cricket in South Africa. In keeping with the dictum of Howa's SACOS, the SACB armed itself with the slogan, 'No normal sport in an abnormal society'.

In 1984, Mackerdhuj succeeded Howa as SACB president. The Durban scientist was regarded as more of a hardliner than his predecessor, and he set out with missionary zeal to bolster the campaign to deny the SACU its much sought-after recognition abroad.

Bacher by this stage had risen through the Transvaal Cricket Council and was the SACU's first managing director. Each time he went to London with the annual, ill-fated SACU mission, he found the doors barred at Lord's. The ICC maintained that, until such time as there was one unified body governing cricket in the republic, it could not entertain any claims for membership by any of the current 'representative bodies'. In effect, the SACB had won the war, but the battles raged on.

When, in desperation, the SACU embarked on a revolutionary course of action – largely masterminded by Bacher in the 1980s – to bring rebel international tours to South Africa, Mackerdhuj and the SACB went to war. In spite of their protestations, however, the SACU had its way and the tours went on. Teams from England, Sri Lanka, West Indies and Australia gave sports-starved white South Africa a taste of international competition.

The bubble finally burst in the summer of 1989/90 when Mike Gatting led the second English rebel team to South Africa. Whereas the previous tours were largely the subject of protests abroad, the Mass Democratic Movement in South Africa came out in force amid the looming new political dispensation. For the first time mass demonstrations took place on South African sporting soil. Bacher, like Saul on the road to Damascus, tuned in to the mood and grievances of the anti-tour forces and saw the need for total change.

In a decision opposed by many of his colleagues, he became instrumental in aborting the tour before it was complete and, in a subsequent signed article in a national Sunday newspaper, he wrote eloquently of his vision for South African cricket, promising that the rebel tours were over. It was this article that persuaded Mackerdhuj's SACB to join the SACU for round-table talks aimed at possible unification.

In September 1990 at a meeting in Durban, Ali Bacher and Krish Mackerdhuj met for the first time. The chairman was Steve Tshwete, a high-ranking member of the ANC, one of the political organisations that had been unbanned by President F.W. de Klerk the previous February. Tshwete, once imprisoned with Mandela on Robben Island, was the facilitator for unity in South African cricket. From the position of sworn enemies, Mackerdhuj, Bacher and their colleagues were able to join hands.

As a small but highly significant part of the incredible changes that took place in South Africa in 1990, cricket's once-warring parties were now able to unite under the banner of the United Cricket Board of South Africa (UCBSA). There were no recriminations, no reprisals, no reopening of old wounds. These men were simply driven by a desire to put the past behind them and forge a new future for the game in keeping with their shared vision. Allies six years later, Bacher and Mackerdhuj were driving to Pretoria for an important engagement.

THE OLD WOUNDS in South African cricket went deeper than was generally known. Basil D'Oliveira, ironically, was not always a hero among his own people. To the contrary, he was held to be a 'stooge' and a 'sellout' by many coloured South Africans who suffered under apartheid. This was a view widely embraced by many officials of the SACB whose allegiance lay with the banned ANC of Nelson Mandela.

They maintained that D'Oliveira had failed to take a tough enough stand on sporting relations with South Africa. They believed he should have used his position in England to discourage his fellow players from having any dealings whatsoever with white South Africa. They were incensed that he did not do so, and that he had always taken a soft line in dealing with the South African question.

They were also angered when he once suggested that, although he admired and respected Hassan Howa, he felt the man was too rigid in his outlook. Whereas the non-white cricket constituency had once rejoiced at Dolly's cricketing deeds in England, an influential section of it later turned on him with a vengeance. In short, they told him that he was no longer welcome back home. When he paid the occasional visit to South Africa, they believed he showed little interest in his own community.

Even when the United Cricket Board of South Africa celebrated its formation with a gala banquet on 29 June 1991, during which the old SACU and SACB officials came together as one and the likes of Bacher and Mackerdhuj embraced the new vision, the most glaring omission from the guest list that momentous night was the name D'Oliveira. This was not an oversight; it was a deliberate statement of intent from the old SACBOC 'hawks'.

Perhaps Basil D'Oliveira was too much of a professional sportsman whose naïvety could not embrace the cause and effect of events that were raging in the world outside the narrow confines of the English game. Perhaps he had been away from South Africa far too long to fully appreciate the iniquities of its political system.

Whatever the case, D'Oliveira was clearly victimised by both the system of apartheid and its opponents. It is said he became a bitter man in later years when all the grim realities began to sink in, but it is to his everlasting credit that not once during the nightmares of 1968 did he show any bitterness for the harsh treatment meted out to him by an uncaring world.

WHEN BASIL D'OLIVEIRA returned to South Africa to watch the cricket in the summer of 1995/96, the UCBSA made a telling gesture. They invited him to be their guest in the VIP enclosure at Newlands on the first day of the fifth Test match against England.

When he arrived that day, in the blazer of the Worcestershire County Cricket Club, he was warmly welcomed. Krish Mackerdhuj took him by the hand, and in three words put years of unhappiness behind them: 'Welcome home, Dolly.'

At lunch that day, 2 January 1996, they made a special presentation to him. He was very emotional.

Exactly two weeks later, five men sat down to lunch at the president's residence in Pretoria. Hansie Cronjé observed the event with avid appreciation. In examining the turbulent and tragic history of his country, he knew where they all came from, these five men of like mind – Xhosa, Afrikaner, Jew, Asiatic and Cape coloured. He saw the tears in D'Oliveira's eyes as the old cricketer shook hands with Mandela. He believes he heard him say this was the greatest day of his life. He knew the healing was now complete, and he was not surprised, not even one bit, that at no stage throughout that day did anyone even mention an event that was called the D'Oliveira Affair.

MIKE ATHERTON HAD led his team into South Africa almost four months earlier, the first one to come from England with official status since Mike Smith's side 31 years before. Much was expected of them because earlier in 1995 they had shared a home Test series with the West Indies and had beaten them in the one-day international series. By the end of the tour, however, England's position in the pecking order of world cricket would be cruelly re-examined. But before that happened they would participate in the making of history by becoming the first touring team to play a first-class cricket match in Soweto.

It was a glorious three days of cricket and colour, all African pomp and ceremony. Even President Mandela curtailed an important meeting in the city to announce peremptorily that he was going to the cricket. At very short notice, following one nervous telephone call to the ground by his personal spokesman, the nation's leader arrived unscheduled at the Soweto Cricket Oval, once the site of a vast rubbish tip. He was escorted on to the field to meet the players, causing the drinks interval on the first morning to go on for half an hour. No one much cared, for the sight of the tall and statuesque white-haired man rubbing shoulders with so many admirers encompassed the very reason England was playing cricket in South Africa again.

Cronjé was the captain of the South African Invitation XI that played out a draw with England in Soweto. He scored an entertaining 50 in the first innings, drawing wild whoops of delight from the township youngsters and their mums and dads when he struck left-arm spinner Richard Illingworth for a three-ball sequence of 6, 4, 4. The Invitation XI was a fine mix of experience and youth from all sections of the cricketing community, and included a stylish left-handed batsman from Soweto, Geoffrey Toyana, and an impressive wicket-keeper-batsman, Lulama Masikazana, from the Eastern Cape, who hit seven fours and a six in his carefree knock of 44.

Given the significance of the tour and matches such as these, the England team was accompanied to South Africa by the biggest media contingent to cover a cricket tour of this country. In Soweto, the English journalists searched for further clues to the progress of young black cricketers. They seemed to have made it their mission to unearth the first such player good enough to gain selection on merit to the South African team. Whenever they asked the question – and they posed it to just about anyone who was prepared to give them a moment of their time – they failed to get a definitive answer. The simple reason for this was that no one knew for sure.

At the welcoming press conference on the day the England team arrived in Johannesburg, Ali Bacher was questioned at length on when he expected the first black player to be selected. The chief authority on the development of black cricketing talent in South Africa said he could not say for sure. 'All I can say is that it will happen sooner rather than later.'

Little did he know that this moment would arrive even sooner than he could imagine.

AT ALMOST THE same time as President Mandela arrived at the cricket match, another significant arrival was taking place in the industrial town of Springs, some 60 kilometres east of Soweto. The Western Province B team was paying a visit for a three-day match against Easterns. This was the kind of low-key game that went largely unnoticed in the bigger scheme of things. On that particular day the all-consuming event in Soweto had overshadowed anything else happening in cricket.

Little if any importance would then have been attached to the fact that an unknown teenage spin bowler from Cape Town was about to make his first-class début at Springs. He bowled an unusual delivery – known as the 'chinaman' – with an extraordinary action. His name was Paul Adams and he came from the St Augustine's Club in Cape Town that included among its former members a cricketer named Basil D'Oliveira.

1

New Kids on the Block

O N A DECEMBER morning in 1987 the University Oval in Bloemfontein was preparing to stage an important cricket match. Free State, the home province, was about to play South African Schools. The two schoolboy openers walked out side by side. One was tall and dark, the other short and fair. Both were 18 years old, the short boy a couple of months the senior. The scorers wrote down their names: W.J. Cronjé and J.N. Rhodes.

Cronjé, the tall one, was the captain; Rhodes his deputy.

Cronjé attended Bloemfontein's most famous school, Grey College, which catered for mainly Afrikaans boys in the heart of the Orange Free State. Rhodes's school was Maritzburg College, the pride of the Natal capital of Pietermaritzburg.

Apart from being groomed at two of the better South African schools, the common thread that bound them was an upbringing in the finer qualities of sport. Both came from sporting families, and their schools were acknowledged as among the finest sports nurseries in the land. Among many of its famous sons, Grey was the Alma Mater of Kepler Wessels, who captained South Africa at cricket, and Morné du Plessis, a former South African rugby captain. Maritzburg could boast among its celebrated past pupils the former Springbok cricket captain Jackie McGlew.

Cronjé's winter game was rugby. He had already represented Orange Free State† Schools at No 8. Rhodes played hockey for both Natal and SA Schools.

Cronjé and Rhodes came from totally different backgrounds, but they both loved cricket. They liked to hit the ball hard and they liked

---

† Although the Orange Free State underwent a name change after the 1994 election, for the sake of continuity, the province is referred to as the Free State throughout the remainder of the text.

to run. They had first met five years earlier when they played for their provincial under-13 teams at the national Primary Schools Week. Rhodes had been the captain of the Natal team and had worn a little white helmet with big ear pieces. Cronjé remembered him as a very quick runner between the wickets, an aggressive batsman and a noisy little blighter. 'Looks like a busybody to me,' the young Free Stater had thought at their first meeting.

In time, Cronjé would grow to admire Rhodes for his dynamic batting and fielding and for the fine example he set his team-mates.

In 1986 they both made a dream come true when they were first selected for SA Schools at the end of a Nuffield Week that was staged on the beautiful playing fields of Hilton College in the Natal Midlands. Cronjé gave the selectors no option when he strung together scores of 51, 40, 36, 121 and 86. Rhodes also caught the eye with innings of 130 and 84. The highlight of the week was the traditional fixture between SA Schools and the local senior provincial team. In a drawn match against Natal at Kingsmead, Rhodes opened the innings and was out for 4, and Cronjé, batting at No 4, was run out on 23.

Now, one year later, they were together again, this time as captain and vice-captain, about to open the innings for SA Schools at Bloemfontein. Side by side they walked out: Wessel Johannes Cronjé, known as Hansie, and Jonathan Neil Rhodes, who was simply called Jonty. The bowlers who would take the new ball against them were Allan Donald and Corrie van Zyl.

The immaculate Van Zyl was one of South Africa's best fast bowlers. He sprinted in with impressive deportment, his elbows pointing sharply outward from hands that met across the chest, his shoulders drawn back with military bearing.

The loose-limbed Donald had an easy, rhythmic action, gaining in pace from a long run-up before uncoiling in the delivery stride like a spring, his elbows and knees perfectly synchronised to provide a whippy follow-through. He was a strong lad with loads of stamina. As a boy he had cycled seven kilometres each day to get to school. His deliveries were often misdirected, but what he lacked in accuracy he made up for in pace.

It was not long before he struck.

Rhodes left the field injured before he had scored, a sharp blow to the elbow from a Donald express delivery seeing to that. But Cronjé settled in to score a fine century that included 12 fours and a six. It was a performance that thrilled a hometown crowd, including his father, Ewie, a former Grey College master who had played for Free State for a decade and was president of the Orange Free State Cricket Union. The

University Oval was special to Ewie. After leaving the teaching profession in the late 1960s, he accepted a position as director of sport at the University of the Orange Free State. During that period he was responsible for the construction of a fine sports complex on the campus, the central point being the University Oval where his son was now scoring a memorable century.

Young Hansie was caught at the wicket for 102 after batting for almost three-and-a-half hours. The bowler was Donald.

CRONJÉ AND DONALD went back a long way. Allan was three years older than Hansie and had first struck up a friendship with the elder of the two Cronjé brothers, Frans, in their primary school days.

'My first memories of Allan,' says Hansie, 'were of a thin boy with a very big nose and close-cropped, blond hair. He was very quiet and shy, and he lived for his sport and he lived for his mates.'

He also scared the living daylights out of young batsmen. 'Even at the age of about 13 he bowled the ball with the speed of light,' remembers Hansie, 'and he regularly operated with six slip fielders and a couple of gullies.' He also had an incredible throwing arm. 'He could throw the ball in from the boundary as flat and as fast as anyone five or six years older than him. He had already won many fielding competitions.'

In 1984 Frans Cronjé and Allan Donald were both selected for Free State Schools, and the Cronjé family packed their bags and went off to Cape Town to support their boys at the Nuffield Week. Hansie remembers watching their opening game against Western Province at Newlands where Allan took four wickets to draw immediate attention from the SA Schools selectors.

In those years, Donald bowled from wide of the crease and swung the ball into the right-handers. His raw pace gave most of the batsmen a hard time but he was not consistent enough to gain his first SA Schools cap. Still, the Free Staters were very proud of him when he was named as twelfth man.

The next year there was a rare double celebration for the Free Staters when Allan and Frans were both selected for the SA Schools XI. Together they formed the new-ball attack that lost to the Border senior side in East London. Allan took just one wicket, but Frans was not quite so successful.

The captain of that SA Schools team was a little left-handed batsman from Rondebosch Boys' High named Gary Kirsten. He batted first drop and scored 27, one slot below Louis Koen from Paarl Gimnasium who was out for 12.

MEANWHILE, AT THE University Oval, Jonty Rhodes was trying to recover from his sore elbow. Those who knew him said it was typical of his fighting spirit that he would refuse to let this setback stand in his way. They said he showed his best side when the odds were stacked against him. The last thing he wanted was to give some fast bowler the satisfaction of putting him out of action on such an important occasion.

So, midway through the SA Schools innings, Jonty donned his trademark white helmet and returned to bat. He was soon enjoying himself, regularly converting singles into twos, dot balls into singles, and hammering any loose delivery. Earlier in the week the Natal captain had scored 134 before lunch against Cronjé's Free State side, a match the host province were lucky to draw because of the intervention of rain. Now he was busily sharing an unbroken 91-run partnership in just 39 minutes with Pieter Strydom, a boy from Grey High in Port Elizabeth, a school that people confused with Grey College at their peril. Jonty scored a quickfire 34 not out, and Strydom made 53 to enable Hansie to declare on 267 for six in 64 overs. In reply, the senior Free State team scored 241 for seven and the match was drawn.

The best of the SA Schools bowlers, with four wickets for 67 runs in 10 overs, was a Transvaal all-rounder named Dean Laing from Jeppe Boys' High in Johannesburg, who swung the ball sharply through the air with a compact action. Another member of the attack was a boy from Durban High School – Richard Snell. He bowled a lethal in-ducker from a distinctive action that was characterised by his high, goose-stepping spring in the delivery stride. He was no slouch with the bat either, being a strong hitter of the ball with a sound technique.

Three weeks later, in mid-January 1988, the SA Schools XI travelled to Kingsmead in Durban to beat a strong national under-22 side in a limited-overs match. When the cricketers assembled for the official photograph to commemorate that historic occasion – the first match of its kind – the front row, though insignificant at the time, carried portents of a future of untold possibilities. There were the two captains, Hansie Cronjé and Daryll Cullinan, and alongside them the two vice-captains, Jonty Rhodes and Louis Vorster.

FROM THE MOMENT he overtook Graeme Pollock as the youngest first-class century-maker in South Africa, the right-handed Cullinan was destined for bigger things. In the view of many, however, Vorster was likely to make an equal if not bigger impact on the game. The left-hander's precocious talent had been spotted at an early age when, barely into his teens at the Volkskool in Potchefstroom, he regularly hit big hundreds, sometimes going past the 200 mark. In January 1988 the South African under-22s relied heavily on his input following his career-best 174 for the star-studded Transvaal senior side against Western Province in the previous weekend's Currie Cup match in Cape Town.

The dark and good-looking Vorster had the natural gift bestowed on so many left-handed batsmen – an aptitude for classical, almost lazy shot-making from a perfectly balanced stance and a gracefulness of execution that suggested the second Pollock was indeed beginning to emerge.

Against SA Schools now, Vorster's 75 was the major contribution in a total of 199 for six. He batted at No 4 while, one slot ahead of him, Cullinan was dismissed for 12 by the swing bowler Laing.

The under-22s had not got off to a particularly good start. Their opening batsman, Phillipus Jeremia Rudolf Steyn, was bowled by Snell for 4. Steyn was born and educated in Kimberley, which many decades before had been a powerhouse of South African cricket. He, however, had subsequently moved to Bloemfontein and was a regular member of the senior Free State side. People who knew him were certain that the 20-year-old would go far in cricket. On that day, however, Snell ensured that the farthest he would go was back to the Kingsmead dressing room, a place that in time Rudi Steyn would call his home.

In their turn at bat, the SA Schools XI opened once again with Cronjé and Rhodes. Both were caught by Steyn, a fielder of some repute. Cronjé scored 10 and Rhodes reached 33 before offering up a catch off the bowling of the orthodox left-arm spinner Clive Eksteen, a former SA Schools representative who had finished his school days at Northcliff High in Johannesburg. In spite of the loss of their captain and vice-captain, the schoolboys were well set. Not even the blond fast bowler Donald could make any inroads. He finished the day without a wicket.

The SA Schools XI reached their target quite comfortably for the loss of five wickets. The top scorer with 41 was the middle-order batsman Errol Stewart from Westville Boys' High School in Durban. Although in the years ahead he would become a wicketkeeper, this role in the SA Schools side was occupied by a lad named Udo Goedeke from Maritzburg College. Both Goedeke and Stewart had represented SA Schools at rugby but Stewart would go a lot further in rugby. His cricket career would also blossom, but these were still early days…

A FORTNIGHT BEFORE Hansie Cronjé's century for SA Schools in Bloemfontein, the SA Universities XI had gone into action in a three-day match against Eastern Province in Port Elizabeth. The varsities' captain was a 21-year-old student from the University of Cape Town named John Commins. He was the son of Kevin Commins, a former provincial cricketer who now served as director of administration at the Western Province Cricket Union. Batting at No 4, John scored 25 and 70, which was not enough to prevent his team from losing by an innings. Further down the order, the Stellenbosch student Dave Rundle scored 21 and 45. As the team's first choice offspinner, he bowled many overs but lacked penetration.

Among the specialist batsmen who did not shape were two highly touted cricketers: Joubert Strydom of the University of the Orange Free State and Mark Rushmere of the University of Port Elizabeth. In two innings each, their total contribution was 25 runs, and Rushmere, playing on his home ground at St George's Park, made 21 of them. Their career paths were not dissimilar. Both were former SA Schools captains: Strydom was playing his fifth season with SA Universities, and Rushmere his fourth. Strydom, aged 25 and a former pupil of Grey College, was already the senior captain of his province in the Currie Cup competition, and Rushmere, not quite 23, was an integral part of the Eastern Province Currie Cup side.

From his school days at Woodridge College in Port Elizabeth, Rushmere was held in high esteem. There was always a strong feeling that he would make his mark at a higher level, with some saying he had the hallmark of a future senior captain. Hansie Cronjé didn't know him, but he remembers Ewie and Frans talking very highly of him. 'They agreed that one day he might even captain South Africa.'

Ironically, it was Commins who was the preferred choice as the varsities' skipper, although five years earlier the roles had been reversed when Rushmere captained Commins for SA Schools. That Schools team included Dave Rundle from St Stithians College in Randburg and a young all-rounder from Grey College, Helgard Muller. In time Muller would make his name in a much more physical sport as a rugby international at centre-threequarter, playing more than 200 matches for Free State. One of his team-mates in the provincial rugby arena was Frans Cronjé, a hooker who played 38 times for Free State.

THE ANNUAL NUFFIELD WEEK for provincial high school teams served as trials for the SA Schools XI. In December 1982 Nuffield Week was held in Stellenbosch, where any number of promising young cricketers were on show. The average age of the players in attendance was normally in the late teens, certainly not much younger than 17, so it was always a big talking point when younger players made their presence felt. Playing in Stellenbosch in his second successive Nuffield Week was a lad from Queens College, Queenstown, in the Border region. He had

arrived in Pretoria the previous year as a member of the Border team
– at that stage just 14 years old.

Now 15, Daryll Cullinan kept cropping up in the scoresheets,
notably when he scored 66 not out and took five for 49 with his gentle
spinners in victory over the hosts, Boland.

Another callow youth who was consistently among the runs in 1982
was a Country Districts batsman from the Western Transvaal town of
Potchefstroom named Louis Vorster. He had arrived at the Nuffield
Week two years earlier aged 14 and was appointed the SA Schools'
twelfth man.

Both Cullinan and Vorster, however, had to wait until 1983 before
they finally gained full SA Schools selection under the captaincy of
Rushmere. Also in that team was Daryll's elder brother, Ralph.

The following year Daryll reached the pinnacle by being handed the
SA Schools captaincy at the age of 17, a promotion that was almost pre-
ordained because his star had long since risen.

It was in mid-December 1983 that the Queens College prodigy made
his first-class début, scoring 53 in the second innings of a drawn match
against SA Universities at the Jan Smuts ground in East London. The
varsities used as their new ball attack the Free Stater Corrie van Zyl and
a 21-year-old Cape Town student, Eric Simons, who could also bat a bit
down the order.

AT ABOUT THE same time in far-away Johannesburg, the 1983 national
Primary Schools Week was being staged. One team that didn't shape particularly well was Griqualand West. It included a little chap in short
pants, Gerhardus Liebenberg, whose only notable performance was an
undefeated 22 in a total of 36 for two in a rain-ruined match against
Border. In time Liebenberg would be singled out by Jackie McGlew, the
former Springbok captain and opening batsman, as the most technically
correct young right-hander he had ever seen. At this stage, however, the
11-year-old Gerhardus Frederik Johannes Liebenberg was merely a
mouthful in the junior scorebook.

TEN DAYS AFTER scoring a half-century in his first-class début at East
London, Daryll Cullinan was dismissed for a duck while playing for SA
Schools against Griqualand West in Kimberley. Three days later, in a
busy cricketing December for him, the youngster played his second
first-class game for his province at East London, this time against
Northern Transvaal B. It was hardly worth a mention at the time that a
certain Patrick Symcox opened the batting for the visitors and scored 8
and 20. What was of greater interest was the batting of young Cullinan.

When he had reached 48 in the first innings, closing in rapidly on his second half-century in as many games, the 16-year-old was run out by his partner. The guilty individual was the Border opening batsman, Norman Minnaar, who went on to score 60. Many years later, the popular Minnaar became Sponsorships Manager at South African Breweries, and is still closely associated with the South African Test team through its Castle Lager branding, often sharing a can or two of his company's popular product with Cullinan and his national team-mates in distant places dotted around the cricketing globe.

These, however, were early days, and the liquid that was about to pass across the lips of the youthful Cullinan was to come not from a beer can but from a champagne bottle.

AT THE LOVELY Newlands cricket ground in Cape Town, 1984 was only a day old. The place usually was abuzz with festive cheer, but on this occasion it was positively jumping. Newlands was playing host to a West Indies team, albeit a rebel one that was breaking international sanctions. Lawrence Rowe and his calypso cricketers were in action against South Africa in an unofficial four-day match. The media, encouraged by the South African Cricket Union (SACU), called it a 'Test' but it could never be anything quite as grand as that. Still, the imperious batsmanship of Graeme Pollock came to the fore once more; his 102 in a total of 404 was on everyone's lips.

In the busy press box, however, a piece of information filtered through from a distant quarter gave rise to even greater excitement. While the eyes of the cricketing public had been riveted on Newlands, on Rowe, Pollock and Sylvester Clarke, an historic feat had been accomplished further up the coast at the Jan Smuts ground in East London. In just his third first-class match, Daryll Cullinan had scored 106 not out against Natal B.

Pollock, less than two months from his fortieth birthday, heard the news on the players' balcony. Back in the summer of 1960/61, at the age of 16 years and 335 days, he had become the youngest South African century-maker in first-class cricket. It was at Johannesburg that he passed three figures for Eastern Province against Transvaal B to establish the first benchmark in a career of extraordinary achievement. This was the batsman of whom Sir Donald Bradman had once said, 'Given a normal career, he would have proved to be the best left-hander of all time.'

Pollock's long-standing record had now been broken, for Cullinan was only 16 years and 304 days old. In the view of many, the heir apparent to the Prince of Batsmen had finally made his entrance.

LATER IN 1984 Daryll Cullinan, still a schoolboy, arrived in Cape Town for the next Nuffield Week. The Cronjés were also there watching Frans and his fast bowling pal, Allan Donald.

At the end of the week, Cullinan was appointed captain of the SA Schools XI for which Donald performed the twelfth-man duties. Coming in at first drop, as he always did, the young skipper was immediately out for his second duck in successive years for the Schools team. It is not without good reason that the game of cricket is known as the great leveller because, apart from Cullinan's failure, Louis Vorster showed such poor form throughout the week that he failed to regain selection for SA Schools.

The 15-year-old Hansie Cronjé watched all this from the sidelines. Cullinan was a constant source of interest to him, a talent he had long admired. Hansie knew the Cullinan boys, Ralph and Daryll, from their visits to Grey College as members of the Queens College cricket and rugby teams.

Hansie recalls, 'In 1982 there was great excitement in Bloemfontein because Grey College were due to play against Queens in a big cricket match. We were all there to watch, of course, and were shocked when our school was bowled out for 38. That was when I first heard about the Cullinan brothers because they were two of the Queens College stars. Ralph was a fine medium-fast bowler, and Daryll was an exceptional batsman and a good spin bowler. Helgard Muller was our captain at Grey, and the coach, Johan Volsteedt, was so upset at their performance that he didn't speak to Helgard and his team-mates for the next two weeks.'

A year later the Cullinan boys were back in Bloemfontein, this time for a rugby match between the two schools. Hansie was again on the touchline, yelling encouragement to the Grey College 1st XV. He couldn't believe their luck when Ralph Cullinan missed two penalties from point-blank range in the dying minutes for Grey to triumph 17–16. 'I could see how upset Ralph was when he missed those kicks, and I could also tell how much winning meant to the Cullinan boys.'

Sitting at Newlands watching Daryll dismissed for a duck, Hansie cast his thoughts back to the winter months of 1984 when Daryll had turned up again in Bloemfontein for the big schools' rugby match. As if to atone for his brother's failing the previous season, he played a blinder, scoring most of Queens' points in a 25–9 victory.

'He really is something special,' thought Hansie. 'He can play cricket and rugby and is also South Africa's under-16 squash champion. Pity about the duck, but I'm sure he'll go far in whatever sport he plays.'

AT AROUND THE same time, the 1984 national Primary Schools Week for boys of 13 years and younger was underway in Port Elizabeth. The Griqualand West team was doing much better than the previous year, one reason being the maturing form of Gerhardus Liebenberg. He was 12 years old and regularly among the runs and wickets.

The Free State team at that tournament included a left-hander from Bloemfontein named Nico Bojé. He was just 11 years old and, as things turned out, he didn't do much to write home about. In the years to come 'Nicky' would fall under the influence of Hansie Cronjé at Grey College and Free State, yet little could he imagine that the opportunity would one day come for him to post letters home from such distant places as Calcutta, Kanpur and Ahmedabad.

THE BARREN EIGHTIES rolled on and, but for the occasional visit by a rebel touring team, there was little on the horizon to suggest that there was any great future for the young cricketers of South Africa. The boys from the establishment schools were at least fortunate to have decent coaching and facilities; any number of youngsters from less privileged circumstances were simply lost to the game.

Mindful of this, the SACU was in the midst of a concerted drive to take the game into the black townships of South Africa to ensure that no further generations of players would disappear without a trace. Bankrolled by the business sector, expansive coaching programmes were set up and, backed by generous sponsorships from Bakers Biscuits, a nationwide Mini Cricket phenomenon was spreading cricket's gospel to thousands of underprivileged youngsters.

One winter morning, a group of people drove out of Bloemfontein into the adjoining black township of Rocklands. They were led by Ali Bacher, Ewie Cronjé and Johan Volsteedt, and they had come to introduce the game of cricket to the black youngsters living there. Hansie and Frans Cronjé and their friend Corrie van Zyl put the kids through some rudimentary coaching. 'It's the coldest winter's day I've ever experienced,' said a shivering Bacher, 'but my heart is warmed by what is happening here.'

Further afield, in such places as Alexandra, Atteridgeville, Bisho, Galeshewe, Kagiso, Kwamashu, Langa, Mamelodi, Soweto and Tembisa, the development drive was moving forward. Bacher described it as a revolution. 'Dismantle apartheid?' he asked rhetorically. 'Why, we are destroying it!'

The tragedy, of course, was that Bacher and the SACU were being forced to perform a dangerous juggling act. There was the dire need to keep the game alive at the highest level by signing up rebel touring teams which, in the view of Krish Mackerdhuj's SACB and its political allies, was tantamount to propping up apartheid sport and spending vast amounts of 'blood money' on mercenary foreign teams. At the same time there was the SACU's total commitment to developing the game at grass-roots level in the black townships, where the laws of apartheid were still acutely in evidence.

WHILE ALL THIS soul-searching was going on, Cronjé was blithely scoring a century as SA Schools captain, Strydom was fast making his mark as Free State's adventurous captain, and Rushmere was emerging as the new golden boy of provincial cricket.

Three weeks after failing with the bat for SA Universities at St George's Park in December 1987, Rushmere returned to the same ground to hit an undefeated 136 against Northern Transvaal in a Currie Cup match. He also became the first Eastern Province batsman for three decades to carry his bat, remaining at the crease throughout the 389 minutes. The 22-year-old son of Colin Rushmere, president of the Eastern Province Cricket Union, was attracting rave notices for his mature approach in the first-class game. In the *Protea SA Cricket Annual* of that year he was described as the finest batsman to come out of Port Elizabeth since Graeme Pollock.

In that season of 1987/88, he averaged 61.66 in the Currie Cup, 71.85 in the floodlit Benson & Hedges Series, and 41.50 in the Nissan Shield one-day competition. In all he hit six centuries, prompting the *Protea Annual* to dub him 'a megastar of the future'.

Strydom was not hanging about either. Ten days after being dismissed twice for single figures for SA Universities against Eastern Province, he proceeded to lash 107 off the same attack while leading Free State to a remarkable last-ball victory in a thrilling Currie Cup match at Bloemfontein. This match was notable for a number of achievements, not least of which was the record 355 runs which Strydom and Allan Lamb established for the fifth wicket. Lamb's 294, the first double century of his career, was the highest individual score in Currie Cup history. Lamb had joined Free State on a one-off season contract when he was omitted by England for the Test series in Pakistan that followed the 1987 World Cup on the subcontinent. The former Western Province batsman was disappointed to be cast aside by his adopted country for the Tests because he had been one of England's World Cup stars, helping them reach the final where they were narrowly beaten by Australia. As a professional cricketer who needed to earn a living, he was therefore happy to accept an offer made to him by Mike Procter, Free State's new director of cricket. Back in South Africa, and playing his first Currie Cup match in six years, the dashing Lamb was in compelling form. Joubert Strydom enjoyed the opportunity to bat with him in this mood.

The Strydom family was renowned for its seemingly endless production line of provincial sportsmen from their roots at Grey College. Joubert's father, Steve, had played for Free State as had Steve's three younger brothers, Willie, Piet and Corrie. Their record was quite unparalleled in South African cricket for, in 68 consecutive provincial matches spanning 1960 to 1973, there had always been a Strydom in the Free State team. On several occasions at least three of the brothers were in action on the same side. Apart from being an international rugby referee of note, Steve was also the president of the Orange Free State Rugby Union. As Free State's cricket captain, Joubert continued to keep up the traditions of the great Strydom dynasty. He also had his eyes firmly fixed on the growing batting maturity of one Hansie Cronjé.

THE CRICKETING COGNOSCENTI at large focused their attention elsewhere, notably on the progress of such players as Cullinan, Rushmere and Vorster. In various ways, all three had been likened to Graeme Pollock. Being the only left-hander in this trio, Vorster bore a far stronger resemblance to South Africa's greatest batsman but there, unfortunately, the similarity would eventually end. In the years that followed, his arrival in the middle was always eagerly awaited; everyone so badly wanted him to succeed. Always, though, he lacked consistency, the vital, missing element that meant this wonderfully gifted batsman would never be a great one.

This, of course, was all academic in the summer of '87 because they were young and brash then, and they could only dream of playing Test cricket. Shunned by a world that was fast freezing out the nation on the southern tip of Africa, there seemed little hope for them at all.

2

Donald Ducks

I N ENGLAND IN mid-1987 a total of 17 South Africans were playing county cricket. At the two extremes were Clive Rice, in his thirteenth and final season for Nottinghamshire, and Allan Donald who was playing in his first season for Warwickshire. Rice was 38 years old and supposedly in the twilight of his career; Donald was just 20 and enjoying a meteoric rise.

Rice was an institution in English cricket. When he finally bowed out at Trent Bridge he had played 284 first-class matches for his county, topped 17 000 runs and captured 476 wickets. In 1987 he scored over 1 000 runs for the thirteenth consecutive English season with three centuries and five 50s for a batting average of more than 43. His chief ally at Notts was the New Zealand all-rounder Richard Hadlee. In 1987 Hadlee took 97 wickets at only 11.89 runs a piece, and scored more than 1 000 runs at an average of over 53. Together Rice and Hadlee helped Nottinghamshire win the County Championship that season before both bade farewell to a club at which their names were enshrined forever.

Amid the tearful departures came the joyful arrivals – the new boys to the county circuit. The 1987 *Playfair Cricket Annual* claimed in the player biographies that Allan Anthony Donald had attended school at Grey College.

The English editors of *Playfair* could be forgiven for believing that every top-class cricketer from Bloemfontein inevitably came through the senior Grey ranks but, in Donald's case, this was not strictly true. He had attended primary school there but had then enrolled at the local technical high school, which was a less grandiose place. There was no pretence at sophistication, and his aspirations extended little beyond a desire to bowl a cricket ball faster than anyone else. He had a lean, athletic build and boasted a natural rhythm that was a basic requisite for good fast bowling. In the school's cadet band, he had been the kettle drummer.

In spite of his English-sounding name, Donald was an Afrikaans boy to his roots. When Ewie Cronjé heard the news that the young bowler had been accepted by Warwickshire, he sent for him immediately.

'Listen, boy, if you're going to play cricket in England and live there, you're going to have to learn to speak their language. If you like, I'll teach you what I know.'

When Donald arrived at Birmingham in the spring of 1987, his English was barely passable. In the social graces, too, he was less than comfortable, but he was an impressionable young man and showed signs of learning fast. 'Fast' was a word that was going to sit comfortably on his youthful shoulders.

The young Free Stater came highly recommended to the Edgbaston ground. Alvin Kallicharran, a tiny Guyanan batsman who had been on the club's books since 1971 was one of the senior pros at Warwickshire. He was a veteran of 66 Tests, had scored centuries in his first two Test innings against New Zealand, and had captained West Indies nine times. Kallicharran was five months older than Clive Rice and, like the South African, had been around the cricket block a few times. This included several tours of duty in South Africa where he played for a powerful Transvaal side under Rice's captaincy between 1981 and 1984 before moving on to Bloemfontein to join Free State. It was there that he came to know Allan Donald.

'During my Test career for the West Indies,' said Kallicharran, 'I played with some of the greatest fast bowlers in the world, men like Andy Roberts, Michael Holding, Joel Garner, Malcolm Marshall, Colin Croft and Wayne Daniel. Allan still has a lot to learn, but I reckon he has the potential to become a great fast bowler too.'

TOWARDS THE END of January 1987, with the county circuit still several months away, the Free State team arrived in Johannesburg for a three-day Currie Cup match against Transvaal, the would-be South African champions. The home side, captained by Rice, included some of the finest cricketers in the land. They were Jimmy Cook, Henry Fotheringham, Kevin McKenzie, Alan Kourie, Mandy Yachad, Ray Jennings, Hugh Page and Neal Radford. The Free State team was led by Joubert Strydom in his first season as senior captain. It included the opening batsman Rudi Steyn, the left-handed Kallicharran and the right fast-medium Donald.

Free State batted first and were soon dismissed for a paltry 137. Steyn scored 25; Kallicharran a duck; Strydom 47; and Donald, coming in at No 10 with a fast bowler's pretence at being a batsman, was caught at the wicket for a duck. He was dismissed by a powerfully built fast bowler named Brian McMillan, who a month earlier had celebrated his twenty-fourth birthday and was into his first full season of Currie Cup cricket. His four wickets for 22 runs in 15 overs was by far the best from the Transvaal bowlers.

Rice's men were smiling, but by stumps on the first day they were in deep trouble on 97 for seven. Cook was gone for 14, Fotheringham for 2, Yachad for 10, McKenzie for 4, and Rice for a duck. The top five in the batting order had all succumbed to the fiery fast bowling of Allan Donald. The No 6 batsman, McMillan, was run out cheaply and, when Transvaal were finally dismissed for 139 on the second morning, Donald had claimed the remarkable career-best figures of eight for 37 in 23 overs.

Apart from McMillan, the only other Transvaal batsman who denied Donald was the No 7 batsman, Louis Vorster, who hit the top score of 33.

With Free State all out for 187 in their second innings, Transvaal were able to knock off the required runs for the loss of only one wicket to win very easily. Although Donald could not add to his eight wickets of the first innings, he had done enough to catch the attention of the national selectors and win further approval from the Warwickshire talent scouts. They had been watching his growing maturity for quite some time.

Donald wasn't exactly an unknown entity to Transvaal but, when he had arrived at the Wanderers the previous season at the age of 19, he most certainly was. He was then coming to the end of his final year at school, and Free State, newly promoted to the Currie Cup, took the risk of playing him against Transvaal in his début match. Little was known of him, other than that he was the Free State Schools opening bowler and had been twelfth man for SA Schools in Cape Town a year earlier.

The day before the match the Transvaal players began arriving in ones and twos for their final net session. The Free Staters were coming to the end of their practice so the Transvaal players stood around chatting and watching the goings-on.

'Hey, who's that young bloke with the short haircut?' asked Cook, South Africa's top opening batsman. 'He looks pretty quick to me.'

The tall, wiry youngster was lean and fit. Long bicycle rides to and from school each day had helped to build hard muscles in his deceptively spindly pair of legs. From what the Transvaal players could gather, though, it was uncertain whether the wide-eyed rookie would get a game. He was merely a member of an expanded Free State squad, and they had yet to announce their final XI.

Play, though, Donald did. With his lanky, sinuous build and long legs, he looked like a young giraffe as he sped in on his lengthy run-up to bowl the second over of the morning. Cook, who the previous season had scored some 700 runs in 10 matches, had five runs to his name when a superb delivery from the youngster clipped the outside edge and he was caught at the wicket. It was Donald's only scalp in a match that Transvaal went on to win by an innings, but he performed well enough against the best batting line-up in the competition.

'He's wild and woolly and sprays it around a bit,' said Cook, 'but he's quick all right. When he puts the ball in the right place, you've got your work cut out in keeping him out.'

Boasting Cook as his first victim in first-class cricket, the enthusiastic Donald travelled to Kingsmead four days later for his second Currie Cup match. There he dismissed Natal's charismatic Collis King for 25 following the big-hitting West Indian's 154 in the first innings. The match was drawn, Donald took three wickets in all, and Corrie van Zyl's five for 54 in the second innings earned the ever-improving fast bowler a match haul of seven wickets.

While all this was going on in November 1985, a team of rebel Australian cricketers had arrived in South Africa.

UNLIKE PREVIOUS REBEL tours by teams from England, Sri Lanka and West Indies, the veil of secrecy surrounding the Australian venture was lifted long before their arrival. By the time the 14 players jetted into Johannesburg amid huge public debate for a two-season tour that would earn each of them $200 000 tax-free, a number of sensational headline-making events had already taken place. The SACU and the Australian Cricket Board (ACB) had engaged in a series of heated exchanges. The ACB had issued writs against the tour organiser Bruce Francis, against some of their contracted players and against the SACU before the whole matter was settled out of court. Also, three would-be rebels, Graeme Wood, Dirk Wellham and Wayne Phillips, were reportedly bought out of their rebel contracts by Kerry Packer, the media magnate who effectively ran Australian cricket with the ACB due to his powerful television interests. Packer's Channel 9 network had bought the TV rights for the Ashes series in England that year and he did not want it devalued by a mass exodus of top Test cricketers.

Talk of a rebel Australian tour had been rife for many months, but mostly it was dismissed as rumour. Then, in April 1985, two Australian newspapers published the names of a group of players they claimed had signed rebel contracts to travel to South Africa. As it turned out, they were not far off the mark. The story then gained momentum, and the

ACB and the Australian government began voicing serious concern over a potentially damaging situation.

The real intrigue had, however, begun several years earlier. Francis, a former Australian Test cricketer, travelled to South Africa back in 1982 for preliminary talks after being recommended to the SACU as a likely recruiting officer. Because a rebel West Indies tour was already in the pipeline, the Aussie venture was put on hold, and Francis returned home to sound out several players about their availability at some future stage.

In May 1983 the Australian team, under Kim Hughes, went to England for the World Cup. There, several of the players held secret meetings with Ali Bacher, who had gone to London as the SACU's special consultant and was staying not far from the Waldorf Hotel where the Aussies were based. A system of codes was invented for Bacher and the players to conduct telephone conversations without arousing any suspicion. When the Australians left London to play in Leeds, Bacher followed them. Another meeting was held there.

In matters of secrecy, there is always a risk. One of the players who had talked with Bacher, and whose identity was not revealed, was inspired to leak details of the scheme to a newspaper and the ACB. Bacher was furious but he moved quickly and effectively to defuse an explosive situation. He announced that plans for an Australian tour had been cancelled. He told the players he could not proceed because of the leaks. It was an admission that seemed to appease the ACB.

There the matter rested until an Australian player visited South Africa in August 1984 to reopen talks with the SACU. Francis was also in Johannesburg at the time and, armed with instructions to act with the utmost urgency, he returned home to contact more of the players.

In late September the Australian team attended a training camp in Canberra prior to a series of three one-day matches in India. It was during this camp that Francis held more clandestine talks with the players. The time had come for them to make a decision one way or the other.

Bacher then travelled to Singapore on the pretext of going to England to visit his sister. He booked into the Marco Polo hotel, timing his stay to coincide with the completion of the one-day series in India. Some of the Australian players let it be known that they would be breaking their return journey in Singapore to reconnect to Brisbane. Others decided to stop off in Singapore for some overnight shopping, one being Kim Hughes, who had no inkling about what was going on behind the scenes. A further group of players, who had not been selected for India, slipped out of Australia and went to

Singapore for their secret rendezvous with Bacher. Speed was of the essence because it was vital that they return home within a day lest their absence be noted. They travelled light, one with only his toothbrush.

It was also imperative that Hughes not see them. He had booked into a hotel within a stone's throw of the Marco Polo where Bacher, Francis and the SACU's legal representative had arranged to meet the would-be rebels in the presence of their lawyers. What followed was a series of pre-arranged meetings with small groups of players who, one by one, granted power of attorney to enable a third party to sign the actual contracts at a later stage.

On 9 November 1984, a lawyer representing the players flew to Johannesburg and duly signed the contracts on their behalf. The hush-hush ceremony took place on the eve of the first Test between Australia and West Indies at Perth. Of that 12-man Test squad only three had not been approached to sign the original power of attorney: Kim Hughes, Allan Border and Geoff Lawson.

Now all the SACU needed was a captain of stature to give the final stamp of credibility to their venture.

BORN ON AUSTRALIA DAY, Kim Hughes was a patriot through and through; an ACB man to the hilt. When the Packer revolution erupted in 1977, he refused to be a part of it. And when Francis approached him informally in 1982, he made it clear he was not interested in the rebel tour. As captain of his country he would hardly run the risk of getting involved with some dodgy South African business.

Little did he realise, however, that in November 1984 his days as Australia's cricket captain were numbered.

Hughes's life as captain had never been easy. There was distrust between himself and former Packer players in his team. Most of the older players resented him because of his blue-eyed-boy image. He was often strung up by his detractors in the media because of the team's poor results, and back-stabbing was rampant following Australia's failure to reach the semi-finals at the 1983 World Cup.

On their tour to the West Indies in the first half of 1984, Hughes's Australians lost the last three Tests after drawing the first two. In November that year, the West Indies paid a return visit to Australia for another five-Test series. There was a sense of foreboding in the Australian team; the mood was fraught with feelings of potential disaster.

In the first Test at Perth, the Aussies were bowled out for 76 to lose by an innings. In the second Test at Brisbane, defeat came by eight wickets.

With a record of five Test defeats in a row, the Australian captain was the very picture of despair when he appeared at the post-match press conference at Brisbane. He broke down in tears while he read from a handwritten statement: 'The Australian cricket captaincy is something that I've held very dear to me. However, playing the game with total enjoyment has always been of greatest importance. The constant speculation, criticism and innuendo by former players and sections of the media in the past four to five years have finally taken their toll.

'It is in the interests of the team, Australian cricket and myself that I have informed the ACB of my decision to stand down as Australian captain.' Hughes could scarcely get the words out, but he went on haltingly, 'I look forward to continuing my career in whatever capacity the selectors and the ACB deem fit with the same integrity and credibility I have displayed as Australian captain.

'Gentlemen,' Hughes said as he fought back the tears, 'gentlemen, I wish not to discuss this matter any further and I will not be available to answer any further questions.'

Allan Border was immediately appointed Australia's captain while Hughes was retained as a batsman. In the next Test at Adelaide he was dismissed first ball. In the second innings he scored 2. Australia were beaten by 191 runs. His media detractors were now screaming for him to be dropped once and for all, but still the selectors held on. In the fourth Test at Melbourne he was out for a pair of ducks. Australia drew the match, but it was the end for Kim Hughes. As fate would have it, Australia went into the fifth Test at Sydney without him, and triumphed by an innings and 55 runs.

In March 1985 the Australian team for the forthcoming Ashes tour of England was announced. Hughes was not in it. The selectors told him he did not warrant selection because he had not been scoring enough runs.

As soon as the SACU heard the news, they contacted him. He declined their offer to join the South African tour. A month later, however, he changed his mind and telephoned Bacher to tell him he was prepared to negotiate.

By this stage it was already public knowledge that a rebel tour was imminent, and when, on 13 April, the *Adelaide Advertiser* and *The Australian* newspapers jointly published the names of prospective members, the SACU could deny it no longer. SACU President Geoff Dakin announced in Johannesburg that he had 12 signed contracts with two more pending. He named no names. Neither the *Advertiser* nor *The Australian* had included Hughes in their list.

When the 31-year-old former skipper later agreed in principle to captain the rebel team, he asked to travel to Johannesburg with his wife to meet with Bacher. The couple let it be known in Australia that they were going on holiday to Hong Kong but there, on 11 May, they joined a connecting flight to Mauritius and then on to Johannesburg. In the transit lounge in Hong Kong, Hughes was approached by an autograph hunter. He signed his name without a second thought. Upon returning to Australia, the stranger went straight to a television station armed with the autograph and a photograph of the cricketer about to board a plane bound for Johannesburg. The Channel 10 station broadcast the news on 15 May.

Kim and Jenny Hughes had meantime booked into a Johannesburg hotel under the name of Mr and Mrs Greg Smith. In Australia it was thought they were travelling under the name of Scott. Ironically, a Mr and Mrs Scott from the United States had checked into the same hotel as the 'Smiths', and for the duration of their three-day stay the puzzled American couple constantly answered telephone calls from the Australian media.

Hughes's cover was blown, and he immediately signed a contract with the SACU. There was no point in keeping it a secret any longer. Bacher invited local cricket writers to his home where he introduced them to the rebel captain. Hughes then returned to Perth where he called a press conference. Ever the patriot, he wore an Advance Australia necktie and spoke eloquently about his loyalty to Australian cricket and how he believed this had not been repaid. He was clearly upset that certain players had been bought out of their rebel contracts in order to join the Ashes tour of England and that he, never tainted by any such South African contract, was overlooked for selection.

'I believe that cricket in this country is at the mercy of major business interests and cricket politics. Accordingly, in all the financial countermoves employed to maintain the essential strength of the touring team to England, it seemed clear and obvious that my loyalty to establishment cricket meant nothing. My priorities now lie with assuring my future and that of my family...'

On the political question, Hughes said, 'I am going to South Africa with an open and, I hope, intelligent mind. I will be able to see for myself the truth of the matters which concern the politicians. I believe I have the ability to judge what is right and wrong. I also believe I will be able to comment and suggest ways in which the situation can be improved. Then it can be left to the politicians.'

The ACB and members of the Australian government denounced Hughes's decision, but the public at large came out in support of a man they felt had been hounded out of Australian cricket. Bill O'Reilly, the legendary Aussie spin bowler who had played alongside Don Bradman, summed up this feeling: 'As a thoughtful, ambitious, well-educated family man, Hughes has exercised the right which every Australian considered to be his own from birth. He has made his decision to take advantage of an unparalleled offer to set up his family for life. I'm entirely on his side.'

A four-hour phone-in poll by an Australian television station drew a 79 per cent vote of support for the former national captain.

This, however, did not deter the ACB. It moved quickly to seek a high court injunction to prevent Hughes from going to South Africa. It also issued writs against several other rebel players, and against Bruce Francis and the SACU for allegedly inducing players to break agreements with the ACB.

Dakin retorted, 'The SACU wants no legal confrontation with the ACB over its projected tour. All we want is to play cricket again, but if the ACB declares war by taking legal action, then we will meet fire with fire.'

Lawyers began flying back and forth between the two countries amid the ongoing threats and counter-threats. The ACB was determined to take the matter into the courts of law, and a date was set in early July for the case to be heard in the Melbourne High Court. As the day drew closer a group of SACU officials travelled to Australia and, after a meeting with their ACB counterparts, they left the matter in the hands of their high-powered team of solicitors.

In an atmosphere of high tension, the ACB soon realised that the SACU had a very strong case. If it went to court, the ACB were likely to be embarrassed by the SACU's revelations about the role that various prominent individuals had played in the making of the rebel tour. These included players who were still part of the establishment.

The ACB backed down and agreed to settle out of court. The terms of the settlement obliged the SACU not to undertake any further raids on contracted ACB cricketers and to pay the legal costs. Both sides claimed victory. The ACB's executive director, David Richards, said the terms of the settlement were 'highly favourable to Australian cricket', and the SACU's managing director, Ali Bacher, stated, 'The bottom line is that we have got a tour in November, without having to secure the tour by going to court.'

Kim Hughes enthused, 'We've won; we're free agents!'

The Australian rebels were banned from official international cricket for the next three years. Some would play again, others wouldn't. The fast bowlers Carl Rackemann and Terry Alderman, and the leg-spinner Trevor Hohns were eventually welcomed back into the Australian Test team. Two other fast bowlers, Rod McCurdy and John Maguire, and the most talented batsmen, Kim Hughes, Mike Haysman and Steve Smith, went on to play provincial cricket in South Africa. Many years later some would re-emerge in different roles, Hohns as chairman of the Australian selection panel, and Haysman and Rackemann as well-known television commentators.

Allan Border took the official Australian team to England in 1985 in defence of the Ashes. They lost the series 3–1.

MOST OF SOUTH AFRICA'S top cricketers did not fully understand the ramifications of the rebel tours. All they wanted was to prove their ability in international company. They now had their chance again.

The first two three-day games of the rebel Australian tour were against Free State in Bloemfontein and a President's XI in Pretoria. Allan Donald played in both.

Back home at the Ramblers ground, Donald and Corrie van Zyl took the new ball against the New South Wales openers John Dyson and Steve Smith. The scoreboard was manned as usual by a group of schoolboy enthusiasts who were paid R5 a day each for their services. One of them was a 16-year-old Grey College scholar, Hansie Cronjé. He was very excited because this was a big day for cricket in Bloemfontein and some of his friends were playing.

Dyson, with 30 Tests to his credit, scored 141. His younger partner, Smith, reached 47 when he was dismissed by Donald. Van Zyl struck a big blow when he trapped Hughes for 17, and Hansie and his pals whooped with joy in the scoreboard. Donald's other victim in the drawn match was Hohns for 14, while Van Zyl ended with three wickets in all.

Four days later the two Free State bowlers travelled to Pretoria to join a President's XI that was captained by the Transvaal batsman Mandy Yachad, and included Daryll Cullinan, the promising young Western Province all-rounder Eric Simons, and the veteran left-arm spinner from Boland, Omar Henry. Back in the Seventies he was one of the first SACBOC cricketers to switch allegiance to the SACU, a decision that sometimes made life difficult for him in his coloured community. Simons was the pick of the bowlers, taking six wickets in defeat. Van Zyl bagged another three scalps and Donald took two, including the big prize of Hughes for 73. Henry bowled economically but without reward.

The Aussies went into the match with a four-pronged pace attack of Hogg, Alderman, Rackemann and Maguire. They were a fearsome bunch and had the President's XI batsmen in all sorts of trouble, removing Yachad for scores of 1 and 3 and Cullinan for 14 and 0. The home side were bowled out for 150 in the first innings, and were struggling again on 104 for nine in the second when the No 11, Donald, walked out to bat.

'At junior school,' said Hansie, 'Allan wasn't much of a batsman but he always begged for the opportunity to bat up the order. At under-13 level he once got the opportunity at No 3 and managed very stylishly to leave every ball outside the off-stump. After three overs of this, the coach ticked him off for trying to show too much style without actually hitting the ball. He called him a *windgat* and chased him off the field.'

Donald was determined to show these Aussie fast bowlers he could bat a bit. Rodney Hogg, a man renowned for his mean streak, had other ideas. He immediately unleashed a vicious bouncer that whizzed dangerously past the schoolboy's helmet. Hogg was from the hard school. He had taken 123 wickets in his 38 Tests and he loved nothing better than to make batsmen suffer. Another short-pitched missile screamed past Donald's ear. Hogg advanced up the pitch. 'Listen you little *%#!,' he sneered, 'I'm going to bowl you right back to *%#@! school!'

The wide-eyed youngster was angry and confused. Never before had a fellow fast bowler treated him in this way. It made him more determined. In the face of a barrage of bumpers, he clung on courageously amid Hogg's continued cursing. Ducking this way then that, he thrust his left foot firmly down the pitch and nudged the ball away when it was occasionally pitched up to him. He was eventually run out for 12, and left the field with a feeling of warm satisfaction that none of the fast bowlers, and particularly Hogg, had claimed his wicket. One day, he resolved, he would have his revenge.

IT IS SELDOM that a schoolboy gets to play two Currie Cup matches and two more games against international opposition before he has actually played for SA Schools. It was therefore not surprising that Allan Donald was selected for the 1985 Schools team at East London. Just three weeks after enduring the wrath of Rodney Hogg, he was taking the new ball with Frans Cronjé against Border.

On exactly the same day as Gary Kirsten led SA Schools into action, the Australians were engaged in a limited-overs match against Natal at Kingsmead. The top scorer for the defeated home side was their elegant No 3 batsman, Andrew Hudson, with 43. He was 19 years old and was playing only his second one-day match for the senior Natal team.

He had yet to play Currie Cup cricket.

Five days earlier at Paarl in the Western Cape the national Primary Schools Week had ended. An 11-year-old coloured boy from Cape Town, Herschelle Gibbs, had set tongues wagging when he totalled 208 runs during the five-day tournament. His team ended unbeaten, and much of their success was due to him.

For many of the senior schoolboys playing at East London, the fun and games would soon be over; compulsory military training was the next stop for these young men. Donald was called up for the army and, much to the relief of the Free State Cricket Union, he was based in Bloemfontein.

The Cronjé family saw a lot of him in those days. Because Allan's parents lived far out of town, the Cronjé home was far more accessible to him. Hansie often awoke in the morning for school to find the soldier sleeping in the bed next to him. 'Because of the ridiculous hours he had to work in the army, he would often knock off in the early hours and come to our house and crash. He would then get up later in the day and go to nets before returning to guard duty.'

At the Free State nets, Donald came under the influence of Vanburn Holder, the West Indies and Worcestershire fast bowler, a veteran of 40 Tests who was playing in Bloemfontein in the twilight of his career. Free State's captain at the time was Chris Broad, opening batsman for Nottinghamshire and England. Both he and Holder liked what they saw. Between them they would carry word to England about a young fast bowler who was showing great promise.

EARLY IN JANUARY 1986, Allan Donald was back in the news when he dismissed two Eastern Province batsmen with successive balls in career-best figures of five for 46 in the first innings of his third Currie Cup match.

Cricket fever in Bloemfontein was at an all-time high. Corrie van Zyl's consistently good bowling had been acknowledged with a call-up for the South African team that was due to play the Australians in the third 'Test' at Johannesburg a week later. The previous season he had taken a record 50 wickets for Free State to push his career tally in first-class cricket to 116 in just 21 matches. Against Eastern Province now, he celebrated with five wickets in the match, twice dismissing their best batsman, Mark Rushmere, for 78 and 40.

The pick of the bowlers, however, was a member of the visiting team. Tim Shaw, a tall left-arm spinner, brought victory to Eastern Province with career-best figures of seven for 79 in the second innings to claim 10 wickets in a match for the first time. Aged 26, he was into his fifth season of provincial cricket but, for all his promise, he continued to live in the shadow of the country's first choice spin bowler, the big and reliable left-arm Alan Kourie of Transvaal.

The captain of the Eastern Province team was the wicketkeeper, Dave Richardson. He scored 50 in the second innings while batting at first drop. Richardson was a neat and undemonstrative keeper; a quiet and affable 26-year-old law student who at national level had been forced to play second fiddle to another Transvaal star, the more excitable and acrobatic Ray Jennings. Richardson's supporters believed their man was underrated. They were confident his time would come.

Shaw and Rushmere had travelled to Bloemfontein from Port Elizabeth where they had been members of an SA Universities team that came dangerously close to beating Hughes's Australians. The Universities' batting line-up was a strong one that included Roy Pienaar, the captain from the University of Cape Town (UCT); Daryll Cullinan, studying at Stellenbosch University; Joubert Strydom from the University of the Orange Free State (UOFS); and Rushmere from the University of Port Elizabeth (UPE). In their first innings, however, they were all upstaged by UPE's Shaw, who hit a top score of 66. Bowling on his home track at St George's Park, he could take only one wicket in the match.

By far the most spectacular bowling from either side came from a big, blond bear of a man from UCT who bowled left-arm fast over the wicket. Brett Matthews restricted the Aussies to a one-run first innings lead by firing out four top-order batsmen, including Hughes for 1, in figures of four for 43 in 26 overs. Set to score 237 for victory, the rebels again had difficulty against the big fellow, hanging on grimly to survive at 203 for nine with Matthews taking three for 49. The 23-year-old fast bowler was clearly a player for the future, but his progress to A Section cricket would not be easy because the Western Province team was blessed with a battery of fine fast bowlers that included the Springbok opening pair of Garth le Roux and the left-arm Steve Jefferies, plus Eric Simons and a young newcomer, Adrian Kuiper.

It was of no significance at the time that Matthews had a brother, Craig. He was two-and-a-half years younger and little known outside club cricket in Cape Town where he played as an all-rounder for Pinelands.

CORRIE VAN ZYL went to Johannesburg to join the South African team in place of Steve Jefferies. The previous two 'Tests' in the best-of-three series had been drawn, so this was the decider. When Corrie dismissed Kim Hughes with the first ball, the cheers could be heard in faraway

Bloemfontein. In the second innings, the Aussie skipper again faced only one delivery, which was caught behind by Ray Jennings to become the middle victim of a Garth le Roux hat trick. Set to score 250 for victory, the Aussies were bowled out for 61, with skipper Clive Rice performing the hat trick as well, the first of his career. Dyson carried his bat for 18 runs, the lowest score ever in such circumstances in South African cricket.

South Africa had won the series, and Van Zyl ended his first major match with five wickets, a performance that cemented his place in the team for the entire six-match limited-overs series that was soon to follow. Into that squad also came Simons and Shaw, but neither would meet with any great success.

South Africa's strategy throughout the rebel era was to bolster the side with fast bowlers and use the left-arm spin of Alan Kourie as the foil. Most of the time it worked perfectly, and Kourie's reputation grew in leaps and bounds. In the tunnel vision of South African cricket, many rated him as the best bowler of his kind in the world. Yet, against the Australians, he was exposed to dashing batsmen like Hughes who were prepared to use their feet and hit him off a length. His confidence fell sharply and, in a move once considered unimaginable, he was dropped. His replacement, Shaw, was used only sparingly.

Simons's promotion to the national squad was due to an exceptionally productive season with Northern Transvaal the previous summer when he was named one of South Africa's six Cricketers of the Year. Based in Pretoria for his military service, the former Western Province journeyman topped the Currie Cup table with 51 wickets at 14.25 runs apiece.

In addition, he played several match-winning innings down the order to finish second in the Northerns' batting averages. At the start of his golden season of 1984/85 he had played only 11 first-class matches and had taken just 26 wickets. By the end of it he had increased his number of matches to 22 and his wicket-tally to a remarkable 77.

His return to Western Province for the 1985/86 season did not bring him anything like this kind of success, but in January he was named in the South African team. After being on the losing side in the first two limited-overs matches, he was summarily discarded.

THE DAY AFTER South Africa had levelled the one-day series 2–2 in Cape Town, Donald began his fourth Currie Cup match for Free State. With Van Zyl committed to the national team, the Free State selectors were forced to find another fast bowler. They opted for the 19-year-old Meyrick Pringle.

He came from the little town of Adelaide in the Eastern Cape but was based in Bloemfontein on military service. He had never before played in a Currie Cup match but was invited to share the new ball with Donald against Border at East London. Neither bowler made much headway. In a rain-ruined match, Donald took one wicket and Pringle none, but the new lad with the broad and impish grin at least had the satisfaction of scoring 26 runs as a tail-ender. Joubert Strydom also had the pleasure of scoring 100 not out.

Five days later, Free State were back at the Ramblers for their final Currie Cup match of the season against Northern Transvaal. Van Zyl had also returned from national team duty having helped South Africa win the limited-overs series 4–2, so Pringle didn't get a game. Donald did, and he ended on a high by taking a new career-best five for 43 in a narrow defeat for his team.

It had been a highly impressive début season for the young fast bowler. In his seven first-class matches he took 21 wickets, including five in an innings on two occasions. His 17 wickets at an average of 21.50 for Free State in the Currie Cup was bettered only by Van Zyl's 20 wickets at 21. Not shabby by any means, said the critics, and the *SA Cricket Annual* agreed. It named Donald as one of its five Promising Young Players of the Year.

SIX MONTHS LATER, and coming to the end of his national service, Allan Donald was selected for the SA Defence Force team against Griqualand West in a three-day match at the De Beers Country Club in Kimberley. Also named in the Force's side were David Callaghan and Meyrick Pringle. Unlike Donald, they were the products of one of the country's great hotbeds of cricketing talent.

The 21-year-old Callaghan was born in Queenstown, the small Border town where Daryll Cullinan grew up, and he spent part of his schooling at the famous Dale College in the Eastern Cape. Pringle, now 20, had attended Dale and Kingswood Colleges and had been a team-mate of Callaghan's for Eastern Province Schools. For the photograph of the 1983 SA Schools XI, Cullinan, Callaghan and Pringle stood alongside each other in the back row behind their captain Mark Rushmere.

At Kimberley now, victory for the soldiers came easily by 10 wickets. The hero was Donald, who took seven for 63 in the second innings for a match haul of 11 wickets. He was certainly living up to the promise of the previous season.

One of the few Griquas players Donald did not dismiss was a medium-paced bowler named Warren Symcox. He had a 26-year-old cousin, Patrick, who had been playing B Section provincial cricket since the age of 17 but was seemingly destined to remain in the lower divisions of the game. After five seasons with Griqualand West, Patrick was now playing his fourth season in Pretoria, still struggling to make the step up to Currie Cup cricket from the Northern Transvaal B team.

As a promising player at Kimberley Boys' High, Patrick had gone to the 1977 Nuffield Week in Durban as a member of the Griqualand West team but failed to gain SA Schools selection. That team was captained by a strapping 18-year-old all-rounder from Bishops in Cape Town, Adrian Kuiper. During the course of the week, he compiled scores of 43 not out, 78, 20, 62 and 71 not out for Western Province, but was dismissed for single figures in the showpiece SA Schools game against the senior Natal provincial team at Kingsmead. Still, Kuiper was a cricketer to be reckoned with, and within days of the Kingsmead match he was invited to make his first-class début for Western Province B. Against Northern Transvaal at Newlands, he scored 18 and took two wickets.

Patrick Symcox, too, made his first-class début before the 1977/78 season had ended. The tall teenager was included in the Griqualand West team that travelled to Pretoria to play Northern Transvaal. In the first innings he scored 12 before being caught by the wicketkeeper, Trevor Quirk, and in the second he made 19. He did not bowl; in fact, he wasn't really a bowler at all.

Symcox left Kimberley in 1983 to try his luck in Pretoria. 'I want to play A Section cricket,' he told his friends, 'and this move could do it for me.' By the time he arrived in Pretoria he had played a mere 17 first-class matches for Griquas in B Section cricket. He had a batting average of 23.60 and had taken only 12 wickets as an occasional bits-and-pieces bowler at the high average of 41 runs each. In the Datsun Shield 55-overs competition, he had played three matches, the best of them in October 1982 when he hit the top score of 67 as the No 4 batsman against Northern Transvaal.

In the same game, he emerged as something of a bowler in sending down 11 overs for 35 runs. As a bowler, however, he did not have a real identity. Depending on the situation, he would bowl spin and then change to seam. Cricket in the smaller provinces is a bit like that. In truth, if Symcox had any real claim to fame, it was not as a cricketer but as a national-grade badminton and squash player.

By the time Donald took his seven for 63 at Kimberley in October 1986, Symcox was still a regular member of the Northern Transvaal B team. Earlier that year, after scoring a maiden century against Transvaal B at Pietersburg, he briefly gained promotion to the senior team for four Benson & Hedges (B&H) Series 45-overs floodlit games.

He scored 7 not out, 4, 8 not out and 7, and at no stage was he called on to bowl.

The last of these four matches was the B&H Final against Western Province at the Wanderers Stadium in March 1986. Symcox, coming in at No 3, was one of the three top-order batsmen clean bowled by the big left-armer Brett Matthews, who duly took the bowling prize and was named the 'find' of the season. Victory went to Western Province which had already won the coveted Currie Cup. It was a joyous time for Adrian Kuiper, enjoying his second season as the senior captain, and for their coach, the former England fast bowler Robin Jackman.

By 1987 the Datsun Shield had been renamed the Nissan Shield, but Symcox's career bowling figures remained unaltered. In October 1982, they had read 11–0–35–0; by February 1987, they still read 11–0–35–0. During the course of the 1986/87 season he was called up by Northerns to play in three of these 55-overs matches, thus boosting his tally of Shield outings to six in all since his début in the competition for Griqualand West way back in 1980. Three games for Northerns yielded a further 28 runs in all and, of course, he did not bowl a single ball.

IF THE NORTHERN TRANSVAAL B team wasn't exactly providing the spring-board the exuberant Patrick Symcox had sought, it most certainly was for a fun-loving youngster named Petrus Stephanus de Villiers. He was born and brought up in the industrial heartland of the Vaal Triangle but had moved to Pretoria where he was studying to be a teacher. As a useful fast bowler in club cricket he generated a lot of pace from a strong upper body and powerful shoulders, a result of being a highly-rated javelin thrower with provincial colours.

He was a charming young man with a mischievous twinkle in his eye and was immensely popular among his fellow students. He was a typical *boereseun* and they knew him as Fanie.

A fortnight after his twenty-first birthday in October 1985, Fanie de Villiers made his first-class début for Northerns B against Natal B at Berea Park in Pretoria. After failing to take a wicket in the first innings, he charged back in the second to produce remarkable figures of five for 33 with his impressive away swingers. One of his victims was the teenage opening batsman Hudson. The attractive stroke-player had scored 62 in the first innings and was then bowled by De Villiers for 71, his highest score in seven first-class outings. Hudson was already catching the eye as a classy young batsman who was seen as a natural successor to one of the province's senior openers, Brian Whitfield or Mark Logan. Within two months he would bat behind them at first drop and top score in the one-day match against the Australians. It seemed as if the former Kearsney College scholar had a bright future in the game.

Northerns B, meanwhile, had travelled to Pietersburg for their match against Transvaal B. It was there that Pat Symcox scored his maiden century of 107 which, as it turned out, would be the only hundred he would ever score throughout a career that was to carry him to untold heights. De Villiers was not there to see it. He had been named in the senior Northern Transvaal team to play the Australians in a 50-overs day/night match in Pretoria on the same day. This followed hard on the heels of his Currie Cup début against Western Province when he took one wicket, but a very important one at that. The man he removed for 41 was Peter Kirsten, far and away the country's best No 3 batter and a former South African captain. Kirsten's scoring feats and his insatiable appetite for runs were already legend. In the final County Championship season of his five-year stint with Derbyshire in 1982, the little batsman had hit eight centuries, four of them in five innings and three in succession. He was right up there with the world's best.

De Villiers, too, felt on top of the world as he prepared to take on the Aussies; sadly, it was they who took him on. Bowling at first-change, he was hammered for 48 runs in eight overs. His captain, Lee Barnard, immediately took him off and, in order to make up the remaining two overs, handed the ball to Roy Pienaar. It didn't help; those two overs of medium pace went for 35 runs.

A MONTH AFTER Allan Donald's seven for 63 for the soldiers at Kimberley, Kim Hughes led his team back to South Africa on the second leg of their tour. In preparation for their opening first-class match against Free State, the Aussies invited a group of local school-boy cricketers to bowl to them in the nets and to help out generally at their practices. Among the willing helpers was Hansie Cronjé, who was delighted to be in such top-class company as he prepared himself for the forthcoming 1986 Nuffield Week that was to be staged at Hilton College.

'Do me a favour, mate. Give me a hand with this bowling machine.'

Hansie was happy to oblige the likeable Aussie captain. 'Okay, Mr Hughes!' he replied enthusiastically, and fed the balls into a device which then spat them out in the direction of the batsman.

Hughes was obviously readying himself for a torrid time from the Free State fast bowling duo of Van Zyl and Donald.

'Listen,' he told Hansie, 'I want to set this thing for short-pitched balls, and I want you to push the speed as fast as it can go.'

'Okay, Mr Hughes!'

Cronjé watched in awe as the tigerish little batsman withstood the full venom of the bowling machine, never once flinching as the missiles screamed past his head.

'*Jislaaik,*' Hansie told his pals later, 'that oke is totally mad. He was picking bumpers right off his face and he didn't even wear a helmet!'

The next day Cronjé and his friends had a busy time operating the scoreboard when Hughes, who often batted like a madman, led an assault on the Free State bowlers. On a dead Bloemfontein pitch, the Aussie skipper smashed 100 in 119 balls as his men powered to 313 for five in 73 overs. When the declaration came at 412 for nine on the second day, Donald had taken two wickets for 104 runs, and Van Zyl three for 79.

The Free State batsmen also took full advantage of the flat wicket, and their total of 367, which included 110 from Alvin Kallicharran, steered the match towards a tame draw.

Rodney Hogg did not play in that match at Bloemfontein, but he was back in the side three days later to play a President's XI at the Harmony Oval in the gold mining town of Virginia. As was the case the previous season, Donald was among the President's men.

Hansie Cronjé had become quite partial to Hogg, who took a shine to the youngster while he was bowling to the Aussies at their nets. 'Come here, matey. You want to be a fast bowler? I'll show you how to be a fast bowler.'

Cronjé wasn't exactly an athletic sort of boy. He trundled in slow medium pacers with an ungainly action. He would relish any kind of advice from such a great bowler.

'What you have to do, mate, is get as high as possible off the ground in your delivery, like this…' Hogg demonstrated. 'Pull your left shoulder right across your body, like that … get side on like this, and keep your left eye fixed on the batsman and your head very steady. Then, like this,' he continued the demonstration, 'you get your right arm up high and close to your ear and you swivel your shoulders, like so, before following all the way through. Gottit?'

Gottit? Sure he had got it! Hansie resolved there and then to start working much harder on becoming a better bowler. The next day his muscles were so stiff and sore he could hardly move, let alone bowl. But he was determined to carry through the lessons he had learned from the friendly Aussie. His admiration for Rodney Hogg, however, was not shared by his buddy, Allan Donald.

AT THE HARMONY OVAL, the Aussies and the President's XI had completed a three-day match on a graveyard pitch that didn't assist the fast bowlers, and both teams were now enjoying themselves in a low-key limited-overs game. Hughes and his men were looking for batting practice, and their fast bowlers didn't think they would get a chance to bat. Hogg and his mates were fooling around in the dressing room when wickets suddenly began falling and there was a mad scramble to pad up. Hogg didn't take batting too seriously and was having difficulty even finding his gloves and helmet.

When he finally got his act together and walked out to the middle, he was in a jovial mood. The result of the match didn't matter and everyone seemed to be having a jolly good time. He chatted happily with the fielders and poked fun at them as he took his guard. The bowler, Allan Donald, walked back to his mark.

Crash! The ball hit the batsman's helmet above the ear as he tried in vain to duck out of its way.

'Jeez, what the...?' said Hogg, slightly dazed, as he reorganised himself. 'What the hell is this bloke trying to do?'

The close-in fielders smiled. They knew what the bloke was trying to do, and they were loving it.

Hogg then had to endure a series of short-pitched balls that went screaming past his head and sent him ducking and diving and sprawling. The Aussie was hating every minute of it. As one of the world's leading fast bowlers, he was not accustomed to this sort of treatment. No one bowled short to Rodney Hogg.

Tell that to Allan Donald. Deadly serious, he continued to give the hapless batsman the full treatment. Hogg was growing angry. 'What's this bloke playing at?' he asked the fielders. 'I mean, what's he trying to prove?'

Donald knew what he was trying to prove. So did his team-mates.

'Remember Pretoria,' they said, 'remember Pretoria last season when you made his life a misery and threatened to bowl him back to school?'

Hogg remembered; Donald had not forgotten. Revenge is sweet.

BRIAN MCMILLAN WAS a member of that President's XI, which included a number of players who were being groomed for bigger things. Unlike the majority of his team-mates, McMillan had grown into the game from unfashionable roots. His family were mining folk from the northern Free State goldfields, and he had completed his schooling in the Western Transvaal town of Carletonville, which was not exactly renowned as a centre of cricket culture. There were no Nuffield Weeks for him and no chance of playing for SA Schools. When he moved to Johannesburg in the early Eighties, it was not to further a burgeoning cricket career but to study instead as a primary school teacher. Transvaal cricket in those years was the hardest of any province to break into.

The famed 'Mean Machine' provincial team under Clive Rice consisted of a galaxy of stars, and in the wings were any number of young hopefuls. McMillan was spotted playing club cricket, and the talent scouts saw in him the makings of a useful all-rounder. He bowled deceptively fast from a slow, loping action, and his exemplary straight bat made him a difficult man to dislodge. In 1984, they gave him a tryout in the Transvaal B team. He batted 10 innings that season and totalled 113 runs. As a fast-medium bowler he showed more promise by taking 20 wickets.

His first-class début was against Northern Transvaal B. It produced nothing of note, but it did give him the chance to meet Pat Symcox for the first time. The No 6 batsman for Northerns B was even given an opportunity to bowl exactly one over as an afterthought in a seven-man attack.

In his second home game that season, McMillan took six wickets against Boland but failed in both innings with the bat. Each time he was dismissed by Gordon Parsons, a young fast bowler from England who was in his second season with Boland. In a remarkable demonstration of straight, fast bowling, the Leicestershire professional took every wicket but one in the Transvaal B first innings for figures of nine for 72. Parsons liked South Africa, and in the years ahead he would take his talents to Griqualand West and then to Free State.

It was when he moved to Bloemfontein that Parsons married Hester Cronjé to become brother-in-law to Frans and Hansie Cronjé.

BRIAN MCMILLAN'S CAREER suddenly took off like a rocket. In November 1985 he and the Transvaal B top-order batsman Mark Venter shared in a record 318-run stand against Eastern Province B at the Wanderers. Venter scored 225 not out, and McMillan's 129 was his maiden first-class hundred. It was a performance that would take McMillan into a senior Transvaal side that was beginning to show signs of wear and tear and was badly in need of new blood. On his Currie Cup début at Newlands he and Jimmy Cook fashioned a partnership of 113, and McMillan showed his liking for the Cape Town wicket by scoring a solid 85 off 227 balls. It was an innings that would secure his place in the team and inspire him to lift his game yet another notch. Batting at No 6 in the Currie Cup semi-final against Northern Transvaal, he put together scores of 80 and 53 to gain him promotion to the No 3 batting berth for the final against Western Province at Newlands. There he scored 4 and

34 in a drawn match, which was enough to give Western Province the Cup because they had finished on top of the league log.

Transvaal were not without their glory. They beat Western Province by seven wickets in the final of the Nissan Shield 55-overs competition at the Wanderers, with McMillan scoring 39 not out and earning the fielding prize for his magnificent work in the outfield. He was now also an integral part of the bowling attack, although his batting and fielding stood out.

By the end of his first season in A Section cricket, McMillan had topped Transvaal's Currie Cup batting averages with 54.20, and had accepted an invitation for a one-off season in England. There he fell just one run short of scoring 1 000 runs in 12 first-class matches for Warwickshire; struck three centuries, including 136 against Clive Rice's Nottinghamshire; and returned home with a batting average of 58.76.

It was hardly surprising that he was included in the South African team when Hughes's Australians returned for their second tour. At age 22 he was the baby of the side in terms of years but not in size. He was known to his team-mates as 'Brian Mac' to distinguish him from his illustrious colleague Kenny McEwan, whom everyone knew as 'Kenny Mac'. As well as both being shy and reserved, the other characteristic these two cricketers had in common was an iron-like will on the field of play.

In the years ahead, and once McEwan had bowed out of the game, 'Brian Mac' would become the beloved 'Big Mac' of the South African team.

DURING THE YEARS of isolation, Kenny McEwan, like Peter Kirsten, was one of the modern 'greats' of South African cricket. He was educated at Queens College, and captained Border and SA Schools. In the Currie Cup he played initially for Eastern Province, captaining them for a time before moving on to Western Province to become their best batsman. He also played two seasons with Western Australia and 12 glorious years with Essex in the County Championship. Had South Africa played Test cricket in the Seventies and Eighties, he would have been a masterly member of a masterful team.

At Essex he was nothing short of a giant; this short, clean-cut, compact man with a batting ability that was surpassed only by the kindest nature one could ever wish to find in a human being. In his dozen seasons in England he amassed over 18 000 runs, scored 52 centuries, 82 half-centuries and had a batting average of 43.05.

He twice scored eight centuries in a single season, once hitting 218, 102, 116 and an undefeated 106 in successive innings. In another season, he scored six centuries, two of them coming before lunch on the first day. Essex named Allan Border as McEwan's replacement when he finally said farewell in September 1985, inspiring cricket writer Peter Sichel to suggest, 'Essex will miss him enormously and Allan Border, superlative cricketer that he is, will strive mightily to emulate the extraordinarily high standards set by this distinguished son of South Africa.'

At Western Province in 1985/86, he transformed the side. That season, Western Province scored four centuries, and McEwan owned all of them. By the end of the summer, his province had won four trophies, including the Currie Cup and, more than anyone else, McEwan had got them there. In his six Cup matches he totalled more than 500 runs at an average of 71.57.

Kenny Mac was a good guy to play with, and Brian Mac could now consider himself fortunate to be one of his team-mates for South Africa. One day, too, he would become a Western Province star.

CORRIE VAN ZYL was named Man of the Series for the four day/night internationals that followed. As Garth le Roux's new-ball partner, he bowled with great economy throughout and picked up vital wickets, helping South Africa win the series 2–1 with one match abandoned. Behind him in the new-look line-up came Brett Matthews, Brian McMillan, Clive Rice and the big Transvaal all-rounder Hugh Page, a hugely popular and capable player who had not quite lived up to Rice's early prediction that he would become the 'second Ian Botham'.

This was a very good attack that was at its best in the third match at Newlands. Van Zyl quickly ripped out the openers, and Le Roux then took five wickets in 30 balls on his home ground leaving the Aussies reeling at 15 for seven. In the end it was nothing less than amazing that they actually totalled 85.

Such was the public frenzy that accompanied South Africa's startling performance in Cape Town that little notice was taken of the national Primary Schools Week that had got underway earlier that day in Pretoria. Apart from their families and schoolmates, no one much cared that 12-year-old Herschelle Gibbs had hit 79 or that Nicky Bojé, the 13-year-old spin bowler from Bloemfontein, had taken five for 51.

Of greater importance was the tidy start Brian McMillan was making to his international career. In his first day/night international, he took two for 47 in his 10 overs at Centurion Park, and in his second at the Wanderers he bagged four for 35. He was now an integral part of the South African side and retained his place for the four-day 'Test' series that was soon to begin.

THE FACE OF the South African team was changing. Alan Kourie played in the first two 'Tests' without much success, and was then dropped in acrimonious circumstances to make way for Omar Henry. It was the coloured left-armer from Boland's lifelong ambition to play for his country, and here he was making his international début at Kingsmead a week before his thirty-fifth birthday. What's more, in his following 'Test' at St George's Park, he came within a whisker of performing the hat trick.

Kourie's days were over. Sadly, he had made some unseemly public remarks when he was axed from the side, and he headed off into retirement after taking 421 wickets and scoring 4 459 runs in 126 first-class matches. One of his great allies in Transvaal and South Africa, wicket-keeper Ray Jennings, also fell from favour. Dave Richardson, quiet and reserved but unshakeable in the quest for his goals, was the preferred choice as South Africa's keeper. At the age of 27, he was determined to turn this into a long-term arrangement.

Richardson had been used as a makeshift opener during the day/night international series after Jimmy Cook's regular partner, Henry Fotheringham, was injured and ruled out for the rest of the summer. It was important, though, that a specialist opener be found for the forthcoming 'Tests', so the choice went to Whitfield, the high-scoring Natal batsman. Such were South Africa's riches in the middle order that even McEwan was not a first choice at the start of the four-day matches. Kevin McKenzie, the stylish Transvaal batsman, was the selectors' preference at No 6.

Corrie van Zyl and Brett Matthews were being used exclusively as limited-overs bowlers. The fast-bowling spearhead for the 'Test' attack revolved around Garth le Roux, Steven Jefferies, Hugh Page, Brian McMillan and Clive Rice.

The face of the Australian team had also changed, largely due to the inclusion of Kepler Wessels. The South African-born batsman had returned home after eight years abroad – the last four as a Test cricketer for Australia – to strengthen Hughes's outfit. In the four one-day internationals at the end of the tour, he was named Man of the Series. This was ironic because many critics maintained the circumspect Wessels wasn't much good at playing limited-overs cricket. His scores in those matches were 122, 35, 43 and 26, but South Africa still triumphed 3–1 in the series.

Allan Donald took eight for 37 against Transvaal during the week that separated the third and fourth four-day 'Test' matches. While he was busy skittling Transvaal at the Wanderers, the Aussies were up the motorway at Verwoerdburg in a three-day match against Northern

Transvaal. Fanie de Villiers, opening the bowling for his province, was battling to take any wickets. The national selectors were looking to beef up the Springbok attack, and Donald emerged as the answer to their prayers. They immediately named him for the fourth and final 'Test' at St George's Park. In order to make place for him, they dropped Brian McMillan.

NOTHING COULD STOP the Cronjé family from making the trip to Port Elizabeth. They simply had to be there for Allan Donald's international début, and they wanted to see Kepler Wessels, the boy from Bloemfontein who had finally come home. It was also to be Graeme Pollock's final 'Test' before his retirement, and they didn't want to miss seeing the master batsman one last time. They were not to be disappointed.

In the 'Test' series up until then, Wessels's scores read 0, 49, 36, 0 and 2. At St George's Park, he scored 135 and 105 not out and was named Man of the Match. In growing awe, Hansie Cronjé watched every shot he played. He marvelled at the man's power of concentration, his ability to play any kind of bowling, and a batting technique that was rock solid.

He also yelled with delight when his friend Donald clean-bowled Kim Hughes in both innings. This was the stuff of a young boy's dreams – his friend, just a year out of school, playing for his country and dismissing the great Australian captain. He thought how great it would be to be out there with his pal, playing cricket for South Africa.

Graeme Pollock knew what it meant to play for his country. He had made his Test début in Australia at the age of 19 years and 283 days, and now, just over a month short of his forty-third birthday, the colossus was walking back on to the ground where he had first made his name. It was the last time he would so.

The 12 000-strong crowd rose as one and applauded him every step of the way to the wicket. Save for the handful of Australians, everyone wanted him to bat and bat and bat. Rodney Hogg, naturally, wanted to spoil the party. The first ball he bowled to the maestro might have been the best ball he had ever bowled. With tremendous velocity and pinpoint accuracy, it swung through the air and then cut viciously off the pitch to leave Pollock groping unashamedly. The ball clipped the edge of the bat but, with the rapt crowd sensing a terrible disaster, it fell just short of the wicketkeeper. The next two deliveries were equally lethal, but the great left-hander survived. He settled in, made it through the first 20 runs – always the most difficult for him – and then he flourished. In a fairy-tale ending to an extraordinary career, Pollock batted for almost four-and-a-half hours and scored 144 runs. There were 22 fours and a six before Hogg finally bowled him.

St George's Park rose to bid him farewell. Nothing quite like it had been seen there before. Perhaps Sir Donald Bradman was right; perhaps he might have been the greatest left-handed batsman there ever was. In any event, his Test batting average of 60.97 was second only on the world all-time list to Bradman's 99.94.

McEwan was a right-handed batsman whose range of shots was equal to the best. With McKenzie dropped from the side, it was up to him to continue the scoring tempo. For the next six hours he occupied the crease, scoring a glorious, undefeated 138. McEwan couldn't have known it, but it was to be his last 'Test' for South Africa. Sadly, unlike Pollock, he never had the opportunity to represent his country in an official Test match but, when his cricket career finally ended, his place in history was secure – 26 309 runs in first-class cricket with 73 centuries for an average of 41.63.

The 18-year-old Hansie Cronjé was there to see him that day in February in Port Elizabeth, blazing away against the Australians. Later Hansie whooped and yelled again as Donald, bat in hand and no *windgat* by any means, hit out lustily to score a career-best 21. Rodney Hogg took five for 95, but he didn't take Donald.

Omar Henry, meanwhile, had caused a little sensation of his own in only his second 'Test' appearance. Looping up his accurate left-arm spin, he dismissed Steve Rixon and Hogg with successive balls and, with his next delivery, had a very debatable lbw appeal against Rod McCurdy turned down.

What a match it had been. South Africa had won the series, and the Cronjés went home to Bloemfontein with so much to tell their friends.

IN RETAINING HIS place in the South African squad for the four one-day internationals, Donald effectively squeezed Brett Matthews out of the international picture. The younger of the two Matthews brothers, Craig, was concurrently starting out in first-class cricket. The fourth 'Test' in Port Elizabeth coincided with his début match for Western Province B against Northern Transvaal B at Verwoerdburg. In the second innings, he took four for 57 in 24 overs as the opening bowler.

In the one-dayers, Donald and Corrie van Zyl became interchangeable in the South African attack. On one occasion at Centurion Park they bowled together for their country.

Jimmy Cook also received a new opening batting partner in the classy Roy Pienaar. Ten years earlier he had made his provincial début at the age of 16 while still a scholar at St Stithians College in Randburg, he had since played starring roles for a variety of provincial and representative teams. He had captained SA Schools, SA Universities and the President's XI, and had always been viewed as an international all-rounder in the making. He scored a fine 74 in the first one-dayer but did little of note in the others. Still, time was on his side, provided of course that South Africa could continue to find teams willing to play them.

THE BUSY DOMESTIC season of 1986/87 was over and the players went their separate ways. Allan Donald busied himself in nervous anticipation of his first trip to England and Warwickshire. He was not alone in his excitement. His fast bowling ally, Corrie van Zyl, was also going to join Glamorgan.

Before he left, Allan visited the Cronjé family. 'Remember your English, boy,' chided Ewie.

'Good luck, pal,' said Hansie. 'Give it your best.'

'I will,' promised Allan, 'I will. I want cricket to be my life. I want to earn my living playing this game.'

Hansie smiled his encouragement. He knew how determined Allan was, but he wasn't yet sure that he was good enough to make a full-time profession out of cricket. Still, you never know, you just never know...

THE BIG-NAME OVERSEAS professionals on the county circuit are often West Indians, mostly fast bowlers. At Edgbaston, Allan Donald encountered two of them. One was the Barbados-born Gladstone Small, who had qualified to play for England. The other was the Antiguan Tony Merrick. Both were considerably senior in years and experience to the 20-year-old South African.

Until midway through the season Small was out through injury but, once he returned, Warwickshire decided to stay with a Merrick–Small opening attack. In the meantime, Donald had made a very good impression. In the English press he was being referred to as the fastest white bowler in county cricket, a description that didn't sit particularly well with some people. The English cricket writers were merely trying to make a derisory point about the state of England's fast bowling arsenal and the potential fire power Warwickshire had at its disposal.

Donald played 10 Championship matches that season and took 37 wickets at 26 runs a piece. He was at his best against Essex at Chelmsford when he bagged six for 74, following which Warwickshire announced they would be happy to have him back the following year. The critics felt sure he would bowl even better then.

Van Zyl's term at Glamorgan was far less happy and productive. Before breaking down with a stress fracture after a couple of months, the 26-year-old paceman found himself bowling on the flat wickets of Swansea and Cardiff in a team that placed greater store in the spin bowling of the Indian Ravi Shastri. Corrie played only six Championship matches, took 11 wickets at 39 runs each, and had a best return of three for 35 against Yorkshire at Leeds.

Roy Pienaar was another of the 17 South Africans who went to England. He managed to play seven matches for Kent after their overseas professional, the West Indian Eldine Baptiste, was injured. Against Derbyshire, Pienaar hit a career-best 153, and returned home with a batting average slightly higher than 40.

WHEN ALLAN DONALD returned to Bloemfontein, his friends could not believe the change in him. From being a quiet, shy boy, he was now totally outgoing. He was also remarkably fluent in English and had picked up a wonderful Birmingham accent. He enjoyed a beer and was clearly one of the boys. 'England is obviously good for him,' Hansie told Ewie. 'And you know what, Dad, he told me again that cricket is going to be his life. It sounds like a terrific idea.'

3

The Import/Export Business

In the years that followed the D'Oliveira Affair, South African cricket entered a decade of gloomy isolation. In the midst of this upheaval, some huge talents emerged that South Africa alone could no longer sustain or retain. The most gifted of these players faced an agonising choice of whether to stay or to go.

Kepler Christoffel Wessels went.

At Grey College he had played 1st XI cricket at the age of 14; at 15 he was selected for SA Schools; at 16 he made his first-class début for Free State. The third of his SA Schools caps also brought him the captaincy. His side included a fast bowler from Johannesburg, Neal Radford, and a batsman from Natal, Chris Smith. They also went – Radford to Worcestershire and then Lancashire; Smith to Hampshire. They both later qualified to play for England.

After representing Free State for three years as a schoolboy, the 19-year-old Wessels left Bloemfontein to continue his studies at Stellenbosch University. He was immediately included in the Western Province team, where three of his contemporaries were Allan Lamb, Peter Kirsten and big Garth le Roux. They went, too – Lamb to Northamptonshire, Le Roux to Sussex, and Kirsten to Sussex and then to Derbyshire where he achieved legendary status.

Kirsten and Le Roux eventually returned, but Lamb remained. Lamb had lived in South Africa for more than 20 years, and he loved Cape Town more than any other place, yet he knew that his dream of playing international cricket could not be fulfilled at home. So he went and he stayed, and in time he would play 79 Tests and 122 one-day internationals for England.

Wessels, too, was getting itchy feet. After a season playing for the Sussex 2nd XI, where he scored over 2 000 runs, he was persuaded by the county captain, Tony Greig, to return on a three-year contract in 1977.

As captain of Sussex and England, Greig had watched Wessels with growing interest during his early forays in the county game. The year was 1977 and big things were afoot behind the scenes in international cricket. Mr Kerry Packer and Tony Greig were talking turkey.

At Tunbridge Wells, Wessels went in to bat for Sussex against Kent. Derek Underwood, the deadly Kent and England left-armer, was bowling beautifully, yet Wessels proceeded to score 138 not out. Afterwards, Greig took him aside: 'How would you like to go to Australia with me to play cricket for Kerry Packer?'

'I'd love to,' replied Wessels without hesitation.

So Wessels went, but things were not as he had thought. Instead of joining Greig's World XI alongside his fellow South Africans Mike Procter, Barry Richards, Clive Rice and Garth le Roux, he was instructed by Packer to link up with the Australian XI who were in need of an opening batsman. His new captain was Ian Chappell, and his team-mates included Ian's brother Greg, Dennis Lillee and Rodney Marsh. They were a tough crew, but Wessels was a tough young man.

It was a mind-boggling time for the boy from Bloemfontein. He had never before known cricket like this. Five-day Super Tests were being played for the first time under floodlights by cricketers in coloured clothing; the series was surrounded by amazing razzmatazz and huge commercial hype; he was on a contract worth $30 000, money he had never dreamed of.

The detractors in the establishment dubbed World Series Cricket the 'Kerry Packer Circus', but the reality was that Wessels, at the age of 20, was being paid to play with and against the best cricketers in the world for a very demanding boss.

After scoring 8 and 46 in his first Super Test against the World XI, he was confronted by Packer in the dressing room: 'We don't import people to score 40s, now get your arse into gear!'

Kerry Packer was a big bull of a man, rich and dictatorial. He hired and fired employees with alacrity. People were terrified of him. They didn't talk back. Wessels just nodded.

The next Super Test was against the West Indies. They had the most feared fast bowling attack in world cricket. Wessels was hit on the head by a Colin Croft bouncer and then felled by a delivery that hit him square in the groin. He fainted on the pitch, was revived and, against medical advice, continued his innings.

When he finally returned to the dressing room, he had scored 126.

Packer was there but it was Ian Chappell who spoke. 'So, Kerry, is that the sort of innings you expect from an import?'

Kepler Wessels had arrived in the big time. By the time World Series Cricket was wound up he had a better batting average than any of his team-mates. He enjoyed Australia, he liked the Australians, and he married his Australian sweetheart Sally.

Returning to England, he grew unhappy with the set-up at Sussex. He didn't enjoy the way Greig was running the team, the way he persuaded the county to employ so many overseas professionals that their chances of playing on a regular basis became too limited. After almost six seasons of county cricket, he decided to move on again. Just for good measure, he scored 254 against Middlesex before bidding farewell to Hove. In his 53 matches for Sussex, he had scored over 4 300 runs, had compiled 10 centuries and 28 half-centuries. He had a batting average of 52.16.

Back in Australia, Wessels joined Queensland under Greg Chappell, was awarded Australian citizenship and, after serving a residential qualification of four years, was selected for his new country against England. The selectors had no option. The previous summer Wessels had become only the seventh batsman along with Bill Ponsford, Don Bradman, Norman O'Neill, Barry Richards, Greg Chappell and David Ogilvie to score more than 1 000 runs in a Sheffield Shield season. In 11 matches he had hit five centuries, including one innings of 220 against Tasmania, for a batting average above 60. The sheer weight of runs from the determined Brisbane-based batsman forced the selectors to drop Graeme Wood and install a new opening partner for John Dyson. It was November 1982, Wessels was 25 years old, and Australia, under Greg Chappell, were intent on winning back the Ashes that had been in England's possession since 1977.

The teams lined up at the Gabba in Brisbane, Kepler's new home ground. It was the second Test in the five-match series, the first having ended in a draw. The Australian team was Kepler Wessels, John Dyson, Allan Border, Greg Chappell, Kim Hughes, David Hookes, Rodney Marsh, Bruce Yardley, Geoff Lawson, Carl Rackemann and Jeff Thomson. The England team included Ian Botham and Allan Lamb. As Wessels's innings blossomed, Botham called Lamb aside: 'Why don't you use some Afrikaans swearwords and upset his concentration a bit?'

Lamb did. It didn't help. Then Lamb taught Botham some Afrikaans swearwords and he tried them on Wessels. That didn't help either. Wickets continued to fall around him, but on he went. After seven-and-a-half hours he was out for 162.

Only 12 Australians had previously scored centuries on their Test débuts; only two of them had gone beyond 162.

Australia won the Test and the Ashes 2–1. Wessels's scores in his four matches were 162, 46, 44, 1, 47, 14, 19 and 53. He then went with Australia for a one-off Test in Sri Lanka and scored 141.

In his first season of Test cricket, Wessels had made the long journey well worth his while. Brisbane was now his home, Australia his country. It was there that he would stay; a man whose determination to occupy the crease was matched only by his obsession with physical exercise. Like a Spartan of old, he trained his body relentlessly till it was as tough as teak. He also conditioned his mind to resist any influence that might sway him from his one-track mission to make an indelible mark for his adopted country in the unforgiving world of Test cricket.

THE TOWNSFOLK OF Bloemfontein were filled with admiration for the son they had lost. Kepler Wessels might have been batting for Australia but, in their hearts, he was batting for them. Free State had never produced a better or more famous cricketer. Perhaps it would never do so again.

Hansie Cronjé was 13 years old when Kepler scored his magnificent maiden Test century. He felt terribly proud that Grey College, a school renowned only for its rugby heroes, had finally put a cricketer on the world stage. The next time he picked up his cricket bat, he gripped it just that little bit tighter.

KEPLER WESSELS MADE one big mistake. He signed power of attorney in 1984 with the South African Cricket Union (SACU). He did not want to join the rebel Australians in South Africa, but he signed the document just in case he ever changed his mind. He told the SACU he was not signing a contract but merely putting his name to an informal agreement that would keep his options open. It was all top secret, of course.

Wessels was also feeling the pressures that preceded Kim Hughes's tearful departure from the Australian Test captaincy. In seven consecutive innings against the West Indies, Wessels's scores were 4, 20, 4, 4, 13, 0, 0. In the second innings of the Brisbane Test, he came good with a much-needed 61, and then completed the series with scores of 98 and 70 at Adelaide, 90 and 0 at Melbourne, and 173 in victory at Sydney.

He was an automatic choice for the tour to England that followed and, although he passed 50 only twice in his 11 innings in that Ashes series, he had already decided not to join the rebels on their tour later that year. What's more, he believed the power of attorney would become null and void.

What Wessels did not know was that the Australian Cricket Board (ACB) had got wind of it. They had always suspected he was involved in recruiting rebel players, and now they believed they had the evidence to support this belief. Wessels vehemently denied the charges but the damage was done. Systematically, he found himself being driven out of the Australian cricket establishment. He realised he was not wanted when the ACB offered him a new contract of the kind that was normally awarded to players starting out in Test cricket. He had already played 24 Tests and 54 one-day internationals, and on the Ashes tour he was on a top-level contract reserved for the most senior players. Now they were asking him to sign a new deal that effectively demoted him to the lowest rung on the salary structures.

A bitter and disillusioned man, he had no option but to reject it. He was 29 years old and his cricket career for Australia was over. There was only one way to go.

He returned to South Africa, accepted a long-standing offer to captain Eastern Province, and later joined Hughes's team on the second leg of their rebel tour. They were in need of a batsman of his class and he did not disappoint them. Neither did he disappoint his new provincial bosses.

In his first Currie Cup match after his return, he scored 133 and 78 against Free State at Port Elizabeth and, in spreading his talents between Eastern Province and the rebel Aussies, he had such a glorious summer that he was named as one of South Africa's Cricketers of the Year. His total of 1 160 first-class runs was surpassed by no other batsman, with four of his five centuries scored on his new home ground at St George's Park.

For many years Eastern Province had been a perennial also-ran in provincial cricket but now, under his strict, autocratic and disciplinarian rule, the team was re-inventing itself. Wessels led by example and he demanded that his team-mates follow. So tough was the training regimen he imposed on the players that some of them cried off and simply left the province. Those who remained were in awe of his expectations; they were prepared to follow him anywhere and to do his bidding without complaint. It was the beginning of the new golden age of Eastern Province cricket.

One of Wessels's converts was Mark Rushmere, who immediately impressed his new skipper with his innings of 124 against Free State. He would later stand in as Eastern Province captain when Wessels was on international duty with the Aussie rebels, a position that further enhanced the view that here possibly was a future South African captain in the making.

ON THE DAY that Hansie Cronjé scored a century as SA Schools captain at Bloemfontein, Western Province and Natal were completing a Currie Cup match at Kingsmead. The visitors were blooding two new players. One was the seam bowler Craig Matthews and the other was the offspinner Dave Rundle. Matthews took no wickets and did not bat, but his fellow rookie, Rundle, was the toast of his team with a remarkable match return of 11 wickets for 96 runs. One of his five victims in the first innings was Andrew Hudson, batting at No 3 behind Brian Whitfield and Mark Logan, for a top score of 72. Only a week earlier Hudson had opened the batting for the second-string Natal B team, but a career-best score of 148 against Griqualand West catapulted him back into his province's senior side. They were happy to have him aboard again.

The previous two winters Hudson had travelled to England to play club cricket in the Huddersfield League. He first went there in 1986 when he won a Natal scholarship for being the batsman with the best potential in the Durban Inter-City League. On the damp, uncovered wickets of Yorkshire, he developed the art of back-foot play. It was there that he learnt how to cut and pull.

When he wasn't playing cricket, he worked as a plumber's assistant for a coloured man from Cape Town who had carved out a new life for himself and his family in the north of England. The young Hudson, meanwhile, was intent on carving out his own career in cricket. He seemed to know where he was going in life, but he was a philosophical young man, quiet and unassuming, and he was happy for things to take their natural course. What puzzled his team-mates was that he never showed outward signs of anger or frustration when things did not go his way.

Western Province's next match at Newlands gave Craig Matthews his first chance to bat in the Currie Cup. The requirements were simple: his team were looking for every run they could possibly get. They were facing something of a crisis, yet, in an amazing contest against Northern Transvaal, they contrived to triumph within two days of being put out in their first innings for 120. This result had hardly looked possible after they had collapsed to a woeful 22 for six against the impressive fast bowling of Fanie de Villiers and his new partner Tertius Bosch. Both took four cheap wickets before some lower order heroics – including 20 invaluable runs from Rundle – took the home side against the odds into a three-figure total. Matthews scored eight runs before he fell victim to Bosch.

Like his mate Fanie, the 21-year-old Bosch was born into an Afrikaans family in Vereeniging. Neither could boast any real pedigree in a game that was hardly fashionable in the Vaal Triangle. They were both keen and eager, though, and liked bowling fast. Bosch was into his first season of senior cricket, and De Villiers was quickly establishing himself in the side. It was not for nothing that his pals were already calling him 'Vinnige Fanie'.

Nonetheless, in spite of their fine bowling at Newlands, the Vereeniging boys were upstaged by the Springbok left-arm paceman Steve Jefferies. He captured nine wickets in the match, and his five for 48 in the second innings snuffed out Northerns' challenge and left them stranded on 96 all out.

It is just possible that the visiting batsmen were psyched-out by the presence of Jefferies because of a remarkable feat he had performed three weeks earlier. It was against Free State, in the same week that Cronjé scored his SA Schools century, that the Western Province left-armer became the first bowler in 80 years to take 10 wickets in an innings in a first-class match in South Africa.

In 23 overs and five balls, Jeffries scythed through the second innings to finish with 10 for 59. Free State were bowled out for 113, but not before Allan Lamb and Allan Donald had put on 49 runs for the tenth wicket. Donald eventually fell victim to Jefferies for 25, and Lamb was undefeated on 30.

Just 10 days earlier, Lamb had scored his record 294 against Eastern Province in Free State's famous last-ball victory. The scene of that triumph was the University Oval in Bloemfontein where Kepler Wessels, as the visiting captain, was able to renew some acquaintances. Perhaps as a treat for his old home town or perhaps as a rejoinder to Lamb's double-century, the Eastern Province skipper unveiled all his batting skills. In rekindling memories of his performance in the last of the rebel Aussie 'Tests' in Port Elizabeth, he produced scores of 101 and 130 to join Graeme Pollock and Peter Kirsten as the only batsmen to score two centuries in one match on two occasions.

'If Grey College can produce such a batsman,' thought Hansie Cronjé, 'then surely he must be my hero.'

Two days later on the same ground, the SA Schools captain scored 102 against Free State.

ALLAN LAMB'S SHORT-TERM contract came with conditions laid down by the player himself. He was organising his benefit season with Northamptonshire when he joined Free State on the understanding that he be allowed to return to England during the South African season to take part in benefit events. It meant that he was not always available to play for them.

When Free State travelled to Johannesburg in January 1988 for a Currie Cup match against Transvaal, Lamb was not in the country. Free State did not have to look very far to find a replacement. They called on Cronjé.

Skipper Joubert Strydom took the 18-year-old rookie under his wing. He wanted to make the transition as easy as possible for the young batsman. The day before the match was due to begin, he took the newcomer down to the Wanderers Stadium to show him around and let him get a feel for the place. Cronjé, of course, had never played there before. Together they walked on to the big oval and out to the middle of the deserted, cavernous stadium.

'Hey, Joubert, which pitch are we going to play on?' asked Hansie.

'I don't know, your guess is as good as mine!'

The former Grey College boys stared at the huge square of turf that contained half a dozen pitches side by side. Cronjé had never seen anything quite like it. In Bloemfontein, he knew exactly where the pitch was because the strip was brown and closely cropped, making it easily distinguishable from the rest of the turf table. Here the entire square was green; you could hardly tell one pitch from the other.

Welcome to the Wanderers, Hansie!

That night, Strydom called Cronjé aside and had a long chat with him. The Free State captain was a born leader and a batsman who led by example. He was well liked and respected by his team-mates. The two cricketers chatted about the game in general, how to bat against different bowlers on the Wanderers 'Bullring', and the requirements of Currie Cup cricket. Strydom was doing his best to put Cronjé at ease and make him feel welcome in the team. He was down to bat at No 6, one spot below his captain.

A look at the green wicket might have unleashed fear in the hearts of the batsmen, but the fast bowlers looked upon it with relish. This was clearly going to be a fast bowlers' war and, in preparing such a pitch, Transvaal were obviously backing their own pace attack against that of the visitors. This was a big risk because the spearhead of the Free State bowling was the notorious West Indian speed merchant Sylvester Clarke who, on this ground five years earlier, had wrought havoc among South Africa's top batsmen in taking seven wickets for 34 runs in a crunching 'Test' victory for the rebel West Indians. It was reckoned that his fastest delivery was faster than any other in world cricket, and there were a few South African batsmen who could readily vouch for that. Also, the Free State attack included the Springboks Allan Donald and Corrie van Zyl, both of whom were likely to flourish in this paceman's paradise.

Ranged against this trio would be the old warhorse Clive Rice, the left-arm Gordon McMillan, the sharply accurate Justin Hooper, and a West Indian named Rod Estwick, Clarke's half-brother from Barbados who was enjoying a wonderfully productive first season with Transvaal. Still, an important cog was missing. Neal Radford, the province's most consistent fast bowler, who earlier that season had taken 11 for 80 against Natal, had qualified to play for England and was touring in New Zealand. On paper, Free State's attack looked more lethal.

Mike Procter, the Free State coach, said he could not fathom why Transvaal had produced such a green wicket. 'Without Radford, they've got the weakest attack in the competition.'

Albie During, the Transvaal cricket chief, rose to Procter's challenge. 'Without Allan Lamb, Free State have got the weakest batting line-up in the competition.'

The game was on! It was clear from During's statement that Transvaal believed their more experienced batsmen – the likes of Rice, Cook and Henry Fotheringham – were more than equal to the challenge. They also boasted the gutsy Mandy Yachad, who had once scored a century on début against the West Indians on the same ground.

Free State batted first and were soon reeling on 46 for six against the almost unplayable bowling of Estwick and Rice. Cronjé did not last long, bowled by Rice for 2. The shell-shocked visitors did well to total 163. On that pitch, it looked like quite a good score.

Clarke, determined to rough up the province he had once played for, tore venomously into the Transvaal batsmen. Not far behind him was Donald who, despite battling to find his line on the sharply tracking wicket, still joined in the mayhem.

The top six batsmen were dismissed for single figures, and the innings was all over within 52 overs. Louis Vorster, batting at No 4 in Graeme Pollock's old spot, took a sickening blow from a Clarke missile flush on his trademark maroon helmet, and fell straight into his stumps. Transvaal were all out for 130, Clarke had taken seven for 48, and Donald three for 48.

If the Transvaal innings were a hopeless shambles, this was nothing compared to the carnage still to come. In their second turn at bat, four of the top five Free State batsmen were dismissed for ducks as the scoreboard read an astonishing seven for 5. With Estwick taking five for 17, Rice three for 9 and Hooper two for 5, the Free Staters folded for 51. Only two batsmen managed double figures: Van Zyl was 10 not out, and Cronjé hit a top score of 16. Transvaal reached 85 runs for victory for the loss of only one wicket.

It was a Currie Cup début that Cronjé would not forget – top scorer for his province, and 16 runs at that. Welcome to the Wanderers, Hansie!

CENTURION PARK WAS the scene of Free State's next match. Hansie Cronjé was again down at No 6, and Frans Cronjé was named one slot below him. It was not a good time for the Cronjé brothers. Hansie was dismissed for ducks in both innings, and Frans was out for 0 and 4. De Villiers and Bosch again bowled in tandem and took two wickets each.

Once again, the Free State bowling hero was Clarke. He took nine wickets in all, removing the left-hander Mike Rindel cheaply in both innings, and clean bowling De Villiers twice.

Free State's victory meant they had qualified to meet Transvaal in the Currie Cup final, a high-water mark in the province's history. The match was to be played at the Wanderers Stadium, and Hansie Cronjé was stood down to make way for the return of Allan Lamb.

Not that the England batsman made much difference. He was soon trapped by Brian McMillan for 8. Alvin Kallicharran, who like Sylvester Clarke was a former Transvaal import, had something to prove against his old province. The former West Indies captain was bowled by McMillan for 7. Alistair Storie, the Scottish-born, Johannesburg-educated English professional, also failed to reach double figures. So, too, did Joubert Strydom, while the opener Rudi Steyn made 12. At one stage they were teetering on 76 for eight, but a few lower order saviours – notably Corrie van Zyl with 31 – helped them total 144.

Transvaal survived some early hiccups against Donald's bowling to total 279 after Ray Jennings and Rod Estwick had put on 74 runs for the tenth wicket. Donald picked up four wickets but, for once, Clarke was not a threat. Free State relied very heavily on their West Indian fast bowler, but this time he took only one wicket.

Trailing by 135 runs, the out-classed visitors totalled just 166 in their second knock. Steyn was out for 2, Storie for 9, Kallicharran for 10, Strydom for 1, and Lamb scored 33. Brian McMillan, who had taken three wickets for 18 runs in 17 overs in the first innings, now returned figures of three for 7 in nine. Cook and Fotheringham had no difficulty knocking off the necessary 32 runs. Estwick was named Man of the Match for his eight wickets and 43 not out. And, in their first Currie Cup final, Free State had been beaten by 10 wickets.

It was not a happy time in Bloemfontein. Elsewhere there was a feeling that Free State had relied too heavily on too many itinerant overseas professionals. There was no long-term future in players who were there one minute and gone the next.

No, the province would have to start building a winning team of home-grown talent.

It was hard to say what the young cricketers could look forward to. The rebel tours had dried up and world opinion was mounting against South Africa. Promising players continued to flourish, but their future looked uncertain. The two young Eastern Province stars Mark Rushmere and Dave Callaghan were named among the Cricketers of the Year for 1987, but there was no chance for them to prove themselves against the best in the world. Twenty-year-old Gary Kirsten had scored an undefeated 163 as the No 5 batsman for Western Province B against Border, but it was unlikely he would get the exposure of his elder brother, Peter. Fanie de Villiers ended his first full season as Northern Transvaal's leading wicket-taker but his success extended little beyond the boundaries of Pretoria. Louis Koen had made his first-class début in B Section cricket and, at best, could hope to play in the Currie Cup. And what real chance could there be for 12-year-old Jacques Kallis as he blissfully compiled scores of 72 and 53 at the national Primary Schools Week in Cape Town?

For the older players, time was running out. Clive Rice had ended the season with a batting average of 57, but he was surely nearing the end of his competitive years. Omar Henry's left-arm spin had brought him an impressive haul of 36 wickets that season for Boland, but he was 36 years old and unlikely to scale any greater heights. And Pat Symcox's offspin had produced 30 wickets, more than double the number of any of his team-mates, but he was still playing for Northern Transvaal B and was unlikely to advance above the second-stringers of provincial cricket.

As usual, a steady stream of cricketers made their way to England in the winter. Among them were Pringle, Vorster, Pienaar, Callaghan, Van Zyl and Donald. In most cases their appearances in county cricket were limited, but for some there was much to write home about. Pienaar had a wonderful 1988 season for Kent, scoring over 1 200 runs and hitting three centuries and seven fifties. Donald took 26 wickets in seven matches for Warwickshire. Pringle played five games for Sussex. Van Zyl made just four appearances for Glamorgan, while Callaghan played only once for Nottinghamshire. Vorster had wretched luck. He was initially refused entry to Britain because of work permit problems and, after playing one match for Worcestershire, was forced to return home to do his national service.

Free State's overseas professionals had now departed. In Bloemfontein, a group of players were discussing the road ahead. They were Joubert Strydom, Allan Donald, Corrie van Zyl, Rudi Steyn, and Frans and Hansie Cronjé. They had grown tired of reading in the papers that they were still a Cinderella province who 'bought' fleeting success from foreign imports. They wanted to turn things around; to become a force on their own. They made a promise to themselves that they would practise and train as hard as it took to turn Free State into a respected entity in South African cricket. They were determined to win some trophies.

4

'Mister Bob'

T HE KIRSTENS' REPUTATION preceded them. Peter Kirsten was South Africa's best No 3 batsman, whom Hansie Cronjé greatly admired. Gary Kirsten was a useful left-handed batter who had captained SA Schools and was playing first-class cricket. Noel Kirsten, their father, was a former provincial wicketkeeper who became head groundsman at Newlands. He knew a lot about the game, and it rubbed off on his boys. They lived in a house nestled behind the famous oaks that flanked one side of South Africa's loveliest cricket ground. Cronjé was very envious when he heard about this. Imagine living inside Newlands Cricket Ground!

In December 1988, Gary Kirsten was appointed captain of an SA Universities team that included Cronjé, Rudi Steyn, Dave Rundle and Tertius Bosch. The younger Kirsten had a nonchalant, laid-back air about him, a sort of beach-boy, 'no problems' approach to life. Hansie took one look at his new skipper's long, bleached hair and thought, 'Well, that figures; he's from Cape Town University after all.' In his view, the cricketers from UCT – and Cape Town in general – were totally different from the rest, so casual and detached in their outlook and lifestyle. It was quite an eye-opener for him, a clean-cut Bloemfontein boy from a more conservative and regimented upbringing.

Still, Cronjé had great admiration for these players' cricketing ability and, being something of a rugby nut, too, he respected the fact that Gary had played Craven Week rugby for Western Province. Most important, he was Peter Kirsten's brother, and that alone spoke volumes for his prowess on the sports field. As a rugby flyhalf, Peter had been touted as a future Springbok by none another than Danie Craven himself and, at cricket, he was one of the class acts of the game. It came as no surprise to Cronjé that Gary lived up to the family reputation that

79

December by scoring a lot of runs and being the dominant skipper at the 1988 Universities Week at Stellenbosch.

Jonty Rhodes was also there, representing the Pietermaritzburg campus of Natal University. He was as bouncy and chirpy as ever but, although he won the prize for the best fielder at the tournament, he was not selected for either the SA Universities A or B team. The Player of the Tournament was awarded to Clive Eksteen of Rand Afrikaans University, who shone with both bat and ball. He scored a century against Natal University and was regularly among the wickets with his tight, left-arm spin. His reward was being named in the SA Universities B team alongside Richard Snell of Wits University and Frans Cronjé of UOFS.

A new captain, meanwhile, was about to emerge elsewhere. At the Nuffield Week at Grahamstown later in December, Derek Crookes of Hilton College and Natal Schools was named to lead SA Schools against Eastern Province. He batted at No 8, was bowled for a duck by Tim Shaw, and sent down 12 tidy overs of offspin. Derek had a good pedigree. His father Norman was an offspinner who had toured England with South Africa in 1965.

The SA Cricket Union's development programme was also conjuring up exciting new possibilities. A select XI named at the end of the national under-15 tournament in Pretoria included several black youngsters. It was reckoned to be a sure sign of the direction that cricket was taking that two of these boys had the first names of Peace and Harmony. What's more, Peace Nkutha had a brother named Justice, who also played a good game of cricket. They were held up as shining examples for the rest of the country to follow. More than any other sport, cricket was breaking down barriers.

THE CENTENARY OF Test cricket in South Africa was being celebrated. The SACU decided to do it in style. They invited a galaxy of past and present Test cricketers to a party that went on for two weeks. Among those who came from England were Denis Compton, Fred Trueman, Trevor Bailey, Peter May, Alec Bedser, Tony Lewis, Mike Smith, John Edrich and Geoff Boycott. From Australia came Lindsay Hassett, Keith Miller, Ray Lindwall, Ian Craig, Ian Meckiff and Norm O'Neill. The New Zealanders included John Reid, Bert Sutcliffe, Lance Cairns and Walter Hadlee. The rebel teams were represented by Kim Hughes of Australia, Gregory Armstrong from West Indies, and Tony Opatha of Sri Lanka. A veritable who's who of South African cricket also went on show. The fortnight-long celebrations included any number of events and matches, including a series of one-dayers between teams of Golden Oldies from South Africa and abroad.

The international team of past players was captained by Tony Greig and included a former England top-order batsman, Bob Woolmer, who was 40 years old and had played 19 Test matches between 1975 and 1981.

Woolmer had been living in Cape Town for four years, but his connections with South Africa went back much further. He was first brought to the country in 1970 to coach the boys at four Afrikaans primary schools in Johannesburg. From once being derided as the 'Englishman's game', cricket had become a very popular summer sport in the Afrikaans community, and there was a concerted effort to improve standards. Woolmer lent a hand with a salary of R200 a month but, of more lasting value, he immediately fell in love with this sunny country. In 1973 he returned to take up a three-year contract with Natal and to coach its university from being an outfit of also-rans to victors at the SA Universities Week.

Woolmer continued to play for Kent and England, and also followed Greig to Kerry Packer's World Series Cricket (WSC) in 1978. After the birth of their first son the following year, the Woolmers returned to South Africa on holiday in 1980 to show off baby Dale to Gill's parents on their farm in Tzaneen. On the flight from London, Woolmer met Stephen Jones, a left-arm fast bowler from Cape Town who tried to persuade the Englishman to join Western Province. Woolmer promised to think about it. While in Tzaneen, he received a phone call from Eddie Barlow, whom he had come to know at Packer's WSC in Australia. Barlow was director of coaching at Western Province and he made Woolmer a firm offer. At least Woolmer thought it was a firm offer – the line was so bad on the Tzaneen farm's crank-phone in the midst of a howling storm that the two cricketers had a tough time making intelligible conversation.

In later talks with the Western Province Cricket Union, Woolmer's only insistence before accepting the offer was that he be assigned as a coach to a coloured club in the Cape. At the Avendale Cricket Club he single-handedly took charge. When he joined them, they had three teams. Four years later, that number had grown to 16. He was responsible for building proper practice and playing facilities, teaching youngsters the basics of the game, establishing a junior section, playing for the senior side, and instructing officials on all manner of administrative matters, including how to make a profit at the bar. Woolmer immersed himself in the affairs of Avendale. He fell in love with the place and with its people.

Amid the squalor of the Cape Flats, he conducted cricket clinics for coloured children who were always delighted when 'Mister Bob' paid them a visit. He became so involved with township cricket that, after one season playing for Western Province, he told them that he was too busy at Avendale and in the townships to play provincial cricket as well.

Woolmer was still dividing his year between England and South Africa but, after a one-season coaching stint with Kent, he decided for his family's sake to settle in the Cape.

He became involved in the new Plascon Cricket Academy which the SACU had set up as a sort of finishing school for promising young players. For a week each year, top coaches and experts in related fields were called in to help groups of hand-picked players make the transition from school to provincial cricket. It was during these sessions that Woolmer met the up-and-coming cricketers of South Africa, among them Hansie Cronjé.

At the same time Woolmer suffered a major disappointment. Western Province were advertising for a full-time coaching co-ordinator in the development area, a post for which Woolmer felt he was tailor-made. He had been working in the townships for several years, had devoted his life to coaching coloured children, and had a very fond relationship with those people. He confidently applied for the position.

The Western Province Cricket Union gave the job to Freek Burger, who was better known as a top provincial rugby referee. It was a decision that hurt Woolmer very deeply. He then turned his hand to teaching coloured kids how to play hockey.

THE SHOWPIECE OF the centenary celebrations was South Africa's equivalent to a Test match – the five-day Currie Cup final. It was booked for St George's Park, the ground where South Africa played their first Test match against England in March 1889.

Transvaal, who had won the first Currie Cup 99 years earlier, arrived in Port Elizabeth in March 1989 intent on retaining the trophy they had held for the previous two seasons. They were to play the home team, Eastern Province, which had never won the most coveted prize in provincial cricket. Kepler Wessels wanted nothing more than to deny Clive Rice a hat trick of championship titles. There was no love lost between the two teams or the captains, but there was mutual respect.

In a league match two months earlier, these two sides had played out a draw at the Wanderers, an occasion when Neal Radford took a remarkable nine for 102 in Eastern Province's only innings. Transvaal's top batsman was Brian McMillan with scores of 77 and 43 not out; for Eastern Province, Wessels scored 60 and Mark Rushmere 43.

At St George's Park, Wessels won the toss and batted on a good pitch. Rushmere was soon out for 3, and his skipper for 11. The total was 42 for two. When the next wicket fell, it was 379 for three.

For just over seven hours the Transvaal bowlers and fielders were tormented by Kenny McEwan and Philip Amm. They were finally parted when McMillan dismissed McEwan for 191, the partnership of 337 being a new record for the Currie Cup. Wessels's instructions were clear, and Amm pushed on. After 11-and-a-half hours he was finally stumped by Jennings off Eksteen. He had scored 214. Still, Eastern Province batted on.

Into the third day they went amid growing alarm in the pavilion that Wessels was ruining the match as a spectacle for the large assembly of VIP guests. Wessels did not care; he wanted to grind Transvaal into the dust and so demoralise them that they would be easy pickings. Eastern Province batted all the way through and were eventually all out for 561. Transvaal had no hope of winning the match. They were required to bat out two-and-a-half days to secure the draw.

All out for 203 in their first innings, Transvaal were asked to follow on. Rice was determined not to buckle to Wessels's plan. He batted doggedly for five-and-a-half hours in the second innings to score 75, agonisingly taking the match into the final session on the fifth day. Then the breakthrough came and, with three wickets falling without a run being added, Transvaal finally folded for 255, beaten by an innings and 103 runs with only an hour left to play. It was their first Currie Cup defeat in seven seasons – an incredible run of 58 matches unbeaten. And for Eastern Province and Kepler Wessels it was the most glorious moment in the province's history. The VIP guests nodded their approval. Tim Shaw put his tired feet up for a deserved glass or two of champagne. His match figures read 92 overs, 59 maidens, 70 runs, six wickets.

FREE STATE'S CELEBRATIONS were on a far less grandiose scale. While the Currie Cup final was underway in Port Elizabeth, Joubert Strydom's team were heading for victory in a promotion-relegation match against Border in Bloemfontein. It was sad – but true – that the previous season's Currie Cup finalists were now required to play for their future existence in A Section cricket. Without overseas stars, Free State had finished bottom of the log with four defeats in seven matches.

Hansie Cronjé had become Rudi Steyn's new opening partner, but had scored only 170 runs in 12 first-class innings for an average of 15.45. Steyn, on the other hand, had prospered. He topped his province's batting averages with 38.30, and his 383 runs included a magnificent 178 against Western Province at Newlands. He also scored 57 not out, and carried his bat in a total of 98 against Eastern Province at St George's Park. In the match against Transvaal on the University Oval, Jimmy Cook had been the dominant figure. He scored 133 and 180 not out.

In the promotion-relegation match, there were half-centuries from Steyn, Strydom and Van Zyl, plus seven wickets each from Van Zyl and Donald, allowing Free State a comfortable victory by 10 wickets. A new member of their side was the English professional Gordon Parsons who had moved on after two seasons with Griqualand West.

A player who had moved back to Griquas after an absence of five seasons was Pat Symcox. All his time with Northern Transvaal he had worked and lived in Johannesburg and commuted to practices and matches in Pretoria. Having grown tired of all the travelling, he readily accepted a position to open a new private hospital in Kimberley. Back with his old province, he scored 59 runs in three first-class matches and took 10 wickets. It seemed as if his cricket career was finally winding down.

A cricketer whose career was just taking off was Jonty Rhodes, who was called on to play A Section cricket for Natal. The 19-year-old responded perfectly by achieving the rare feat of scoring a century in his Currie Cup début against Western Province at Kingsmead. He ended his first full season with 321 runs in seven matches at a tidy average of 32.

His team-mate Andrew Hudson played only two Currie Cup matches in which he totalled 44 runs, but he did perform better in the Nissan Shield, where he opened with Brian Whitfield and scored 70 in a quarter-final against Free State before being dismissed by Parsons.

IF FREE STATE did not perform too well in the Currie Cup, the same could not be said for their showing in the other competitions. If anything, they were emerging as a team of limited-over specialists whose enthusiasm and nerve in both the Nissan Shield and the Benson & Hedges Series was at times spectacular. One of the key players in this vibrant, young side was Hansie Cronjé. In the two Shield quarter-finals against Natal, he scored 46 and 91 not out, only for his team to be knocked out in the semis by Transvaal.

It was in the Benson & Hedges Series, however, that the teenage batsman and Free State went top of the class. Against Transvaal at the Wanderers, Cronjé scored 63; against Western Province at Virginia he made 36 before being bowled by Craig Matthews; against Northern Transvaal he was dismissed by Tertius Bosch for 12; against Natal he scored 38; and, in achieving a personal milestone, he batted through the innings to score an undefeated 105 in the semi-finals against the Impalas.

Free State were through to the final. Their opponents were a high-riding Western Province team that had won eight matches on the trot and were out-and-out favourites on their home ground. Also, three weeks earlier Western Province had beaten Transvaal in the two-leg Nissan Shield final. Skipper Adrian Kuiper, Peter Kirsten, Daryll Cullinan, Eric Simons and Dave Rundle were all in good nick.

Kuiper must have been supremely confident leading his team out in the B&H final. In the conclusive leg of the Shield final at the Wanderers he had plundered an unbeaten 42 off just 23 balls, and had then taken a career-best five for 47 to win the Man of the Match award. In the first leg, Cullinan had scored a sparkling 75 not out in 71 balls; at the Wanderers it was Kirsten's turn to hit top score of 73; and in the same match Simons had taken four for 44, with Rundle the very picture of offspin economy throughout.

Free State were no less confident. Earlier in the season at Virginia they had beaten Western Province by five wickets on a night when Parsons bowled particularly well to take three for 29 in his nine overs. At the start of the season the Free State players had promised themselves that they would make their mark on South African cricket. Now was their big chance under the Newlands floodlights.

In their bright-orange night-series uniforms, they batted, bowled and fielded like men possessed. Cronjé anchored the innings to score a wonderful 73, but it was Allan Donald's bowling that ultimately stole the show. In defence of a total of 213, he ripped into the batsmen to take four wickets for 18 runs. The defiant Peter Kirsten's 72 stood out like a beacon as Western Province were shot out 62 runs short of the victory target. Cullinan was dismissed by Donald for a duck, and Kuiper was out for 5.

Donald was named Man of the Match, and Cronjé later confided, 'I don't think I've ever seen him bowl so well. He was so charged up it was unbelievable. If he continues in this vein, I think he can make a very big impact on cricket for a long time to come.'

Joubert Strydom and his boys were ecstatic. Victory away from home without the aid of any big-name foreign players had brought the province the first trophy in their history. The Free Staters had made good their promise; they were now a team to be respected in South African cricket. But they did not sit back on their laurels; they vowed to get even better in the years ahead.

It was also a pivotal moment in the career of the young Cronjé. He was named as vice-captain to Strydom for the following season.

FANIE DE VILLIERS'S meteoric rise in the game hit a new high. Only three years before, he was just another young fast bowler in B Section cricket. Now he was named one of South Africa's Cricketers of the Year. After taking a modest 25 wickets the previous season, someone offered him the reward of a cricket book if he could surpass 30. He went much further than that in the summer of 1988/89. He took 43 first-class wickets and, in the powerful Western Province first innings at Newlands, he knocked over six for 47. Allan Donald, by comparison, took 28 wickets. Also named among the Cricketers of the Year was Mike Rindel, Vinnige Fanie's team-mate at Northern Transvaal. In his third season of A Section cricket, the cavalier left-hander totalled 711 runs at an average of almost 65. Kepler Wessels, on the other hand, averaged 57. He and Rindel each notched up two centuries and five fifties.

A few months later, Jimmy Cook went to England and upstaged them all. At the age of 35, he accepted a contract to play for Somerset to prove what many already believed. Throughout the Eighties Cook had been South Africa's outstanding opening batsman – a key figure in the Transvaal 'Mean Machine' that had dominated provincial cricket. As an automatic choice for all the rebel series, he had represented South Africa in more unofficial internationals than any other player, yet South Africa's continued isolation prevented him from proving himself on the real stage of world cricket. There had been previous offers to play county cricket, but he had declined them because he could not get extended leave of absence from his job as a primary school teacher. Accepting a position in the sports department at Rand Afrikaans University allowed him to be away for the winter months. Taunton would become his temporary new home, and English cricket would become his realm.

In 23 matches for Somerset, he amassed a staggering 2 241 runs, the only batsman in England to exceed 2 000 in 1989. He scored eight centuries – four in a row, and five in six innings. Against Nottinghamshire he became only the second cricketer in history to carry his bat in both innings with undefeated scores of 120 and 131. He needed just seven matches to move his aggregate of runs from 1 000 to 2 000, and he ended the season with a batting average of more than 60. When Somerset invited him to return to Taunton the following year, no one was surprised.

Elsewhere in England, South Africans were meeting with success. Roy Pienaar had another golden season with Kent, scoring 1 321 runs and hitting four centuries in quick succession, while Allan Donald was doing a different kind of damage at Warwickshire. Bowling at lightning pace against Lancashire at Old Trafford, he struck opener Gehan

Mendis on the toe and put him out of the game for a week; he hit Wasim Akram in the mouth and sent him away for 15 stitches; and he forced two other batsmen to retire hurt with hand injuries. Against Surrey he took five for 18. In his next match against Middlesex he bagged seven for 66, and against Kent at Canterbury he had one devastating spell of five for 9 in 24 balls. In 19 championship matches in total, Donald took no fewer than 86 wickets. His fans were calling him 'White Lightning'.

THE START OF each cricket season in England is prefixed by a grand occasion in London known as the Wisden Dinner. In 1989, Ali Bacher was invited as the guest speaker. There was much sympathy in English cricket for the SA Cricket Union's non-racial constitution and the work it was doing in the black communities. There were many people in England who believed that South Africa should be readmitted to the International Cricket Council, yet the ICC continued with hardline and punitive measures against the unwanted nation. In a passionate and eloquent address to a distinguished audience, Bacher detailed at great length the advances being made in South African cricket to break down racial barriers. He spoke of the revolution that was taking place in cricket's fight against apartheid.

'I would like tonight to bring a message from those involved in cricket in South Africa. Out of Africa will come something new. It will be dazzling, it will be strong and it will be good...' He was given a standing ovation.

Back home a palace revolution was underway in the ruling National Party. The more enlightened F.W. de Klerk had assumed control of the party from State President P.W. Botha. Untold political change was in the wind.

5

Kaalgat at Springbok Park

IN 1988 EWIE CRONJÉ took his two sons to England on a month's holiday. They stayed in Birmingham with Alvin Kallicharran, and watched Allan Donald and his Warwickshire team-mates in action at Edgbaston. They also went to watch the tennis championships at Wimbledon where they bumped into Ali Bacher, Geoff Dakin and Joe Pamensky.

The trio of high-ranking SA Cricket Union officials were on their annual pilgrimage to London in an attempt to get the International Cricket Council to see reason on the South African question. Two member nations apparently voiced support for some form of reconciliation, but the ICC, as usual, was not playing ball. South African cricket's isolation would continue.

Because of Ewie's position on the SACU executive, his boys, Frans and Hansie, were sometimes privy to the inner workings of the game's administrative affairs. 'I pretty much had an idea about what was going on and how hard they were trying to get South Africa back into international cricket,' said Hansie.

Year after year the SACU trio would visit London in the hope that the ICC would hear their case. Each time they were rebuffed. Even after Bacher had made such a positive impact on the Wisden Dinner in April 1989, the ICC refused to debate the issue. All the SACU officials were asking was that the ICC send a fact-finding mission to South Africa to see what was happening in cricket, but all they received was another resounding snub.

Bacher, Pamensky and Dakin knew there was only one road to follow – they would have to talk directly with the English players. What followed was the ill-fated Gatting tour that unwittingly paved the way for unification between the warring parties in South African cricket.

Unlike the other rebel tours, arrangements for this team of 16 English players to tour South Africa under the captaincy of former Test skipper Mike Gatting were known well in advance. The English cricket authorities certainly knew what was afoot; in some cases they were sympathetic to South Africa's need to have some form of international competition. Bacher himself had warned officials at the Wisden Dinner that if they did not admit South Africa through the front door, then South Africa would find a way in through the back door.

Bacher and company were well versed in the business of arranging unofficial competition and certainly appreciated the sensitivities. The SACU's township development programme was burgeoning and black players, coaches and officials were coming into the game. There was a feeling among cricket people of various persuasions that for the game to continue in South Africa, gate money from big tours was vital. Bacher knew that cricket, his beloved game, would die if there were no international competition.

The SACU had been criticised for forking out vast amounts of money to lure foreign cricketers to South Africa. Its detractors called it 'blood money', and pointed to the poverty that existed in the townships. They asked why the money lavished on overseas teams was not spent on upgrading underprivileged people.

For the SACU, it was a vicious circle: they needed more money for their development programmes but they also needed tours to bring in the cash. Also, overseas opposition was essential to improve standards in the game.

In organising the Gatting tour, the SACU hierarchy decided that the days of offering 'telephone number' cheques to the players were over. A system of remuneration that was market-related was devised, offering the players not much more than they would earn if they stayed within the English establishment.

It was claimed that the figures were based on the going rate in international cricket, and the SACU argued that they were effectively ridding the ventures of the 'rebel' tag they so despised. The players, they said, were by no means 'rebels', but rather professional cricketers opting for alternative employment. Their contracts also stipulated that they would have to spend time coaching at development clinics, and that a big percentage of the tour's profits would be sunk directly into the township development programmes.

In South Africa, meanwhile, the political picture was changing. F.W. de Klerk had been voted in as the new state president and was making conciliatory noises that suggested big things were afoot.

IN SEPTEMBER 1989, Bloemfontein unveiled a new cricket ground complete with floodlights. It was called Springbok Park, and Ewie Cronjé was instrumental in its making.

'What's the biggest crowd you reckon it will hold?' he was asked.

'I'd say about 9 000,' Ewie replied. 'There again, if we ever get 9 000 people at a cricket game in Bloemfontein, I'll strip and run naked around the ground during the lunch break!'

No one knew the Free State sporting public better than Ewie Cronjé. While tens of thousands would turn up for rugby games, barely hundreds watched the cricket. When he spoke of 9 000 fans, he was just being hopeful.

The opening of the new ground was celebrated with a floodlit match between Free State, the defending Benson & Hedges Series champions, and a Rest of South Africa XI. Fielding on the boundary, Dave Callaghan dived for a ball and inadvertently lost his trousers. With the ball clutched in one hand, and his flannels sitting around his ankles, the red-faced Eastern Province player was frozen for a moment with indecision … to return the ball or to pull up his pants? There were far fewer than 9 000 people in the ground that night but there were still enough spectators hooting with laughter to inspire Callaghan to get dressed before worrying about how many runs were being scored. The wicketkeeper Dave Richardson, known to his teammates as 'Swinger', had tears rolling down his cheeks. 'I've never seen anything so funny on a cricket field and I doubt I ever will.'

Things hadn't been going too well for Callaghan. He had been bowled by Allan Donald for 2 before losing his trousers. The Rest XI were restricted to 190 for five, of which Mike Rindel hit 66 not out in 67 balls.

Hansie Cronjé made a good start for Free State, but when he reached 59 he was bowled by Clive Rice. This wicket seemed to inspire the Rest's skipper, who then took four more wickets to pull off victory by six runs. Things, meanwhile, had improved for Callaghan. He conceded only 26 runs in his nine overs of seam bowling to keep the scoring rate in check. It took him a while, though, to get over his earlier embarrassment.

HANSIE CRONJÉ'S FIRST Currie Cup match as Free State's vice-captain came shortly after his twentieth birthday – against Northern Transvaal at Centurion Park. It was not a particularly happy one for him or his team. They had little answer to the fiery fast bowling of Fanie de Villiers and Tertius Bosch who shared 14 wickets in a nine-wicket victory.

Cronjé was castled by Fanie for 2 in the first innings, and dismissed by Bosch for 10 in the second. Free State's best batsman was their new acquisition from Boland. At age 37, Omar Henry had scores of 32 not out and 78. The fast Centurion pitch did not help his slow bowling, so it was the pacier Gordon Parsons who did the most damage with his five for 65. For once, Donald and Van Zyl were off the boil.

At Kingsmead, meanwhile, Adrian Kuiper was positively cooking. In response to a decision to axe him as the Western Province skipper in favour of Lawrence Seeff, the stocky apple farmer produced a wonderful all-round performance against Natal. He lashed an undefeated 161, took four wickets for 29 in 13 overs and held two splendid catches.

The Western Province team also had a new member. After five seasons with Transvaal, Brian McMillan had moved to the Cape for what was to be the start of a glorious career. Against Natal on this occasion, he scored 44 and 41.

The Western Province attack was also undergoing change. Meyrick Pringle had joined from Eastern Province, Eric Simons was struggling to hold down a place in the Currie Cup line-up, and Craig Matthews was fast enhancing his reputation as a fine, penetrative seam bowler. His brother Brett had since departed, first to Eastern Province and then briefly to Transvaal, his heyday as a strike bowler apparently over.

Natal also had a new captain. With no future back home in Australia, Kim Hughes had returned to South Africa.

CLIVE RICE LED Transvaal against SA Schools at the Wanderers. He had scored just one run when he was caught by Gerhardus Liebenberg at slip off the bowling of Brett Schultz. The veteran all-rounder made a mental note of their names.

Liebenberg was a shy, polite Afrikaans boy from the Diamantveld High School in Kimberley, a tall, gifted batsman with a copybook technique. Schultz came from Kingswood College in the Eastern Cape. He had big, broad shoulders, a mop of blond hair, and bowled left-arm fast. He wasn't afraid of telling the batsmen exactly what he thought of them. He was anything but reserved.

During the preceding Nuffield Week, Liebenberg had hit successive scores of 100 not out, 84 and 110 not out and now, opening the batting against Transvaal, he made 25. Schultz had had a quiet sort of week, but he reserved his best for last. Counting Rice as his prized wicket, he returned bowling figures of five for 39 in 18 overs against a powerful batting side.

The SA Schools squad, which included the Grey College left-arm spinner Nico Bojé, then embarked on a short coastal tour. Against

Western Province Colts, Schultz again wrought havoc with six for 29 in a total of 113 for seven. His next opponents were a strong SA under-21 XI that included Hansie Cronjé, who immediately made a mental note of Liebenberg's name when the Kimberley boy scored an immaculate 103.

In his turn at bat, Cronjé was going along very nicely on 77 when the blond bombshell from Kingswood College nipped him out. As Cronjé tucked his bat under his arm, Schultz ran down the wicket and raised a threatening finger at the departing batsman.

'That's number one, that's number one!' he repeated at the top of his voice as if to say that their encounters had just begun.

'Noisy fellow,' muttered Hansie to himself as he glanced over his shoulder, 'but not a bad bowler.'

The Eastern Province selectors agreed. Two days later the 19-year-old paceman was in the province's B team for his first-class début at Kingsmead. In Natal B's first innings he took six for 72 and, batting at No 11, he scored 29 not out. Kepler Wessels made more than a mental note. He immediately contacted his fellow selectors. Four days later Schultz made his Currie Cup début at Springbok Park, forcing his way into an Eastern Province team that already boasted Rod McCurdy and John Maguire as its new-ball bowlers. His sole wicket of the match was Hansie Cronjé's. The Free State opener left one alone and was surprised to be clean bowled for 21.

Schultz ran down the wicket at the departing batsman. This time he raised two threatening fingers.

'That's number two,' he yelled, 'that's number two!'

Cronjé turned and smiled. He was beginning to enjoy the antics of this brazen youngster.

THE SOUTH AFRICAN selectors, led by former Springbok captain Peter van der Merwe, were also making notes. Callaghan had scored 107 and 47 against Free State, Rudi Steyn had hit 95, and Donald had taken nine wickets for 96 runs. Elsewhere, Daryll Cullinan had added an innings of 137 against Northern Transvaal to his 140 against Transvaal the previous season, Wessels had scored 182 against Northern Transvaal, and Rushmere was consistently hitting big scores at the top of the Eastern Province batting order. Louis Vorster was less fortunate. He had been dropped from the Transvaal Currie Cup squad.

THE NEW STATE PRESIDENT continued to make favourable political noises, and Ali Bacher wondered what they meant. He asked the advice of a political analyst. The man assured him there was no immediate chance of the apartheid laws being scrapped; in his estimation they would probably remain on the statute books for the next 10 years at least.

If that were the reality, thought Bacher, then the sporting boycott would remain in force. The SACU would have no option but to press ahead with the Gatting tour. Deep down, though, Bacher felt uncomfortable. The political climate that had surrounded the previous rebel tours was such that it was almost justifiable. Now somehow it was different; there was a discernible change of climate. Bacher could not put his finger on it, but the looming venture just didn't seem right.

Little did he realise that it would be so fraught with problems from day one that a stage would be reached when, for the first time in his life, he would feel that he had lost control of events.

From the moment they set foot in South Africa, Gatting and his men were the target of confrontational anti-tour demonstrators. Never before had cricket in this country been threatened by angry protestors – indeed, in the totalitarian days of grand apartheid, demonstrations were not permitted by law – but now, in the process of political change and marshalled by the relatively unknown ANC-aligned National Sports Congress (NSC), the process of playing sport was under heavy fire from the Mass Democratic Movement of young black activists. Gatting, the very picture of diplomacy and control, constantly invoked his democratic right to play cricket wherever he chose. Whenever he opened his mouth, though, the English tabloids would find ways to interpret his comments as 'insensitive remarks'. He was in a no-win situation.

During the opening tour match in Kimberley, Bacher found himself in an even tighter situation. Despite the threat of violence outside the ground, he stepped into the vice between demonstrators and armed police to appeal for calm and good sense. He exchanged harsh words with policemen who were bent on disrupting a peaceful protest; he telephoned at least two cabinet ministers and a range of municipal officials; and, after hours in the cauldron, succeeded in winning the demonstrators the right to continue their protest in a designated area. There was just a hint of a suggestion that his courage and sincerity had gained him new respect among people who were trying to ruin his cricket tour.

But where the Gatting tour went, the demonstrators went. Although the matches proceeded, they were surrounded with an air of foreboding. People debated whether it was all worth the trouble.

In the meantime, Cronjé and Rushmere had achieved new milestones. As captain of the SA Universities team in the second match of the English XI's tour at Springbok Park, Cronjé hit his maiden first-class century. His 104 was the standout performance in a talented team that included Steyn, Hudson, Eksteen and Bosch. In the next tour match at Pietermaritzburg, Rushmere opened the batting for Roy Pienaar's SA Invitation XI and was undefeated twice with scores of 150 and 151, the first South African to hit two 150s in a first-class game. In a high-scoring match, Pienaar made scores of 63 and 81, and Cullinan hit 77 not out. The best of the home bowlers was Omar Henry with three wickets in each innings, and even Jonty Rhodes was given the rare chance to bowl four overs for 11 runs.

On the day that separated these two matches, President F.W. de Klerk made his opening address to parliament. It was 2 February 1990. De Klerk told a hushed gathering and an incredulous world that he would lift the ban on political organisations such as the African National Congress, and would effectively begin the dismantling of apartheid. What's more, he suggested that Nelson Mandela would 'soon' be released from prison.

THE SELECTION OF the South African team for the first 'Test' caused different shock waves. Clive Rice was not only axed as captain but also dropped from the side. Jimmy Cook was amazed when Peter van der Merwe invited him to take over the captaincy. The rest of the team was Fotheringham, Wessels, Peter Kirsten, Pienaar, Kuiper, McMillan, Jennings, Rundle, Snell and Donald.

Wessels's selection was not universally popular. It was felt that he had not been back in South Africa long enough to shed his Australian identity. Some of the senior South African players believed he was keeping out a 'local' batsman, and that he should serve a much longer residential qualification before becoming eligible for selection. But Van der Merwe, who doubled as convener of selectors and vice-president of the Eastern Province Cricket Union, was adamant. Wessels would play.

With spotter helicopters hovering over the Wanderers Stadium, and a huge police presence around the perimeter of the ground, the 'Test' match got underway in surreal circumstances. It was all over within three days. Gatting's team were bowled out for 156 and 122, and South Africa triumphed by seven wickets. Donald took eight wickets in the match, Snell six and McMillan four. Cook was out for 20 and 15, Wessels scored 1 and 2, McMillan got a duck, and Adrian Kuiper was the match top scorer with 84.

THE DAY AFTER the 'Test', two extraordinary events took place. Nelson Mandela walked out of prison and Kepler Wessels walked out of the South African cricket team.

On any other day the news of Wessels's departure would have dominated the headlines. Now it was only of some relevance to the cricket community. Mandela's release from the Victor Verster Prison was televised live to a rapt mass audience, the vast majority of whom had never seen him before. The sight of the tall, white-haired, old man walking triumphantly out of the prison grounds gripped the emotional nation and stunned the world. He had been incarcerated for over 27 years. It was 11 February 1990.

Wessels, meanwhile, decided he wanted to play no further part in the Springbok team. The innuendo surrounding his controversial selection had reached his ears, making him feel uncomfortable among teammates who did not want him, and he confessed that the pressures had grown too great. He wanted out, and no amount of cajoling could persuade him to stay. It was still 11 February 1990.

Another significant event was taking place. Ali Bacher met with the NSC in Johannesburg and agreed to curtail the Gatting tour. In exchange, the NSC would hold off its demonstrators. The planned second 'Test' in Cape Town would be cancelled, and the six limited-overs internationals would be reduced to four. 11 February 1990 continued to produce unprecedented turnabouts.

The cricket was now almost secondary to the incredibly dramatic political changes unfolding around it, but at least it continued unencumbered, with the fireworks and drama being confined to a more regular sporting variety. Rice was back in the team, but still not as captain. It seemed that someone believed that he and Wessels could not play in the same team at the same time, but no one really spelled that out. Others who received their turn to play at national level were Rushmere, Shaw and the effervescent De Villiers.

The major highlight, and low lights, came at Springbok Park when the belligerent Kuiper bludgeoned a century in 49 balls before one of the four giant floodlights fused during the English innings. Kuiper's 100 included eight sixes and seven fours, and he was eventually out for 117 in 66 deliveries.

Hansie Cronjé watched in awe and amazement from the pavilion. 'It's the most unbelievable innings I've even seen!' he told Ewie. 'I'm sure we'll never see anything like it again.'

His father nodded in agreement, but his thoughts were elsewhere. He was wondering what the future held for South African cricket; what the game in the years ahead would mean for Springbok Park.

'One other thing, Dad,' Hansie interrupted, 'how many spectators have we got here tonight?'

'They tell me 10 500,' said Ewie cagily.

Then both of them burst out laughing. Try as he might, Hansie couldn't imagine his father running *kaalgat* around Springbok Park. Neither, for that matter, could Ewie Cronjé.

BACK IN PORT ELIZABETH, Wessels's bitterness had turned to determination. He was a man who thrived on adversity and he communicated this quality to his Eastern Province team-mates. People elsewhere were calling him a quitter which, in Kepler's case, was akin to waving a red rag at a bull. His team had already won the Nissan Shield with back-to-back final victories over Northern Transvaal, as well as having drawn the Currie Cup final against Western Province. It was in the latter match that Gary Kirsten opened the innings with a career-high 175, and brother Peter followed with 128. Still, the draw meant that Eastern Province retained a share of the gold trophy they had won outright the previous season.

The only competition still to be decided was the Benson & Hedges Series. The Eastern Province captain badly wanted the treble. At Kingsmead, the two skippers tossed for innings. They were Kim Hughes of Natal and Kepler Wessels of Eastern Province, two Aussie mates who, sometimes together, sometimes alone, had travelled a long and tough road in the world of cricket.

Natal batted first and totalled 202 with Hughes scoring 43 and Hudson 35. Eastern Province followed; Wessels made 41 and Callaghan 65. With one ball remaining, the total stood on 201 for nine, McCurdy on strike. He hit a four.

When Wessels returned home, he was smiling again.

JIMMY COOK RETURNED to Somerset in the South African winter. There he scored 2 608 runs in 24 first-class matches for an average of 76. That season he hit nine centuries and 11 fifties. Against Glamorgan at Cardiff he compiled a career-best 313 not out, batting for just under nine hours and hitting 43 fours. In one of his several limited-overs centuries, he scored 100 in 75 balls against Hampshire, and hit the great West Indies fast bowler Malcolm Marshall clean out of the attack. No one was particularly surprised when Somerset invited him back for a third season.

Among the other South Africans on the county circuit was Adrian Kuiper on a one-off contract with Derbyshire. In a Sunday League game against Sussex, he caned 53 not out in 28 balls; against Essex, he reached his 50 in 31 balls. English critics called him a second Ian Botham.

At Kent, Fanie de Villiers was having fun. He liked to boast that he was a *boereseun* but he loved the English way of life for all its pomp and circumstance and its great sense of history. There was nothing he enjoyed more than learning about other people's customs and cultures, and he was an inveterate sightseer and explorer. As the new member of the Kent team he took 25 wickets in 12 matches, including six for 70 against championship leaders Middlesex at Arundel.

Allan Donald was back again at Warwickshire, intent on making cricket his life. Sadly, a series of injuries severely restricted his appearances, but against Kent at Edgbaston he still managed to take three wickets in five balls.

6

'What are you doing on Thursday?'

THE ABORTED GATTING tour was a crisis for South African cricket. The venture had been scheduled for two legs spanning successive seasons, but Ali Bacher's agreement with the National Sports Congress (NSC) included an assurance that the return visit would be cancelled in its entirety while the first leg of the tour would be curtailed. He acted outside his mandate from his board in making this concession, and Geoff Dakin, the SACU president, was not pleased. Dakin accepted that there was no option other than to curtail the first leg but he was adamant that only his full board could stop the second.

Dakin was in a difficult position because he had to walk a delicate tightrope in a sharply divided SACU boardroom. As the president, he owed it to his members to consider all arguments and counter-arguments before any decision was reached but, unlike Bacher, he had no hands-on dealings with the anti-tour forces.

Bacher, on the other hand, was a lone wolf. He knew what cricket had to do and he was prepared to put his job on the line in order to achieve this. He made no bones about it.

Tensions were running high. The SACU board met. Bacher did not beat about the bush. He knew what was going down. He had seen the anger of the people, he was fearful of compromising the hard-won friendships of cricket's township allies and he knew better than most that the enthusiasm in the development programmes was being seriously eroded. His message would not have escaped even the most hardline cricket official, and the board duly agreed to cancel the return visit by Mike Gatting's team. Bacher's vision was also rewarded. He was asked to investigate the way forward for South African cricket. It would be his task alone, but this time he had an official mandate.

It was a masterstroke. Having been caught in the verbal crossfire of the anti-tour demonstrations and hearing first hand the complaints of the masses, Bacher had quickly tuned into the anger and aspirations of a turbulent nation. Clearly in sympathy with the mood on the ground, he knew that swift and decisive action on cricket's part was absolutely essential. He immediately announced that rebel tours would cease.

This was seen as an undisguised invitation to the rival SA Cricket Board (SACB) of Krish Mackerdhuj to put its cards on the table. Mackerdhuj was also a vice-president of the NSC, so he was equally in touch with the political climate surrounding cricket. At the next board meeting, the SACB agreed that round-table discussions should take place with the SACU.

At a Durban hotel on 8 September 1990 the executives of both organisations held exploratory talks. It was the first time that Bacher and Mackerdhuj had met, the first time in fact that any of the officials gathered that day had been in such close contact. The meeting was chaired by Steve Tshwete.

Tshwete had recently returned from life in exile after serving a jail term as a Robben Island political prisoner, and was the ANC's 'shadow' sports minister. In his role as a facilitator between two organisations with so little in common politically, he was the key player.

He would later become known as 'Mr Fixit' for the shrewd and sagacious guidance he brought to the conference tables of so many rival sporting bodies seeking to establish unified structures.

Cricket was the first sport to get it right. Out of the ashes of the aborted Gatting tour rose a phoenix that would carry the sport back on to the world stage and inspire Mackerdhuj to deliver an eloquent summation when the United Cricket Board of South Africa (UCBSA) came into being on 29 June 1991: 'From that tentative, tense beginning on a beautiful spring day in Durban in September 1990, sometimes with faltering steps, the Board and the Union found each other, developed a working relationship and eventually trust.'

The trust was all-embracing and all-important. It superseded the distrust and suspicions of the past and brushed aside the old, insurmountable obstacles with the power of a bulldozer. Even the emotive issues of emblems and symbols were quickly overcome without rancour – the UCBSA would have a new identity and the old Springbok badge of the apartheid years would cease to be.

ALI BACHER, IN the meantime, had been a busy man. In April 1991 he was escorted to a house in the unfashionable Johannesburg suburb of Mayfair where he was introduced to a number of high-ranking ANC officials. Among them were Thabo Mbeki and Joe Modise. Later, with Steve Tshwete as his ubiquitous companion, Bacher paid visits to the London high commissions of the world's cricket-playing nations. The two South Africans carried with them a letter from Mbeki, the ANC's foreign affairs spokesman, in which he appealed to those governments to recognise South Africa's new unified cricket body. 'A positive decision in this regard,' he wrote, 'would play a crucial role in encouraging forward movement within South Africa towards the complete desegregation of sport in general. This in turn would have the important impact on the processes in which we are engaged directed at moving the millions of South African people, including the youth, towards a non-racial and democratic order and a peaceful and stable society.' Mbeki's letter, a gesture of goodwill, was the direct result of Bacher's insistence that the Gatting tour be scrapped and that the rebel era come to an end.

'For the first time,' said Bacher, 'I saw first hand the power and influence of the African National Congress. At the High Commission of Guyana in London I noticed a portrait of Fidel Castro hanging on the wall. I thought, "What chance do I have here?", but Steve as usual opened the batting. He said, "You asked us to isolate South African cricket and we did it. If you want them back, we'll do it."

Bacher was in awe of Tshwete. In the space of only a few months he had grown to know him well. On a train trip between London and Birmingham, Tshwete had opened his heart to Bacher to describe in graphic and shocking detail the torture inflicted on him by security policemen during his first 24 hours on Robben Island.

Bacher was amazed that, despite the terrible privations of 15 years of imprisonment, there was not an ounce of bitterness in the man. 'His only desire was to heal the wounds of the past and build for the future.'

Bacher and Tshwete were also invited to address high-ranking cricket officials in the famed Committee Room at Lord's Cricket Ground. Tshwete's message was pungent: 'South African cricket is an embryo that needs oxygen to grow. To suffocate it now would be terrible.'

A week after the formation of the UCBSA, a four-man delegation returned to London for the annual meeting of the International Cricket Council (ICC). They were the UCBSA president, Geoff Dakin; the vice-president, Krish Mackerdhuj; the managing director, Ali Bacher; and Steve Tshwete. Proudly, they walked side by side through the fabled Grace Gates at Lord's.

On 10 July 1991, the ICC readmitted South Africa as a full Test-playing member. South Africa's application for membership was supported by India, a country that had been at the forefront of the anti-apartheid struggle since 1948. All the years of trying to gain entry through the back door had come to nought; now South African cricket was being shown the red-carpet treatment through the front door.

BACK HOME, EXCITEMENT and expectations were running at fever pitch. What would happen next? How soon would South Africa be playing official international cricket? The incredible pace of change had stunned South African cricketers. From being outcasts one minute, they were fully fledged members of the international community the next. They were anxious to know what the future held for them, and Free State's new captain – their youngest ever – was no exception.

At the age of 21, Hansie Cronjé had succeeded Joubert Strydom at the province's helm. Bloemfontein had been Strydom's home all his life but, at the end of the previous season, aged 27, he packed up and left to further his professional business interests in Johannesburg. It was, in a sense, the end of an era for Free State cricket, and Strydom spent most of the summer at his new province playing for Transvaal B.

Cronjé took over the reins with enthusiasm. He was well liked and respected by a young team that now included the valuable 18-year-old SA Schools prodigy Gerhardus Liebenberg, who had recently moved from Kimberley to Bloemfontein. Also, the arrival of specialist opener Mickey Arthur from Griqualand West gave Rudi Steyn a new batting partner and allowed Cronjé to operate at either No 3, 4 or 5 in the order. The young captain had a strong ally, too, in the team's manager/coach, Johan Volsteedt, his former mentor at Grey College.

Although 1990/91 turned out to be a fairly average season for Free State, it was a most productive one for their new captain. In his second Currie Cup† match in charge, he hit 95 against Transvaal, and then went to Durban to score his maiden Currie Cup century, declaring immediately on reaching 100. One of the first men to congratulate Cronjé was the Natal captain, Kim Hughes. It was not clear whether he remembered him as the schoolboy who had once operated the bowling machine for him in the Bloemfontein nets.

Jonty Rhodes, meanwhile, was having trouble again with Allan Donald. With his score on 42 in the first innings, he was struck on the head by a short, fast delivery and was forced to retire hurt. In typical fashion, he returned in the second innings to hit a half-century. The top scorer for Natal in his first season in senior cricket was Errol Stewart

---

† The Currie Cup underwent various name changes over the years but, for the sake of continuity, the premier first-class provincial competition is referred to throughout the text as the Currie Cup.

with 76 not out. He was a fine all-round sportsman who was already playing provincial rugby for Natal at centre three-quarter.

Cronjé's second Currie Cup century came at Springbok Park. Wickets were tumbling quickly to the superb swing bowling of Fanie de Villiers when Cronjé came to the wicket at first drop. A total of 69 for six became 279 all out against Northern Transvaal with Cronjé standing on 101. At the end of the season he was atop the provincial batting averages with a total of 715 Currie Cup runs. He was also using himself occasionally as a change bowler.

EWIE CRONJÉ WAS still a board member of the Free State provincial cricket union and retained contacts within the new UCBSA. Still, he was reluctant to make any bold predictions about South African cricket's immediate future when Hansie quizzed him on the issue.

'It's hard to say, son,' he replied cagily. 'Dr Bacher has already said that we shouldn't be in too much of a hurry. The timing has to be right so that we have the support of the whole country, and any decision will have to be taken in conjunction with the National Sports Congress. We shouldn't be impatient, Hansie. It'll happen in good time.'

The young Cronjé, like all South African cricketers, was naturally impatient. The World Cup was to be played in Australia and New Zealand early in 1992, and he had heard suggestions that South Africa might be invited to take part. Not that Cronjé expected to be there himself – although his batting average of 69.88 in the Nissan Shield and 39.23 in the Benson & Hedges Series suggested otherwise – but he wanted nothing more than to see South Africa competing. His feelings mirrored those of the entire cricket community.

The ICC chairman, Colin Cowdrey, was not holding out any hope of South Africa's World Cup chances.

The tournament had been long in the making, and by mid-1991 the competing nations had already been announced, the fixtures were set, and the ticketing process underway. Cowdrey thought it unlikely that the organising committee could accommodate another team at this late stage. He was wrong.

The organising committee announced that it would consider South Africa's position. This prompted the UCBSA, with the backing of the NSC, to apply immediately to take part. The ICC called a special meeting at Sharjah in the United Arab Emirates in October 1991, and a UCBSA delegation, armed with a letter of support from Nelson Mandela himself, travelled there to put its case. A function had been arranged in a Sandton hotel to coincide with the ICC meeting, and a satellite telephone link-up was set up to connect Dakin, Mackerdhuj and

Bacher with the guests back home. In a festive mood, a large group of officials, politicians, players and journalists stood around expectantly over drinks and snacks waiting for the news out of Sharjah. There were wild whoops of delight when it finally came. Dakin's booming voice was crystal clear on the line as he announced with unbridled joy that South Africa would play at the 1992 World Cup. The party began.

The South Africans in Sharjah immediately headed off on a pre-arranged goodwill mission to India, Pakistan, Sri Lanka and Kenya. The object of the expedition was simply to introduce themselves to their cricket counterparts in those countries.

In South Africa people could only talk about the World Cup, but in India a more urgent matter had arisen. Pakistan had cancelled an imminent tour of that country for security reasons, and the Indian cricket team were suddenly without opponents. Because of this, the Indian Cricket Board would lose income, and its coffers were in bad shape. When they arrived in Calcutta, the South Africans were told of the impasse. The Indian officials were in a fix. They had to find a solution and they had to do so without delay. The first match of the aborted Pakistan tour was already scheduled for 10 November 1991 and tickets had been sold. It was now 29 October. They appealed to Dakin and his colleagues to send a South African team in Pakistan's place.

In Johannesburg, four days later, the UCBSA called an emergency board meeting. It was crazy, said several officials, to undertake a tour at such short notice and so early in the new season, but Bacher reminded them that South Africa was indebted to India for backing its application for readmission to world cricket. The board agreed. South Africa had to go. It was Sunday 2 November. The plane would leave on Thursday.

The administrative infrastructure of the defunct SACU formed the backbone of the new UCBSA. This was just as well because the SACU office staff had vast experience of crisis management from the days of the rebel tours. The well-oiled machine clicked into gear with Bacher at the helm. There was just one small problem: South Africa didn't have a cricket team.

THE 1991/92 SEASON was barely underway and most of the players were still brushing away the cobwebs of a winter's inactivity. There was hardly any current form to go on. The first priority was to find the right team in time for the World Cup in February and March. No one was expecting anything like this.

The selection committee convened. It was a new one, made up of former SACU and SACB officials. They hardly knew each other. Their brief was simple: select a 14-man South African squad and do it now. The convener was Peter van der Merwe. What on earth did he have up his sleeve? It was still Sunday, 2 November.

The selectors agreed there was only one way out. They would have to choose a team based on the previous season's performances. They would need as many of the older, experienced players as possible – and particularly Clive Rice. Van der Merwe phoned him at home.

A year before Van der Merwe had axed Rice as captain and dropped him from the team for the Gatting series. Now he was asking him to captain the first official South African team to India. Rice was surprised and overjoyed. Twenty years earlier, he had been selected as a 22-year-old to tour Australia with the Springboks. Because of politics that tour never got off the ground.

His team now was Jimmy Cook, Peter Kirsten, Kepler Wessels, Mandy Yachad, Andrew Hudson, Dave Richardson, Adrian Kuiper, Brian McMillan, Tim Shaw, Clive Eksteen, Allan Donald, Richard Snell and Craig Matthews. It was a squad based largely on form and statistics from the past year and partly on reputation: Yachad, the country's chief run-getter, with 994 Currie Cup runs and four centuries; Wessels, with an aggregate of 871 and a knock of 197 against Northern Transvaal; Hudson, 673 runs in the Currie Cup and an innings of 184 not out against Transvaal; McMillan, 632 runs for an average of 45; Matthews, named Player of the Year after topping the Currie Cup bowling averages with 47 wickets; Shaw with 40 scalps; Snell with 35.

Cook picked himself. The opening batsman had again surpassed himself in England when, in his previous season at Somerset, he had scored more runs than ever before, an incredible 2 755 in first-class matches with a record 11 centuries and a highest score of 210 not out. Donald, too, had had a golden summer on the county circuit where his 83 wickets included four five-wicket hauls – known in modern cricket-speak as 'fifors' – in successive innings.

Kuiper had enjoyed only moderate success in the champion Western Province team of the previous season, but his track record as a combative all-rounder booked his place. So, too, did Peter Kirsten's distinguished batsmanship, which had not enjoyed its normal, free-wheeling exposure after his move from Cape Town to help the Border province gain promotion to the Currie Cup.

Some players were unlucky not to get a trip. Mark Rushmere was astonishingly overlooked, especially since he was averaging more than 40 in limited-overs cricket; Roy Pienaar's return to Transvaal from Northerns had not brought the usual mountain of runs, but the classy pedigree remained; Transvaal strike bowler Steven Jack's astounding 54 wickets in his maiden Currie Cup season, including eight for 51 against Eastern Province, and a limited-overs best of five for 20 against the Impalas went unrewarded. And Tertius Bosch's 42 Currie Cup scalps for Northerns and his seven for 75 against Free State did not win him the vote.

Daryll Cullinan was hardly out of form, but he had not helped his cause by being dropped from the Western Province team for an 'attitude problem' involving differences of opinion with the team leadership. Cullinan's response was to pack and leave for Johannesburg where he joined Transvaal. His replacement in the Western Province middle-order was the 16-year-old Herschelle Gibbs.

JONTY RHODES HAD been knocking on the door, too. He was already acclaimed as the most spectacular cover-point fielder in the country, his spring-ball athleticism and dazzling speed across the ground matched only by his uncanny presence and bull's-eye accuracy. He had also developed into an extremely audacious limited-overs batsman whose unorthodox, risk-taking approach made him a huge hit wherever he played. In a Benson & Hedges Series semi-final eight months before the India tour, he brought the Kingsmead crowd to its feet and Transvaal to its knees in quite the most extraordinary climax in the history of the floodlit competition. Natal needed seven runs off the last ball to win the match. Rhodes had 80 runs and was on strike. Snell was the bowler. He was so intent on not overstepping the crease and giving away a no-ball that he delivered a short-pitched ball which Rhodes crashed away over mid-wicket for a six. 'No-ball!' The umpire ruled it had passed above waist height. An extra ball had to be bowled. Rhodes hit it for four.

For all these heroics, Natal cricket continued to flatter to deceive under the captaincy of Kim Hughes. Once the dominant force in South African cricket, Natal had last won the Currie Cup in 1980/81, the B&H Series in 1983/84, and the Nissan Shield in 1986/87. For all his achieve-ments as a great all-rounder and captain, Mike Procter had yet to win a major trophy as their new director, and Hughes, likewise, had yet to taste real success. They were surrounded by talented personnel, includ-ing an enthusiastic fitness trainer named Clive Barker – who would one day become a household name in South African soccer – but the lean spell endured. For the second successive season, they lost the B&H final, soundly beaten by Western Province at Newlands.

Among the newcomers in Procter's expanded provincial squad was the itinerant Patrick Symcox. He had been posted to Pietermaritzburg by his company to open a new hospital in the Natal capital. All the seasons of trying to play Currie Cup cricket had finally brought their reward. Thirteen years after making his provincial début for Griqualand West, he was at last selected for his first Currie Cup match. Against Free State at Kingsmead, the 30-year-old Symcox took three wickets and scored 21 not out and 1. In the same match, the 21-year-old Hansie Cronjé reached his maiden Currie Cup century.

Symcox played only one other Currie Cup game in the 1990/91 season. Against Eastern Province at Pietermaritzburg he again took three wickets and scored 12 runs. He also failed to get a game throughout Natal's exciting B&H campaign that summer.

THE FREE STATE CRICKET UNION had made a very important appointment in September 1991. They hired former Springbok all-rounder Eddie Barlow as their manager-coach in place of Johan Volsteedt. This was not an easy decision to make because Free State cricket ran deep in Volsteedt's blood. The man who replaced him, though, was an institution in South African cricket. Barlow played 30 Test matches in the pre-isolation years and was vice-captain to Ali Bacher in the team that thrashed Lawry's Australians in 1970. Throughout his playing career he had exhibited incredible self-belief and a fighting spirit. His team-mates said of him that he didn't *think* he could walk on water, he *knew* he could. In provincial cricket, he had been an inspirational leader who had taken his teams to dizzy heights, and in Test cricket he averaged over 45 as a top-order batsman and took 40 wickets. In Australia in 1963/64 he scored 201 in the Adelaide Test, and for a Rest of the World XI in 1970 he performed the hat trick, and took four wickets in five balls against England at Headingley.

'Bunter' Barlow was just the man Free State needed to pull their fortunes around, yet he had set his goals even higher. At his first practice with his new team at Bloemfontein he startled the players when he declared, 'I am here to prepare you for international cricket!'

At that stage none of them was even contemplating playing international cricket. Although the country had been welcomed back by the ICC, the prospect of playing Test cricket was still a distant one in their minds. Their only goal was to take Free State cricket to the top of the heap in the coming 1991/92 season.

As the weeks went by, Barlow continued to drum home his message to his young charges: 'The reason we're running so hard today, boys, is that when you get out there at the Melbourne Cricket Ground and the Sydney Cricket Ground, you've got to be ready!'

Barlow had foresight of what was to come. Within two months of his arrival in Bloemfontein, the gates of world cricket were beginning to open.

Cronjé adored Barlow. He believed he could do nothing wrong as long as he had Bunter to guide him on his way.

THREE NIGHTS BEFORE Clive Rice's team departed for India, Hansie Cronjé received a telephone call from Ali Bacher.

'What are you doing on Thursday, Hansie?'

'Oh, well, I have to ... um... Why do you ask, Dr Bacher?'

'I was wondering whether you'd like to go to India for 10 days.'

Hansie could not believe it. The team for India had already been announced and here, out of the blue, this strange telephone call.

'Er, what exactly does this mean, Dr Bacher?'

The managing director explained that the UCBSA had decided to send four 'development' players with the team, and that Cronjé was one of them. The others were Natal's Derek Crookes, Western Province's Faiek Davids and Transvaal's Hussein Manack. They would not actually play but would go along for the ride in order to get a feel for conditions in India in preparation for possible future tours of the Asian subcontinent.

Cronjé couldn't believe his ears, but he had one big problem. That Thursday he was due to sit his final exam for his B.Comm. degree at the University of the Orange Free State. 'Can I ring you back, Dr Bacher?' he stuttered, 'I ... I need to make a ... a few enquiries.'

Hansie immediately phoned his lecturer to tell him of his dilemma. 'Is there any way I can maybe postpone writing this exam?' he asked breathlessly.

'Of course you can, Hansie. This is a great chance for you and you can't afford to miss it!'

'Thanks very much, Mr Smit.'

'Hang on, Hansie, one other thing...'

'Yes, sir?'

'Just make sure you use this to get into the World Cup team and go to Australia, too!'

'Thanks, Mr Smit, that'll be nice.'

A CHARTERED AIRLINER was laid on for the trip. Cricket officials, their families and friends hastily booked their places, among them Ewie and San-Marie Cronjé. There was also place for a contingent of cricket supporters that included a group of Asian South Africans eager to return to the land of their forebears in support of the team.

The four development players nervously boarded the aircraft at Jan Smuts Airport (now known as Johannesburg International Airport). As non-playing members of a South African squad, they felt somewhat surplus to requirements. There was nothing to worry about, however; they were made to feel totally welcome by the team members. As the tour progressed they were included in all the team talks, they heard all the planning and all the strategy. In fact, they became an integral part of everything that went on behind the scenes.

'I mean, we knew nothing, let's face it,' said Hansie afterwards. 'Now we were among great players like Clive Rice, Kepler Wessels, Jimmy Cook, Peter Kirsten, Adrian Kuiper – in the dressing room with my heroes. Although I had been playing against them in provincial cricket, they were sort of, well, right up there – untouchable. But here we were pulled into the whole thing: part of the team talks, the practices, throwing balls to the batsmen, helping them to prepare – everything!'

Nothing was overlooked. The four development players were even given the team's regular meal allowances. 'I thought it outrageous that we should be getting so much money,' said Hansie. 'It was the same as the players were getting – $20 or so a day – and I was very impressed. We got everything the team got. The only thing, of course, was that we didn't get to play any cricket.'

The actual cricket – three limited-overs internationals in the space of five days – was almost a sideshow for a South African team that was mobbed and acclaimed from the moment it arrived in Calcutta. As Cronjé later recalled, 'We were told that it normally takes about 20 minutes by bus from the airport to the hotel. That day it took us three-and-a-half hours with 300 motorbikes in front of us. It was an incredible experience – thousands of people lining the route, waving and shouting and smiling up at us in the bus. It was one of the more moving experiences of my life. We stopped several times along the way and each time there were more speeches. The people seemed so happy to see us. They were genuinely pleased we were back in world cricket, and I think they also saw us as saviours for the cancelled Pakistan tour. In those 10 days we probably had a function every night, and to get to some of them we had to travel up to four hours there and back.'

Eden Gardens is one of the great cricket grounds of the world. It was there, on 10 November 1991, that South Africa re-entered international cricket. More than 90 000 people came to watch. The South African players were overwhelmed by the scene.

'When we walked out on to Eden Gardens in front of this huge crowd at the start of that first match,' recalls Cronjé, 'I remembered Ali Bacher telling us at the team talk how important it was to acknowledge the crowd. We walked out there in this incredible atmosphere, bowing our heads and putting our hands together in greeting. The crowd just cheered and cheered. I'll never forget it.'

When Cook and Hudson walked out to open the batting, their eyes were as big as saucers. Andrew Hudson, in the biggest match of his life, was out to Kapil Dev after facing three balls. Later he mused, 'If I had to do it all over again, it wouldn't be much different – I'd still be out for nought. The emotions running through me were overwhelming. I guess you could say I wasn't really in control. I mean, it was my first exposure at international level and it was South Africa's historic return as well. I just didn't feel right about concentrating on my batting.'

Cook scored 17, Wessels 50 and Kuiper 43 in a total of 177. Then the South Africans had their first look at the 18-year-old boy wonder Sachin Tendulkar. He scored 62 before becoming one of Donald's five victims, and India won by three wickets.

The second match was at Gwalior two days later. 'It was here that we got a good taste of what it was like touring India,' recalls Cronjé. 'The day before the game the guys went off to practice but their kit never arrived. They sat around for two hours waiting for the kit but it never pitched up. They eventually gave up.'

Even with Tendulkar failing to reach double figures, caught at the wicket this time off Matthews, India still mounted a good total of 223 for six. South Africa fell 39 runs short but Wessels was well pleased with his second successive half-century, this time scoring 71. In the third and final match in New Delhi, the Eastern Province captain went one better.

So did South Africa. India again lost Tendulkar for a single-figure score, dismissed again by Allan Donald, but opener Ravi Shastri and Sanjay Manjrekar both lashed aggressive centuries in a 175-run partnership, making India's total of 287 for four look well beyond the South Africans. Amazingly, only four batsmen were needed: Cook 35, Wessels 90, Peter Kirsten 86 not out, Kuiper 63 not out. And South Africa, thanks to their experienced top order, had triumphed by eight wickets with more than three overs to spare. At last, back on the world stage, they knew they could win.

Hansie Cronjé watched the amazing run-chase from the pavilion. 'How important it was for me to see how the batsmen set about getting those runs. It was incredible. I learnt so much about one-day cricket that day from Kepler, Peter and Adrian – just the way they played it in very difficult and demanding circumstances.'

Ten days in India had come to an exhilarating end and Hansie returned home with an amazing tale to tell. 'We even got to see Mother Teresa,' he told Frans excitedly. 'We were in the room when Ricey met her. She didn't shake hands with all of us, but she handed out her cards. We also saw the Taj Mahal. It's so big and magnificent…'

It had been a such a huge experience in his young life and he knew he would cherish it forever. 'Also, one of the really good things was that it gave us a chance to get to know people like Krish Mackerdhuj, Morris Garda, Goolam Rajah, Rushdie Majiet – South African cricket officials whose names we had never even heard until this tour, people we never knew existed. Now we had the chance to hear all their stories about cricket. On the plane coming back I sat next to Krish Mackerdhuj. It was the first time I had met him. We had a great chat.'

IN PIETERMARITZBURG, Patrick Symcox was immersed in his work. As manager of the new private hospital, he was constantly on call and finding less and less time for leisure activities. Although he had played two Currie Cup matches the previous season, he knew he was only a fill-in player for Natal. It was also becoming increasingly difficult to travel several times a week to Durban for provincial practices, and people like Procter and Hughes were not exactly sympathetic. He could see no real future for himself in the game.

It didn't exactly make headlines when Pat Symcox announced his retirement from provincial cricket before the start of the 1991/92 season. Those who knew him were not surprised. He had had a long innings.

A FORTNIGHT AFTER his return from India – where he shared the Man of the Series with Manjrekar – Kepler Wessels led his Eastern Province team in a four-day match against Border in Port Elizabeth. The home team had a new player in its ranks. He was Louis Koen, 24 years old and still trying to find a home in first-class cricket. Koen started out at Western Province where his undoubted talents were not rewarded beyond regular games for the provincial B team. Frustrated and disenchanted, he left for the neighbouring Boland, a B Section outfit that happily welcomed Cape Town-based cricketers unhappy with the setup in Western Province. It was at Boland that he came under the influence of Bob Woolmer who, himself disillusioned with Western Province affairs, had taken up as their new coach. Koen was an immediate success, scoring a spectacular maiden first-class century against Griqualand West at Stellenbosch in just 95 minutes before lunch and ending undefeated on 177. With a top batting average of 65 in the 1990/91 season, it was hardly surprising that he caught Wessels's talent-spotting eye and agreed to leave Boland for Eastern Province.

Making his Currie Cup début against Border, Koen did not disappoint his new captain. He scored 121 not out.

Another player who had transferred to Eastern Province was the broad-chested fast bowler Rudi Bryson. He came from the industrial and mining town of Springs, east of Johannesburg, and had first played provincial cricket for Northern Transvaal B before becoming another important catch in Wessels's nationwide recruitment net. With the Australians Maguire and McCurdy having faded from the scene, Bryson was sharing the new ball with Brett Schultz.

Against Border he took six wickets in the first innings and five in the second.

IN POTCHEFSTROOM, the future of South African cricket was taking on a new hue. At the Nuffield Week, two black cricketers were chosen on merit for the first time for SA Schools. They were Lulama Masikazana, a wicketkeeper-batsman from the Eastern Cape; and Morgan Mfobo, a seam bowler from the Western Cape. The SA Schools XI was captained by Nicky Bojé, the left-arm spin-bowler from Grey College, and included a fast bowler from Northwood High School in Durban named Shaun Pollock. Herschelle Gibbs, the prolific batsman from Bishops in Cape Town, was also in the frame and was later appointed vice-captain of an SA Under-19 development team to undertake a six-match tour of the West Indies. The world was getting bigger for South Africa's young cricketers.

THE LOOMING WORLD CUP was occupying the minds of everyone involved in cricket. The South African players knew they could beat India, but what of Australia, West Indies, Pakistan and England? And what of the team? Who would go?

Hansie Cronjé remembered it well: 'There was big excitement throughout that 1991/92 season. Everyone was picking their teams and speculation was running wild. Every time somebody scored an 80 off 80 balls in a one-dayer, he was in the team. Then this guy was in the team, and that guy was in the team, and no one really knew exactly what was going on. On the question of the captaincy there was no doubt. Clive Rice was everyone's choice.'

Not exactly everyone. When Van der Merwe announced a preliminary 20-man squad, Rice was not in it, and neither was Jimmy Cook nor Peter Kirsten. The convener of selectors suggested that Rice (42), Cook (38) and Kirsten (36) might be a little too old to stand up to the rigours of the trip. So much for experience. At age 34, Kepler Wessels was awarded the captaincy. He said he was as surprised as anyone to hear the news.

Van der Merwe emphasised the squad was only 'preliminary' and that other players could still make the final 14. But people were in a rage that no amount of reasoning could quell; they couldn't believe what the selectors had done. Neither could Rice.

He went live on television and denounced them. It was probably an undignified thing to do but dignity was hardly in vogue at the time. Any chance of Rice forcing his way back into the select 14 now disappeared amid the mud slinging. He was never the sort of man to go down silently anyway.

In keeping with his new youth policy, the Port Elizabeth-based Van der Merwe called up Cronjé, Rushmere and Rhodes. Hudson, after batting just once in India, was also retained. The new recruits should have been overjoyed, but they received the news with mixed feelings.

'We were suddenly the ones,' says Cronjé, 'who were replacing these great players. I was seen as taking Kirsten's place; Hudson in Cook's place; and Rushmere and Rhodes, the young guns, were in there … and it was actually disappointing for us because here we were seen as the youngsters taking the places of players whom the whole country wanted. Now we had to sit and watch television interviews with Clive Rice having a go at the selectors and we began feeling almost guilty. Of course, it was good for us to be in the squad, but it was also disappointing.'

The young guns found themselves under further pressure. Van der Merwe's statement that those outside the 20 could still make the final 14 merely heightened the frenzy. Who was to say that the selectors would not bow to the mounting pressure and throw out the youngsters?

Cronjé's response was spectacular. He pushed up his Nissan Shield career batting average to 74, and his B&H average to 39.95. In three Currie Cup matches before the World Cup, he batted at an average of 66.50, and at St George's Park over the New Year weekend his fine innings of 112 could not quite match the back-to-back centuries by his hero Kepler Wessels.

A fortnight later, the spotlight again fell on St George's Park for a Nissan Shield semi-final between Eastern Province and Northern Transvaal. The 14-man World Cup squad would be selected that night. Tertius Bosch was the bowling hero, removing Wessels and Rushmere for ducks in his five for 56. Koen was EP's best batsman with 86. Among the visiting batsmen, Mandy Yachad hit 56 and Mike Rindel 41 not out. The pick of the home bowlers were Bryson and Schultz with a couple of cheap wickets each.

The honour fell to Geoff Dakin, the Port Elizabeth-based cricket president, to announce the World Cup squad. He read out the names:

Early days...

Hansie Cronjé (above), aged 13 at Grey College, shows that he can hold the bat all right. At the 1988 Wimbledon tennis championships (left) a chance get-together involving Ewie Cronjé, Corrie van Zyl, Ali Bacher, Geoff Dakin and Frans Cronjé, and (below) the young Hansie with Wessels, coach Johan Volsteedt and Joubert Strydom. Volsteedt had the rare distinction of coaching two South African captains in Wessels and Cronjé, and a Free State captain in Strydom.

Photos: Hansie Cronjé collection

Hansie Cronjé made great strides under the influence of his hero, Kepler Wessels, who (below) offers some advice during the one-day international against Pakistan at Centurion Park in 1993 when Cronjé hit some lusty blows.

Photos: (left) Jon Hrusa; (below and bottom) Danie Coetzer

Always in the thick of things...

Hansie Cronjé runs down the wickets to dismiss Australian opener Matthew Hayden at St George's Park in March 1997 as Jonty and the others gather for the celebratory 'high fives'. Cronjé (below), a highly effective bowler in limited-overs cricket, shows his style against the Aussies.

Photos: Jon Hrusa

Valentine's Day flowers from Australia was the start of a romance that led to the big day when Hansie Cronjé married Bertha Pretorius in Bloemfontein. A busy day (below) for Hansie in Soweto as eager young fans jostle for his autograph.

Photos: (above) Renier Brönn; (below) Chris Collingridge

The hero returns to his Alma Mater...

Hansie Cronjé was the centre of attraction when he returned to Grey College after being appointed South Africa's captain to talk to the pupils and revisit some old haunts.

Photos: Hansie Cronjé collection

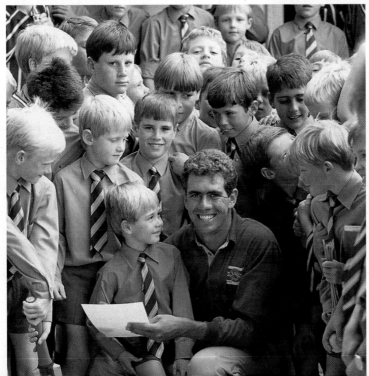

Big days at Lord's Cricket Ground...

Krish Mackerdhuj waves the national flag from a jubilant dressing room balcony after victory over England in 1994. It all started when Andrew Hudson and Gary Kirsten (left) became the first South African Test cricketers in 29 years to walk on to the hallowed ground and (below) Pat Symcox's rags-to-riches story continued with a meeting with Queen Elizabeth II.

Photos: (above) Frans Cronjé; (left and below) Touchline Photo

The famous five-run Test victory at Sydney had a lot to do with Fanie de Villiers and Hansie Cronjé (above) and Allan Donald (right). The squad (below) in the SCG dressing room.

Photos: (above and right) Touchline Photo; (below) Hansie Cronjé collection

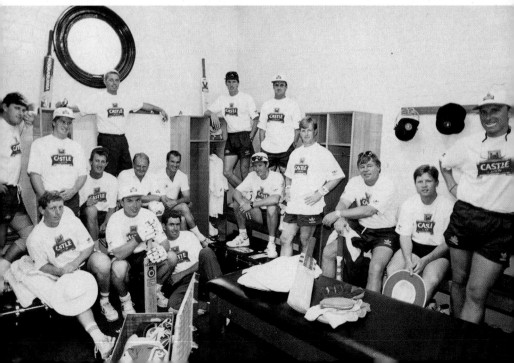

Stalwarts of the South African team show their style...

Daryll Cullinan (top left) and Brian McMillan (below left) and the immaculate Dave Richardson (bottom). The fans at Newlands (below) wanted 'Swinger' for President after he scored a maiden century against New Zealand, a feat that brought smiles to the faces of Bob Woolmer and Hansie Cronjé.

Photos: (left) Touchline Photo; (below) Sunday Times; (bottom) Jon Hrusa

Wessels, Hudson, Rushmere, Peter Kirsten, Kuiper, Cronjé, Rhodes, McMillan, Richardson, Snell, Donald, Henry, Bosch and Pringle.

Omitted from the original 20-man squad were Rindel, Bryson, Schultz, Cullinan, Jennings, Craig Matthews, Shaw and Van Zyl. Of the team from India, four players who did not warrant a second glance were Rice, Cook, Yachad and Eksteen. Despite his three extraordinary seasons at Somerset, Jimmy Cook had apparently not scored enough runs at home to justify selection. Still, Van der Merwe made good his promise that players not named in the original 20 could force their way into the final 14. Those who came in from the cold were Kirsten and Pringle.

At the World Cup, Kirsten would be his team's top run-scorer and, even before the 20-man squad was chosen, Pringle's outswingers had brought him 31 wickets in only four matches for Western Province.

The selectors went away confident they had finally managed to get it right. Hansie Cronjé went away to write his final exam and was awarded his B.Comm. degree. Eddie Barlow went away to join Transvaal as their new cricket manager. In his sole season with Free State, he had instilled a new belief in those players, and guided them to their first Nissan Shield title. Six months earlier they had laughed when he promised them international honours.

'He had a way of telling us that we were the best players in the world,' says Cronjé, 'and we believed every bit of it. I was very, very confident heading for Australia. So, too, were Allan Donald and Omar Henry.'

BEFORE THEIR DEPARTURE for their greatest adventure, the chosen 14 attended a training camp in Cape Town. At the Newlands nets, the Western Province players were just finishing their practice when the World Cup squad arrived at the head of a huge entourage. Craig Matthews was the very picture of dejection as he walked past Hansie Cronjé. The young Free Stater muttered, 'Bad luck. You came so close.'

Later, Cronjé confided, 'It really hurts me a lot to see another player's disappointment. I guess it makes you want to try your bollocks off because you realise that there are 10 other players who would like to be there as well.'

Mike Procter was again named as the team coach after securing the appointment for India. He was well known to all the players, but some of the younger ones, including Cronjé, did not know their new team manager. He was Alan Jordaan, a captain of Northern Transvaal in the Seventies and that union's current president. At the team's first meeting

in their Cape Town hotel he addressed the players, opening his speech
with the words, 'For those of you who are wondering who this big
@*&%! is standing before you, I'm Alan Jordaan.'

The big, bluff Afrikaner played life with a straight bat. He would earn
the players' respect.

7

Flowers for a Friend

O N THE EVENING of 25 February 1992 the South African players gathered in the team room of their Sydney hotel. Kepler Wessels arrived with a man that they knew by reputation but had never met – Alan Jones, the former Australian rugby union coach and popular radio talkshow host.

Jones was renowned for his motivational talks. A big part of the Wallabies' success story during the Eighties was due to the spirit and resolve he instilled in his rugby team. He was a highly intelligent and articulate man, and he knew just which buttons to press. He was about to share some of his magic with the South Africans, an ironic situation given that he was a fair dinkum Aussie and they were due to play Australia the next day.

He spoke; they listened.

'There are four things in life that never return: a spoken word, time elapsed, a shot arrow and a lost opportunity. Remember that, and remember that tomorrow is your opportunity to beat the world champions on their home turf!'

The next day South Africa emerged under the blazing floodlights of a jam-packed Sydney Cricket Ground to beat the Cup-holders and favourites by nine wickets in a dream start to the 1992 World Cup.

Pandemonium reigned afterwards as the South Africans and their officials celebrated what many had believed was the impossible. In the build-up to the tournament the visiting teams had been subjected to constant media hype about the all-conquering strength of Allan Border's team. The parochial Channel 9 commentators in particular had acclaimed Australia as the team of the moment and the team to beat. Now the Aussie dressing room was in total disarray. It was their second defeat in as many matches, following the shock setback against New Zealand in Auckland four days earlier in the opening game of the

115

tournament. The Aussie commentators were stunned into silence; the Sydney crowd rubbed their eyes in disbelief. In the South African dressing room, they were whooping it up. Steve Tshwete had tears rolling down his cheeks, his round spectacles misted up. The ANC's Mr Fixit embraced Wessels in a huge and lingering bear hug, and everyone else was slapping backs and squeezing hands and throwing arms around their neighbours.

Mike Gatting walked in to offer congratulations. He was attending the World Cup as a member of a television commentary team. Tshwete hugged him lovingly, and so too did Krish Mackerdhuj.

Hansie Cronjé watched and wondered at the miraculous healing power of sport – enemies one minute, friends the next.

THE SOUTH AFRICANS had arrived in Australia by way of Zimbabwe where, at the Harare Sports Club, they played a one-off game against their northerly neighbours. In the days when Zimbabwe was known as Rhodesia they had played as a province in the Currie Cup, for a time under the shrewd and successful leadership of Mike Procter. Now, as Zimbabwe, they were hosting a South African cricket team for the first time.

From the moment he was omitted from the preliminary 20-man World Cup squad, Peter Kirsten had something to prove. Being a sensitive man, he responded dogmatically to injustice, so at Harare he hit a top score of 64 in a six-wicket victory.

For the next fortnight, the South Africans experimented with various combinations in warm-up games at Perth, Adelaide, Bowral, Canberra and Hobart. Their goal was to find the right team for the World Cup opener against Australia, but it did not help that their preparations were being hampered by the inclement weather. Wessels was growing increasingly irritable. His batting form seemed to have deserted him, and the bleak, rainy days were not helping his mood. After another washout at the Bradman Oval at Bowral, the captain was sitting alone in the dressing room, his furrowed brow more deeply creased than usual.

'Come on, guys, we have to cheer up the skipper,' whispered the mischievous Adrian Kuiper. He produced a pair of handcuffs. 'Borrowed 'em from a policeman,' he smiled wickedly. Brian McMillan and Cronjé liked the idea so the trio strolled nonchalantly up to Wessels, leapt on him and tried to cuff him. The captain was not in a playful mood. He often worked out in the boxing ring, was trained in martial arts, and had picked up some street-fighting skills at a tough gym he had frequented when he lived in Brisbane. He head-butted Kuiper so hard that he saw stars. He then set about wrestling the other two to the floor. 'Big Mac' was the biggest man in the team but he was no match for the older man. It was clearly not the right time for fooling around. The defeated trio quickly backed off.

'Kepler was a lot of fun in many respects,' says Cronjé, 'but we realised that there were times when he was best left alone. This was one of them.'

Other players who tried to be left alone were in for a rude shock. The warm-up game against the Australian Academy XI at Adelaide was due to start at 11 am. With 10 minutes to go, a dishevelled Tertius Bosch and Allan Donald came running frantically into the ground. They had over-slept and missed the bus.

The previous night they had discovered a distraction that was foreign to most South Africans – a casino, where they had enjoyed themselves till the early hours of the morning. Both were fined $500 by the team management for being late, but Tertius wasn't upset. 'Ag, it's nothing,' he told his roommate Cronjé, 'I won $8 000 on the tables last night!'

The distractions in Australia were many and varied for the inex-perienced world travellers, prompting Cronjé to describe the situation as a 'nightmare'.

'We were young and naïve, and suddenly we found ourselves staying in five-star hotels with mini-bars in our rooms. I mean, we had never seen a mini-bar before and we found out, to our detriment, just how expen-sive they are. We were prepared to try anything, see everything and do everything all at once. We were trying to experience the whole of Sydney in one night.

'I looked out of my hotel room on the forty-third floor and saw there were other buildings even higher than that. When you come from Bloemfontein, that's something!

'Some of us ended up not getting very much sleep, not because we were messing around or anything like that, but because there was so much to see and do. It was like being thrown at the lions and I, for one, didn't know what it really took to be an international cricketer. I was enjoying life, getting stuck into fast foods, having a good time and a few beers. We went over with two suitcases each and came back with seven. How can you resist buying all that stuff, souvenirs and CDs and hi-fis, when it's all so new and different?'

But if Cronjé were eager to learn what it took to be an international cricketer, he was in good hands. Wessels was a strict disciplinarian and he and Jordaan saw eye to eye. Procter was a more easy-going man, but he knew what it took to play hardball in Australia. Jordaan became a sort of father figure in his dealing with the younger players. He came from the old school of respect and discipline, and he made it clear that they should know their place. He was a lawyer by profession and used all his skills to ensure that the South African players, at a delicate time in their country's history, were allowed to get on with the job without interference from outside. He was also quite skilled in public relations.

Back home, F.W. de Klerk had called a referendum in which he sought backing to continue his unprecedented programme of reform. He was simply asking the white electorate to vote 'yes' or 'no' for change.

The South African cricketers in Australia were portrayed as the positive face of the reform movement, and the entire team made a public show of casting their ballots in the Australian capital of Canberra. The players were genuinely positive about the changes taking place in their country and made a point of conveying this message throughout their travels. Back home, the 'yes' vote prevailed.

Valentine's Day dawned and Big Mac made a deal with the international florists Interflora for the players to send gifts to their wives and sweethearts. Cronjé didn't have a steady girlfriend but he did know a young woman, Bertha Pretorius, who lived down the road from him in Bloemfontein.

He decided to send her a bunch of flowers and a Valentine's Day card, but he didn't sign his name. If he thought he could keep his identity a secret, he was in for a rude surprise. McMillan's deal with Interflora gave them the right to generate whatever publicity they could at the other end. When the delivery man arrived at Bertha's house with her bouquet, he was accompanied by a photographer from a Bloemfontein newspaper. The story was all over town. 'That's funny,' said Bertha, 'because I have a boyfriend already!'

If Cronjé weren't exactly growing closer to Bertha, he was at least developing an important understanding with Wessels. All his life, the South African captain had thrived on constant practice and hard training. In the young Cronjé, he found a soul mate. Whenever he needed someone to throw balls at him in the nets, Cronjé was there. When he wanted to go out for a training run, he knew where to find a partner.

In Sydney, the two cricketers would run up and down the long and steep flight of steps at the Opera House. Cronjé imagined these exhausting runs as the ladder to success at the World Cup. Each time he reached the top he pictured it as the pinnacle of South Africa's triumph.

Wessels was Cronjé's inspiration. The young man enjoyed a strict training regimen and he was delighted to have such a great man as his mentor. He also developed a deep respect for this person who, in spite of his established success and fame, was still prepared to go that extra mile and put more work into his game than lesser players.

Wessels's inspiration right then was seated in his return to a country where he had achieved all his international success. He had left Australia under a cloud and now he was coming back to take on the world as South Africa's captain. His team-mates appreciated and understood his situation. He had their total support.

The rain persisted. The World Cup opener was drawing closer and Wessels was unhappy with his team's lack of preparation. All the usual practice facilities in Sydney were under water, and scheduled net practices were becoming a lottery. The South African players completed their final preparations in an Action Cricket indoor arena which was hardly the ideal place to practise for the biggest game of their lives.

THERE WERE 40 000 people in the Sydney Cricket Ground (SCG). They were curious to see the South Africans, but they had come to celebrate an Australian victory. Although Border's Aussies had already lost their opening match to Martin Crowe's New Zealand, the fans did not think South Africa would pose a big problem. The mood in the South African dressing room was razor sharp.

'As far as motivation went, no one needed to say a word,' said Cronjé. 'I mean, we just ran on to the field and were like tigers out there.'

It all happened in a blur. 'We're running on to the field now, so pumped up, and the first ball from Allan gets a wicket. We're all running up the track cheering and shouting and the umpire says "Not out!" We couldn't understand what was going on. We had all seen Geoff Marsh edging the first ball to Dave Richardson off Allan Donald. The umpire just said he didn't see any deflection or hear any sound either.'

Cronjé later spoke to the umpire, Brian Aldridge of New Zealand. 'He said he was so surprised at Allan's pace. He was looking down at the line where Allan's foot was landing and when he looked up again the ball was already past the batter. He was just so surprised by the speed it was too difficult for him to pick up the ball. There was also so much noise coming from the crowd that the sound of the ball hitting the edge of the bat was drowned out.'

Out on the field, the first three or four overs seemed to last half an hour. 'It wasn't because there were so many wides and no-balls,' said Cronjé, 'it was just because of all the excitement and everything out there. We had never experienced anything like it before.'

The players who had the good fortune to experience it were Wessels, Hudson, Peter Kirsten, Cronjé, Kuiper, Rhodes, McMillan, Richardson,

Snell, Pringle and Donald – the chosen XI to open South Africa's campaign. In their new green uniforms, they were taking on the yellow-clad warriors of Australia.

Marsh went on 25, caught Richardson, bowled Kuiper. This brought Border to the wicket. He was cheered all the way. First ball from Kuiper bowled him off the pads. Tom Moody survived the hat-trick ball. The Aussies were on the back foot now, and Cronjé was marvelling at the amount of swing the bowlers were getting on the SCG. Pringle, Donald, Snell, McMillan and Kuiper were all producing extravagant movement through the air. It augured well for the match and for the tournament as a whole.

Jonty Rhodes's fielding was also looking promising – a lightning-quick return left Craig McDermott stranded a metre short of the crease. Australia were restricted to 170 for nine; the match was South Africa's if they wanted it. Did they ever want it!

Wessels and Hudson put on 74 runs for the first wicket before Hudson was bowled by the offspinner Peter Taylor for 28. Then Wessels and Kirsten knocked off the remaining 97 runs without further loss. Kirsten was undefeated on 49, and Wessels, revelling on his old stomping ground, hit nine fours in his 81 and was crowned Man of the Match. Victories don't come much sweeter.

IF SOUTH AFRICA could whip Australia in Sydney, they would surely have a good chance against New Zealand in Auckland. Even though the Kiwis were off to a good start, they did not look like a team that could sustain a winning streak. That, at least, was the popular theory. The fans in South Africa were excited and expectant. They were happy to get up in the early hours of the morning or even sit up all night to watch the direct telecasts.

The nation was in the grip of World Cup fever. People who had never watched cricket before became instant converts.

In Auckland, the players checked into their hotel. Standing next to Hansie Cronjé at the reception desk was a man wearing jeans and a denim jacket. Cronjé vaguely recognised him.

'Are you here for the cricket?' he asked the man by way of starting up a conversation.

'Well, yes and no. I'm actually here to do a few gigs in the city. Maybe I'll catch some cricket, too.'

'Where are you from?'

'Oh, I'm down from the UK.'

Cronjé was intrigued by the man's references to 'gigs'. He glanced over his shoulder at the name on his room card.

'Excuse me, but are you Feargal Sharkey, the pop singer?' he asked disbelievingly.

'Well, yes, I am...'

'Gee, I've been a big fan of yours for a long time! I loved your songs, "A Good Heart" and "You Little Thief", and your latest hit is also great. It's called "I've Got News for You", isn't it?'

'Yes, that's right,' smiled the singer. 'I'm actually over here promoting it.'

'Gee,' said Cronjé in wide-eyed wonder, 'that's great... Listen, if you're really interested, I can get you some tickets for the cricket.'

'Oh, I'd like that very much.'

'Done!'

Cronjé was thrilled to meet one of his pop music idols. '*Jislaaik,* Tertius,' he told his roommate, 'here's this little oke from Bloemfontein and guess who I bump into in Auckland? I tell you, this is the life, man!'

Cronjé was in high spirits, and so too were his team-mates. They had already beaten Australia and fancied their chances against New Zealand who might just have scored a freak win over the Aussies.

The practice facilities in Auckland were far from ideal. The South Africans went into the match with very little knowledge of local conditions.

The New Zealanders were at home, and they were ready. They had studied the South Africans during their victory at Sydney, and devised a plan to nullify the fast bowlers at Eden Park mainly by preparing a very flat wicket that produced little pace on to the bat. The South Africans had just come off a fast SCG wicket, and the batsmen would surely struggle to time the ball on a slow, low track. The New Zealanders also loaded their side with slow-medium bowlers, not unlike Cronjé himself, who bowled back-of-a-length and made it very difficult for the batsmen to play their shots.

These bowlers were Rod Latham, Gavin Larsen, Chris Harris and Chris Cairns. The New Zealanders were unconventional in their game plan. The South Africans were still somewhat naïve about the nuances of limited-overs international cricket. The wily Crowe further perplexed his opponents by tossing the new ball to his spin bowler, Dipak Patel. He reckoned he could make it through his allotment of overs before the batters had got into their stride. In the final master-stroke of innovative thinking, the New Zealand skipper called up the belligerent left-hander Mark Greatbatch to open the innings for the first time.

Crowe's plans were made in heaven; everything he tried worked a treat. Patel bowled Hudson for 1 while conceding just 28 runs in his 10 overs. The medium-pacers reduced the runs to a trickle and picked up important wickets amid the drought-induced panic. A total of 190 for nine, including a gutsy 90 from Kirsten, did not look enough.

It wasn't. At home on the slow wicket, Greatbatch took the attack apart at the seams. He plundered 18 runs off Kuiper's only over, hit most of the other bowlers out of the attack, and needed only 60 balls for his 68 runs.

Feargal Sharkey watched from the grandstand as yet another Greatbatch six sailed high over the roof. It was great spectator value, but the Irish singer felt a twinge of sadness for his new pal Hansie. New Zealand's seven-wicket victory arrived with a remarkable 15 overs to spare.

Tertius Bosch was one of the fast bowlers who took the brunt of the Greatbatch onslaught. The pitch was totally unsuited to his bang-it-in style of fast bowling and his two-and-a-half overs cost 19 runs. That night, Cronjé commiserated with his crestfallen roommate. Cronjé felt very sorry for him. It was the only World Cup match Bosch ever played.

The South Africans were impressed with New Zealand's ploy to use a big-hitting batsman at the start. It made a lot of sense because the fielding restrictions during the opening 15 overs permitted only two fielders outside the 15-metre circle.

Moving on to play Sri Lanka at the Basin Reserve in Wellington, they adopted the pinch-hitter strategy for the first time. They promoted Kuiper to open the innings. It didn't work.

Bemused again by a slow wicket, the normally aggressive batsman took too long to get used to the slow pace and the awkward Sri Lankan bowlers. His 18 runs came off 44 balls and, with the exception of Rhodes, the other batsmen were also bogged down. Wessels scored 40 from 94 balls, and Kirsten 47 off 81 balls but Jonty, improvising, hit 28 runs from 21 balls. The South Africans were all out for 195.

'It was the first sign,' says Cronjé, 'that South Africa had never played regularly on the Asian subcontinent where slow wickets are the order of the day. All the other teams had played there many times before and had learned how to adjust quickly, but on Asian-type wickets in New Zealand, we were battling to get the ball off the square.'

Profligate bowling in defence of a small total did not help either. All in all, there were 13 wides and four no-balls. Only three quick wickets by Donald hauled South Africa back into the game. In the end it was close, but Arjuna Ranatunga's undefeated 68 steered Sri Lanka to a three-wicket win with one ball to spare.

SOUTH AFRICA'S PRE-TOURNAMENT plan was going badly awry. They figured they had a good chance of beating New Zealand, Sri Lanka,

India, Zimbabwe and maybe England, but would battle against Australia, West Indies and Pakistan. In three matches, that logic had been turned upside down.

Next up was West Indies in Christchurch, their final game in New Zealand. It was probably South Africa's best performance of the tournament and, with it, the logic again came unstuck.

It was a tough time for Hansie Cronjé. He was dropped from the team for the first time. In his first two knocks he had scored 7 and 3.

'You learn to take things like this in your stride, but I was young and new so I didn't really know how to handle it. I was very, very disappointed. I felt that batting at No 6, 7 or 8 in one-day cricket one didn't really have a chance to prove oneself. I had scored very heavily in South Africa that season and I felt I could make a contribution now. It felt like my world had fallen apart.'

Mark Rushmere replaced him. He was out for 10. The South Africans had been asked to bat first on a greenish Lancaster Park pitch that would obviously move around quite a lot. The West Indies' pace attack included some of the best bowlers in the world – the likes of Marshall, Cummins, Winston Benjamin and Ambrose. It was a track tailor-made for them. Wessels was dismissed by Malcolm Marshall for 1, and Hudson made 22 before falling victim to Anderson Cummins.

Still, thanks to yet another half-century from Kirsten, the South Africans did well to total 200 for eight.

The downside was that the valiant Kirsten tore a calf muscle during his innings and was out for the rest of the match. The upside for Cronjé was that he made it on as the substitute fieldsman. The five-man pace attack of Donald, Pringle, Snell, McMillan and Kuiper could not wait to get back on. They were dying to have a go on this helpful pitch. They bowled the West Indies out for 136.

It was South Africa's first encounter with a left-handed batsman named Brian Lara. He was promoted to open the West Indies innings for the first time. From the outset, the South Africans could see he was a good batsman. In the first couple of balls he got stuck into Meyrick Pringle and was hitting very cleanly. 'We have to get this guy out,' commanded Wessels.

Off Pringle, Lara hit with great force and timing in the air towards cover point, where Rhodes was fielding. The ball came to him so hard it knocked him off his feet. But still he held it. It was a wonderful catch that swung the whole game. Pringle went on to take four for 11 with his swing bowling in that spell, and it also helped that the excellent slip cordon of Wessels, McMillan and Richardson pouched the five catches that came their way.

Pringle was a constant source of mirth. The story goes that while bowling in one mark, he was on his way back to his bowling match when he inquired, 'How many balls, Mr Ump?' The umpire held up three fingers. 'Is that three bowled or three to come?' asked 'Pring' innocently.

Kirsten's unfortunate injury gave Cronjé a lifeline into the next game against Pakistan at Brisbane as the No 6 batter. He responded well to his recall by hitting 47 not out in 53 balls in a 71-run stand with McMillan, who scored 33. Wessels's failure to get out of the blocks again – seven runs in 26 balls – put pressure on the top order, but Hudson's 54 and Rushmere's 35 saw the South Africans total more than 200 for the first time. This was no small achievement, considering they encountered the concept of reverse swing for the first time. The left-arm paceman Wasim Akram, in particular, had perfected this strange phenomenon – an ability to get the old ball to swing in the opposite direction to its normal trajectory, which caught a lot of the batsmen by surprise.

The South Africans were confident of defending their total of 211 for seven in 50 overs, but rain put a damper on things. When the weather finally lifted, a puzzling mathematical process was applied to set the Pakistanis a tough, revised batting target of 194 in 36 overs. Inzamam-ul-Haq, their big-hitting No 3 batter, seemed determined to take them there. He had lashed 48 runs from 44 balls when he played a ball into the gully and set off for a run...

Rhodes at cover point raced across to cut it off. Imran Khan, sensing danger, yelled to his batting partner to get back. Inzamam slammed on the brakes and turned clumsily. By that stage Rhodes had the ball but, instead of shying it at the only stump he could see and possibly missing, he decided to run down his quarry. Inzamam was powering towards the crease at full tilt but Rhodes was eating up the ground square of the wicket. Then Jonty dived.

He dived like no cricketer had dived before, kicking out his legs straight behind him and stretching his arms to their limit, ball in hand.

Like a guided missile, perfectly horizontal to the ground and barely 20 centimetres above it, he launched himself hands-first into the stumps to execute quite the most astonishing run-out ever seen in world cricket.

It was the turning point in a match South Africa clinched by 20 runs, and words and images of Rhodes's stunning dive were flashed around the world. Cronjé was overjoyed at his little friend's achievement. 'I thought I had batted pretty well for my 47, but afterwards no one was interested in me. No one wanted to discuss any batting or bowling – they just wanted to speak to Jonty. He had made an incredible impact.'

The sporting goods company Adidas were also overjoyed. They had just developed a new cricket shoe and needed someone to try it out. Before the match, their representative brought a pair into the South African dressing room to ask whether there were any takers. It just so happened they were exactly Rhodes's size so he volunteered to use them. In the photograph of his famous dive, the shoes, with their distinctive logo, received more mileage than Adidas might ever have dreamed of. The company immediately adopted the photo as a marketing statement.

The team was overjoyed to have beaten the powerful Pakistan in yet another contradiction of the pre-tournament logic. Mike Procter told the players, 'Well, that's them out of the tournament! At least we've knocked out one of the teams.'

To have any chance of qualifying for the semi-finals, Pakistan would need to win all their remaining matches against Australia, Sri Lanka and high-riding New Zealand, who had yet to lose a game.

SPIRITS IN THE South African team were high as a possible semi-final berth beckoned. Before leaving Brisbane, the players took time out to relax and have some fun. They visited the Warner Bros. studios where they made a music video featuring Cronjé and Rhodes miming on guitars, and Omar Henry and the ubiquitous M-Net television anchor man Louis Karpas on vocals. They also whooped it up a bit at the Surfer's Paradise holiday playground on the Gold Coast of Queensland.

Brisbane also marked the start of the famous room-to-room battles. It was raining and the players were bored, so room warfare commenced in the team's hotel. Cronjé was sharing with Rushmere, and Wessels and Kuiper were roommates. There were no rules. The only object was to make life as difficult as possible for the occupants of the other rooms. Dustbins filled with smelly water were balanced against bedroom doors. Knock, knock, guess what's about to come in? Rushmere was made to suffer in different ways. He was one of the neatest members of the team, a man who always ensured his belongings were packed away in the right place, so Wessels and Kuiper regularly sneaked into his room, pulled his bed apart and turned everything upside down. Most of the rooms received similar treatment, but very few of the players knew where it was coming from. Who the heck put shaving cream on the toothbrush?

'Kepler was always up to something,' remembers Cronjé. 'It was a side of him the public never saw.'

The next stop was Canberra to play Zimbabwe.

'FOR THE FIRST TIME,' recalls Hansie Cronjé, 'I saw how much pain a player was prepared to endure in order to play.'

Peter Kirsten was still battling with his torn calf muscle. Craig Smith, the physiotherapist, advised him not to play, and Procter said he definitely should not play, but Kirsten was adamant. He was going to play. And what a match he had.

With his offspin he took three wickets – narrowly missing a hat trick as well – and then scored 62 not out to claim Man of the Match. Cronjé was impressed: 'If you need discipline and determination and guts to make it in international cricket, this was a very good example.'

The seven-wicket victory over Zimbabwe also brought Cronjé his first wicket in international cricket. His victim was the opening batsman Andy Flower, and later he took another wicket for figures of two for 17 in five overs. 'Afterwards, I took a bet with Kepler that I would one day better his figure of 18 wickets in limited-overs internationals.'

The South Africans then started to worry about their run-rate. It had taken more than 45 overs to knock off the required 164 runs against Zimbabwe, and they were concerned they might be counted out of the semi-finals because of slow scoring.

'We were discussing things like changing the batting order and being more positive at the start of our innings. Proccy wasn't happy that we had won with only a couple of overs to spare, but Kepler didn't seem to mind. Proccy felt we should have won with eight overs to spare to get our run-rate up, but the skipper didn't exactly see it that way.'

Omar Henry was also growing more and more frustrated. At this stage he had played only one game, when he bowled well against Sri Lanka to take one for 31 in his 10 overs, so he now turned his hand to commentating for television viewers back home instead. Players like Rushmere and Bosch also found themselves on the sidelines as the South Africans stuck with their winning combination.

Again, at the Melbourne Cricket Ground (MCG), South Africa went in with an unchanged team against England, relying on the four-pronged pace attack of Donald, Pringle, Snell and McMillan, and allowing Kirsten and Cronjé to share the fifth bowler's duties.

There was also more talk of upping the scoring tempo although a simple victory in this match would automatically book them a place in the semi-final. Nonetheless, with Wessels and Hudson putting on 151 in the first 36 overs, they were able to post their biggest total so far – 236 for four.

A group of about 3 000 English supporters (members of the notoriously noisy 'Barmy Army') were in the crowd of 25 000, making up about a quarter of the great ground's capacity. When the South Africans went out to field, the English fans began to make a huge racket, singing and chanting like soccer supporters at a cup final.

Cronjé had never experienced anything like it before. 'I was amazed at the amount of noise a few thousand people could make. Until now, everybody seemed to fancy South Africa because of our return to international cricket and because we had been doing quite well. We had been getting a lot of support but suddenly, for the first time, people were against us rather than for us. They actually succeeded in putting us off our game, and we weren't as focused as we usually are.'

Big Mac was intent on upsetting a different kind of focus. Ian Botham, England's pinch-hitter, scored 22 runs before McMillan cartwheeled his middle stump out of the ground, the same stump housing the tiny television 'stump camera' that gave viewers the chance to see the batman's perspective. The stump was broken in half but, amazingly, the miniature camera was not damaged. It lay on the ground, transmitting pictures of the sky – until McMillan approached and gave it a quizzical look at close range.

There was great mirth back home as a distended, close-up picture of McMillan's happy face was beamed into South African television rooms.

There was less happiness when the unpopular rain rule again came into play after the heavens opened over the MCG. According to the formula, South Africa's slowest scoring overs would be reduced, and England were asked to score 225 in 41 overs. It was a close call in the end, and their No 9 batsman, Phil DeFreitas, hit the winning run with one ball to spare. England's three-wicket victory – their twelfth in a row in limited overs cricket – meant that South Africa would have to win their next match against India to qualify for the semis.

Pakistan, meanwhile, had beaten Australia, while New Zealand's incredible run of victories extended to a record-equalling six with their triumph over India.

At Adelaide, the South Africans were in a must-win situation and under real pressure. It was also raining. It rained the day before the game and the following morning as well. It never looked as if the teams would make it on to the field. At lunch the weather broke and the match was reduced to 30 overs a side. In that kind of game, anything can happen.

'Please don't do this to us,' pleaded Cronjé to no one in particular. 'We've waited 21 years to get back into international cricket and our most important game is now down to a 30-over lottery!'

South Africa needed 181 to win at six runs per over. It was the kind of scoring rate they had spoken about but never before achieved. Peter Kirsten was asked to open the batting with Hudson. They were both positive players who could score quickly. And they did. Kirsten's 84 and Hudson's 53 carried them close and, although there was a little flurry of wickets, the winning runs came with five balls remaining.

The excitement in the dressing room afterwards was tempered by the intervention of Geoff Dakin. The UCBSA president announced he would withdraw his team from the semi-finals if F.W. de Klerk's all-white referendum two days later rejected the reform process in South Africa. The threat turned out to be academic as white South Africans came out in force to back their state president on his road to democracy.

Before the tournament the players had worked out they would need to win five of their eight league matches, or at least four of them with a good run-rate, in order to qualify for the knockout stage. So far they had won five and were through to the semis with New Zealand, England – and Pakistan. Imran Khan's team had confounded expectations. After winning only one of their first five matches, they took three in a row and inflicted New Zealand's only defeat in eight starts.

There was anguish in Australia because their team had not qualified.

AT THE SCG, Hansie Cronjé experienced the raw emotion of watching grown men cry from bitter disappointment. There were tears shed in the dressing room balcony as the ridiculous rain rule conspired to count South Africa out of the World Cup in the cruellest way possible. They had needed 22 runs from 13 balls with four wickets in hand to beat England. Then the earlier drizzle turned to rain and drove the players from the field for just 12 minutes. When they returned, the rain rule dictated they then needed 22 runs from one ball. The South African players could not believe their eyes as the impossible new requirement was flashed up on the big scoreboard. It was all over. Before the stoppage, Brian McMillan and Dave Richardson had scored 25 runs from 18 balls and looked well set. Big Mac disdainfully pushed the final ball away for a single, and then sloped off the field in disgust and dejection.

'We weren't too happy with Allan Lamb,' said Cronjé. 'We felt he was the one who pushed Graham Gooch into leaving the field. England's captain told the umpires he couldn't go off, but Lamb urged him to do so. I think he wanted so badly to beat the South Africans.'

The crowd of 35 000 were in total sympathy with Kepler's men.

'Come on, guys, let's go and thank them.' The captain indicated to the players that they should all walk out on to the field. In a hugely emotional cameo, the defeated players jogged around the SCG in a lap of honour, waving to the cheering, appreciative crowd.

'We just wanted to thank the people for having us back in international cricket,' said Cronjé afterwards. 'It was just amazing, seeing the people accepting us so wholeheartedly. Even those noisy England fans applauded us.'

It was an unforgettable sight. Adrian Kuiper, with no time to change back into his clothes before his team-mates began their spontaneous run, hurriedly joined them on the field, dressed only in socks and shirt with a towel wrapped jauntily around his waist. And Jonty Rhodes, the superb athlete, struggled to finish the lap of honour because of a sudden attack of leg cramps.

South Africans hypothesised for an eternity about what might have been had the final two overs of the match been allowed. Cronjé was confident they would have scored the 22 runs for victory. 'I mean, it was getting a little bit wet because of the drizzle, and the ball was getting slippery. Had we stayed on, the odds would have been in our favour because the bowlers and fielders would have battled to control the slippery ball. Mac and Swinger were also batting very well at the time.'

THREE DAYS LATER at Melbourne, Imran Khan proudly held aloft the Waterford crystal trophy. Pakistan, the team South Africa thought they had eliminated in the round robin section, were the new World Cup champions. More than 87 000 spectators applauded their feat while, in Pakistan, millions of people celebrated. They had come from behind to beat New Zealand by four wickets in the semi-final before conquering England in the final. Ironically, their margin of victory was 22 runs.

THE SOUTH AFRICAN players were nonetheless in high spirits on the long flight back. They had been away for two months and could not wait to get home. They were a lot richer in experience and a little wealthier financially. Each of them was paid R20 000 for playing in the tournament – about R2 200 per match. There were no player contracts so they were happy to get some form of remuneration. 'The big thing, really,' said Cronjé, 'was to be able to represent South Africa. That was enough reward for the guys.'

On the plane, David van der Sandt, an SABC television reporter, conducted some taped interviews. After a little gentle persuasion, he and his cameraman were 'relieved' of their equipment by Meyrick Pringle and Kepler Wessels. 'Pring' took over the camera while 'Chopper' commanded the microphone as the pair of pranksters staged their own impromptu interviews with various players. One of them was Hansie Cronjé, who entered into the spirit when asked a series of ribald questions by his captain. He didn't mind because he knew the interview would never be publicly aired.

At Jan Smuts Airport a large crowd had gathered to welcome the team. There were chaotic scenes when they eventually arrived three hours late. The arrival was broadcast live on television. Van der Sandt handed his video tapes to his producer. Thinking nothing of it, the man unwittingly plugged them into the telecast while the players were waiting for their luggage to come through. Cronjé was horrified. His interview with Wessels was being beamed live to the nation!

'It was very embarrassing, and I was quite upset with David. I realised later that it was just a bit of a misunderstanding between him and his people, but I still copped quite a bit of flak from conservative people in Bloemfontein for the things I said.'

Ewie and San-Marie Cronjé were among the well-wishers at the airport, and they joined in an official reception party for the team.

After overnighting at an airport hotel, the players boarded an open-roofed bus the next morning to be paraded through the streets of Johannesburg on the first ticker-tape parade for a sports team. Cronjé remarked to Wessels that he didn't think too many members of the public would be interested, but the people of Johannesburg came out in their thousands to cheer the players and wave congratulatory banners. At least most of them were congratulatory – one simply pleaded, 'Marry me, Snell!'

8

In the Fast Lane

ANDREW HUDSON LAY awake in bed in his hotel room in Bridgetown, Barbados. He was struggling to fall asleep. The next day would see South Africa's return to Test cricket against the West Indies. The honour of opening the innings was his. Against him would be ranged a fearsome West Indies fast-bowling battery that was epitomised by the intimidating shape and form of the brooding giant Curtly Ambrose.

'You just have to survive out there,' Hudson told himself. 'You don't want to get pinned and end up being concussed or something.'

After a restless night, he and his team-mates arrived at the Kensington Oval where the West Indies were defending an incredible 57-year unbeaten record. It was here that they had also won their last 10 consecutive Test matches.

Hudson was his normal quiet and introspective self as he contemplated life in the fast lane. Someone asked him what was going through his mind.

'Survival,' he replied.

It was not the first time Hudson was facing the might of the West Indies pace attack, but this was a début Test match so it was different. His record against these fast bowlers in limited-overs matches was not altogether bad: against them at the World Cup he had scored 22 and, in the three one-day internationals leading up to the Test, his scores were 50, run out 6, and 30. At least he had survived till that point without being seriously pinned.

Still, he knew that a début Test would always be different...

WITHIN DAYS OF parading the Benson & Hedges Series trophy at the Wanderers, Kepler Wessels was again at the helm of the South African team *en route* to the Caribbean. Corrie van Zyl was back in the squad to replace the injured Brian McMillan.

After all the hype of the World Cup, the players had to reset their sights quickly on another tough assignment. In the space of 16 days, they would play the West Indies in three one-day internationals and a five-day Test match.

It was going to be tough. But even worse, after the slick organisation of the World Cup, the team was in for a shock. Practice facilities were almost non-existent, playing conditions were far from ideal and, in spite of the political reform process taking place at home, the people of Jamaica did not exactly extend a warm hand of friendship to a party of white South Africans whose sole non-white member was Omar Henry. Still, they came out in their hordes to watch the one-day series which, much to their delight, the home team completely dominated.

Inspired by two glorious back-to-back centuries by Phil Simmons and consistently good batting by Brian Lara, the West Indies won the first match at Kingston by 107 runs, and the second and third at Port-of-Spain by wide margins of 10 and seven wickets.

At Kingston, Cronjé was patrolling the outfield when, suddenly, he heard someone in the crowd call his name. He turned around, half surprised. A man was standing beyond the boundary proffering something through the wire fence. 'Hey, South African, come have a smoke with me, mon.'

A little bemused, Cronjé took a step towards the stranger. In his hand he held a smouldering joint of marijuana. 'Have some, mon,' urged the local fan. 'It's very good for your fielding, mon.'

Cronjé smiled politely, declined, and took up his fielding position again. The boy from Bloemfontein had never before been offered dope, let alone out on the field in an international match.

Off the field, there was a lot of fun – social events, fishing, sunbathing and day trips to the various islands. But there were also a few unfortunate incidents. Pringle and Snell were body-surfing and horsing around when Snelly collided with his partner in the surf and badly injured Pringle's ribs. Pringle was still in a lot of pain when he took the new ball in the third one-dayer, yet, in a sensational start, he bowled the great Desmond Haynes first ball. At the end of five overs, the grimacing Pring had to call it quits with figures of one for 6.

Snell, meanwhile, caused another scare while out swimming. This time he was practising his butterfly stroke, arms flailing all over the place, when he hit Richardson in the eye. It was serious enough for the keeper to sit out the next practice while Kirsten, Kuiper and Cronjé took turns keeping wicket, just in case. Fortunately, Swinger regained his vision to play in all the matches.

In Barbados before the start of the Test, the players were pleasantly surprised to meet up with the two Western Province batsmen Gary Kirsten and Kenny Jackson. These two were on their way to New York on holiday and decided to pop in to watch the cricket and experience some Caribbean nightlife. The only problem was that their connecting flight to the US would leave before the start of the fifth day...

THE FAMOUS KENSINGTON Oval was near deserted when the Test began. Cricket-mad Barbados was in the grip of cricket politics, and the fans were boycotting the match because of the non-selection of local hero Anderson Cummins.

The South Africans were very disappointed when no more than 300 people pitched up at a ground renowned for the atmosphere created by its noisy and knowledgeable crowds. Hudson, meanwhile, was thinking only of survival, and most of his team-mates had similar thoughts. With the exception of Wessels, they were about to play their first Test match.

The South African XI consisted of Hudson, Rushmere, Wessels, Peter Kirsten, Cronjé, Kuiper, Richardson, Snell, Pringle, Bosch and Donald. Rhodes was the twelfth man. Wessels, who had played 24 Tests for Australia, became the thirteenth cricketer to represent two countries in the Test arena. Kirsten, at age 36, was the second-oldest South African débutant after Geoff Chubb, who was 40 when he played his first Test against England in 1951.

Cronjé, aged 23, felt confident enough. In the one-dayers, he had scores of 42, run out 22, and run out 23, and he was hitting the ball well. He wasn't too concerned about the West Indies fast bowlers because he had benefited at Free State from facing Allan Donald and the province's West Indian speedster Franklyn Stephenson on an almost daily basis in the nets. 'I'm quite used to pace,' Cronjé said confidently.

Cronjé didn't last long. He was caught on the cut by Brian Lara, playing his second Test match, to give Jimmy Adams his first wicket in Test cricket. Cronjé was upset with himself. It was a stupid shot to play.

Hudson, meanwhile, was surviving quite splendidly as the South Africans set out to overhaul the West Indies' total of 262. At the close of the first day he had nine runs. At stumps on the second he was on 135 not out. He was eventually the seventh batsman out, bowled by the newcomer Kenneth Benjamin for a historic 163 that took him eight hours and 40 minutes. It was the first time a South African had made a century on début. He had survived, and then some.

South Africa's total of 345 gave them a handy 83-run lead, which was good enough to put them into a winning position when the West Indies were reduced to 184 for seven by the close of the third day. Only Lara had made a meaningful contribution with his maiden Test half-century, but Jimmy Adams was still there with 23 not out. He was to prove a thorn in the flesh of the confident South Africans.

Adams eventually ran out of partners but not before he had scored an undefeated 79 and, with tail-ender Patrick Patterson, put on 62 runs for the last wicket. The West Indies' total of 283 meant that South Africa needed to score 201 runs for victory.

Things did not look promising when Hudson departed for a duck and Rushmere for his second 3, but Wessels and Kirsten pulled things around, and at stumps on the fourth evening the total was 122 for two. Wessels was on 74 and Kirsten on 36.

The younger Kirsten and his mate Kenny Jackson had, meanwhile, been having a ball. They tore around the island in a hired beach buggy by day and burnt the candle at both ends by night. They were both beach-boy types, and they loved the Caribbean lifestyle. Gary was also enjoying the atmosphere surrounding the cricket Test. 'If this is what international cricket is all about, I want to be part of it,' he told Cronjé. 'Tell you what, Hansie, one of these days I'll be in this team!'

Cronjé wasn't too certain that Gary's batting form was quite up to it yet, but he had no doubt about the man's determination. 'I'm sure you will, Gazza,' he nodded before bidding farewell to the two Western Province players as they left for New York.

The final morning dawned with attendants carrying crates of beer and champagne into the South African dressing room. The supporters were readying themselves for the victory party, and had a music box set up for the expected festivities.

Says Cronjé, 'We were very positive going into that final day. We only needed 79 runs and had eight wickets in hand. We had a team talk on the fourth night. We were all saying, "Well done, it's been a great effort" and "To come here and to play well and to beat these guys is really very special." Then Kepler cautioned, "Remember, the game's a long way from over yet. You have to be very careful on the last day of a Test match. A lot of things can happen. For all we know, they may bowl us out for next to nothing tomorrow."'

Twenty minutes before lunch it was all over. South Africa's last eight wickets crashed for 26 runs – all out for 148, defeated by 52 runs.

It was cricket's ultimate horror show as Curtly Ambrose and Courtney Walsh bowled the innings to tatters: Wessels 74, Kirsten 52, Cronjé 2, Kuiper 0, Richardson 2, Snell 0, Pringle 4, Donald 0 and

Bosch 0. In a devastating 11-over spell, Walsh took four wickets for eight runs; and Ambrose picked up the rest, including Cronjé's wicket when he chased a wide delivery and was caught at the wicket. He was upset with himself. It was a stupid shot to play.

The South Africans were devastated. They had not survived.

For both Rushmere and Bosch it was their one and only Test match. Rushmere scored a total of six runs, and Bosch bowled well to get three wickets in all. 'It wasn't an easy time to be playing your first Test match,' says Cronjé ruefully.

In New York, Gary Kirsten and Kenny Jackson were still having a ball. After a couple of days there, they found a newspaper with a report on the Barbados Test. The news was shocking. They had left Barbados on the fourth night of the match after congratulating their countrymen on their expected victory. They could not believe what they were reading.

LIKE BASIL D'OLIVEIRA many years before, Hansie Cronjé's first taste of English cricket was in the Central Lancashire League. He went there after the West Indies tour to play for Norden Club. He had applied through an English agent for a position as a club professional and had been successful. Among the other South Africans playing in the leagues was his Free State team-mate Bradley Player.

After a week, Cronjé phoned home.

'How you enjoying it over there, Hansie?' asked Ewie.

'I don't know, Pa, it's not much fun.'

'Why's that, son?'

'I thought it would be quite easy over here. You know, playing a bit, earning a little money and then coming home. I didn't realise they expect the pro to do most of the work around the club and also perform better than anyone else. I just can't get used to it, and the weather is also terrible. You know, in the West Indies the wickets were hard and the bowling was pretty quick, but here you're batting on these pudding wickets. I tell you, Dad, the pitches get so wet that the mud splatters your pads when the ball pitches.'

Ewie Cronjé listened to his boy's complaints. 'Hansie, this is a great experience for you. Stick with it, boy. To be a good batsman you have to be able to play on all sorts of wickets and under all sorts of conditions. I know you can do it.'

In his first game, Cronjé scored 63, took three wickets, held a couple of catches and led Norden to victory. He then collected three ducks in a row. Because of the slow wickets, he was hitting through far too early, completely at odds with his timing. He also began imagining that the

members of the club, the people who were paying his salary, were starting to mutter about wasting their money on a no-hoper. He was hating
every minute of it.

After a month there was little improvement. 'I'm fed up, Bradley,
there's no ways I want to stay here. I think I'm going to pack up and go
home.'

Player advised him to lighten up. 'Listen, Hansie, the idea is to have
fun. Just relax and enjoy yourself. The wickets are going to get better
as the season gets older. Just wait, you'll see.'

Like the frustrated and embarrassed Basil D'Oliveira all those years
before, Cronjé stayed on. The wickets did get drier and better, and his
scores did improve a bit. Yet, by his own high standards, he still wasn't
very happy with his batting form. Then one day he took a train trip down
to Birmingham to visit Allan Donald, who by now was a senior member
of the Warwickshire county team. It was a happy reunion and they had
a lot to talk about.

In the Edgbaston club house Cronjé was describing his English
experiences to his pal when a man walked in.

'Hey, Hansie, meet our coach. Bob Woolmer, this is Hansie Cronjé.'

Of course. They had met a couple of years before at the Coaching
Academy back home.

'Nice to see you again, Bob.'

Cronjé continued talking about the battle he was having putting bat
to ball. Woolmer listened intently.

'Why don't you come down to the nets and I'll throw a few balls at
you,' offered the Warwickshire coach.

Cronjé wasn't angling for this, but he eagerly accepted the offer. He
had nothing to lose by it. Woolmer threw; Cronjé batted. No problems.
The Englishman was directing his throws rhythmically on to a good
length. The batsman hit them back without any fuss. Then suddenly
Woolmer held one back. Cronjé was fooled, and he lost his balance. The
ball beat him completely.

'That's it, Hansie, you're not standing still! On English wickets you
really have to wait for the ball. You have to stand really, really still until
you pick up the length. Let's try again.'

In his next game for Norden, Cronjé scored 130. The little net
session at Edgbaston was to be the start of a long and fruitful relationship with Woolmer.

Donald, meanwhile, was also reaping benefits from his relationship
with the shrewd Warwickshire coach. He again finished the season in the
English top ten with 74 wickets, including six 'fifors', in his 21 matches.

GRAHAM FORD, NEWLY appointed as Natal's director of playing affairs, made an appointment to see Patrick Symcox in Pietermaritzburg. It was shortly before the start of the 1992/93 season.

In his dual role as player-coach for Maritzburg University the previous summer, Ford had played against the Zingari Club for whom Symcox was a weekend cricketer. He was impressed with what he saw: a classy spin bowler who could also hit the ball pretty well and was obviously enjoying his cricket.

Symcox ushered Ford into his office at the private hospital he managed. 'What can I do for you, Graham?'

'Well, Pat, it's like this. I know you didn't play any provincial stuff last season, but I reckon you still have a lot of cricket in you. I'm really here to ask you to give it another go for Natal.'

'I've retired, Graham. You know that. I'm through with the game, man.'

'Come on, Pat, think about it. We could still use you. Why don't you come down to the nets and see how it goes?'

'Hell, I don't know, Graham, I mean, is it really worth it? You might use me once or twice and then chuck me out. I don't know if it's worth my while. Also, I'm still pretty busy here and I don't know that I have enough time to attend practices in Durban.'

'I promise you, Pat, we can use you all right. As for your job, we'll work out a way to accommodate you. A lot of guys still travel down from Maritzburg – Jonty, all of them. Just do me a favour and think about it.'

Symcox thought about it. The Natal management had changed, Kim Hughes was no longer part of the setup, Rhodes was the new captain and Clive Rice had joined them from Transvaal. Also, international call-ups could create more opportunities in the provincial team and, yes, deep down he still felt he had something to offer.

Patrick Symcox decided to come out of retirement.

HANSIE CRONJÉ WAS back from England, a wiser man for the experience. The local season was just underway, and a 55-overs provincial match was to be played at Empangeni on the Natal North Coast between a Natal Country Districts XI and his Free Staters. The day before the match Cronjé was driving a hired car from Durban airport along the North Coast road. It was dusk and visibility was poor.

A group of children was walking along the side of the road as the car neared. Suddenly, a six-year-old girl broke away from her friends and dashed out in front of the car. Hansie saw her at the last instant. He braked and swerved, but it was too late. The girl died as a result of the collision.

Cronjé was overcome with shock and grief. Tragedy like this had never touched his young life before. The next day he went out and scored a century in a big Free State victory, but he didn't much care. Cricket seemed so pointless after what had happened the previous evening.

On his return to Bloemfontein he was consoled by his family and friends. Bertha Pretorius came around to his house daily. She became a very special friend, inviting him to join her at her Bible study group and in prayer meetings she liked to attend. Cronjé also met Pastor Ray McCauley, head of the Rhema Church. Hansie liked him, and he liked Bertha. They grew closer and closer.

Cronjé knew what he had to do. He resolved to hand over his life to Jesus Christ; to become a born-again Christian. It became a source of great comfort.

FOR TWO MONTHS solidly, Cronjé worked on his fitness. He had never trained harder in his life. He went on a diet, drank only mineral water, and brought his weight down from 93 kilograms to an ideal 83 kilograms. He knew he was under pressure from players like Roy Pienaar and Mike Rindel, who were knocking at the door of national selection. He went to a team training camp in Cape Town where he proved to be the fittest player.

'If there are few players vying for the same berth,' he told himself, 'then at least no one is going to be fitter than me.'

India was due to tour South Africa for the first time and he was determined to feature in the series. He also concentrated on his bowling in order to give him an edge over his rivals. He had bowled a lot for Norden and had taken his fair share of wickets. He watched video tapes of India's games against England the previous season, studying them carefully, working out batting strategy against their bowlers. A week before the first Test at Kingsmead, he captained a President's XI against the Indians and scored 73 and 53. He felt fit, confident and well prepared.

When the selectors named the Test team, Cronjé was the twelfth man. After only one Test in the West Indies, he was on the sidelines. He felt hurt, but he was not alone. Rushmere, Kuiper, Bosch and Snell were also axed.

The real debate, however, did not concern these five players. It involved Jonty Rhodes. His wonderful performances at the World Cup had his fans clamouring for his Test call-up, but there was stern opposition from established critics and former players who maintained he was not a genuine Test batsman. 'He doesn't have the batting technique,' they lamented, 'and you can't afford to pick a specialist fielder.'

In the raging, pre-selection debate, the best most of these critics could do was to include Rhodes as the twelfth man. His supporters hit back. They saw his infectious spirit as integral to South Africa's cause. They believed he had the guts and determination to perform well at whatever level he played. They saw him as the fresh new face of South African cricket; the perfect role model for the game's growing band of young followers. They argued it would be an absolute folly to leave him out.

The selectors picked him. On his home ground, cheered by his adoring fans, he scored 41 and 26 not out, and fielded brilliantly. They also recalled Jimmy Cook. He was dismissed by Kapil Dev off the first ball of the match in South Africa's first home Test in almost 23 years.

Snell's place in the attack was taken by 22-year-old Brett Schultz. He had bowled himself into the team the previous week when, for Cronjé's President's XI, he took five Indian wickets for 35 runs in their first innings. Now, at Kingsmead, he took one wicket before hobbling off the field with a hamstring injury without completing his fifteenth over.

The drawn Test was hampered by rain and produced little sparkling cricket, but it did give the international game its first-ever decision by a third umpire studying line decisions on a television monitor. In this way, Sachin Tendulkar was adjudged run out for 11, beaten by Rhodes's throw.

For the second Test at the Wanderers, the selectors announced two changes. Craig Matthews made his début in place of the injured Schultz, and Cronjé came in for Omar Henry.

'I was so nervous I couldn't hold the bat,' Cronjé confessed later. But hold the bat he did, occupying the crease for 84 minutes during a tricky period to score eight runs. Rhodes hit a wonderful 91, and McMillan, after five hours at the crease, fell two runs short of his maiden Test century. In their second turn at bat, Cronjé made 15, Rhodes 13, and McMillan 5, while Swinger Richardson celebrated his maiden Test fifty.

Meyrick Pringle, meanwhile, was in serious trouble. A short, fast delivery from Javagal Srinath squeezed between the visor of his helmet and fractured his skull near his left eye. Deprived of a key bowler, Wessels called on Cronjé. He had yet to bowl in a first-class game for Free State, but bowl he did, sending down 35 overs in the match and dismissing Tendulkar for 111.

In the Wanderers nets, Cronjé had called on the assistance of Anton Ferreira, the former Northern Transvaal and Warwickshire all-rounder who was coaching at Transvaal. 'I asked him a little bit about my bowling, how I could improve it, and so on. He gave me a few tips.'

Cronjé also remembered the words of Gordon Parsons who once strongly advised him to work on his bowling. 'Believe me,' said his brother-in-law, 'if your batting form is not up to scratch, your bowling will often pull you through.'

In an exemplary display of tight seam bowling, Cronjé conceded just 54 runs in those 35 overs, sending down no fewer than 17 maidens. As South Africa's No 6 batsman, his bowling was pulling him through. He was retained for the third Test at St George's Park.

Wessels wanted badly to win. The first two Tests had ended in draws prompting the critics to rant about the dull, negative cricket. It was time for a turnaround on the same ground where South Africa had won its last Test match in 1970 against Bill Lawry's Australians. Schultz and Henry were back; Pringle, of course, was out; Cook was dropped; and Peter Kirsten was going through a bad trot. Wessels decided to promote Cronjé to No 3.

Wessels won the toss and put India in. Donald found his rhythm, bagged five for 55 – his first 'fifor' in Test cricket – and the innings closed on 212. Wessels was bowled fourth ball by Manoj Prabhakar. Cronjé was in at the deep end, but he was ready.

'I had set myself a goal of batting for two days because I knew this was a golden opportunity at No 3 to establish myself in the team.'

After almost eight hours at the crease, he nudged his score to 92. Anil Kumble was bowling. The delivery was just wide of the leg stump. Cronjé clipped it for four. The next ball was short and outside off-stump. Cronjé cut it to the boundary. In what he laconically described as an 'emotional moment', he had scored his maiden Test century. He went on to reach 135 before he was bowled by Kumble. He had occupied the crease for eight hours and 51 minutes.

Although he admitted batting for a 'ridiculous amount of time; very, very slowly', Cronjé's landmark innings gave South Africa a crucial 63-run lead on the first innings.

By the end of the third day India were in tatters on 31 for six against the rampant fast bowling of Donald and Schultz. Yet, in an innings in which no other batsman scored more than 17, Kapil Dev somehow managed to hit a magnificent 129. Donald's figures read seven for 84, and Richardson's nine catches in the match was a record by a South African.

South Africa needed 153 to win. 'Remember Barbados!' the cry went up. Wessels needed no reminding. He hit 95 not out, Cronjé was undefeated on 16, and victory was theirs by nine wickets.

The fourth and final Test was another tedious draw at Newlands. Into the side for the first time came Daryll Cullinan to hit 46 and 28. Wessels was bowled third ball for a duck by Prabhakar, and Cronjé scored 33 and 0. He was also called on to bowl again. In 18 overs and four balls in the first innings, he took two for 17. In the second innings he sent down three overs, all of them maidens. As the new No 3, his bowling and batting were pulling him through.

As for Jonty Rhodes, he made his critics eat their words by topping the Test batting averages with 45.83. Not bad for a man they did not think was up to it.

FANIE DE VILLIERS was a happy man. His excellent swing bowling had been rewarded with a call-up by the selectors for the seven-match limited-overs international series. At Newlands he joined in the fielding practice the day before the first game.

Crash! De Villiers and Kepler Wessels collided head-on as they both raced to get under a steepling catch. At top speed, their eyes on the ball, they ran full tilt into one other and clashed skulls with a sickening crash that reverberated around the ground. Severely dazed, and with blood seeping out of facial wounds, they were both rushed to hospital. Wessels took 35 stitches in his forehead while De Villiers needed 17 in his eyebrow. It was not the first time Vinnige Fanie would be involved in a freak accident, but he was a tough guy. The next morning he insisted he was well enough to make his international début. Wessels, too, was black and blue but refused to stand down. It was the kind of dedication their team-mates admired.

At the end of a six-wicket victory, the admiration of the fans was reserved for Hansie Cronjé. Still not established as a front-line bowler, he sent down his full quota of 10 overs and took five for 32, an extraordinary return in limited-overs cricket. Then, with South Africa needing six runs from four balls to win the match, he walloped Prabhakar into the crowd beyond mid-wicket. There was no other candidate for Man of the Match.

In the next match at St George's Park, the so-called 'Friendship Tour' suddenly turned sour. The Indians became annoyed that Peter Kirsten was constantly backing up out of his crease. Kapil Dev had warned him about this on a few occasions, and at Newlands had actually pulled up in his delivery stride and made as if to knock off the bails. At St George's Park, Wessels was facing Kapil Dev, and Kirsten was at the non-striker's end with five runs to his name. The Indian bowler again pulled up before releasing the ball and, in a flash, whipped off the bails and appealed. Kirsten was out of his crease and, upon Kapil Dev's insistence, was given out. Out in the middle of the pitch, strong words were exchanged between the two players. Kirsten gesticulated wildly and cursed. Wessels tried to intervene, but Kapil Dev was unrepentant. He claimed he had already warned Kirsten three times in previous encounters.

Back in the dressing rooms and in the crowd, the mood had turned nasty. There was still lingering anger out in the middle when Wessels, turning for a second run, swung his bat around in time-honoured fashion and cracked Kapil Dev a hard blow on the shin. At a subsequent inquiry by match referee Clive Lloyd, Kirsten was fined half his match fee for offensive behaviour – the first South African to be punished under the ICC's new code of conduct – but no case could be proved against Wessels. Had the South African skipper been found guilty of deliberately hitting the Indian bowler, the UCBSA would probably have been left with no option but to strip him of the leadership.

South Africa won the match with a delightful unbroken partnership of 78. The batsmen who shared in it were Cronjé and Dave Callaghan, now a member of the national one-day squad.

At Springbok Park in Bloemfontein, now hosting its first official international match, South Africa took an unassailable 4–1 lead in the series. It was there that Andrew Hudson, already the standard-bearer in the Test arena, scored 108 to become the first centurion for South Africa in limited-overs internationals. When South Africa finally wrapped up the series by five matches to two, Hudson's batting average was 39.71, Wessels was tops on 48.85, Cronjé had 47 and Callaghan 38. The best of the bowlers was Craig Matthews with 11 wickets in all. It had not been a particularly high-scoring series, neither was the run tempo very good, and the debate began all over again in the South African dressing room over scoring rates at the top of the innings.

THE TRICK WITH a triangular series is to make sure the home side qualifies for the final. From the host nation's perspective, this means that one of the two foreign sides must be capable of being eliminated. South Africa's first triangular series soon after the India tour departed sharply from this script. The invited teams were West Indies and Pakistan. It placed the South African team under enormous pressure.

In fairness to the UCBSA, the country was fresh back in international cricket and they wanted to get as many top teams to South Africa as quickly as possible. Unfortunately, South Africa failed to qualify for the final. It was won comfortably by the West Indies who beat Pakistan by five wickets at the Wanderers. Earlier in the series, they had bowled out the Pakistanis for an astonishing 43 on a poor wicket at Newlands.

The series gave the South Africans the opportunity to welcome a new member to their squad. Errol Stewart joined the team as a hard-hitting wicketkeeper-batsman. He and Richardson played three matches each, but neither did much with the bat. The South Africans in general had trouble against the Pakistani pacemen Wassim Akram and Waqar Younis, who were the world's leading exponents of reverse swing at the time. At East London, Wassim picked up four wickets in 13 balls as the South Africans crashed from 151 for three to 162 all out. Cronjé's innings of 81 stood out like a beacon on an island strewn with wreckage.

The reverse swing phenomenon was occupying the minds of the players in the South African dressing room. All sorts of theories abounded on how best to play it. Eddie Barlow phoned Cronjé.

'Get a bowling machine out, Hansie. Set it on high speed at yorker length and make it swing into the bat. That way you'll maybe work out the best way to play these guys.'

The next game at Newlands was against the West Indies. It took place 12 days before Pakistan's 43-run debacle, but already the wicket was in poor enough shape for Wessels to describe it as 'disgraceful'. The South Africans managed just 140, with Kirsten and Cronjé catching a lot of flak from the spectators for their slow rate of scoring. Cronjé made 31 and Kirsten 30 which, as it turned out, were pretty good scores under the circumstances.

During the break between innings, the South Africans were sitting around looking glum. Cronjé piped up, 'Come on, guys, buck up. We can defend this total.'

His team-mates looked at him in disdain. One of them replied, 'I'm pleased you think so.'

Cronjé shot back, 'I'm telling you, that wicket's doing a lot!'

The West Indies were bowled out for 136. Cronjé took three for 27 and was named Man of the Match for the second time in a limited-overs international on that ground. His reputation was growing as an all-rounder of note.

HANSIE CRONJÉ'S BURGEONING international prowess was seen as the reflected glory of his feats with the Free State team. Under his impressive leadership the province had become the country's top outfit, winning both the Currie Cup with a wonderful first-ever victory over Western Province, and the Total Power Series (formerly the Nissan Shield) through a Cronjé-inspired triumph over Eastern Province. Cronjé's Currie Cup average was an astonishing 98.75, inspiring the 1993 *Protea Cricket Annual* to describe him as 'a national treasure'. In the maiden victory over Western Province, he scored 161 not out, and in the Total Power Series final he hit top score of 75. His captaincy potential was also advancing match by match.

ELSEWHERE, PAT SYMCOX had become a regular member of the Natal senior side, as was the young fast bowler Shaun Pollock.

9

Heir Apparent

THROUGHOUT THE WESSELS era, the South African captaincy was an emotionally charged issue. Kepler Wessels was the man in possession but a lot of people did not think he was right for the job. He had received the appointment because he was the only player in South Africa who had experience at Test match level. In that respect, he was a man apart.

His detractors did not like the fact that a former Australian was captaining South Africa. They claimed that a man who had left his country for another should not have his cake and eat it.

Those who had originally supported Clive Rice must have known he did not have time on his side. He was already 42 when South Africa returned to international cricket, and he probably got the job for India in return for his long years of service. Re-entry had come at least half a dozen years too late for him. In any event, some powerful officials did not like his style of management. His days were always numbered.

If there had been other candidates, they too had the odds stacked against them. Jimmy Cook was not getting any younger at the time of readmission and, despite his three exceptional seasons in England, was in danger of losing those elements of batting form that are almost impossible to rekindle once the fire of age has consumed them. Peter Kirsten, too, was deemed to be heading into the twilight of his great career, and the once-cavalier Adrian Kuiper had all but shed the fresh bloom of youth.

Back in international cricket, South Africa had to catch up with two lost decades in the shortest possible time. To do so, they would have to learn quickly about the pitfalls and the opportunities in the dog-eat-dog world of the international arena. They would have to become competitive and disciplined without delay and have shrewd, uncompromising and experienced leadership.

Given the limitations of South African cricket, Wessels was reckoned to be the only real candidate for the job. His strength was his battle-hardened background; here was a man who, in the face of adversity, had endured, survived and then flourished in the unforgiving, white-hot crucible of Australian cricket.

His problem was that he carried the kind of excess baggage that suggested his appointment could not be of a long-term nature.

To build a team for the future, South Africa would need to groom a younger, more flexible and adventurous captain. He would have to be a man with all-round cricketing skills yet, more importantly, he would have to possess extraordinary leadership qualities and a vision that would mirror the spirit of his country's quest for democracy. He would need to learn at Wessels's knee, then emerge as his own man with an exceptional personality.

The issue was largely confined to cricket's inner sanctum. The man in the street neither knew of these priorities nor did he much care. For him, South Africans were playing international cricket again, and it was important that they did well. When another captain was appointed one day, so be it.

In the team itself the immediate needs lay elsewhere. Wessels was well received as the captain, and the players respected him for his knowledge of the game and disciplined approach. They knew they could learn from him, and they were happy to be taught. The vice-captaincy mattered little to them. Wessels was the captain and that was all that counted.

It was different in the game's inner sanctum. The vice-captaincy was seen as an important issue. On the basis of sheer seniority it was easy at the outset to award it to the likes of Cook, Kuiper and Peter Kirsten, who all had the necessary experience to take over in times of emergency. The issue of the captaincy was more critical because the vice-captain's role carried with it the very future of South African cricket.

The game's custodians had to be certain that whomever they chose would develop into the kind of leader South Africa needed. If they picked the wrong man, they would lose the initiative.

Elsewhere in Test cricket, the appointment of the vice-captain might be regarded as reward for services rendered; in the South African team it became a position that commanded far deeper appraisal. The vice-captain would have to be a new-generation man free of prejudice, a role model for the youth of his land, a strong and statesman-like figure. He would also have to be a very good cricketer and a fine tactician.

There had been some fine young captains in recent years – Rushmere, Rhodes, Cronjé, Cullinan, Strydom, Commins, Pienaar,

Matthews, Gary Kirsten – but some had faded, others remained, and a few besides may have lost the cutting edge.

Wessels was by no means ready to abdicate, but he had already identified his successor. His choice was Hansie Cronjé, and he made his thoughts plain in official circles.

IN AUTUMN 1993, Hansie Cronjé was appointed vice-captain of the South African team to tour Sri Lanka, India and Australia the following summer.

The young Free State skipper was glad for the opportunity, but he did not read too much into it. He saw it as a 'passive position' that would only become active if the captain were not available. Wessels was still the man in control and he was not planning to relinquish power just yet. 'Just make sure you're ready to fit in if ever I'm injured' was Wessels's advice to Cronjé in the days before the flight to Sri Lanka.

Cronjé liked and admired Wessels. They had come from the same school and a similar Afrikaner background and, given the age gap, there was more than a hint of hero worship. Cronjé saw Wessels as a father figure, and he was delighted to be his deputy. As a young and already successful provincial captain, Cronjé knew he could learn a lot more from him. He had already shown himself to be a fast learner.

HANSIE CRONJÉ KISSED Bertha Pretorius goodbye and promised to phone her whenever he could. Then he left for Sri Lanka, vice-captain of a South African team that included some interesting personnel.

Jimmy Cook was back as a middle-order batsman, Peter Kirsten had been dropped, and Brett Schultz's high-octane bowling made him a popular selection. Clive Eksteen's consistently impressive left-arm wicket-taking for Transvaal had earned him a recall in a close run contest with Free State's unlucky spin-bowling hero Omar Henry. Another spin bowler was deemed necessary on the slow, turning pitches that characterise Sri Lankan cricket.

The selectors' choice was Pat Symcox who, rejuvenated by his return to the Natal side, had suddenly emerged as the best off-spin bowler in the country. He had been travelling four times a week between Pietermaritzburg and Durban for practices, Natal were encouraging him, and he was regularly taking wickets for them. The last thing he expected, though, was a call from the national selectors. At the age of 33, 'Symmo' was about to write another chapter in the most incredible rags-to-riches story in South African cricket.

The first Test at Moratuwa began a fortnight into the tour. The South Africans got off to a good start with a century opening stand from Wessels, who scored 47, and Hudson 90. Then they found themselves in awful trouble, particularly against the dangerous offspin of Muttiah Muralitharan. He took career-best figures of five for 104. Only Symcox, in his Test début, was prepared to take him on. He scored 48 off 63 balls.

Set to score 365 to win, the South Africans lost quick wickets and looked to be heading for a big defeat. That they managed to hold out for a draw against the odds was due to heroic rearguard batting from Rhodes and débutant Eksteen. Rhodes scored his maiden Test century, ending on 101 not out after 262 minutes of sheer vigilance. Eksteen was undefeated on 4, keeping out 89 balls in the process.

'Jonty's innings was the best I've seen him play under pressure,' enthused Cronjé. 'I was very proud of him.'

Cronjé himself scored 17 and 1. That night he telephoned Bertha. He sounded distraught.

'Are you okay, Hansie?' she asked anxiously.

'I don't know, Bertha, I might have chucked my chances out of the window,' he replied.

'Why, what's happened?'

'My back's packed up. I can hardly move.'

He then reminded Bertha how, when he had been moving house before the tour, he had manually shifted some big rocks in his new garden. He remembered feeling a little twinge of pain at the time, but thought nothing of it. In the Moratuwa Test he had bowled 34 overs which had only compounded the problem.

'It's just got worse,' he complained, 'and it's so bad that I definitely won't be able to play the second one-day match in three days' time. I'm flat on my back. I feel like this is a turning point in my career. Other guys in the team are starting to do really well and I can't even move. I don't know, I'm sort of worried about what's going to happen.'

Bertha comforted him as best she could. She promised to pray for him and told him it would be all right.

In the next few days, Cronjé received several faxed messages of encouragement from Bertha, her family and from his own folks at home. The support from Bloemfontein spurred him on. It made him more determined to get better. He also had the support of his teammates. They ragged him about shirking his duties.

Cronjé was a spectator when South Africa won the second one-dayer in great style. The Sri Lankans were bowled out for 98, and Brian McMillan scored 35 and took three for 12 to be named Man of the Match. With the first one-dayer abandoned due to rain, the South Africans led the series 1–0.

The third one-dayer took place two days later. Cronjé had been receiving intensive treatment from physiotherapist Craig Smith for his strained back, and he was feeling much better. Wessels asked him if he'd be fit to play. Yes, he said, and he was out for 2. Sri Lanka won by 44 runs when South Africa failed to chase a target of 198, and Cronjé grew more depressed. His back was holding up, but he desperately needed to score some runs.

THE SOUTH AFRICANS were learning some valuable lessons about how best to play spin bowling on an island that boasted several spin wizards. They were also finding out about Asian fireworks.

Shortly before the team's arrival in Colombo, the Sri Lankan head of state was assassinated in a car bombing in the street outside the Taj Samudra hotel where the players would be staying. Upon arrival, they felt a little uneasy as they surveyed the terrible black marks on the pitted road where the explosion had taken place. It was a touchy time in the Sri Lankan capital and fireworks were banned by the authorities.

The deputy head of state accepted an invitation to watch the cricket. He was surrounded by bodyguards as he sat in the main pavilion. The players' enclosure was not far away.

'Boom!' The huge explosion sent the dignitaries and bodyguards diving for cover.

'Sorry, guys,' said a grinning Symmo, 'maybe this isn't such a good time to be lighting up firecrackers.'

It certainly wasn't. The dignitaries were not amused. The mischievous 'old man' was told to refrain from the practice.

In the privacy of the team bus, Richard Snell decided to light a firecracker that, in truth, was nothing less than an explosive device. It went off in his hand and he had to have stitches in a nasty gash.

FOR THE SECOND TEST held at the Singhalese Sports Club in Colombo, the South Africans made two changes. After going wicketless at Moratuwa, Eksteen was left out, and Snell was recalled to the Test team for the first time since the one-off match against West Indies 17 months before. Cook, who had scored a total of 31 runs batting at No 5 in the first Test, was replaced by McMillan.

Jimmy didn't know it at the time, but his Test career was over.

Symcox, who picked up three second-innings wickets at Moratuwa, was retained as the only spinner. He was not needed. The four-pronged pace attack of Donald, Schultz, Snell and McMillan scythed through the brittle Sri Lankan batting. Snell took five wickets, Donald four, and McMillan two, but the real heroics belonged to the blond bomber

Schultz. He bowled extremely fast to take five for 48 in the first innings, and four for 58 in the second.

South Africa began their first innings in the final session of the opening day. They had bundled out their opponents for 168 shortly after tea, and it was vital that they compile a match-winning total. Cronjé was determined to get among the runs, and the openers, Wessels and Hudson, provided the perfect platform for him. When he walked out to bat at No 3, there were already 137 runs on the board.

When he finally departed six hours and 50 minutes later, he had scored 122, his second century in Test cricket.

There were wonderful supporting roles in what at times was a painfully slow but nevertheless effective batting effort. Wessels scored 92, Hudson 58, Cullinan 52, Symcox 50 and Snell 48. Muralitharan was called on to send down no fewer than 54 overs of spin and, although he again took five wickets in an innings, it did not prevent the rampant South Africans from totalling a massive 495.

Sri Lanka faced the daunting task of scoring 328 runs to make South Africa bat a second time. They did not even come close. Thanks to the charged-up fast bowlers, they were humbled for 119. It was a huge personal triumph for Schultz, and his nine wickets in the Test earned him the Man of the Match award. It was also a moment of great satisfaction for Cronjé who, after scoring his fine century, confided, 'It was a big turning point in my career. I needed it badly.'

FANIE DE VILLIERS was hatching a devilish plan. He left the Taj Samudra and walked to a nearby shop. There he bought a freshly caught fish and wrapped it in a newspaper.

Back at the hotel, he let himself into one of the rooms. It was in an awful state: kit and belongings lying all over the place, beds unmade, clothes and wet towels strewn over the floor. Vinnige Fanie pulled up his ample nose.

'I'll teach them for being so untidy.'

He unwrapped the fish, climbed on to a chair and gently squeezed it into the air-conditioning unit. Then he slipped out of the room and visited the others in quick succession to tell his team-mates what he had done. All the players were staying on the same floor at the Taj Samudra. They waited and watched.

By the next day the fish was coming on very nicely in the ventilation duct. Allan Donald turned to his roommate Richard Snell: 'Hey, Snelly, what's the pong?'

'Not me,' said Snelly, 'but it's not too good, whatever it is.'

The other players waited and watched.

First, the shoes came out of the room, but that didn't help. Next, it was time for some laundry, so the two fast bowlers washed all their clothes. Then they washed all their bedding. But still it didn't help.

'I don't know, Snelly, but this pong is just getting worse,' moaned Donald. 'Let's go through the room and see if we can find what's causing it.'

The other players continued to watch as the two troubled room-mates began carefully spring-cleaning their room. Fanie smiled his approval as the clean clothes were neatly stacked in the cupboards, the kit stashed away in its right place, and the bathroom tidied up.

After several days, the smell disappeared. Fanie slipped back into the room and opened the air vent. The fish had dried out completely, so he removed it. No one told Snelly and Sling what had caused their discomfort, but at least they had learned a lesson in personal house-keeping.

THE THIRD TEST at the Tamil Union Cricket Club was the scene of Daryll Cullinan's maiden century. Almost 10 years had passed since he became South Africa's youngest centurion. Now, in his fourth Test match, he was playing a very important innings of grace and concentration. With five wickets down and 128 runs on the board, South Africa badly needed a major contribution. This was provided by Cullinan and Richardson, who set about putting on a vital 122 runs for the sixth wicket.

Cullinan occupied the crease for four minutes short of six hours to finally reach his 100 with a copybook offdrive. Although he perished two runs later, the rescue act had been achieved. Richardson's 62 was his highest score in Test cricket.

Schultz again was raring to go. This time he produced figures of five for 63 to keep his team in the ascendancy. As it turned out, rain had the final say, washing out the entire fifth day's play for the match to peter out into a draw. The series was won, and Cronjé was not unhappy with his batting form. He produced scores of 24 and 73 not out.

BRETT SCHULTZ WAS undoubtedly the bowling success of the series. On pitches that normally aid spin bowlers, the 'Bear' had taken 20 Test wickets at 16 runs apiece. Still, the rough-and-ready 23-year-old had a bit to learn on the question of subtlety. This was no better illustrated than in the third and final one-dayer in Colombo where the South Africans were struggling to get Aravinda da Silva out. Wickets were falling around him, but he looked well set. If only they could dismiss him, they might be in business.

Wessels, fielding at slip, hit on a plan. He called Rhodes across from point and explained, 'To get this guy out, we have to attack his leg stump. Look how he's shuffling across. I reckon we can bowl him around his legs. Pass it on.'

So the message was relayed quietly from slip to point, from point to cover, and from cover to Cronjé at mid-off. He walked across to the bowler Schultz. 'Listen, the captain wants you to attack his leg stump because he's shuffling across. Maybe you can bowl him around his legs.'

Shultz nodded and walked thoughtfully back to his bowling mark. Then he turned and yelled down the pitch at Wessels, 'If you want me to bowl at leg stump can I have my fine leg a bit finer, please!'

De Silva's ears pricked up. Smiling, he went on to score 61 not out, and Sri Lanka won by 44 runs to share the series 1–1.

THE VISIT TO Sri Lanka provided the first real sign of disagreement between Kepler Wessels and coach Mike Procter. It was again sparked by a debate over the scoring rate in the first 15 overs of the limited-overs matches. Procter's view was that the team needed to hurry things up during this period of a match when fielding restrictions were in place. Wessels believed that the best strategy was to exercise greater caution and build a big platform. The commentators began taking sides with Procter, and Wessels started to become a bit uptight because his authority was apparently being challenged.

'What worked for us at the World Cup apparently isn't good enough any more,' complained Kepler. 'In fact, whatever we do is wrong. If we try to build an innings, we're told we're too slow. If we go for runs and lose wickets, we're criticised.'

Procter represented the other school of thought. Throughout his cavalier playing days, whether for South Africa, Rhodesia, Natal, Gloucestershire or Packer's World Series Cricket, he had adhered to the theory that attack was the best form of defence. 'In my view,' he said, 'you have to attack from the start, even if you lose a wicket or two along the way. You will win more games by attacking than the other way.'

Procter emphasised that his role was not to dictate from the sidelines, so he and Wessels left it at that. The official line was that they had 'agreed to disagree', and only time would tell whose strategy was the correct one.

THE SRI LANKAN TOUR was by no means all serious stuff. The players grew a little bored staying in the same hotel in Colombo for a six-week stretch so they arranged their own entertainment. This sometimes took the form of high-speed races along the beachfront in scooter taxis known as tuk-tuks. These noisy little vehicles are designed to carry only two passengers but three of four players at a time would bundle into them and bribe the drivers with 50 rupees (the equivalent of a month's wages in Sri Lanka) to race each other. In one of these high-speed chases, a tuk-tuk carrying four players, including the captain and vice-captain, overturned. It was agreed to exercise some caution in future.

On his return to Bloemfontein, Cronjé recounted his experiences on the lovely Indian Ocean island. 'It really was a good tour,' he told Bertha. 'They looked after us very well, and I reckon it has to be the best country to visit on the subcontinent. The travelling's not nearly as bad as in India because you only have to travel short distances by bus or coach. Also, we stayed in the same hotel in Colombo all the time, and our rooms were all on the same floor. The only bad thing I can say about the place is the practice facilities. They really aren't up to much.'

DARYLL CULLINAN'S TEST career was coming on nicely. In three matches in Sri Lanka, he had averaged 47.40. In the one-dayers he was less productive with a total of eight runs in his three innings. Back home, he was determined to cement his place in the South African side for the coming tours of India and Australia. He did so in the best way possible.

In a Currie Cup match against Northern Transvaal at the Wanderers, his 337 not out was the highest score by a South African in South Africa. Ironically, earlier that season Terence Lazard had set the record with his 307 not out for Boland against Western Province. He was supported by John Commins on 165.

Jimmy Cook was also back among the runs. In the match at the Wanderers he contributed 102 to a fourth-wicket stand of 283 with Cullinan but, alas, it was not enough to gain the veteran a recall to the South African team.

Cullinan's place in the side was not in doubt, however. Two days before his treble-century, he hammered an undefeated 111 in a night series match.

It was a domestic season of batting feats. Peter Kirsten scored 271 for Border against Northern Transvaal. Against Natal at Bloemfontein, Cronjé scored 150 and 107, and his classy team-mate Gerhardus Liebenberg weighed in with a fine innings of 142. In the same match Jonty Rhodes hit 114.

Gary Kirsten was also making a name for himself with Western Province, hitting 192 against Northern Transvaal and 116 against Eastern Province. The young Herschelle Gibbs blossomed with 152 not out against Eastern Province B, and the exciting Mike Rindel slammed 137 against touring Barbados at Centurion Park.

The country's top wicket-taker was a left-arm pace bowler of extraordinary potential, Aubrey Martyn, who had represented SA Schools in 1990. He took a total of 41 wickets while playing for Western Province and South Africa A.

Eksteen's left-armers brought him 34 wickets for Transvaal and South Africa A, and his match haul of 12 for 95 at Newlands included seven for 29 in an innings. The flame-haired Transvaal fast bowler Steven Jack picked up 33 wickets, while the combative all-rounder Lance Klusener bagged 27 scalps at Natal and was third in the bowling averages.

South Africa was definitely not short of cricket talent, and some members of the national team were already glancing anxiously over their shoulders.

THE INTERNATIONAL ROADSHOW was now in full swing. Next stop was India for the five-nation Hero Cup series of one-dayers. From there the South Africans would head for their first full tour of Australia.

Although the Hero Cup had a grandiose title, it was merely named after its sponsor, which happened to be a bicycle manufacturer. The competing nations were India, West Indies, Sri Lanka, Zimbabwe and South Africa.

The first match against Zimbabwe at Bangalore was rained off after only nine overs were bowled. The damp South Africans returned to their hotel, and management decided there was no better time than the present for a spot of fitness training. Wessels was preoccupied with media interviews, so it fell to Cronjé to take the players on a run. The drizzle was coming down as they set off down the road.

'Come on, Hansie,' moaned Fanie, 'this tar is killing my feet!'

'Keep going, guys,' exhorted Cronjé, 'don't slack. Remember: guts, determination and character!'

The run took them past a golf course. 'Come on, this way,' commanded the vice-captain as he steered the group on to the fairway. 'There, Fanie, we're off the tar. Now we can do some more running on the course.'

The players began getting into the spirit of things. Before long they had lined up in formation like a platoon, with Allan Donald assuming the role of drill sergeant. 'Hup, two, three, four, hup, two, three, four, get those knees up, son!'

The players were having a great time. Cronjé smiled to himself as he watched them leopard-crawling on the wet grass. He could see that, in damp Bangalore, team spirit was taking shape very nicely for the major challenge that awaited them in Australia. There would be times in the months ahead when the going would get tough, when the players would look back on days like these as they dug deep down to dredge up fresh supplies of guts, determination and character.

'Keep it up, guys,' yelled Cronjé.

'Hup, two, three, four,' they chanted.

WHILE THE SOUTH AFRICAN cricketers were leopard-crawling on the golf course at Bangalore, Northern Transvaal were hosting Border in a Benson & Hedges Series floodlit match at Centurion Park. The Border captain, Peter Kirsten, opened the innings and was dropped off Rudi Bryson on 9. He went on to smash a career-best 134 not out in 149 balls. The best of the Northerns' batsmen was the left-hander Mike Rindel with 73.

KEPLER WESSELS AND his men headed for Bombay to meet the West Indies. The South Africans were pumped up. They had a few scores to settle.

The Indian fans packed into the Brabourne Stadium where they soon found a new hero in Rhodes. This was the first time they had seen him in person, and he put on quite a show. When South Africa batted first, he turned on the charm in a delightful innings of 40 at a run a ball. Then, in defence of a 180-run total in a match reduced to 40 overs a side because of early rain, he inspired his team-mates and dazzled the fans with undoubtedly the most brilliant all-round display of fielding yet seen in limited-overs cricket. He took a world record five catches that day, including a breath-taking one-hander at point to get rid of Brian Lara, and a full-length dive at wide mid-on to stop a Phil Simmons onslaught.

After pouching two more catches to dismiss Haynes and Adams, Rhodes had the crowd on its feet. The deliriously happy Indian fans were chanting 'Jonty, Jonty, Jonty!' as if he were one of their own, but his best effort was still to come.

Anderson Cummins was hitting the ball around at will when he got a thick outside edge to a Donald thunderbolt and the ball looped high into the vacant gully area. Rhodes at backward point took off like a bullet. He sped 10 metres then threw himself at full-length into the gully arc, caught the ball one-handed and, propelled by the momentum, slid on his stomach right into the batting crease.

'Jonty, Jonty, Jonty!'

The West Indies were dismissed for 139 – sweet victory by 41 runs with Rhodes awarded Man of the Match. The name of only one cricketer was on the lips of the whole of India that night.

The South African camp was jubilant. Not only had Rhodes excelled himself but Cullinan had batted quite beautifully in scoring 70 not out in 81 balls. 'It's the best I've seen Daryll play,' enthused Cronjé. 'Right now there's no better batsman in the team.'

The downside was that Cullinan had collapsed from heat exhaustion in the sauna-like conditions and had to be carried off the field on a stretcher in the midst of his blazing innings. He was later treated for dehydration, and then picked up a mystery virus which continued to plague him. It did not augur well for the looming campaign in Australia.

The next game against Sri Lanka was at the Nehru Stadium in run-down Gauhati, which one of the players described as 'the worst place I've seen in my life'.

The South Africans went out before the match to examine the pitch. One look at it and Cronjé turned to Wessels: 'This thing's going to break up. We don't want to be batting second on this.'

'You're right,' said the captain, 'but if we bat first, the ball's going to move around a lot. Look at the overcast skies – perfect for swing bowling. This is not a toss I want to win.'

Wessels and the Sri Lankan captain, Arjuna Ranatunga, went out to toss. There was no match referee. 'Heads,' said Wessels. It was tails.

'Let's toss again,' suggested the Sri Lankan skipper. 'Make it best out of three.'

'Heads,' said Wessels. It was tails.

'Ah, I don't know, man,' said Ranatunga. 'Let's forget the first two and toss one final time.'

'Heads,' said Wessels; it was tails.

'Oh, crikey,' said Ranatunga, 'I guess you guys can have a bat.'

The state of the dodgy pitch was soon apparent. The first ball Hudson faced was pitched up to him. He played forward, the ball bounced right over his head and then bounced again before it reached the keeper. He was soon caught at the wicket for 5.

It was left to a half-century from Wessels and another fine knock of 41 by a still ailing Cullinan – who was later too sick to field – to take the South Africans to 214 for seven in their 50 overs. Then, as expected, the pitch broke up. Snell bagged four wickets for 12 runs in seven overs, and Cronjé provided useful backup to claim two wickets at a low cost. The Sri Lankans were bowled out for 136 in 40 overs, and victory was again in the bag.

A week later, at the beautiful Mohali Stadium in Chandigarh, the South African challenge faltered badly. India may have lost the one-day series in South Africa, but they were a very different proposition at home. It didn't much help that Cullinan was too ill to play and that the bowlers conceded a full three extra overs and 19 runs in wides and no balls.

Cronjé was the pick of the bowlers, taking three for 28 in his 10 overs and bowling Vinod Kambli for 86. Still, the target of 222 proved too big and, although Rhodes scored a fine 56, they fell short by 43 runs. The defeat did not bode well for the semi-final against India in Calcutta, but the popularity of the South Africans was not in question.

Outside the Oberoi Grand hotel where they were staying, mounted policemen with long canes were called on to control the crowds that had gathered there to see the team. Most of the people, it seemed, just wanted to meet Jonty Rhodes. The team bus was also given a large police escort, which apparently allowed the driver to propel the vehicle at breakneck speed on whatever side of the road he chose.

At the magnificent Eden Gardens, Cronjé felt all over again the thrill he had experienced when he had stepped on to the ground with Rice's team two years earlier. Then, he was a non-playing member of the inaugural team; this time he would be playing in front of a boisterous crowd of almost 90 000. The noise of the firecrackers was deafening.

Vinnige Fanie bowled magnificently to claim three for 19 in his 10 overs, thereby restricting the Indians to a total of 195. It was a match the South Africans should have won, but their innings again started too slowly and, although Hudson scored 62 and McMillan 48 not out, they fell three runs short of their target. There were three run-outs, including Cronjé for 13.

The team was upset on a number of counts, not least of which was an incident in which Anil Kumble fielded a ball that clearly crossed the boundary. Had the legitimate four runs been signalled, South Africa would probably have won. Unfortunately, international rules had not yet empowered the third umpire to judge boundary calls on his television monitor.

In the other semi-final, West Indies crushed Sri Lanka by seven wickets, but the Hero Cup belonged to India. In the final, they bowled out the West Indies for 123, with the spinner Kumble taking a stunning six for 12.

Cronjé went to watch the final. He had become good friends with Jimmy Adams and Phil Simmons. His world in cricket was continuing to expand.

10

Thanks to Madonna

A USTRALIA HAD A cricketer named Shane Warne. With his first ball in an Ashes series in June 1993 he clean bowled Mike Gatting at Old Trafford. Cricket writers dubbed it 'The Ball from Hell'.

Gatting was back in the England side after completing a three-year ban for his rebel involvement. His score was 4, and England were 80 for one when Warne took the few easy strides that constituted his short run-up. Gatting was rated as one of the best batsmen in the world against spin bowling, so he was relaxed. The first delivery from most bowlers is usually nothing more than a loosener, so England's No 3 was not expecting anything out of the ordinary.

Warne flicked the ball out of the back of his hand with an audible snap of the fingers. It was aimed at the batsman's pads. Gatting watched it carefully as it spun through the air and then dipped away even wider of his legs. He was content to pay no further attention to it because he calculated it would pitch about 20 centimetres outside the leg stump. It did. Then it turned sharply in the opposite direction, ripped across his body and hit the off-stump just below the bail. Gatting was rooted to the spot. He heard the noise and he could not believe what had happened. From the spot where it had pitched, the ball had turned a full 45 centimetres.

Warne went on to take eight wickets in Australia's victory, the best return by an Australian leg-spinner in England since Bill O'Reilly's 10 at Leeds in 1938. He was named Man of the Match, and word of his wrist-spinning dexterity was telegraphed to the most distant corners of the cricket-playing world. In Australia's retention of the Ashes, he topped the bowling averages with 34 wickets and, when the South Africans arrived in Australia six months later, he was the most feared bowler in Test cricket. With no discernible change of action, he varied his leg breaks with the 'wrong 'un', otherwise known as the 'googly', which turned the other way. He had also perfected the mysterious 'flipper', which hurried straight through.

Warne was 12 days older than Hansie Cronjé, but there the similarity ended. The Free Stater had the clean-cut looks of a college boy, was tall, dark and lean. The Victorian resembled a chubby beach boy with his bleached blond hair, daubs of sunblock on the tip of his nose and his bottom lip, and a gold earring. It was said that, as a youngster, he had lacked dedication. His liking for the good life had caused his expulsion from the Australian Cricket Academy three years earlier.

When the South Africans reached Australia, the Aussies were involved in a Test series with New Zealand. This gave Kepler Wessels and his men the chance to study their opponents, particularly the devastating wrist-spin bowling of Warne.

'The only New Zealand player who really could play him was their captain Ken Rutherford because he would step back to give himself enough room to hit him through the offside,' remembers Cronjé. 'A few of us worked out that to handle Warney successfully you had to play him from outside leg stump and not give him a chance to bowl you around your legs. When he bowled the flipper, you had to make sure your pads were outside the line of the off-stump otherwise, if you missed it, you were trapped stone dead.'

Barry Richards, the former South African Test batsman who was living in Australia, visited the team to give them advice on how to counter Warne's menace. To beat Australia, they would have to find ways to keep him out. It would not be easy.

THE MELBOURNE CRICKET GROUND (MCG) was in bad shape. Rock music concerts featuring Madonna and U2 had been staged there a few days earlier, and sections of the turf had been been badly damaged by the thousands of fans. Sea sand had been spread over the field to help it recover but the underfoot conditions in the bowler's run-up and delivery area were unstable. In a warm-up game against Victoria at the MCG, the South Africans paid a high price. McMillan lost his footing in the delivery stride, twisted his knee and tore a lateral cartilage. The following day he underwent key-hole surgery and had to remain in Melbourne for the next three weeks to recuperate.

The South Africans were not in good shape. Many of them had picked up viruses and stomach bugs in India and were still suffering. Cullinan was particularly in distress, Big Mac was out of action and Wessels's right knee, a source of serious discomfort for several years, was playing up again. Also, the original plan for Brett Schultz to join the team had been scuppered because he too had undergone surgery for a knee problem in South Africa and was not yet fit to play.

A replacement was needed for McMillan. An all-rounder would have to be flown out quickly. The selectors opted for Gary Kirsten. In three recent Currie Cup matches, he had scored 58 against Boland, 192 against Northern Transvaal, and 25 and 116 against Eastern Province. More than that, he was bowling impressive spells of offspin, the highlight being his career-best six for 68 at Centurion Park, which took Western Province to victory over Northern Transvaal .

Peter Kirsten had failed to gain selection for the Australian trip, but now his younger brother was there, 24 years old and a month younger than Cronjé. 'I guess I have to thank Madonna for getting me here,' Gary joked.

SOUTH AFRICA'S FIRST international outing was in the World Series Cup one-day triangular series which also included New Zealand. At the MCG against Australia, Wessels's men picked up where they had left off in the World Cup the previous year by winning. Australia started off well, but a century opening stand was broken when Pat Symcox juggled a return catch to dismiss Michael Slater for an impressive 73 in his one-day international début. Jonty Rhodes ran out David Boon for one, and the Australian innings fell away sharply to 189 all out.

In reply, South Africa lost Andrew Hudson quickly, but Wessels and Cronjé put their team in sight of victory with a 140-run partnership for the second wicket. Wessels went for 70 but Cronjé stayed to hit an undefeated 91 in a rollicking seven-wicket triumph and was named Man of the Match.

Cullinan had his first encounter with Shane Warne. He was bowled for a duck by the flipper.

The next game was scheduled for Adelaide against New Zealand. The South Africans were bent on avenging their World Cup defeat but it was pouring with rain. The players were sitting in the dressing room kicking their heels when the rain let up at 2 pm and the umpires suggested that a 15-over game be played. A new member of the limited-overs squad was the hard-hitting, offspin bowler Dave Rundle, who hadn't yet played at all on the trip.

'Dave, we want you to go in as a pinch-hitter,' said Wessels. 'Just get in there and whack it around.'

Unbeknown to the Western Province player, the idea to play a curtailed game had just been discarded and the fixture called off. Blissfully unaware of this, he began strapping on his pads, while Kirsten played along by donning his batting equipment.

'Dave was getting very animated,' recalls Cronjé, 'telling us exactly how he was going to hit every ball. He was so pumped up he was sweating, swinging his arms and warming to the task. We even had a mock team talk and told him exactly what to do. Then we pushed Dave and Gary out of the dressing room. As he got through the door he saw there was not a soul in the ground. We were rolling around laughing, but he was very disappointed and annoyed.'

It was nothing like the disappointment the team were about to experience at the Sydney Cricket Ground (SCG). In their next World Series game against Australia, they were bowled out for a record-low 69 on a green SCG pitch that even the Aussies agreed was not suitable for a one-day game. Things had looked good for South Africa when they had reduced their opponents to 69 for six and 172 all out, with Cronjé taking a tidy one for 14 in 10 overs and dismissing the dangerous Steve Waugh for 13. Then the wheels came off on the dodgy track, not helped by the local umpire Darrell Hair's several dubious decisions. Only two batsmen made it into double figures: Wessels with 19 and Cronjé with 20. And, in his first match for South Africa as Hudson's opening partner, Kirsten was caught behind off Glenn McGrath for four. Warne was not even required to bowl after Paul Reiffel bagged four for 13.

The injury list was also growing. Rhodes, in stopping a full-blooded square cut from Steve Waugh, fractured a bone in his hand.

SHORTLY BEFORE CHRISTMAS at the Woolloongabba in Brisbane, Cronjé prepared himself for the opening Test match by scoring 145 against Queensland. Cullinan with 113 and Hudson with 105 also looked in good nick against a state team captained by the Australian skipper, Allan Border.

It was in another respect altogether, however, that the match would set the tone for the Test series that was due to begin at the MCG on Boxing Day. It concerned the umpires, Jay and Parker. The South Africans were growing more and more suspicious of Aussie umpires in general, and they were again frustrated by a number of appeals that went against them. Fanie de Villiers in particular was having a tough time of it, constantly appealing and constantly being turned down. As the players walked off the field, he raised his voice loudly enough to be heard complaining about 'useless umpires', whereupon Border turned on Fanie and told him in no uncertain terms to stop moaning and shut up. This was all too much for Wessels, who entered into a slanging match with his Australian counterpart and former Queensland team-mate. The argument was only resolved in so far as each skipper assured the other that he could play it 'tough and dirty' if it were necessary.

Back home, the fans were unaware of any bad blood between the teams. All they wanted was for the Boxing Day Test to begin. Wessels's men had shown themselves capable of beating the Aussies in limited-overs cricket, but how would they shape in a full five-day match with the likes of Warne unfettered by over restrictions?

The alarm clocks were set early as the live telecast was to be beamed into South Africa while it was still dark. The fans rose bleary-eyed and excited in the small hours of the morning following Christmas. They were greeted by a sorry sight. The covers were still on – the MCG was soaked with rain.

Wessels and his players were sorely disappointed. They were raring to go, and now this. Wives and girlfriends also sat around gloomily. They had flown in especially for the big match and were as eager as anyone for the action to begin. At least they had all had a jolly time over Christmas lunch the previous day, and Cronjé was particularly happy because Bertha Pretorius had come out to join him.

Wessels, meanwhile, was thinking of his immediate future. During practice earlier in the week, he had stumbled and fallen on the damaged MCG outfield, badly wrenching his already injured knee. He told no one about it because he didn't want to set any alarm bells ringing, but he knew he was in trouble. The knee was badly swollen and he was in constant pain.

Play eventually got underway after tea on the first day, but the entire second day was washed out and there were only two hours of play on the third day.

In the meantime, Wessels had visited a specialist who advocated an immediate operation to his knee. This would put an end to his tour so, although in pain, he declined the offer. At least a pretty meaningless Test match would give him the chance to rest up a bit.

Wessels stayed off the field for a good part of Australia's innings of 342 for seven declared, of which Mark Taylor scored 170 before being bowled by Symcox. In the captain's absence, Cullinan was roped in to take his place at slip, and Cronjé recalls that it was not a happy time for his young team-mate. 'If anyone got a nick, it went straight to Daryll. In fact, they all went to Daryll and he put down four catches. When we finally came out to bat, the ball was getting wet and soft. Hudders and I were going very nicely in a century stand when Warne threw a ball and hit Andrew on the elbow, forcing him to retire hurt on 64. So Daryll came in to bat and, just as he arrived, they changed the ball because it was too soft and wet. He had been watching us bat and it had looked quite easy from the dressing room. But McDermott now had a nice, hard ball in his hand. Daryll pushed forward to the only ball that bounced in the entire Test match, and he was caught off the shoulder of the bat for nought.'

Cronjé went on to score 71 before the match petered out into an inevitable draw. Wessels, batting at No 6 and determined to show his 'softer' team-mates a thing or two about courage, was undefeated with a gutsy 63; and Rhodes, in spite of his broken hand, was with him on 25. In his first Test match, Kirsten scored 16, with the other débutants, Symcox and De Villiers, taking two and one wicket respectively. Fanie was generally regarded as a one-day bowler who had made it on to the Test team only because of Schultz's prolonged injury.

The South African team remained unchanged for the second Test due to begin two days later at Sydney. McMillan failed a fitness test, Wessels was determined to see out the match, and Rhodes announced cheerily that his damaged hand was okay. For Australia, Steve Waugh could not play through injury.

The pitch at the SCG looked over-prepared. It was dusty and worn and would definitely take spin early on...

IN THE BEST bowling performance in a Sydney Test this century, Shane Warne ripped the South African innings apart with figures of seven for 56. From 91 for one they were bowled out for 169 on the opening day which, in Test cricket's traditions, was pretty much an instant recipe for defeat. The only standout for the South Africans was a gutsy 90-run stand between Kirsten and Cronjé.

As a newcomer to Test cricket, Gazza was a natural target for vocal abuse from the Aussies and McDermott in particular. 'You're the worst batsman I've ever seen!' he snarled at him on more than one occasion. Kirsten refused to be intimidated.

'Be cocky, be confident, be cool' was the mantra he constantly recited to himself on his way to a fine 67. Apart from that knock and Cronjé's 41, there was little else to distinguish an innings that capitulated to the wiles of the destructive Warne.

Blond hair bobbing and a toothy grin fixed across his rosy cheeks, Warne bowled Cullinan with his flipper, trapped Rhodes plumb with a similar delivery, drew Kirsten out for a stumping, induced Wessels to return an easy catch, had Richardson and Matthews caught at slip, and clean bowled Symcox. In one devastating 15-over spell, he took seven wickets in a row at a cost of only 28 runs.

Wessels was furious. His knee was giving him hell and he felt that some of the batsmen had not shown enough character under fire. The only way out was to bowl fast and straight and restrict the Aussies to as small a lead as possible. His bowlers responded magnificently, forcing the batsmen to score very slowly. Donald and De Villiers picked up four wickets each, Symcox bagged two, and Matthews conceded only 44 runs in his 28 overs. Restricting the Australians to a lead of 123 runs was as good as Wessels could have hoped for, but the South African captain had picked up another problem.

In diving for a catch from Ian Healy that was falling short, he had jammed his left hand into the turf and split the webbing between the last two fingers. He left the field with blood dripping from a deep gash and, in spite of protesting that it was no big deal, he was persuaded to go for X-rays. It was then discovered that he had suffered a bad fracture of the hand.

It was now up to the other batsmen to wipe out the Aussie lead and build a big enough total to put the Australians under pressure when they batted last on a wearing pitch. At 110 for five – still 13 runs short of making Australia bat again – the South Africans looked on a hiding to nothing. Wessels had earlier felt the need to promote himself to No 4 in order to shore up an innings that looked in danger of floundering. He cut open his glove to accommodate the splint on his broken hand and, wracked with pain, he batted for over an hour to score an invaluable 18 runs before being bowled by Warne. Still, with Hudson out for one, Kirsten for 41, Cronjé for 38, and Cullinan trapped by Warne's flipper for two, the South Africans were in need of a batting saviour.

It came in the form of Rhodes who, in the same manner as his match-saving innings in Sri Lanka, hit an unbeaten 76 in the face of unrelenting pressure. Refusing to buckle to the scheming Warne, he first shared a 72-run stand for the sixth wicket with Dave Richardson and then found a willing partner in Donald – the *windgat* batsman who had once been chased from the field by his schoolmaster – who together added 36 gilt-edged runs for the tenth wicket. South Africa had recovered magnificently to 239 all out, Warne had taken another five wickets, and Australia needed just 117 runs for victory with the fourth day far from over.

Wessels, in the meantime, reluctantly conceded to the chairman of selectors, Peter Pollock, that his match and his tour were over. He might have been able to bat, but there was no way he was going to field. He would have to hand over the captaincy at a critical stage in the Test match, and a replacement for the rest of the tour would have to be flown out from South Africa. On the question of the replacement, Pollock made a telephone call to East London, where over the New Year's holiday at the same time as the South Africans were watching the rain fall in the first Test at Melbourne, Peter Kirsten had scored a magnificent 271 while opening the batting for Border against Northern

Transvaal. It was his highest first-class score and the eighth double century of his career – and it earned the 38-year-old batsman a recall to a South African team that had discarded him at the end of the previous season.

On the question of the captaincy, there was no debate. 'Just make sure you're ready to fit in if ever I'm injured.' And Hansie Cronjé was ready all right. He had never been more ready.

Cronjé admired Wessels for his courage in going to bat with a tortured knee and a smashed hand, and he was determined not to let his mentor down. He encouraged his team-mates to follow this example of guts, determination and character, and he found a willing ally in De Villiers.

The wiry pace bowler immediately skittled Slater for one and, after Taylor and Boon had put on 47 for the second wicket, he single-handledly reduced Australia from 51 for one to 54 for four, three batsmen departing in the space of five deliveries. De Villiers had changed his line of attack to bowling off-cutters on the responsive pitch, while Cronjé was exerting further pressure by setting attacking fields with three men in catching positions ahead of the bat.

With each wicket-fall Vinnige Fanie exhorted his team-mates to be ever-alert to the possibilities. 'Don't give up! One more wicket and we're in!' was his constant cry as Australia struggled to the close of the fourth day on 62 for four, still 55 runs short of their target with six wickets in hand.

Afterwards, De Villiers was much in demand at the media conference. 'Do you believe you can win this match?' he was asked.

'South Africans never quit,' he replied.

Cronjé admired Fanie's conviction because he knew him to be a very determined man. He remembered his first meeting with him more than five years earlier when Cronjé went to Centurion Park for his second Currie Cup match and was out for a pair. 'Both sides were loaded with fast bowlers and there was a big rivalry between Corrie van Zyl and Fanie. Corrie beat him with an away swinger and then said, "Now watch out for the one that comes back." Anton Ferreira, who was fielding nearby, just laughed and said that not in a month of Sundays could Corrie nip one back, but he did exactly that with the next ball and beat Fanie all ends up. Corrie then had something more to say to Fanie when he left the field. They were not exactly friendly words.

'After the match, which we won, we were leaving the stadium when Fanie and the late Gerbrand Grobler set upon Corrie and pulled him back into the change room. Fanie wanted to wallop him. Some of the other players intervened to stop a nasty little incident.

'I think the problem was that both Fanie and Corrie saw each other as a threat. When they were on the field they both wanted to be in charge and they wanted to be the best.'

At Sydney, Fanie de Villiers was taking charge of a Test match that was hanging in the balance.

THAT NIGHT, CRONJÉ visited Bertha Pretorius at her hotel where he treated them both to a milkshake. Somehow he managed to bump his full glass off the table and on to his shorts. He was looking an awful mess when he left the hotel later that night, and he hoped he would not meet anyone he knew. In the hotel lobby, he bumped, red-faced, into Ali Bacher and Peter Pollock. They ignored his shorts but said, 'Good luck tomorrow. What do you think is going to happen?'

'I have no doubt we're going to win the game,' shot back Cronjé. He wasn't trying to impress them or act like a big deal. Deep down he just knew it. He also knew that Fanie knew it, and he believed the others knew it, too.

At the team talk at the warm-up the next morning, Cronjé gathered his mates around him. 'Guys, it's never easy chasing a target on the fifth day of a Test match. Just remember what happened to us at Barbados. The same can happen to them now. Never quit.'

The fateful fifth day was upon them, and Cronjé tossed the ball to Allan Donald. The second over would be bowled by De Villiers. 'Fanie was full of confidence,' remembers Cronjé. 'He was an inspiration to all of us. You couldn't get the ball out of his hand and his true colours came out as a genuine Test bowler.'

In a match where Warne's 12 wickets should have earned Australia the spoils, it was De Villiers and Donald who brought South Africa a famous victory. Donald struck first in the opening over when the dangerman, Allan Border, let three balls go by, only to watch the third track back suddenly and clatter into his unguarded off-stump (63 for five). Donald then released a perfect yorker to trap Mark Waugh plumb in front (72 for six). The rampant De Villiers, still bowling his deadly off-cutters, continued the mayhem by bowling Healy (73 for seven), and an inspired Cronjé then returned a perfect throw into the stumps from the deep to run out Warne (75 for eight).

The tail-ender, McDermott, suddenly became a real threat. He refused to let the pressure get to him and hit out lustily from the outset *en route* to a quickfire 29 not out. The score crept past the 100 mark and then to 110 when Damien Martyn, who had kept a determined 106-minute vigil for his six runs, lost his head and his wicket in a spooned catch to Hudson in the covers off Donald (110 for nine).

There were just five runs in it at the end when, in the perfect finale, De Villiers pouched a return catch from the ashen-faced McGrath to complete figures of six for 43 in the innings and 10 wickets in the Test. Australia were all out for 111.

The South Africans were beside themselves with delight. Cronjé recalls, 'I immediately ran off the field to say well done to Kepler and Proccy and everyone, and then I ran back on again. When I came back, McGrath was still standing in the middle with his head hanging. He just couldn't believe what had happened. Everyone was jumping on top of one another, and I can remember carrying Fanie off the field.'

Peter Kirsten arrived in Sydney that night. When he had boarded the plane in Johannesburg, he had heard the Aussies needed only 117 runs to win the Test.

When he arrived at Sydney's Kingsford Smith Airport, he heard the result for the first time. It was the best news he could receive, and it set the tone for the rest of his tour.

Cronjé's ninth Test appearance had been a memorable one in more ways than one. He had batted for 41 and 38, fielded brilliantly and, at the business end of the Test match, had shown rare captaincy skills in the face of mounting pressure.

The critics applauded his willingness to take the fight to the Aussies through his audacious field settings and the encouragement he gave his bowlers. Some of them saw in him the very antithesis of Wessels – an uninhibited young man who was willing to turn defence into attack and to accept the consequences. 'Hansie was brilliant,' enthused Procter.

Cronjé shrugged off his own role in the victory. 'Fortunately, Kepler was still in the dressing room, and he and Proccy were helping me from the side. I also had Fanie, Allan, Craig and Symmo as a very experienced bowling attack. Fanie was bowling almost unchanged from one end so that made it a lot easier for me, too.'

Wessels's role should not be underestimated. He thoroughly briefed his deputy before the final day and also sent tactical instructions out to him on the field. The important thing, though, was that Cronjé made the plan work. In so doing, he displayed so many of the fine attributes the selectors were looking for in a future Test captain.

As for De Villiers, in only his second Test match the 29-year-old fighter was the very epitome of guts, determination and character. He had bowled unchanged for almost two hours on that final day to justify his contention the previous night that South Africans just aren't quitters. He also silenced those critics who maintained he was only a one-day bowler. By the end of the series he would head the Test bowling averages.

THREE DAYS AFTER 'Fanie's Test' at Sydney, a one-day cricket match was staged at the Wanderers Stadium. It was between the SA Colts and SA Schools XIs, and was watched by about 100 spectators. At No 4 for SA Schools was a big, strong batsman from Wynberg Boys' High in Cape Town named Jacques Kallis. He scored 27 and later took a wicket. Chasing a target of 173, the SA Colts cruised home with seven wickets to spare. They were led to victory by 19-year-old Herschelle Gibbs who scored 50 not out. The best of the Colts' bowlers, with three wickets each in their 11 overs, were two 20-year-olds, the Natalian Shaun Pollock and the Free Stater Nicky Bojé.

HANSIE CRONJÉ WAS soon brought back to earth at the Woolloongabba in Brisbane.

With Wessels out of the tour, he was in charge at the age of 24. At the 'Gabba' he would have the opportunity to lead his country for the first time in the limited-overs arena. Lying ahead were two World Series matches on successive days.

In both games, against New Zealand and Australia, Cronjé won the toss and decided to field. South Africa lost both, mainly due to their failure to chase targets, but Cronjé inwardly blamed himself for making two wrong decisions in his first two games. In the second game – which ended in a 48-run defeat by the Aussies after Cronjé had promoted himself to open the innings with Gary Kirsten and was out for 17 – he was so disappointed that he refused to attend the post-match media conference.

Later he chided himself. 'That was really arrogant and stupid of me. I can't just run away from things like this. My inexperience is really showing.'

Cronjé was not the only one who was disappointed. Dave Callaghan was so upset at not being chosen for either of the Brisbane matches that he gave away some of his kit, including his spiked cricket shoes, to the dressing room attendant.

For the next two one-dayers the South Africans travelled to Perth with only a slim hope of qualifying for the World Series Cup finals. At the WACA ground, they would have to beat both New Zealand and Australia by big margins.

Cronjé and Procter called the players together. The young captain addressed them: 'Guys, it's very, very important that we decide where we're going in the one-day game.' For the next 90 minutes they discussed their tactics, and eventually agreement was reached. At their next net practice, the players would attempt to hit the ball as hard as possible to get used to scoring more quickly.

•

'For us to reach the finals we have to score at a very, very fast rate,' Cronjé told his team-mates. 'We have no option but to really bang it.'

New Zealand won the toss and batted. Donald took three for 15 in eight overs, and New Zealand were bowled out for 150. The Kirsten brothers were asked to open the innings for South Africa for the first time, and they put on 80 for the first wicket in 112 balls. Gary was felled by a blow to the helmet but went on to score 50. Then Cronjé bludgeoned 40 from 35 balls. South Africa won with almost 10 overs to spare. The plan had worked; the run-rate was motoring.

THE RUN TEMPO wasn't the only thing that was motoring. Vinnige Fanie, always the jester, had bought himself a radio-controlled model bakkie complete with 'fat takkies'. He brought the house down at the WACA when, during the drinks breaks, he steered the chunky little truck out to the wicket with the batsmen's cold drinks nestled snugly in the back. Fanie proved to be a very deft driver. He had perfected the radio-controlled operation while steering his bakkie around the corridors in the team's hotel the previous evening.

It was small gestures like these that made the South Africans a popular team in Australia, and it wouldn't be the last time De Villiers would delight the fans with his famous bakkie.

ON THE SUNDAY of the Australia match at Perth, Peter Kirsten climbed out of bed in high spirits. He was looking forward to batting with his younger brother again. Thirteen years separated them and it was such a proud feeling walking out together in the national colours. It was a beautiful morning and Peter, often quiet and introverted, amused his team-mates by waxing lyrical. 'What a lovely day!' he enthused. 'Look at the sunshine, feel the breeze, hear the birds chirping… Oh, it's great to be alive!'

Three hours later he was in hospital with a depressed fracture of the cheekbone.

Australia won the toss and sent South Africa in. Peter had five runs to his name when he ducked into a short-pitched delivery from McGrath that never got up. Thud! Down he went, poleaxed. A great day to be alive had turned out to be a terrible one to be playing cricket.

The dazed and distressed batsman was helped off the field in agony and taken away for emergency surgery. What was left of his unexpected tour was now in the balance.

In the meantime, brother Gary had hit another half-century, setting the Aussies a target of 209. Would it be enough? Yes, replied the bowlers, and they all chipped in, Snell leading the way with three for 26.

Callaghan also bowled very tidily for two for 15 to follow his quickfire knock of 26, but Cronjé was puzzled as to why he kept losing his footing.

'Sorry, Hansie, I gave my spiked shoes away the other day!'

Australia were bowled out for 128, Callaghan was named Man of the Match, and South Africa were a step closer to gate-crashing the World Series finals. All they needed was for Australia to eliminate the Kiwis in the final league match.

THE WORST BUSH fires in history were wreaking havoc on the outskirts of Sydney when the South Africans returned to the New South Wales capital. A relief fund had been set up and there were widespread appeals for support.

The South Africans decided to do their bit by organising a fund-raising game against the local state side. It was a gesture that was very well received by the people of Sydney, and about 10 000 spectators pitched up. The fun-loving De Villiers was again in his element, steering his model bakkie around the perimeter of the SCG, imploring the patrons to fill it with their donations.

South Africa beat a strong New South Wales team and the next day Allan Border wrote in a newspaper article that he was starting to get worried about the burgeoning strength of the tourists.

THE NEXT STOP was Melbourne where the team visited Flinders Park to watch the Australian Open tennis championship. Steffi Graf was playing against Nicole Provis when the South Africans heard that Australia had beaten New Zealand. Jubilation greeted the news, and Cronjé was particularly excited because his heroine Steffi was winning, too.

The joy continued at the MCG where the never-say-die Peter Kirsten declared himself well enough to play and scored 28, and where brother Gary, just five weeks after playing his first match for South Africa, hit a magnificent 112.

'Thanks, Gazza,' said his team-mates.

'I told you,' he smiled, 'don't thank me, thank Madonna!'

With Snell also grabbing the limelight by taking five wickets for 40 runs, the South Africans were home and dry and 1–0 up in the best-of-three finals. Cronjé was a happy man. Not only had he scored 40, but he had led the South Africans to three international victories in a row plus a win over New South Wales. Just one more victory and he would have the World Series Cup in the bag.

Back at the SCG, the ground curator was busy ensuring that the wicket would favour the spin bowlers and all but nullify the South African pacemen.

The spin twins, Tim May and Shane Warne, took four wickets between them, Peter Kirsten was run out for 11, and Mark Waugh and Dean Jones made merry in a 175-run stand for Australia to level the series 1–1. Two days later on the same ground, Allan Border played his last international game at Sydney by way of celebrating another Aussie victory and the series triumph. Peter Kirsten was again run out for a low score, and Cronjé was out for a duck without facing a ball when a straight drive by Gary Kirsten was deflected on to the stumps at the bowler's end. The stand-in skipper was feeling the heat again, but it was nothing like the pressure he would feel at Adelaide where he would lead South Africa in a full five-day Test for the first time.

COMING OFF TWO one-day final defeats, the new captain allowed irrational thoughts to get the better of him in planning the strategy for the third and final Test match. So did the other members of the team management.

One–nil up in the series, they erred towards caution in selecting as many all-rounders and batters as possible so as to secure a draw. They decided against playing either of the spinners, Symcox or Rundle, and went in with the all-seam attack of Donald, De Villiers, Snell and McMillan, who was still not entirely match fit after his long injury lay-off.

As the Aussies ground their way to a massive 469 for seven, Cronjé was forced to call on the two Kirstens to provide some variation with their part-time spin bowling. Although Gary took a wicket with his ninth ball in Test cricket, it didn't help much because Steve Waugh, back from injury, and Border put on 208 runs to break a fifth wicket record that had stood for 85 years. In scoring 84, the Aussie skipper exceeded 11 000 runs in Test cricket.

After commanding centre-stage with his six-hour 164, Waugh then took four wickets for 26 runs to play the South Africans right out of contention. They knew that the task of scoring 321 runs in the fourth innings would be too great. They would have to bat for one-and-a-half days to save the Test.

Peter Kirsten, who had scored 79 in the first innings, and the night watchman, De Villiers, did a fine job. Fanie again proved he was no quitter in facing 170 balls for his 30 runs and, on the fifth day, the gallant pair batted out the morning session and well into the afternoon.

When the courageous Kirsten was given out leg before wicket after seeing off 229 balls for his 42 runs, it was the last straw in more ways than one. It was the fourth lbw decision of the innings and the eighth in total the South Africans had suffered in their 20 dismissals. Of their 13 dismissals, only one Aussie batsman had been given out this way.

At the centre of the controversy stood the imposing figure of Darrell Hair, the umpire South African fans had grown to hate. Each and every time this Australian had officiated in tour games, there had been some highly questionable decisions. In the report cards that are filled in after every game, the South Africans scored him consistently low, and by the time the third Test arrived they reported that, in their view, he was not fit to stand in first-class cricket. The authorities refused to act on this recommendation, and Hair himself remained unrepentant. He continued to give a series of hair-raising judgements that finally inspired Peter Kirsten to sound off publicly against him after the Adelaide defeat. For his trouble, the feisty little South African was fined R1 500.

Back home, armchair viewers, who sat up regularly through the night to watch the telecast, were incensed by Hair's performances. A group of Johannesburg musicians instantly produced a catchy little ditty, 'Stick Your Finger in the Air, Darrell Hair', that pilloried him in the best (or worst) way possible.

At the same time an 'I hate Darrell Hair' lobby of fans willingly offered to send Kirsten the R1 500. In their view, Kirsten's criticism of the umpire was worth every cent.

The one thing the South African players did enjoy at Adelaide was meeting the great Australian batsman Sir Donald Bradman. He visited them in their dressing room where one of his biggest fans turned out to be the team manager, Robbie Muzzell. In Cronjé's words, 'Robbie was all over him all the time', and after that he was known to his players as 'Sir Don'.

HANSIE CRONJÉ WASN'T exactly criticised for the defeat at Adelaide, but some critics questioned a style of captaincy that seemed to have taken a backward step from that wonderful day at Sydney. Although the South Africans had shared the Test series, they had still lost three matches in a row. Cronjé bore the brunt of the disappointment. His last three scores read 0, 0 and 3.

The captaincy question was a big debating point. Cronjé's supporters believed he should be allowed to continue and, even if Wessels were fit in time for the return series that was soon to follow in South Africa, he should play under Cronjé. Back home, Wessels said he didn't mind one way or the other. He would be happy to serve under his protégé if need be. Cronjé himself hoped that Wessels would be fit enough to take over the leadership again in South Africa. Some of his supporters accused him of being too charitable.

As for Daryll Cullinan, his wonderful treble-century earlier in the season and Cronjé's claim that 'he's the best batsman we've got' were now distant memories. In the Hero Cup one-dayers in India he had totalled 121 runs in three knocks. In the World Series he scored 122 runs in nine knocks and was dropped for the third leg of the finals at Sydney. What's more, in the Test series he had scored only 26 runs in five innings with a top score of 10. People claimed it was Warne who had got his number, but that was not the whole truth at all. On the 11 occasions he had batted against Australia, Warne had dismissed him only four times.

Back home in Bloemfontein, Hansie was telling Ewie about his team-mate's plight. 'Gee, there were lots of things that went against poor Daryll. The problems started in India when he fell seriously ill and never properly recovered. Then he came up against Warne, who regularly bowled wicket-taking balls to him. Also, he had terrible luck. In the Melbourne Test he got out to the only ball that bounced in the entire match and, when he was asked to field at slip, he dropped every catch that came his way because he had difficulty in sighting them. You see, Melbourne is a very difficult ground to pick up the ball against the big crowd. And talk about awful luck, in the last Test he ducked under a ball from McDermott, left his bat up in the air and got the faintest of touches to Healy, who dived full stretch to catch it. When it doesn't run for you, Dad, it just doesn't run.'

11

The Scourge of the Aussies

A DAY AFTER THE Adelaide Test, Free State were in Cape Town for the first leg of the Benson & Hedges Series semi-final. Under the caretaker captaincy of Corrie van Zyl they were bowled out for 118 in pursuit of Western Province's 192. The second leg was in Bloemfontein two days later. It was a match they had to win to stay alive.

Hansie Cronjé was on his way back from Australia. He lost two nights of sleep on the long return flight to Johannesburg and, when he eventually arrived home in Bloemfontein, the start of the second-leg semi-final was only a matter of hours away. In the Springbok Park dressing room his provincial team-mates welcomed him with open arms. No one needed to force him; he was soon changing into his bright-orange night cricket uniform.

There were only five runs on the board when the exhausted Free State skipper walked out to bat. When he finally returned to an ecstatic dressing room, he had scored 120.

Later that night he took two wickets, including the big one of Adrian Kuiper, for Western Province to be dismissed for 174 in the quest for a 238-run target. Cronjé was named Man of the Match.

The third and deciding leg was played 48 hours later. This time Cronjé scored only one run and took no wickets, but his team-mates were inspired enough to pull off an exciting five-run victory. In the process they ran out four Western Province batsmen.

Free State had qualified for their first B&H final in five years. Their opponents would be Natal.

IN 103 YEARS of competition, Free State had never beaten Transvaal in the Currie Cup or its equivalent. Ten days after the disappointments of Adelaide, Cronjé changed all that when his men achieved an historic victory at the Wanderers Stadium. In a bold move that was acclaimed by the critics, he declared 91 runs behind to throw down the gauntlet to Jimmy Cook's Transvaal. His shrewd use of the rotund, part-time offspin bowler Kosie Venter was also judged to be a touch of genius. Venter claimed five wickets for 14 runs to bowl out Transvaal for 118 in their second innings.

Free State were left to score 210 in a possible 65 overs, and they got there with four wickets in hand, mainly due to Venter's purposeful 31 and Gerhardus Liebenberg's anchoring 62.

Cronjé was out cheaply in both innings, but his captaincy was his strong hand. Free State were now top of the Currie Cup log and well set to win their second successive four-day championship. Their next first-class outing would be against the Australians in less than a fortnight, but Cronjé would meet them a lot sooner because the one-day international series was about to begin.

THE WANDERERS STADIUM was filled to its 30 000 capacity. The Aussies were in town for the first time and no one wanted to miss them. Kepler Wessels had recovered well enough from his injuries to again take charge of a South African team that had the added firepower of Adrian Kuiper and Eric Simons.

In the famed 'Bullring', the atmosphere was electric. Every anti-Aussie banner and slogan that could be devised was on show, and the fans were baying for blood like never before. They also badly wanted a hero.

Cronjé obliged. He scored 112 from 120 balls and, in the process, brought the entire stadium to its feet when he twice hoisted Shane Warne high over the mid-wicket fence, and once deposited Steve Waugh over the long-off boundary. South Africa won by five runs, and Cronjé was named Man of the Match.

The next day's action was at Centurion Park, and again the 'House Full' signs were up long before the start. When Cronjé walked out to bat, the fans cheered him all the way. 'More, Hansie, more!'

He gave it to them. This time he struck Warne for three sixes over mid-wicket, and there were eight fours as well. When he had reached 97 from 102 balls, he scampered through on a quick single and was beaten by Allan Border's direct throw on the stumps. The jubilant crowd cheered him all the way back, but the mayhem was far from over. To the crease strode the belligerent figure of Kuiper. The overs were running out so he unsheathed the long handle. Craig McDermott was bowling fast. Kuiper hit him for three successive sixes. The last over produced a staggering 26 runs, and Kuiper was undefeated at the end. He had scored 47 runs in 22 balls.

South Africa's 265 for five was far too big a target for the Aussies. They went 2–0 down in the series, and Cronjé claimed another Man of the Match award.

Pulverised in two successive matches, the Aussies fought back gamely two days later in Port Elizabeth. Victory was theirs by 88 runs. But the top-scorer again for South Africa was Cronjé, this time with 45. Was there any end to the scourge of the Australian bowlers? Apparently not.

In Durban two days later, Cronjé's purple patch continued when he scored an undefeated 50 in a seven-wicket victory. Wessels chipped in with 40 not out, and the two Grey College old boys shared a glorious, unbroken 88-run stand. Just for a change, Craig Matthews was named Man of the Match, which he certainly deserved for his bowling figures of four for 10 in eight overs.

South Africa's victory at Durban brought about an interesting change in pattern. In every limited-overs match so far between the two countries, the team that had won the toss had batted first and won the game. Now at Kingsmead the Australians won the toss and duly batted, but their 154-run total was overhauled.

Cronjé also made an interesting observation. 'When we reached Port Elizabeth, Shane Warne's bowling got a lot better. The same at Durban. I know it sounds silly, but I think he is a better bowler at the coast than at the high altitude grounds like the Wanderers and Centurion. I don't know, he seems to have far better control at the seaside.'

With South Africa now holding a handy 3–1 lead in the eight-match series, the hectic one-dayers went into recess to accommodate more sedate matters.

THE AUSTRALIANS WERE battling to make inroads against the obdurate batting of the roly-poly Kosie Venter. Tim May was wheeling down his accurate off-breaks but the cautious, corpulent Kosie would have nothing to do with them. Another chubby player, David Boon, was positioned at short leg with Mark Waugh stationed at silly point, both almost in touching range of the batsman.

May was giving the ball a lot of air, using all his wiles to tempt Venter to leave his crease and have a go. Kosie would still have nothing of it. He remained anchored behind the line, occasionally stretching his short legs to prod away ball after ball.

'Hey, Junior,' yelled Mark Taylor to Mark Waugh, 'why don't you toss a Mars Bar on to the pitch and see if that'll tempt him out of his crease?'

'Won't work,' replied the junior of the two Waugh twins, 'Boony will get to it first!'

Venter was eventually dismissed by May for 13, one of five wickets the offspinner picked up in Free State's first innings. Cronjé scored 44, which included two sixes off Warne, but his team's 264-run total was well short of the Aussies' 450 for eight declared. The Waugh twins both scored centuries and shared a 232-run partnership.

The Australians continued to dominate the four-day match at Springbok Park. Eventually they set Free State the impossible task of scoring 457 runs for victory. By stumps on the third day, they were 102 for one with Cronjé undefeated on 50.

For much of the pre-lunch session on the final day the notorious Australian fast bowler Merv Hughes tried manfully to intimidate the Free State batsmen. The rough-hewn character had picked up the first couple of wickets and was resorting to all sorts of gamesmanship, including the constant use of the bouncer, to unsettle the men at the crease. By lunch Cronjé was still undefeated. He had taken his score past the 100 mark.

Hughes was brought back into the attack for the first over after lunch. Cronjé was at the striker's end. The coarse Aussie began his run-up but when he reached the bowling crease he continued to gallop down the pitch. Cronjé was startled. He stood up in his guard and watched curiously as the burly, snorting figure fast approached. Hughes stopped right in front of the batsman. Then he lifted his leg and released a resonating fart.

'Ah, that's a lot better, mate,' he grinned cheekily. 'Now we can get on with the game.'

If that piece of ungentlemanly conduct could not unsettle the astonished Cronjé, then nothing would. Wiping tears of mirth from his eyes, he took guard again and waited for Hughes to bowl the next ball. The game was on, and the batsman was determined to have the last laugh.

Free State were eventually all out for 396 runs, of which their captain had scored 251. It was a glorious innings that, with each mighty blow from his trusty County bat, brought cheers of approval from his adoring home town fans. His last 50 runs came in only 23 balls, which included three successive sixes off May. 'That's for getting me out in the first innings,' he jested, 'and for getting Kosie out, too!'

No bowler was spared, the least of whom Hughes, who went for 127 runs in 23 overs. Warne again felt Cronjé's wrath. By the time the gallant batsman offered a tired catch in the deep, he had lashed 136 of his runs in boundaries. He had also taken Free State to within 61 runs of a famous victory.

'Nice knock,' said the Aussies afterwards, 'but it's a good thing you're getting your runs now because they're bound to dry up in the Test matches!'

Hansie enjoyed the Aussies. He admired them for the tough way they played the game, and he laughed at their silly antics. Let's see what happens in the Tests, he thought.

Although they had lost the match, the Free Staters celebrated long into the night in Bloemfontein. Down at Newlands, Western Province had lost by one wicket to Border, which destroyed their chance to tie Free State at the top of the Currie Cup log. For the second year in a row, Cronjé's boys were the South African provincial champions.

The first Test match was just four days away...

SIX MONTHS AFTER claiming his maiden Test century in Sri Lanka, Daryll Cullinan was cast into the international wilderness. So, too, was Richard Snell, both of them axed from the team that had lost at Adelaide. Again there was no call for a spinner. In their places at the Wanderers Stadium were Wessels and Matthews. Both would do their bit, but it was Cronjé, freed from the burdens of the national captaincy and revelling in his incredible batting form, who was to steal the show again.

After hitting a carefree 21 from 39 balls in the first innings, he was leaving the field when McDermott ran past him. 'Looks like your luck's finally changed, mate,' shot the smug Aussie paceman.

Cronjé smiled back. 'Yeah, could be.'

In his second turn at bat, South Africa's No 3 occupied the crease for four hours to score a splendid 122. It was his eleventh Test match, his third Test century, and his best innings by far. His two previous hundreds, against India and Sri Lanka, were both precursors of South African victories.

The crowd knew what a Cronjé century meant, and they loved every minute of it. They also seemed noisier and more excitable than ever before. The Australians, it seemed, brought out the best and worst in South African spectators. Warne and Hughes, in particular, were players they loved to hate.

Anti-Aussie banners were again everywhere. Ribald abuse was hurled at them from the shirtless, sun-baked *manne* who pressed their beer-bloated bodies against the boundary boards. Tensions were running high.

Hughes, especially, was feeding the frenzy with his intimidatory tactics against the South African batsmen. Gary Kirsten became the target of his crude barbs, and the crowd, tuning into the vibe, turned up the volume of their scorn. Warne, too, continued to get stick from loutish elements. To them the blond 'Fat Boy', with his designer sunglasses and diamond earstud, was a fair dinkum example of Aussie arrogance. That he was also the world's best spin bowler did not impress them; it merely added to their disdain for him. Coming from a country well versed in the art of belittling foreign sportsmen, Warne had finally met his match. He reacted in the worst way possible.

His target was Andrew Hudson, cricket's most thorough gentleman. The South African opener had reached 60 in the second innings when the ace spinner bowled him round the legs with a perfect leg break. That moment of triumph for the Aussie also popped his cork. All the anger and rage that had been building up inside him suddenly exploded. He turned on the hapless Hudson and verbally abused him for what seemed like an eternity in full view of the angry crowd.

In that single moment, Warne ensured that he would be roundly booed at every South African cricket ground for as long as he played in this country. Later he apologised to Hudson. 'That was disgraceful behaviour,' he conceded. 'I don't know what came over me. I'm sorry, mate.'

THE WANDERERS FANS were again searching for heroes. When Cronjé reached his century, they erupted in unbridled adulation. When at one stage he hit 26 runs in 11 balls, they were beside themselves. For the two hours between lunch and tea on the third day, they cheered non-stop as Cronjé and Wessels added a cracking 119 runs. And when Cronjé was eventually caught at point off Hughes with the new ball, they stood and yelled his name as he walked all the way off the field and up the dressing room steps. In eight successive innings against Australia, he had amassed 742 runs at an average of 106.

Cronjé's departure brought to an end a 135-run partnership with his captain, whose own 50 was yet another signal for the crowd to go dilly. For Australia to win the match they would be required to score the highest fourth innings total in Test match history. The target was a mammoth 454 runs.

At 191 for six, they were well and truly out of it. Allan Donald was in the process of accumulating a match haul of five wickets, and De Villiers, Matthews and McMillan were on their way to bagging four scalps each.

At 235 for nine, it was all but over. The tea interval on the fifth day had not even arrived. Hughes and May were the last two batsmen, their ears ringing from the chanting, happy crowd. The minutes ticked by … 5, 15, 25, 45, 60… Hughes and May refused to be parted. What's more, the almost obligatory storm clouds were growing ominously dark over-head as the crowd grew more anxious by the second.

Could it be that these two tail-enders, with a little help from the heavens above, would contrive to deny South Africa a victory they felt was theirs? Shortly before tea, with light rain falling, the umpires made to take the players from the field, but almost immediately changed their minds. Play continued, but for how long?

Cronjé had not been called on to bowl at all in the match. Confident and defiant, he said to Wessels, 'Give me a bowl, skipper. I'm sure I can do it.'

Wessels was willing to try anything. He tossed the ball to his vice-captain. With his third delivery Cronjé removed May.

THE CROWD WAS not yet through with Hughes, who had scored 30 not out, and it did not take long for him to snap. The big fellow operated on a pretty short fuse and the bomb finally burst as he clambered clumsily up the dressing room steps, with words of abuse ringing in his ears. One uncouth individual was directing personal insults at him at close range.

Big Merv of the shaven head and earring could take it no more. Before he had reached the top of the steps, he stopped, turned and, in a rage, slammed his bat into the advertising hoardings separating him and the spectators. He then poked the bat menacingly through the security fence at the offending spectator. Fortunately, he did not make contact with the man, but more choice words fell before the fuming Aussie made it back into the dressing room.

Hughes and Warne were later fined by match referee Donald Carr for their verbal abuse of batsmen. The Australian Cricket Board was not satisfied. It docked both players their full match fees.

Relations between the dressing rooms was not at all bad. Out on the field it was tough and uncompromising, but off it there were moments of shared fun. There was a mutual respect between two teams that played the game hard but were prepared to swop yarns and share a beer or two once the day's play was over. Rhodes and Warne, for example, became firm friends, and the Aussies enjoyed and respected McMillan for his willingness to give as much as he took in the heat of battle. Big Mac had a dry sense of humour and had become renowned for his ability to have the last laugh in the verbal exchanges. At one point during the Test, he exchanged some harsh words with Border while bowling to the Aussie captain. The cussing and snarling continued, and when the luncheon interval arrived, the good-humoured South African decided that more action was called for. With South Africa approach-ing its first democratic elections, the political climate was particularly sensitive, and big public events were seen as possible targets for fanatical elements. A high security presence was mounted around the Wanderers dressing rooms and the players had come to accept the armed guards in their midst. Big Mac borrowed a .38 Special from one of them and strode into the Aussie dressing room. He pointed the weapon at the astonished Border.

'One more bad word from you and I'm going to wipe you off the face of the earth!'

Then Big Mac burst out laughing. The pistol, naturally, was not loaded.

FREE STATE WERE after the 'double'. They had already won the Currie Cup and wanted the B&H trophy. Throughout Cronjé's reign as captain, Free State had been hailed as the most competitive and enthusiastic young team in the floodlit competition, but each year the title had somehow eluded them.

Three days after the Wanderers Test, Cronjé and his boys travelled to Durban. The B&H final had arrived.

Such was Free State's dominance in nothing short of a mismatch that their innings began before the supper break. They had routed Jonty Rhodes's Natal for 103, with Andrew Hudson's 47 and Derek Crookes's 13 the only two individual scores to reach double figures. Bradley Player had taken five for 27, and Allan Donald four for 21.

Free State knocked off the runs in 28 overs to win by seven wickets. Kosie Venter hit 37 not out, and Cronjé blazed a quick 20 after opening his account with a six and a four.

The new double champions had been crowned, the whole of Bloemfontein was celebrating, and Cronjé was riding the crest of a wave.

FOR THE SECOND Test series in a row against Australia, South Africa were 1–0 up after the first match. Their 197-run triumph at the Wanderers was exactly what they needed to rub out the disappointments of Adelaide, but Cronjé, crowned Man of the Match again in the midst of an incredible run of form, was keeping a level head.

'Make no mistake,' he told Ewie, 'this is a good Aussie team. We can't underestimate them, but we can't let them get off the hook again either.'

A fortnight later at Newlands, South Africa let Australia off the hook. The team remained unchanged from the Wanderers, only this time they changed their character. Maybe too eager to defend the 1–0 advantage, they now showed lack of composure. Three run-outs in a Test match should never happen and, what's more, these dismissals claimed the wickets of top-order specialists Hudson, Gary Kirsten and Wessels. Hudson's demise was the biggest tragedy because, on his twenty-ninth birthday, he had just reached a wonderful century that included 52 runs from boundaries.

Peter Kirsten and McMillan both scored 70s before Warne sent them back, but South Africa's 361 would not be enough. A 70 from Taylor, 96 from Boon, 45 from Border, 86 from Steve Waugh, and 61 from Ian Healy ensured a 74-run lead.

Hudson's 49 was the best there was to offer second time around as Steve Waugh, unquestionably the world's best all-rounder at the time, ripped the heart out of the second innings. He took five for 28, Warne claimed three more victims, and it was all over on 164. Set to score 91 runs for victory, Australia were not about to do another 'Sydney' and they cruised home with nine wickets in hand.

Cronjé could look back at scores of 2 and 19. He had also bowled 13 overs without a wicket. The tide, it seemed, had suddenly turned.

IN A BUSY season for South African cricket, England A had been touring as well. In the opening match of their first visit to South Africa, they had the distinction of being the first overseas team to play in Alexandra, the teeming, ramshackle township on the north-eastern outskirts of Johannesburg. On the spanking new Alex Oval, into which the British government and local industry had sunk some considerable money, England A played an Invitation XI that included several township cricketers. The young Derbyshire all-rounder, Dominic Cork, took five wickets for nine runs in the English team's victory.

Against Transvaal a week later, victory also came with ease. The hero this time was the Essex left-arm fast bowler Mark Ilott, who took six for 61 in the second innings. England A continued to suggest that, based on the fine exploits of this talented team, the England Test selectors should have no cause for concern. It added to the mystery of why England were not a greater force in international cricket. Against Eastern Province, Lancashire's Jon Crawley scored 286, and Sussex's Alan Wells 126.

After winning seven matches in a row, England A finally lost their way against Natal. More specifically, they lost the match by an innings because of the rampant fast bowling of a 22-year-old newcomer named Lance Klusener. He took seven wickets for 98 runs and hit 20 not out while batting at No 10 in his début season in first-class cricket. After taking 12 wickets in four matches for Natal B, he was soon promoted to the senior provincial side where he took another eight wickets in his first two Currie Cup matches. He was known to his team-mates as 'Zulu' from the language he spoke fluently as a child before he had even learnt to speak English. He was educated at Durban High School, over the years a rich nursery for the game, but other than that he had no cricket pedigree to speak of.

Steven Jack also came from Durban, but he had moved to Johannesburg and was playing regularly for Transvaal. His best season had been three years before but he was starting to draw attention to himself again. In his latest appearance at Kingsmead, the wild redhead took the new ball against Natal. It was Klusener's second Currie Cup game and Jack bowled him for a duck. In the second innings, the Transvaal paceman took six for 30 to wrap up nine wickets in the match.

For the last game of their tour, England A travelled to Port Elizabeth for a five-day showpiece against South Africa A. In a match that meandered towards an inevitable draw, Gerhardus Liebenberg scored 79, Eric Simons 88, Rudi Steyn 69 and Derek Crookes 41. Of the home bowlers, the most successful was the left-arm paceman Aubrey Martyn with five for 95. For England A, Ilott took nine wickets and Darren Gough, a feisty Yorkshire fast bowler, landed seven. They seemed to enjoy bowling against South Africans.

AT KINGSMEAD, THE Test series was in the balance. Since the start of the summer, five matches had been played between South Africa and Australia, and no team had yet claimed an overall ascendancy. The three-match series in Australia had been shared, and the current one stood at one match each. Would a victor finally emerge?

Adhering to the theory that you must first ensure you cannot be beaten before thinking of victory, South Africa effectively batted themselves out of the game. In reply to Australia's 269, they occupied the crease for 14 hours and faced 205 overs in amassing 422. Wessels's solitary run stood out among a number of big double-figure contributions by the recognised batsmen, with Cronjé's 26 being the second lowest.

The Australians ensured that the South Africans would stay in the field until the end. When the captains eventually agreed to call off the match 50 minutes early, Mark Waugh was undefeated on 113, and his skipper, Border, had 42. It was Border's final Test appearance for Australia. He had captained them in 93 consecutive matches.

If the Test series could not produce an ultimate winner, surely the one-dayers would? Four more limited-overs matches lay ahead, and South Africa were already 3–1 up. At East London, Australia won by seven wickets. At Port Elizabeth, South Africa prevailed by 26 runs to take a 4–2 lead that ensured they could not lose the series. At Newlands, Australia were the victors by 36 runs. And finally at Bloemfontein, at the end of a long, hot summer, South Africa needed six runs off the final over with three wickets in hand. At the crease were Dave Richardson and Tim Shaw. Victory would give them the series.

McGrath, Reiffel, Warne and Steve Waugh had all completed their 10 overs. Damien Fleming, the least experienced of the bowlers, had sent down nine. Border tossed him the ball. He never wavered. Single, dot, single, dot, dot. Four runs needed and one ball remaining. Swinger smote it to long off and the batsmen started running. One run, two runs, now back for the third that would tie the match. Richardson run out!

Australia had won by one run to tie the series, just a solitary single in it at the end of eight hard-fought matches. As in the Test series, no team could claim the spoils and, for all of Shane Warne's menace, South Africa had refused to buckle.

Cronjé's final four scores of the series were 10, 11, 37 and 18. They were numbers that came nowhere near his scoring feats earlier in the campaign, but there was one particular figure at Bloemfontein that day that made him smile. No fewer than 16 500 spectators had packed into Springbok Park for the grand finale, so he looked at Ewie and grinned, 'Only 9 000 maximum, eh, Dad?'

Ewie Cronjé just buttoned up his jacket.

12

A Call from Scarborough

IN THE FINAL WEEK of April 1994, South Africans flocked to the polls to cast their vote for freedom. It was an epoch-making moment in the history of human dignity that none would ever forget. Within a fortnight, Nelson Mandela was sworn in as the country's president. Political leaders and statesmen from all over the world came to witness it. In the shadow of Pretoria's imposing Union Buildings, Mandela's words rang out: 'We, who were outlaws not so long ago, have today been given the rare privilege to be host to the nations of the world on our own soil...'

It was done, at last.

For South Africa's cricketers another rare privilege waited on the soil of another land where, once the outlaws, they would be welcomed with open arms. They were going to play in England.

This was the tour most cricketers dreamed of because England is the birthplace of cricket, and Lord's Cricket Ground is its spiritual home. On 21 July, Andrew Hudson and Gary Kirsten stepped side by side on to the playing field of the great London ground, the first South Africans in 29 years to do so in a Test match.

On a heady summer's day when the 'House Full' signs went up before the first ball was bowled, there seemed to be as many South Africans packed into Lord's as there were Englishmen. Everyone who was anyone in South African cricket was there, and a lot more besides. Jackie McGlew, who had bagged a pair of ducks in a Lord's Test almost 40 years before, took ages to make the normally brief walk from one side of the ground to the other because of the many people who stopped him for his autograph and for a chat along the way about days gone by.

At the head of the large and impressive South African contingent was Thabo Mbeki, South Africa's senior deputy-president, whose arrival bore testimony to the significance the new Government of National Unity attached to the South African cricket team's presence in

185

England. That so powerful a figure should be dispatched to London was indicative of Mandela's own views on sport. The new president saw in South Africa's national teams the perfect ambassadors to carry the message of the new, united South Africa to the world. He viewed sport as an important catalyst for further change, and he held the cricket team and those who were shaping it in the highest esteem. The players were now wearing the brand-new King Protea badge that cricket had adopted as its national emblem and that, in time, would become the symbol of the shared identity of South African sport.

The badge was not the only new acquisition; there were also changes in personnel. Aubrey Martyn, the impressive Western Province left-arm fast bowler, received his blazer and so, too, did Gerhardus Liebenberg, whose batting had blossomed under Hansie Cronjé's captaincy at Free State. The spin bowlers were Pat Symcox and the left-arm Tim Shaw, both of whom were productive with bat and ball in the county games but were unwitting victims of South Africa's strict adherence to an all-pace and seam attack in the Test series. Martyn definitely featured in these plans, but tragedy struck early in the tour when he suffered a stress fracture while bowling at practice. He returned home without playing a match and was replaced by Richard Snell. Liebenberg did not show enough consistent batting form in seven county games to advance his case for a Test cap.

Cronjé did not forget a promise he had made as a boy to Johan Volsteedt, his former schoolmaster and coach. He sent him two air tickets and a week's free accommodation in London so that he could be at the historic opening Test. Volsteedt remembered the day when the 10-year-old boy had made his promise to him: 'Mr Volsteedt, if I ever play for South Africa at Lord's then you will be there. I promise you that.' Volsteedt was overwhelmed when Cronjé kept his word. 'I never expected him to remember this. I'm very proud of him.'

ANDREW HUDSON, MEANWHILE, was trying to come to terms with yet another emotional, heart-stopping moment in his international career. As South Africa's regular opening batsman it was his privilege to make history wherever he played. At Calcutta in 1991 he was quite overcome by the moment. Now, at Lord's, he was trying to get a grip on himself again. His stay was a short one. Hooking at Darren Gough, he was caught by Graham Gooch at long leg for 6. Cronjé did not last long either. He was out for 7 to a sharp catch at short leg. Gary Kirsten seemed unfazed. He continued in the company of his captain, and together the two left-handers put on 106 runs for the fourth wicket before the opener was out for a fine 72.

Kepler Wessels had played in a Lord's Test once before. Nine years earlier, in the baggy green cap of Australia, he was dismissed by Ian Botham for 11 and run out for 28. Now he was back there, this time as South Africa's captain, and he embraced the moment. Head down, as resolute as ever, and carefully countering the reverse swing Gough had learnt from its Pakistani inventors, he became the first South African since the dashing Roy McLean in 1955 to score a Test century at Lord's. His memorable innings of 105 set up an impressive total of 357.

It was the England batsmen's turn, and they proved woefully inept at countering the highly motivated Allan Donald and Fanie de Villiers. Between them they took eight wickets, with Donald finishing with five for 74, and England were bowled out for 180. A first innings lead of 171 became an overall 455, with Hudson being the only recognised batsman to fail in the second innings. The scorecard read: Gary Kirsten 44, Cronjé 32, Wessels 28, Peter Kirsten 42, Rhodes 32, McMillan 39 not out, and Matthews 25 in a total of 278 for seven declared.

Worse was to follow for England. They were demolished for 99 in the final innings – their lowest total at Lord's this century – with Craig Matthews and Brian McMillan taking three wickets each to complete a crushing 365-run victory, the biggest in South African history.

It was a woeful time for the England captain, Michael Atherton, who, after scores of 20 and 8, had to talk his way out of a damaging situation when he was accused of tampering with the ball during South Africa's second innings. The famous 'dirt-in-the-pocket' incident earned him a hefty fine and almost cost him his job after he first denied and later admitted to using sand in his trouser pocket to keep the ball dry.

South Africa's captain had nothing to answer for, save for the question of whether his team would in future consider going a little easier on an England outfit that looked totally ill equipped to come back from the huge setback of this dismal defeat. John Woodcock wrote in *The Times*, 'As they played while losing to South Africa, this England team would struggle to finish in the first four of the County Championship. For long periods of the match, large crowds sat more or less in silence, waiting in vain for England to assert some semblance of authority.'

All the authority had belonged to the South Africans and to Wessels, of course, who was named Man of the Match. The only disquiet for the tourists came from the rigid traditions associated with Lord's Cricket Ground. First, they were instructed to remove the rainbow flag of their new country which Mike Procter had proudly hung over the dressing room balcony. Then Archbishop Desmond Tutu was initially refused entry to the hallowed pavilion because he was not wearing a tie.

In the moment of triumph, however, South African dignitaries joined the jubilant players out on their balcony, and Procter and company waved the flag like never before. Even at Lord's, no one dared stop them.

BEHIND THE SCENES, the future shape of the South African team was under scrutiny. Ever since the tour of Australia there had been speculation about how long Wessels would retain the captaincy. He had fought back valiantly from injury but his troublesome knee was still a problem he had to face up to. He knew, as did everyone, that his term of office was drawing to a close, and he let it be known that he was preparing himself to hand over the leadership. It was no secret that Cronjé would succeed him. The question was when.

In England, Ali Bacher took Cronjé into his confidence. 'I just want you to know that you're definitely going to get the job. If anyone should ask you about this, don't say that you're not yet ready or anything like that. Just tell them that you'll be happy to take it when the time comes.'

The plan, said Bacher, was for Cronjé to be appointed as captain after the England tour and to lead South Africa to Pakistan for a triangular limited-overs series against the host country and Australia a month later.

FOR THE THIRD time in eight months, South Africa were in front in a three-match series. But in the second Test at Headingley, South Africa found themselves in awful trouble. They had slumped to 105 for five – Hudson 9, Gary Kirsten 7, nightwatchman Dave Richardson 48, Cronjé 0 and Wessels 25 – in pursuit of an astonishingly rejuvenated England's 477 for nine. If ever they needed an injection of guts, determination and character it was now, and it came from Peter Kirsten.

He had scored more than 50 first-class centuries in his long career but, in scope and emotion, none matched the 104 he scored that August day at Leeds. Along the way he survived a nasty blow to the head from the paceman Gough to become, at the age of 39, the second-oldest cricketer to score a maiden Test hundred. He also inspired a remarkable lower-order recovery in which Rhodes hit 46, McMillan 78, Matthews an undefeated 62 in 100 balls, and Donald 27 for South Africa to reply with 447. The Test was saved by their courageous efforts and, in the second innings, Hudson was out for 12, Wessels for 7, Gary Kirsten for 65, and Cronjé – well, he laboured for two hours for his 13 runs. The heir apparent was battling to rekindle the form that had characterised his great season back home.

For the third Test at The Oval, Hudson was axed. He had arrived in England as one of the form batsmen but in four Test innings had totalled only 30 runs. Back in the team came Daryll Cullinan, and the two Kirsten brothers were asked to open the innings. Both of them failed, and Cronjé, another pre-tour form batter struggling to come to terms with his game, scored 38 in the first innings and was bowled for a duck by the Jamaican-born fast bowler Devon Malcolm in the second. Cronjé seemed to have developed a problem with fast bowling and, by his own admission, looked dreadful against the barrel-chested Malcolm.

In South Africa's first innings of 332, Malcolm had given only the faintest clue to his true menace when he bowled Peter Kirsten for 16 for figures of one for 81 in 25 overs. He did succeed, however, in forcing Rhodes to retire hurt on 8 when he felled him with a fierce delivery to the head. The little Natalian was taken to hospital for a brain scan and spent the night there under observation.

Malcolm was ranked only twenty-eighth in the world ratings, yet, in his only appearance of the series, the 31-year-old Derbyshire strike bowler managed to transform most of the South African batsmen into apprehensive novices. Single-handedly, he wrecked their second innings, recording the fourth-best analysis by an England bowler in Test cricket and the sixth-best overall in the history of the game. His figures read nine wickets for 57 runs in 16 overs and three balls.

Amidst the shambles, one batsman stood head and shoulders above the rest. In the first innings, Cullinan was dismissed by Phillip DeFreitas for 7, but in his second knock he refused to defer to Malcolm's menace. With grim tenacity and concentration he hit 94 runs from 134 balls before finally surrendering his wicket to Gough to be the eighth batsman out on a total of 175. No more runs were scored as Malcolm mopped up the mesmerised tail.

South Africa were bowled out for 175, England won by eight wickets, and the series was shared.

FROM THE HIGH of Lord's to the low of The Oval, the South African tour was not looking in good shape. In two one-day internationals, England had been runaway winners by margins of six wickets at Edgbaston and four wickets at Old Trafford. To top it all, Allan Donald was struggling with a nagging foot injury.

It was during the first one-dayer in Birmingham that Bob Woolmer, the Warwickshire coach, heard whispers that Procter's job might be in jeopardy. He shrugged it off as the sort of gossip and rumour that normally afflicts a team that is not doing particularly well. As a coach, Woolmer knew only too well where fingers were pointed when a side was on a losing streak.

One of the problems with the South Africans was that they had not bolstered their Test squad with one-day specialists. There was no Adrian Kuiper, no Dave Callaghan and no Eric Simons. In the first game they barely made it past 200, and in the second they were restricted to 181, neither total creating any real problem for England to overhaul. The only half-century for the South Africans came from Cullinan before he was run out at Old Trafford. It just wasn't good enough.

In his two one-dayers, Cronjé scored a total of 36 runs, and in the Test series he had only averaged 18. He was not a happy camper. People who knew him also believed he was trying too hard to mimic the stony-faced Wessels. Some said he thought this was the right way to act, although all the time he was just dying to smile.

The tour ended at Scarborough where the South Africans were again outplayed, this time by a President's XI in a rain-hampered match that was reduced to two days. Cronjé, captaining the side, scored 36 and took a rare wicket, but his team were probably saved from defeat by the inclement weather.

Procter had been watching Cronjé closely for several weeks. Although the Bloemfontein boy had performed well enough in the county games earlier on tour – where he had scored 108 against Nottinghamshire, 94 against Sussex, 52 against Gloucestershire and 54 against Leicestershire – his game had fallen away alarmingly in the international matches.

The team's coach picked up the telephone in his hotel room at Scarborough and dialled a number in Durban. It was that of Peter Pollock, chairman of the selectors.

'Peter, I'm worried about Hansie. His batting form is down and his head is starting to hang. I think we'll be making a big mistake if we make him captain for Pakistan. It's the kind of tour where things can really get rough and, if things do go wrong there, it could break him. I really think we should ask Kepler to stay on as captain.'

THERE WAS ONE final engagement before the tired, tour-worn players could finally travel home – the match against Holland.

It was to be played at the Royal Hague Cricket Club, 40 overs a side, and no one in the South African camp was taking it particularly seriously. The tour management, comprising manager Fritz Bing, Procter, Wessels and Cronjé, decided it was not necessary for the entire squad to make the trip over the English channel.

A 12-man team would go, under Cronjé's captaincy, and the rest would remain in London until it was over and then reassemble for the return flight to South Africa. The stay-behinds included Wessels and Procter.

What should have been a low-key, goodwill game made banner headlines. South Africa lost by nine wickets to one of the minnows of world cricket. On a matting wicket in the Hague, they scored 134 for eight.

The media climbed into the team for suffering what it termed the ultimate humiliation. As if it weren't bad enough to be beaten in three successive matches by England, they were now being thrashed by the lowly Dutch. Where was Wessels? Where was Procter? Where were Rhodes and Donald? The critics wanted to know.

'It was very tough for us because we were catching the flak,' remembers Cronjé. 'I mean, it was supposed to be a hit-and-giggle game and, if it were really that important, why didn't the coach and the captain come along? We were all thinking about returning home after a long and tough tour so it was very difficult for us to focus properly on the cricket. In the end, those of us who went were made to look really silly.'

Procter was furious that the media had made such a meal of the defeat. 'It wasn't as if it were the first time this sort of thing had happened. Other Test-playing teams had also come unstuck before in Holland. You play on matting wickets over there and it's easy to get into trouble. I think the newspapers blew the whole thing up out of all proportion.'

ON 9 SEPTEMBER 1994, the UCBSA was due to meet to name Hansie Cronjé as the successor to Kepler Wessels. A meeting of the board, however, confirmed Wessels as captain for the coming Pakistan tour. Discussing Cronjé's situation, Peter Pollock told reporters, 'It's a matter of timing. We don't think that now is the right time to make him captain.'

Wessels, still struggling with his chronic knee problem, had acceded to a special request to stay on for one more tour. After that he would relinquish the captaincy. It was his own decision.

Later that month the UCBSA met again to decide whether or not to renew Procter's contract as coach. He did not get much support. The view was that he and Wessels had not always seen eye to eye and that he lacked the proper communication skills. As great a player as he had been, he somehow could not translate his vision into coaching realities.

Just hours before the board reached its decision, Procter was rushed to a Durban hospital with chest pains, and admitted to the intensive care unit. His condition was diagnosed as inflammation of the tissue around the heart, and he was under sedation when Bacher telephoned him in his hospital ward to tell him his contract had not been renewed. Procter was deeply hurt. He was expecting a call consulting him on the selection of the team for Pakistan, certainly not one to tell him he had got the bullet. In a press interview conducted in his ward, he had some strong things to say about the way the game was being run in South Africa. He later made a public apology and telephoned Cronjé to assure him of his full support in the future.

Subsequently, Bacher spoke of Procter's 'enormous contribution to the progress of South African cricket' but said the role of the coach had to be redefined after the introductory phase in international cricket. The man the UCBSA wanted would need to have greater technical skills as a coach.

IN ENGLAND, BOB WOOLMER was caught up in an exciting period as Warwickshire's coach. It was the year they won an unprecedented three major trophies, including the County Championship for the first time since 1972. The Sunday League was to be decided in the last game of the season against Gloucestershire. During the course of this match, two journalists approached him to tell him Procter had been fired and that his name was being mentioned as a likely successor. The former England Test batsman was taken aback. His immediate plans were to accept a lucrative new offer from Warwickshire and to resign from his coaching job at Boland where he was not altogether happy with the setup. He had already helped the B Section province gain promotion to the Currie Cup but, for some strange reason, the Boland Cricket Board were now talking of reducing his salary and taking away his sponsored car. He was puzzled and annoyed by this arrangement but overjoyed that Warwickshire wanted him so badly that they had made him an offer that included a staggering £12 000 in guaranteed bonuses for the next season.

Even though Transvaal were also after his services, he saw his long-term future in England, and he was hoping his successes at Warwickshire would in time lead to some sort of involvement at national level, perhaps with the England under-19 team or England A.

At 8.45 the next morning, following Warwickshire's title-clinching victory over Gloucestershire, Woolmer received a telephone call from Bacher in Johannesburg. 'Bob, we're looking for a new national coach,' said the UCBSA's managing director, 'and I was wondering whether you'd be prepared to fly to South Africa for an interview … that is, if you're interested?'

Woolmer had no hesitation: 'Of course I'm interested!' He loved South Africa so much that he considered the country his first home. His years there had been very happy ones, and he had built up 10 years of senior coaching experience. Of course he was interested in coaching an international team! Woolmer's original intention had been to fly to South Africa to tell Boland what they could do with their job, but now he had a much more pressing engagement. The UCBSA had narrowed the shortlist down to three candidates: Eddie Barlow; Duncan Fletcher, the former Zimbabwe international who was coaching Western Province; and Woolmer. They were interviewed at cricket headquarters in Johannesburg. Woolmer was asked whether he believed he could work with Kepler Wessels. He replied, 'I can work with anyone as long as we have the same philosophy.'

Four days later, on 24 September 1994, Woolmer was in Potchefstroom where he was working on a two-day coaching engagement with Western Transvaal. His cellular phone rang at 5.30 pm. It was Bacher.

'Bob, the job's yours!'

South Africa had a new national cricket coach, and Woolmer could not believe his good fortune. The Pakistan tour was looming and he immediately announced his intentions. First he wanted to meet with Wessels and then 'set about earning the respect of the players, the captain and the public.' Later, he would publicly reassure South Africans that, although he was an Englishman by birth, his cricketing loyalties lay with South Africa alone. Even if his adopted country were to play against England with him as their coach, there would be no divided loyalties.

Dennis Amiss, chief executive at Warwickshire County Cricket Club, let it be known that South Africa would be getting the services of 'far and away the most brilliant mind in cricket today'.

THE TEAM FOR Pakistan included five changes from that of the England tour. Left out were Allan Donald, who was recovering from a foot operation; Peter Kirsten, who had cause to feel aggrieved after his magnificent century at Headingley; Gerhardus Liebenberg, Richard Snell and Pat Symcox. Earning a recall were Adrian Kuiper, Eric Simons and Meyrick Pringle. Clive Eksteen would complete a hat trick of Asian tours, having been to India in 1991 and Sri Lanka in 1993. The only new cap in the 16-man party was Derek Crookes, the 25-year-old Natal offspin bowler.

On the eve of their departure, Wessels called for more urgency from his squad. 'Part of the strength of South African teams is that they run on adrenalin. That's what we ran on in the first two years and we achieved superb results when we sometimes played well above ourselves. I think it was one part of our game that was lacking in the latter part of the England tour and we need to find it all over again.'

Bacher was more forthright. 'The honeymoon,' he said, 'is over.'

Cronjé was wrapped up in his own thoughts. 'This is probably your last tour,' he told himself, 'so make the most of it.'

He genuinely believed his days in the national team were numbered. The tour to England had not been good to him, and he came home feeling distraught and disillusioned. When the media had speculated on who would be selected for Pakistan, several columnists and ex-players could not even find a place for him in their guesswork teams. The fact that he had not been awarded the captaincy also had him believing the selectors were having second thoughts.

'Whatever you do,' Cronjé told himself, 'just enjoy yourself. You may never get another chance.'

SOUTH AFRICA LOST all six of their matches in Pakistan.

After defeat to Australia in the first game, Woolmer told the players, 'Don't look on each game as being the be-all and end-all. Obviously the result is important, but get out there and enjoy yourselves. Don't be afraid to play your shots and take the bowlers on. I want you all to develop a free spirit.'

In the next game, Pakistan crushed them by eight wickets, then Australia won by 22 runs, and so on, and so on...

Back home, there was a feeling of utter dejection. From the end of Australia's tour and including the Holland debacle, South Africa had now lost 11 one-day internationals in a row.

Amid the ashes, however, Cronjé's phoenix rose again. Relishing the invitation to become a 'free spirit' and believing that he had nothing to lose, the vice-captain was the only glowing success of the tour. Against Australia he scored 98 not out, 64, and 100 not out in 118 balls. Against Pakistan his scores read run out 21, run out 53, and 18.

In all, he had scored 354 runs at an average of 88.50. Gary Kirsten totalled 162 runs, Rhodes's aggregate was 150, and Wessels's 143.

Cronjé's confidence was soaring. Gone were the dark and dismal thoughts of his looming demise. Now in their place came the realisation that a cricketer's form is a cyclical thing, and that no player should ever grow so despondent as to believe that it cannot be rediscovered. Peter Pollock recognised the positive signs and called Cronjé aside in Pakistan to tell him that plans were now in place for him to take over the captaincy from Wessels immediately when the tour was over.

Cronjé recalls, 'I think Kepler saw us talking and thought we were trying to push him out or something. It wasn't the case at all. Peter simply asked me whether I would still like to have Kepler in my team once he stepped down. I said there was no question about it. He was still a very good player, and in Test cricket he could continue to make a big contribution because of all his experience. I wasn't too sure that he would make himself available for the one-day games but for the Tests there was no doubt that I wanted him.'

Wessels told reporters, 'I would like to think I can still play Test cricket, and not being the captain would take a lot of pressure off me.'

At a team meeting at about this time, Cronjé also voiced strong opinions about the best approach to one-day cricket. 'I wasn't having a go at anyone or anything like that, but what I did say was that we needed to score our runs more quickly and particularly at the start of the innings. I was not being critical of Kepler, but I think he believed I was.'

The Pakistan venture may have been a disaster in terms of results, but it had one positive spin-off for the South African players: it taught them about playing conditions in Pakistan where, in 1996, they would play all their league matches in the next World Cup.

13

Hansie and the Boys

THEY WERE ALL so very proud, the folk from Bloemfontein. There were Ewie and San-Marie, Frans, Hester and Gordon, there were the Volsteedts and the Strydoms, and there was Bertha Pretorius. They were thrilled, each in their own way that day in November 1994 when Hansie Cronjé was named as South Africa's new cricket captain for the coming international season. In the same week two years before, he had been twelfth man for the Test against India in Durban. Now he was the first name on the team sheet.

He was proud, too, but not of himself. He was proud for the people of Bloemfontein, for the Free Staters, for the Grey College fraternity, for everyone who had played their role in helping him achieve this rare success.

At 25, he was the second-youngest South African captain since Murray Bisset's appointment at age 22 against England in 1899. Bisset went on to play against W.G. Grace when, in 1901, he took a South African team to England in the bitter aftermath of the Boer War. As Sir Murray Bisset, he would later become the Chief Justice of Rhodesia and the country's acting governor. Like Cronjé, his leadership and states-manlike skills were recognised at an early age. Both were mature beyond their years and, in different ways in a political context, both featured prominently in delicate, transitional times for their country.

The big day, 7 November 1994, should have been a time of rejoicing for the new skipper but, sadly, it was not. He was in trouble.

On the eve of his national appointment, Cronjé led Free State in a Currie Cup match in Durban. The defending champions were up against it, facing defeat by Natal, when the captain was given out on 21 to a disputed catch. This was a time for reluctant acceptance, no matter how great the disappointment or how harsh the judgement, but, amid the tension, frustration and final letdown, the young man lost his cool.

196

He disputed umpire Wilf Diederick's decision and, in showing such dissent, had crossed the line that no cricketer may cross. Hauled on to the carpet for the first time in his career, he was fined R500 and given a suspended sentence. The Free State captain felt ashamed and annoyed and, on top of it, his team was beaten by nine wickets.

In the Natal dressing room, there was little sympathy and much celebration. The Man of the Match was the fast-bowling colt Shaun Pollock, who had taken seven wickets to upstage both Natal's famous West Indian import Malcolm Marshall and the former Test bowler Tertius Bosch, who had recently moved to Durban after eight seasons with Northern Transvaal. Marshall, Bosch and Pollock formed a three-pronged pace attack of quality, experience and raw ambition, yet significantly, it was the most junior partner who took the honours – the 21-year-old redhead who was all elbows and knees and had a toothy grin.

Cronjé's appointment, announced two days before New Zealand began their first tour of South Africa in 33 years, continued to grab the headlines. Led by the dashing batsman Ken Rutherford, New Zealand's opening game was a warm-up against the Nicky Oppenheimer XI at Midrand, north of Johannesburg. Cronjé was included in the mining magnate's team, and duly lashed 34 runs in 28 balls. There was no better way to relieve the stress of a burdensome period than to crack a leather cricket ball as hard as he could.

Later, in the comfort of the stately pavilion at Oppenheimer's private Randjesfontein Oval, he was relaxed and articulate in discussing the challenges that lay ahead. He needed no reminding that the New Zealanders were the team South Africa had to take to the cleaners to reclaim credibility after the Pakistan debacle, and the burning question on everyone's lips was whether there would be a marked change of approach in the immediate post-Wessels era.

'Kepler and I have a lot in common,' said Cronjé. 'I have learned a lot under his captaincy, but I have a few ideas of my own that I want to try out. The last thing I want is for the responsibilities of captaincy to change my identity. I have always played the game aggressively and that's how I want to continue.'

In echoing Wessels's credo, he gave the assurance that hard work would be the cornerstone of his approach. 'The only place where success comes before work is in the dictionary.'

Cronjé had shown in Pakistan a willingness to improvise, an exciting quality it was hoped he would instil in his team-mates. 'My plan is for South Africa to play really positive cricket. We owe it to the spectators who pay good money to watch us play.'

Now there was a change, because Wessels had never said that.

There was also the question of his tiff with umpire Diedricks. 'It won't happen again,' he promised. 'It really just came in the heat of the moment and, fortunately, it was my first offence. I guess it goes to show that we all have emotions. It taught me a lesson, but I have put it all behind me. I suppose we can laugh at it now because today's problems are often tomorrow's jokes.'

Hansie's first priority was to renew his acquaintance with Bob Woolmer and, as luck would have it, Free State's next match was against Western Province in the new coach's home town of Cape Town. Cronjé could therefore kill two birds with one stone, and he completed this assignment with the stylish assurance of a confident man.

Western Province had acquired a new trump card in the veteran West Indian opener Desmond Haynes. Making his provincial début at the age of 38, he was out for 5 in a first innings shambles that descended to 54 for eight before ending on 105 all out. Victory for Free State seemed a certainty but Haynes's 96 in the second innings left them a tricky target of 276 for victory.

Enter Cronjé. He batted for six hours and 20 minutes to score 111 and take his team to a four-wicket triumph. It was his seventh Currie Cup century in his seventh season in the competition. Bob Woolmer liked what he saw.

THE SOUTH AFRICA A team had been touring Zimbabwe under the leadership of Mark Rushmere, whose work-related move from Port Elizabeth to Johannesburg had also brought him the Transvaal captaincy, succeeding the semi-retired Jimmy Cook. His team in Zimbabwe included top-order batsmen Gerhardus Liebenberg and Rudi Steyn of Free State, John Commins of Boland, the Transvaal fast bowlers Richard Snell and Steven Jack, the promising Northern Transvaal seam bowler Steve Elworthy, and the Free State left-arm spinner Nicky Bojé. There was also the Eastern Province all-rounder Dave Callaghan and the Border wicketkeeper Steve Palframan.

They won all six matches they played with some outstanding individual contributions. Liebenberg hit a century and a fifty to head the batting averages on 95.50, Callaghan scored two centuries for an average of 93.66, Commins made a century off 82 balls, and Bojé, apart from his eight wickets, scored a century and a fifty for a batting average of 79.50. Elworthy was the most successful bowler with 12 wickets, while Jack took 10.

If this were a tour designed to prepare the players for possible higher honours, then the Test incumbents would surely be casting anxious glances over their shoulders. Among the bowlers, the tall

Elworthy, at 29 years of age and in his fifth season of Currie Cup cricket, was pressing hard. Later in the season he would advance his claims by taking seven for 65 for Northerns against Natal at Kingsmead. As a hard-hitting lower order batsman Elworthy would take a 75 off Eastern Province at St George's Park.

There were possibilities all right because gaps were already appearing in the élite squad of players from which the South African teams were generally selected. Adrian Kuiper, for example, needed a third operation to a damaged shoulder and would play little part in the months ahead.

FOLLOWING HIS APPOINTMENT as South African captain, Cronjé phoned Wessels in Port Elizabeth. He wanted to thank the old skipper for what he had done for him on a personal level and for his overall input in helping to shape the team.

'I asked him if he still wanted to play in the Test team, and he said he would think about it and come back to me. He never did, so I presumed he was no longer available.'

Woolmer had told Peter Pollock he wanted Wessels at No 3 because there was no one else with enough experience for that demanding batting position but, when the selectors named the team for the first Test against New Zealand, Wessels was not included. Neither was Allan Donald. The fast bowler was still sidelined through injury and would remain so for the entire series.

The South African attack for the Wanderers Test was De Villiers, Snell, Matthews, McMillan and Eksteen. The rest of the team was made up of Hudson, Gary Kirsten, Cronjé, Cullinan, Rhodes and Richardson.

Woolmer jotted down the names and then, scratching his head, he wrote, 'Who's the number three???!!' He really did not know. He had already decided that Cronjé should bat at No 4, but who would fill the vexed No 3 slot? How about McMillan? Okay.

THERE WERE STILL a couple of matters to be dealt with in Bloemfontein. New Zealand were at Springbok Park for their final four-day match before the Test, and Cronjé was determined to lead his province to their first victory over a touring team. Steyn was also intent on continuing his fine batting form, which he did quite splendidly with an innings of 157.

The Kiwis had their moments too, not least of which was Chris Harris's hat trick to remove Steyn, Wilkinson and Liebenberg with successive balls.

Cronjé scored 56 and 44 not out, Free State achieved an improbable victory by two wickets after being set a mammoth 381 in 84 overs, and, in the crowning glory, the happy captain announced his engagement to the petite, blonde Bertha. They planned to marry at the end of the season.

It was champagne stuff all round, with the Test match only three days away.

ONE OF THE most important things Cronjé had learnt from Wessels was to do his homework. As the big day approached, he scrupulously studied his opponents, watched videos of previous New Zealand matches, and devised his strategy around each and every player. In the final team talk, he told his team-mates, 'Listen, we're a better team than these guys. If we play up to our standards, we'll win this series. Also, I want you to express yourselves in your own particular way. Don't be inhibited out there; just play the game as naturally as you'd like.'

He recalls, 'In my first Test as captain, I was very aware of the need to be positive. I didn't want to make the same mistakes as at Adelaide, where I was far too negative. So everything I did was based on attack. For the fast bowlers, for example, I had no third man to cover the slip cordon but we bowled far too short and they picked up a lot of bound-aries in that area.

'Also, I didn't have the experience to make my thoughts clear to the bowlers. Everything seemed to be happening so quickly and I was not sure that I was making the right decisions or saying the right things. I suddenly realised that I was losing control of the Test match.'

New Zealand were happy to assume control, taking full advantage of the misdirected bowling to total 411. In reply, the South Africans were strangely tentative, slipping to 73 for four (Hudson 10, Kirsten 9, McMillan 5, Cronjé 20) before Cullinan's 58 and Richardson's lion-hearted 93 hauled them up to 279 all out.

A far better bowling performance by the South Africans in the second innings was highlighted by De Villiers's four for 52, but a victory target of 327 on a deteriorating pitch was always going to be tough. Cronjé battled grimly for three hours to score 62, but around him the innings was coming apart and, with eight wickets falling for 59 runs, it was all over on 189 – victory to New Zealand by a whopping 137 runs.

It was a sobering situation for the new South African captain because the team's successive losses now extended to two Tests and 11 one-day internationals. Woolmer's record was: played seven, lost seven. When the team arrived in Cape Town for the first one-dayer against the Kiwis, the Newlands groundsman, Andy Atkinson, a former colleague of Woolmer's at Warwickshire County Cricket Club, remarked facetiously, 'He's the only coach in the world with a 100 per cent record – lost 'em all!'

Woolmer was told of the remark, and he snapped back, 'Don't worry, we'll turn it around. And when we go on to win 30 games in a row, I'll come here specially and shake his hand!'

South Africa won their next three limited-overs matches.

WITH THE TEST SERIES in recess, the action switched to a quadrangular series of limited-overs internationals involving New Zealand, Pakistan and Sri Lanka. The winner would receive the Mandela Trophy – and South Africa wanted it badly.

At Newlands, the South African one-day squad against the Kiwis included Eric Simons and a newcomer in Mike Rindel. The Northern Transvaal left-hander had been waiting for his chance for a long time, and he weighed in on his début to be crowned Man of the Match. First he hit an attractive 32 before being run out, and then he took two for 15 in five overs of swing bowling. Simons was run out for 24 in 30 balls and then took two wickets for 28 runs in nine overs.

Woolmer was initially disappointed with the total of 203. 'I don't think it's enough,' he told Cronjé. But good bowling and catching and a couple of run-outs humbled the New Zealanders for a mere 134.

A win at last! Woolmer had reason to smile, but not nearly as broadly as after the next match against Pakistan at the Wanderers, where Snell's four for 37, Cronjé's 81 and Hudson's 74 brought victory by a smashing seven wickets. The Man of the Match award went to the South African captain.

Hansie and the boys were now getting their act together and, a day later at Centurion Park, they were positively devastating against New Zealand.

The captain remembers, 'This was when the Woolmer–Cronjé combination started to click. Against Pakistan we had noticed how their openers, Anwar and Sohail, blazed away from the first ball so we decided that we wanted to score far more runs in the first 15 overs.'

The South African brains trust was also reminded of a quite sensational innings played by Steven Jack in his role as a pinch-hitter for Transvaal against the Kiwis a week earlier. The specialist fast bowler had turned his hand adeptly to top-order batting with stunning results, hammering 107 runs from just 75 balls with 16 fours and four sixes. It was a quality knock of orthodox, straight hitting, rather than hectic, hit-or-miss slogging, and it told the story of how this approach could bring spectacular results.

Now, at Centurion Park, the South Africans asked Dave Callaghan to do the job.

'In him,' said Cronjé, 'we found the ideal batter to put our plan into effect. If he had failed, maybe we would have laughed the whole thing off and gone back to using a conventional opener but, of course, he didn't.'

Promoted now as a pinch-hitting opener, the pugnacious all-rounder blazed one of the all-time great innings in limited-overs international cricket. Callaghan's South African record score of 169 not out was the fifth highest in international limited-overs cricket and the second-biggest score in a 50-over international match. It came in just 143 balls with 19 fours and four sixes, and was an innings of such rare grandeur that it made anything before or after it seem nothing more than pedestrian.

As if it weren't enough to earn him the Man of the Match award, Callaghan then chipped in with three wickets in an 81-run victory.

Woolmer was grinning from ear to ear. The boys had now won three games in a row and, what's more, they had reached a massive total of 314 in their 50 overs. Cronjé had also produced a gem of an innings, lashing 68 runs from 79 balls, but it paled in comparison to Callaghan's massive effort. There were tears of joy and admiration in the eyes of his supporters as the bashful Eastern Province cricketer went to receive his prize – a young man whose ability to win a cricket match was nothing compared with the courageous battle he had fought and won against cancer a few years before, and from which trauma he had returned in singular triumph to reach the very pinnacle of his sporting profession.

It was due to this incredible example of guts, determination and character that he had crept into the hearts of his fellow South Africans.

Sadly, his extraordinary batting example was short-lived. In the next two games against Sri Lanka and Pakistan, he failed to get out of the blocks, which seemed to have a ripple effect on the other batsmen. Chasing Sri Lanka's 226 at Springbok Park, they succumbed on 191. Their 206 for eight at Kingsmead was never going to be enough against a Pakistan team that included one Ijaz Ahmed.

Ahmed was an interesting character, a thorn in the flesh of the South African team all summer long. According to legend, he had been selected to tour South Africa in unusual fashion. He was the brother-in-law of the Pakistan captain, Salim Malik, and was not included in the original touring team. It was claimed that Ijaz went along to watch the team's final net practice before their departure for Johannesburg, during which Salim unilaterally invited him to make the trip. The selection of Pakistan teams has always been an unconventional business, often involving *ad hoc* decisions, and, in this instance, Salim merely informed one of the other selectors watching the practice that Ijaz was a late selection for the tour.

Why he was left out in the first place remains a mystery. The South Africans first encountered him during their dismal visit to Pakistan when, in two matches against them, he scored 110 in 112 balls and 98 not out in 87 balls. In the Mandela Trophy encounter at the Wanderers, he had hit 73 from 86 balls in a beaten cause and, at Kingsmead, he was Man of the Match after racing to 114 not out in 90 balls. In his four limited-overs matches against South Africa, his grand total of runs stood on 395 for two dismissals in just 375 balls. This now clearly exonerated Salim from any accusations of nepotism arising from the invitation to his brother-in-law to join him in South Africa. The captain was accused of many things in a Pakistani camp wracked with internal strife, but this was one decision he could honourably justify.

Once again the South Africans found themselves under pressure to qualify for a tournament final. New Zealand had been eliminated, Pakistan were already through, and the last match against Sri Lanka at St George's Park would produce the other finalist. By this stage, Woolmer and Cronjé had reached the conclusion that pinch-hitters were fine in certain circumstances but not in all. A lot depended on the state of the pitch and the kind of bowler the openers were likely to face. At Port Elizabeth, the South Africans reverted to an orthodox batting line-up, and the scoring impetus came from more recognisable sources. Cullinan at No 3 hit 63 in 75 balls, and Rhodes at No 5 chipped in with a careful 53. It wasn't all orthodox stuff, however. As part of his innovative views on one-day batting, Woolmer had been encouraging the batsmen to play the reverse sweep occasionally to upset the iine of the spin bowlers. It was a strange shot that required right-handers to suddenly switch to left-handed batting, and it rightly caused frowns of disapproval among the purists and produced only moderate success for the batters. Cullinan tried it and only managed to top-edge the ball straight into his mouth.

Sri Lanka might have fancied their chances of overhauling South Africa's total of 237 for eight but rain disrupted their innings, and they fell 45 runs short of the revised 34-over target of 184.

South Africa had qualified for the best-of-three final, but first there was the small matter of getting even with New Zealand in the Test series.

THE KIWIS WERE in disarray. They had been whipped by Transvaal, had failed to win a match in five starts in the quadrangular series and, in a scheduled three-day warm up for the second Test at Kingsmead, they encountered a scandalous pitch at Paarl, which was deemed so dangerous the match was abandoned after a single over on the second day. Two innings had already been completed on day one: Boland bowled out for 83 and the tourists for 86 in what was a hopeless exercise on an untried wicket at Boland's new headquarters. In Durban, their mood did not improve when it was found that heavy rains had put paid to decent practice facilities.

Later it would also emerge that a group of New Zealand players had smoked dagga one night at a party in the Cape, causing the team to split down the middle in the resulting witch-hunt. It was a scandal that rocked New Zealand cricket to its foundations and later caused a breakup of the team.

The South African problems were only of a cricketing nature. Not surprisingly, the question of the irksome No 3 batting berth resurfaced in the build-up to the Test which was due to begin on Boxing Day. Speculation again suggested that Wessels was the best man to do the job but, on the eve of the team's announcement, the former captain officially announced his retirement from international cricket. It was the week before Christmas, three months after his thirty-seventh birthday, when he called it quits. He never did make his return phone call to Cronjé, nor did he make any fanfare of his decision. Privately he made it known, however, that he had been prepared to play again for South Africa, but only as a middle-order batsman. He was no longer available to do the job as an opener or the No 3. His departure came after 16 Tests for South Africa in which he scored two centuries and six fifties for a batting average of 38.03. In one-day international cricket for Australia, he took 18 wickets with his gentle seamers.

It was the end of his own adventure in the world of international cricket and a turning point in an historic era of rediscovery and re-acceptance for the country of his birth. There were no comebacks. It was now up to Hansie and the boys to do it their way.

John Commins, meanwhile, was making a special comeback of his own. The tall, elegant batsman had been cast into the wilderness by Western Province, ignored by the selectors for the entire 1992/93 season, to find himself suddenly at the crossroads of a career that had started with so much promise. He decided the only way to restore his flagging career and regain some recognition was to move away and make a fresh start.

Lowly Boland had done wonders under Woolmer's coaching to gain promotion to the Currie Cup, so it was to Boland that Commins went. In his first season with his new province, he scored 557 runs at an average of 42.84 with a career-best 137 against Transvaal. When, a season later, Boland hosted the New Zealanders on their parlous Paarl pitch, he was the new provincial captain in place of the enigmatic Terence Lazard, another Western Province batsman who had crossed the border but had not seen eye to eye with Woolmer's philosophies.

South Africa were looking for a new No 3 for the Kingsmead Test. They chose Commins.

It was a low-scoring match in muggy, overcast conditions that favoured the swing bowlers, but the Boland skipper emerged with honour to score 30 in the first innings and 45 in the second. In occupying the crease for almost five hours in total, he ensured that the level of confidence among those who followed him was far greater than at the Wanderers. This was no better illustrated than by Richardson and De Villiers, whose fighting 44-run partnership for the last wicket ensured that South Africa took a crucial 41-run lead on the first innings.

Commins was not the only new boy in the team. Steve Jack's fast bowling for Transvaal and South Africa A was finally rewarded when he was selected in place of Snell, his provincial team-mate. At Kingsmead he took a wicket with his fourteenth delivery in Test cricket to produce the kind of shock bowling that may otherwise have come from the sidelined Allan Donald.

The burden on the South African attack was further increased when Matthews broke down with a leg injury, but Vinnige Fanie again rose to the challenge by taking eight wickets in the match, including five for 64 in the first innings.

South Africa were left to score 152 for victory, and they did it with eight wickets to spare due to solid contributions by Gary Kirsten, Commins and Cullinan.

Cronjé's high spirits at the end of the match were in marked contrast to the Wanderers Test when he had blamed himself for the big defeat. In achieving his first Test win as South Africa's official captain, he bowled out one of New Zealand's few consistent batsmen, Shane Thomson, for 35, which in turn hastened a second innings collapse that devoured the last six wickets for only 48 runs. He also ran out the cavalier Adam Parore after the television replay proved that the batsman had not grounded his bat at the instant Cronjé had thrown down the wickets after fielding the ball off his own bowling.

WHILE THE KIWIS continued their soul-searching, the South Africans were getting down to serious practice in the Newlands nets for the third and final Test match. The new year had dawned, and with it the real chance of winning the series.

As usual, a number of young, local bowlers were given the chance to help prepare the batsmen at the nets. Just as the school-going Hansie had once bowled to the rebel Australians in Bloemfontein, the enthusiastic young Capetonians were getting a similar chance to prove their mettle against their heroes.

One of the recruits was a coloured kid with the strangest bowling action anyone had ever seen.

'We didn't have a clue who he was,' recalls Hansie, 'but everyone felt so sorry for this little guy who was trying so hard to make an impression with his left-arm spin. Every now and again he'd bowl a ball down the leg-side and the batsmen would catch it and say encouraging things like "Keep going, keep trying, keep practising, one day you might might make it", that kind of thing. I think we all knew he wasn't really going to make it with that peculiar action of his.'

The other kids called him Paul, and said he came from the Cape Flats.

NOT FOR THE first or last time in his international career, Andrew Hudson was axed from the team for the New Year's Test.

'We called him "Moon Man",' recalls Cronjé, 'when we played together early in our careers for SA Universities. He seemed to come from another planet, never ever showing any emotion when things were going wrong for him; just never giving a clue what was going on inside his head. He was such a natural batsman – one of the few that I know that doesn't need to practise before going out there and hitting the ball perfectly from the word go – but he seemed to suddenly slip into lapses of concentration that made us think he was an extra-terrestrial visitor.'

As Hansie would later discover, Hudson was a spiritual man who placed all his faith and trust in God. If it were His decision that runs would not flow on any particular day, then so be it. 'I don't easily show my emotions,' said Hudson, 'and people sometimes take that the wrong way. They seem to think that I'm not trying, but what they don't know is that it hurts terribly when I fail. I maintain this inner belief that I'm good enough to play at this level and, in spite of being dropped from time to time, I believe it's that inner drive that brings me back.'

On tour in particular, Hudson drew courage and comfort from talking regularly with fellow Christians in the team. Wessels and the manager, Alan Jordaan, started a Christian fellowship during the World Cup in 1992, and these meetings had developed into an integral part of the team's character. Cronjé was a committed member and so, too, was Rhodes. In time, Hudson became the group's co-ordinator – 'Brother Andrew', as Hansie jokingly calls him – and delegated his like-minded team-mates to give inspirational talks at schools and churches along the way.

'In a men's environment, guys don't like to open up to each other,' says Hudson. 'No one's going to show his emotions during team talks, so some of us find a need to sit down and chat in a natural and uncomplicated way about life's issues beyond the game.'

Sadly, the reality of the cricketing issue right then was that 'Hudders' was in a batting slump with only 26 runs from four successive innings. His place was taken by Rudi Steyn, the 27-year-old opener who had become such an important member of Cronjé's champion Free State outfit that he was worthy now of his first Test cap. He would not disappoint.

Together with Kirsten, he helped end a succession of low opening partnerships by contributing 38 runs to an opening stand of 106. It was just the platform the others needed, and their total of 440 for a first innings lead of 152 looked as if it were altogether too much for the Kiwis to recover.

The bowlers were also firing. Jack took four for 69 in the first innings, and De Villiers later excelled again with five for 61 for his third 'fifor' in Test cricket.

The South Africans' spiralling confidence was also due in no small part to a talisman that had attached itself to the team. On the three previous occasions that Cronjé had scored a Test century, the team had gone on to victory, so his fine innings of 112 was naturally taken as a harbinger of yet another triumph. After taking 72 balls to score his first 17 runs, the skipper cut loose to reach his half-century only 27 balls later. He was on his way to becoming the first South African to score centuries against four different countries.

The real hero, however, was the faithful Richardson who, at 35, was the oldest man in the team and a player who had often rescued them with his boundless supply of guts, determination and character when the chips were down.

This time he and Eksteen, recalled to the team in the absence of Matthews, put on 85 runs for the eighth wicket before Eksteen was out for 22 after almost three hours of watchful assistance. Still Richardson remained. Having come desperately close before to a Test hundred, his position down the batting order sometimes robbed him of partners before he could achieve the feat. But not on this occasion, although it was still desperately close for the No 8 batsman. When the ninth wicket fell, he was on 99, but the reliable De Villiers stayed long enough to ensure his partner would finally reach his first Test century after five hours at the crease.

At the end of a seven-wicket triumph, the beaming Swinger was hoisted on to the shoulders of his team-mates in celebration of his 109, while behind him the fans held up a big banner that read, 'Richardson for president!' He was voted Man of the Match and, for the first time this century, a team had won a three-Test series after losing the first match.

Hansie and the boys were on their way, and their 'old man' Richardson could look back on a series in which his 247 runs for a batting average of 82.33 was far and away the pick of the bunch.

PINCH-HITTERS WERE SUDDENLY in vogue. Franklyn Stephenson was doing the job for Free State, in one match hitting 99 runs in 97 balls. Frans Cronjé's move from Free State to Peter Kirsten's Border also saw him occasionally filling this role. Sanath Jayasuriya had done it spectacularly well with a breath-taking 140 against New Zealand at Bloemfontein. The South Africans naturally believed that they had the answer in Callaghan.

In the first leg of the Mandela Trophy final at Newlands, they realised their folly. Callaghan hit a four and was out immediately, but Cullinan's 64 anchored a total of 215 which proved more than enough when Simons took a match-winning four for 42.

'We suddenly figured that Dave wasn't the right man for the job against a bowling attack that included Wasim and Waqar,' recalls Cronjé, 'but we had another guy in Mike Rindel, who loved to hit the ball from the very start. Also, being a left-hander, maybe he could upset their fast bowlers a bit.'

For the second leg at the Wanderers Stadium, Rindel joined fellow leftie Kirsten to set a new South African limited-overs record of 190 for the first wicket. Rindel was run out for 106 and, after being crowned Man of the Match, he revealed that the only previous time he had opened the innings was in a club game when one of the regular openers had pitched up late. Kirsten's 87 provided the other sizeable chunk of South Africa's impressive 266 for five in their 50 overs – a total that was far too good for the Pakistanis, who now encountered Allan Donald in his first game after his long injury lay-off. The fired-up Sling found an equally inspired new ball partner in Vinnige Fanie, and three cheap wickets each helped skittle Salim Malik's men for a paltry 109 within 33 overs.

The ubiquitous Swinger also got into the act by taking a South African record five catches behind the stumps. And just a week after parading the Castle Lager Test Series trophy at Newlands, Cronjé held the coveted Mandela Trophy aloft to complete a grand double triumph in his first six weeks as South Africa's new captain.

Jonty Rhodes's athleticism in the field became one of the standouts of the South African team, while (below) Hansie Cronjé shows how he feels about the Kirsten brothers, Peter and Gary, after victory over Australia at the Wanderers in 1994.

Photos: (above) Sunday Times; (below) Jon Hrusa

Victory in exotic places included receiving the Pepsi Cup for winning the triangular tournament at Sharjah in the United Arab Emirates in 1996 (opposite). President Nelson Mandela (above) happily donned his team blazer, tie and cap when he handed over the trophy to Hansie Cronjé after the limited-overs series victory over England in 1996. The entire squad (below) celebrate their triumph at St George's Park.

Photos: (opposite) Hansie Cronjé collection; (above and below) Frans Cronjé

Hansie Cronjé is flanked by Kosie Venter (left) and Nicky Bojé (right) as the Free State team celebrate yet another trophy – this time in the night series final over Transvaal at the Wanderers in 1996. The five cricketers of the year for 1996 (below): Allan Donald, Brian McMillan, Daryll Cullinan, Shaun Pollock and Gary Kirsten.

Photos: (above) Jon Hrusa; (below) Andrzej Sawa

Great honours all round as President Mandela and Steve Tshwete congratulate Allan Donald on his presidential award in 1997 (above). Hansie Cronjé, Steve Tshwete and Bishop Desmond Tutu enjoy the spoils of victory over Pakistan in 1995 (below left), and President Mandela finally gets to meet Basil D'Oliveira at lunch in Pretoria on 16 January 1996 (below right).

Photos: (above and below left) Jon Hrusa; (below right) Juda Ngwenya

Hansie and the boys enjoyed showing the flag for their soccer counterparts when Bafana Bafana played Egypt in an African Nations Cup match at the FNB stadium near Soweto in 1996. The soccer fans enjoyed having Paul 'Gogga' Adams in their midst (below).

Photos: (above) Julani van der Westhuizen; (below) Jon Hrusa

Exciting new faces...

Paul Adams, whose bowling action was described as a 'frog in a blender' when he first emerged in senior cricket, bowls to the Australians at the Wanderers, and (below) Adam Bacher celebrates his maiden half-century in Test cricket against Mark Taylor's touring team.

Photos: (above) Ruvan Boshoff; (below) Jon Hrusa

Among the potential new match-winners in the South African team are Shaun Pollock, who celebrates the prized wicket of Graeme Hick in the Test match against England at Centurion Park in 1995 (above), and Jacques Kallis (below left) and Lance Klusener (below right).

Photos: (above) Christine Nesbitt; (below left) Touchline Photo; (below right) Jon Hrusa

There was just one last hurdle and, by all accounts, it would be the biggest challenge of the season. A week later at the Wanderers, South Africa would play Pakistan in a one-off historic Test match. Pakistan were considered to be the best five-day outfit in the world, and could not be judged too harshly on their meek capitulation in the limited-overs finals where, among the failures, Ijaz Ahmed was out for scores of five and four.

IF SYDNEY WERE 'Fanie's Test', what was the Wanderers? In capping the most brilliant season of his life, the 30-year-old war-horse was again the hero of a famous victory. Batting at No 10, he stunned the capacity crowd with an innings of guts, character and determination – not to mention a little derring-do – to lash 66 not out in 68 balls.

Fighting back the pain from his blistered feet and shrugging off a back injury that had plagued him for several years, he then took six for 81 in the first innings and four for 27 in the second to become the first South African bowler after Hugh Tayfield to complete a second 10-wicket haul in Test cricket.

Afterwards, the tired cricketer confided that the stress of playing a long, hard season with painful, unhealing injuries and the pressure of family commitments were beginning to take a heavy toll. There was a good chance that the 1996 World Cup could be his swan song in international cricket.

Right then, however, it was a time for celebration and adulation. South Africa had beaten a woefully disjointed Pakistan by an unbelievable 324 runs, Big Mac had finally broken out of the 90s to complete his maiden Test century of 113, and Jonty had fought through a lingering batting slump to score a fine 72. Among the other tidy contributions were Gazza's 62 and 42, and Hansie's 41 and 48, which all helped to compensate for the low scores of Steyn and the No 3 Commins in both innings.

For Pakistan it was a time best forgotten. Rumour and innuendo in their dressing room suggested dissension and deceit in their ranks and a lack of support for the captain. Allegations of match-fixing in previous Pakistan teams were related by visiting journalists, who spoke darkly of a mysterious coterie known as the 'Bombay Bookmakers', and of the multi-million dollar trade they plied in offering odds to Asian punters on the outcome of cricket matches.

On the field of play, South Africa were spared the menace of Waqar Younis who complained of an injury and sat out the Test. When his replacement, Aamir Nazir, arrived at the Wanderers directly from the airport, the match had already begun. Ijaz Ahmed was among the batting failures in both innings, and Pakistan's ultimate agony dawned when Salim Malik was caught in the gully by Eksteen off Donald for 99.

Cronjé was well pleased. He had faced an agonising decision in the Test when, given the chance to enforce the follow-on after Pakistan were dismissed for 230 in reply to South Africa's 460, he opted against it. He knew that De Villiers was battling with his injuries and he wanted to give all his bowlers more time to recover. It worked a treat. Pakistan were bowled out for 165 in the fourth innings.

SIX WEEKS LATER came the second make-or-break decision for the South African skipper. At Eden Park in Auckland in a one-off Test celebrating New Zealand cricket's centenary year, Cronjé turned the tide that was running hard against his team when he made a declaration that flew in the face of Woolmer's advice.

After reaching his fifth Test century, a rapid 101 that included three sixes, the confident captain headed off the field to leave New Zealand the more than tempting target of 275 to win in 63 overs. He had already discussed his planned declaration with the coach, who had serious misgiving.

'I'm not going to stop you,' Woolmer told him. 'If you think you can win it, that's fine, but if you lose it, Hansie…'

'I'd rather lose trying to win, Bob, than draw this match.'

'Okay, in that case, I'll back you 100 per cent, but I must tell you that my gut feel is against it. As an Englishman who played Test cricket under Brian Close and Ray Illingworth, I know what they would have done. In their book, you drew the match and got done with it.'

Still, Cronjé declared, and it gave Rutherford's Kiwis a sufficient sniff of victory that he knew only too well they would pursue. He recalls, 'At one stage it looked as if the whole thing were going to backfire on us. Ken Rutherford and Stephen Fleming were going well in the chase. With 35 overs to go, they needed 161 and still had seven wickets in hand. The asking rate was now four-and-a-half runs to the over, and our chances didn't look too good.'

Almost immediately, Matthews engineered the breakthrough by ending a threatening 54-run partnership when Fleming was caught at the wicket for 27. Still, Rutherford was well into his stride and, as long as he was there, New Zealand were definitely in the hunt.

Re-enter the heroic Fanie. With one final throw of the dice, he had Rutherford caught by Hudson for 56. New Zealand immediately fell apart. The last six wickets tumbled for the addition of only 36 runs, and De Villiers ended with four for 42. There was no debate, however, on the Man of the Match. It went to Cronjé. Woolmer described his declaration as 'a magical one' that would enhance the pace of the attacking philosophy they would share in the years ahead, and everyone agreed that his sporting gamble had turned the tables to set up an exciting victory.

Fanie and Gazza Kirsten were so delighted with the triumph that they almost single-handedly polished off the magnum of champagne that was part of the winner's spoils. Kirsten, whose 76 in the second innings was his seventh half-century in 14 Tests, was later found lying flat on his back behind a big pot plant in the dressing room. 'You can run ... but you can't hide, sonny!' laughed one of the attendants.

Hansie, meanwhile, was feeling on top of the world after his first season as the new captain. His first-class campaign had yielded a batting average of more than 50, his Test average was around 40, he had scored two more Test centuries, and had led his team to four successive wins. 'At that time I thought I could walk on water,' he confesses. 'It seemed that everything I did was 100 per cent. I had a lot of faith in my bowlers, and they proved me right on so many occasions.'

There was still one area that troubled the captain – the lack of consistency in the dreaded No 3 batting position. Commins was discarded after the Pakistan Test and Hudson was recalled to fill the void behind the openers Kirsten and Steyn.

Hudders faced only eight balls in the first innings and, although he recovered to score 64 next time around, the vulnerability of the position was still exposed. Also, as a Test opener, Steyn was looking more and more inhibited, but there was no doubt that the middle order was in good hands. A Cronjé Test century again set up a victory – the fourth win in a row now under his captaincy to equal Ali Bacher's record in 1970 – and Cullinan's 96 on his twenty-eighth birthday was a gem of an innings.

It was also to South Africa's credit that they had achieved their win without the services of their one genuine all-rounder, Brian McMillan, who had been forced to miss the trip through injury.

'Mac's importance to the balance of the side has always been a critical factor,' says Cronjé. 'When he's injured, you just have to hope that he gets better soon.'

Rindel's first tour had not been a happy one. Against Australia in the opening match of a quadrangular series before the Auckland Test, he scored 14 in a miserable total of 123. He then dropped a dolly catch from Ian Healy – after the Aussies had slumped to 56 for six in reply – to let them in for a three-wicket victory. South Africa subsequently beat India and lost to New Zealand – but Rindel did not play for his country again.

ON THE TEAM'S return to South Africa, Cronjé did three very important things. On 31 March 1995, he hit 101 in 96 balls against Western Province at Newlands to steer Free State into the Benson & Hedges Series final. On 8 April, he married his sweetheart, Bertha. And on 13 April he interrupted his honeymoon to hit 61 runs in 67 balls in a 113-run victory over Wessels's Eastern Province at Springbok Park.

For the second successive season, Bloemfontein rejoiced in their team's capture of the B&H trophy. It was a big moment for the new Free State coach Corrie van Zyl, who had retired from the game because of recurring back problems. But there was still no rest for the captain.

It was during the Headingley Test the previous year that Cronjé had signed to play for Leicestershire in the 1995 English season. There he and Bertha were immediately reunited with old friends. Parsons was still playing for the county, and the team manager was the veteran spin bowler Jack Birkenshaw, who had once spent two happy seasons as Free State's coach.

'I learnt a lot from them,' recalls Hansie. 'In my second game, a one-dayer against Lancashire, I scored 160, took two wickets, and received the Man of the Match. Once again I thought that everything was going my way. I figured that if Brian Lara could score 2 500 runs, why then couldn't I?'

Why not indeed? Well, on the day South Africa's rugby Springboks beat New Zealand's All Blacks in the World Cup final at Ellis Park, South Africa's cricket captain broke a finger in a county game against Northamptonshire.

'It showed me again that life works in circles. One day you're on top of the world; the next day you're right down at the bottom.'

De Villiers, meanwhile, was not taking the risk of coming off his heroic high of the 1994/95 campaign. Resting his tired and tortured body, he was rewarded with fourth place in the Coopers & Lybrand Test bowling ratings for world cricketers. In the most recent calendar year, he had taken 48 wickets in eight Tests. 'He carried our entire attack,' enthused Hansie. 'And to think they once said that he wasn't good enough for Test cricket.'

One player who could rightly feel unhappy about his lack of elevation was Steve Elworthy. He ended the season as Northern Transvaal's highest wicket-taker with 32 scalps, and he proved that he could also bat a bit. Nonetheless, his selection for South Africa A was the highest recognition he would receive.

For other promising young cricketers, there was significant recognition from the selectors that would lead to even greater exposure in the months ahead. During late winter 1995, Woolmer took a South Africa under-24 team on a short tour of Sri Lanka to help acquaint the next generation of cricketers with conditions on the subcontinent. There, a number of players advanced their reputations, chiefly the impressive Liebenberg, who accumulated 516 runs in five matches for an average of 129. Among others to enjoy success were the skipper Dale Benkenstein, who averaged over 100 in four first-class matches; Jacques Kallis, the blossoming 19-year-old all-rounder who had made his Currie Cup début for Western Province the previous season; the combative Lance Klusener of Natal, who took 12 wickets in three first-class games; and Nicky Bojé, who picked up regular wickets with his left-arm spin.

Others in the team included Shaun Pollock, whose father, Peter, had once been South Africa's best fast bowler; and Adam Bacher, a top-order batsman whose uncle, Ali, had been the captain of the conquering South African team in which Peter Pollock had starred all those years before.

14

Gogga, Polly and Kalahari

THE CENTURION PARK press box was going through its pre-match rituals. One reporter was doing the crossword puzzle, another was leafing through *The Pretoria News,* a third was imparting some important information to a colleague about Fanie's latest hamstring problems, and a fourth was trying to find his telephone connection. It was a pretty normal November morning at Centurion.

Northern Transvaal were about to play host to Western Province, but at that stage of a wet summer the main focus lay much further afield at East London where Michael Atherton's England tourists were in the midst of a rain-delayed match against Border. Peter Kirsten and Daryll Cullinan were both playing, and the big by-line cricket writers were gathered there in preference to Centurion Park.

There was a ripple of surprise in the Centurion press box now as word arrived from the Western Province dressing room that the in-form Meyrick Pringle would perform the twelfth man's duties. In his previous match for the SA Invitation XI against the English team at Soweto, the bouncy swing bowler had taken a hat trick for the first time since his junior school days, and by the end of the summer he would be his province's chief wicket-taker in their ultimate Currie Cup triumph. Now he was to be replaced by a player named Paul Adams, of whom the assembled cricket writers knew very little, if nothing at all.

It was presumed by the majority of them that this Adams must be a seam or swing bowler in the Pringle mould because Centurion Park normally favoured such bowlers and, in any event, Western Province already had a spin specialist in the offspinner David Rundle.

No, declared the wise man from *The Pretoria News,* Adams was a spinner who bowled left-arm stuff. The previous weekend he had made his first-class début for Western Province B at Springs and had taken five wickets in the match at pretty high cost. He was apparently still in his teens, was being promoted for no apparent reason to make his senior provincial début, and would be the second spinner on a pitch that normally assisted the seamers. Ah well, the Western Province dressing room must know what it's doing...

After the fall of two early wickets, Northern Transvaal were mounting something of a recovery when the visiting skipper, Eric Simons, tossed the ball to a dusky, chubby little fellow whom none of the handful of spectators had ever seen before. He was the sixth bowler of the day. By a process of elimination, everyone in the press box agreed that this must be the mysterious Adams.

It was late in the morning and the spectators were showing only mild interest when Adams measured out his short run. Well, let's see what this little guy is all about...

It would be true to say that the moment Adams bowled his first ball the entire crowd, if it can be termed such considering its sparsity, was first stunned into silence before it broke into laughter. By the time he had sent down his second delivery, they were almost rolling in the aisles. This was rather embarrassing because the ground was so empty that any noise or comments from the pavilion were sure to carry to the players. Yet never before had anyone seen such an extraordinary bowling action and, as imaginations ran wild, the big man sitting in the second row of the press box rubbed his eyes and declared that it reminded him of a 'frog in a blender'. The cricket writing fraternity, being what it is, gave him the sole rights to use this descriptive phrase in his report for the next day's edition, not that anyone dreamt this metaphor would soon find its way into the columns of many serious newspapers throughout the cricket-playing world and, indeed, into the august pages of the *Wisden Cricketers' Almanack*.

Out in the middle, Brian MacMillan turned to his skipper. 'He reminds me of a gogga!'

Simons grinned his approval because there was something vaguely resembling a creepy-crawly in this contorted bowling action.

The mirth among those watching, however, soon turned to admiration as the seemingly unflappable Adams proceeded to produce an array of stock googlies that turned away from the bat. He also bowled the occasional delivery known as the 'chinaman', that turned into it, from a left-arm wrist-spinner's action that was quite unique. After a spring-heeled leap into the air, the motion of his delivery stride forced his right shoulder awkwardly down and his head sideways as the left arm completed its arc. On closer examination, it was apparent that, for a split second, Adams' eyes were actually averted at right angles from the batsman, thus making his ability to direct the line of flight with any kind of accuracy that much more amazing. There was also no perceptible follow-through as his rigid right leg hit the turf and appeared to take root there.

It was also clear that the batsmen were totally bemused as to what to expect from a bowler who seemed occasionally to grip the ball between only two fingers. Very soon the vastly experienced and somewhat bewildered Roy Pienaar was heading back to the dressing room having been trapped plumb in front by the chinaman.

'Great ball, Gogga. Keep it up!' yelled Big Mac.

Indeed, the earlier laughter changed to whoops of delight and spontaneous applause from those watching. The realisation had dawned that here was something so extraordinarily rare as to be uncommonly special.

It was all so new and unexpected that one of the cricket writers forfeited his lunch to pay a visit to the fine library in the Centurion Park pavilion in order to read up anew on the unusual delivery known quaintly as the chinaman and its practitioners, there to rediscover how a West Indian of Chinese extraction named Ellis Achong had perfected the left-arm slow bowler's 'wrong 'un', and how, when England had visited the Caribbean in 1929, one of the great batsmen of the age, Patsy Hendren, was bowled by such a fizzing delivery at Trinidad. When asked by his team-mates what had happened, Hendren replied, 'I was done by a Chinaman!'

Adams took two wickets in the first innings but gave all the batsmen a difficult time. That he had achieved such wonderful line and length from so awkward an action and grip was so remarkable that one of the cricket writers suggested South Africa could use a mystery spin bowler for the forthcoming World Cup matches in Pakistan. He was only half joking, but he hoped no one would laugh at his proposal.

Ali Bacher had been watching on television and was in a state of some excitement. He immediately telephoned several officials, friends and sports editors. 'Quick, switch on your television,' he commanded. 'There's a spin bowler you just have to see. He's phenomenal!'

Just how phenomenal was not to become truly apparent until Northern Transvaal batted a second time. Elevated by his captain to the No 4 bowler's slot, the teenager sent down 36 overs to take six wickets for 101 and set up an easy victory. Being crowned Man of the Match in his first Currie Cup game was a special moment for the shy youngster, but greater honour was soon to follow. The national selectors immediately included him in the South Africa A team that was due to play England at Kimberley two days later. He was 18 years old and in his first year out of school.

The morning after his Centurion Park début, Adams received a telephone call in his hotel room. 'Hello, Paul, this is Ali Bacher.'

Adams got a shock upon hearing the name of his caller. Was he in trouble? Had he done something wrong? Why should the great man be calling him now? He stammered, 'Er, good morning, Dr Bacher...'

Bacher could hear the nervousness in the naïve teenager's voice so he wasted no time in putting him at ease. 'Paul, I just want to tell you how much I enjoyed watching your bowling yesterday. It really was a great performance in your first game. Congratulations. You must keep it up!'

Adams was relieved. 'Oh, thanks very much, Dr Bacher. I enjoyed it.'

'I'm sure you did and, Paul, if I may give you some advice, there are two things you should remember.'

'Yes, Dr Bacher?'

'Firstly, you must always enjoy your cricket and, secondly, you must always keep your feet on the ground.'

Bacher was speaking figuratively. One thing Adams most certainly did not do when unleashing his teasing spinners was keep his feet on the ground. Both, in fact, were around bail height in his rubber-ball delivery stride.

By this stage, the country was beginning to sit up and take note. At Kimberley, the new bowling sensation did not let them down.

England began confidently enough, but the introduction of Adams into the attack by skipper John Commins immediately had the effect of creating havoc among the experienced visiting batsmen. Adams's second delivery so completely bewitched opener Alec Stewart that it bowled him neck and crop. Graham Thorpe survived 10 balls before nudging a catch to silly point, and Graeme Hick lasted only four balls before offering an easy return catch to the gleeful little bowler. In his first 23 deliveries, he had taken the three biggest wickets of his life at a cost of only one run.

In the pavilion, William Adams could not contain his delight, leaping up and down in celebration of his son's performance. As the captain of a Cape Town fishing trawler he was often away at sea for long periods, and this unexpected break in his working routine was already well worth it. He had bundled the entire family in their car and driven all the way from Cape Town to watch the baby of the family play cricket against England.

In only his third first-class match, young Paul was not about to disappoint them. He ended the first innings with four for 65 in 29 overs. In the second he took five for 116 in 39 overs.

When President Mandela had been introduced to the English team at Soweto two weeks earlier, he had singled out Devon Malcolm, whose nine wickets for 57 at The Oval the previous year was still fresh in the memory. 'Ah, I remember you,' said Mandela, 'you're the destroyer!'

What would the new president now make of the potentially destructive Paul Adams? The nation was certainly agog, enraptured by this kid with the crazy frog-in-the-blender action, an unheralded coloured cricketer from the Cape Flats who was providing the miracle that South African cricket had been praying for. The Western Province Cricket Union immediately awarded him a three-year contract, and newspaper and magazine reporters were falling over each other to acquire his exclusive story.

From unfashionable Grassy Park to the established cricketing nursery of Plumstead Boys' High School, this self-taught player had been included in the Western Province Schools team for the 1994 Nuffield Week. At that tournament one of the SA Schools selectors apparently warned his colleagues that they would make themselves 'a laughing stock' if they selected him for the prestige SA Schools XI. Instead, they named him for the B team that had a much lower profile. Later, he came under the influence of Eddie Barlow at the Western Province Coaching Academy, where it was agreed that any attempt to tamper with his bowling action could be counter-productive. Some things were not worth changing.

THE EUPHORIA RAGING around Paul Adams had the effect of casting several other promising players into the shadows. While it was Gogga's bowling that stole the show at Kimberley, some of the batting was not altogether shabby either. The 23-year-old Transvaal batsman Adam Bacher was called to Kimberley as a last-minute replacement for the pneumonia-stricken Gerhardus Liebenberg, whereupon he opened the innings, batted soundly for five hours, and scored 116.

Bacher's opening partner was Rudi Steyn who, after eight seasons with Free State and three Tests for his country, had recently moved to Natal. His dismissal for 17 at the end of the first hour's play brought to the crease Jacques Kallis. Together, he and the athletic Bacher mounted a richly entertaining partnership that lasted just over three hours and produced 181 runs of which Kallis produced a sparkling 93.

Further down the order at No 6, the Natal all-rounder Lance Klusener underlined his batting potential with a well-crafted 61, but it was Kallis who was creating the most interest. At the start of the season, a month before his twentieth birthday, he had accompanied the Western Province team on a short tour of Australia. Against a strong

Queensland side at the Gabba in Brisbane, he batted for seven hours to score a magnificent 186 not out. It was his maiden first-class century and he shared successive stands of 210 and 183 with the team's other two centurions, Gary Kirsten and John Commins. In the view of the experts, Kallis was well on his way to higher honours.

BOB WOOLMER AND Hansie Cronjé had watched the Kimberley match on television. They were astounded by Adams's performance.

'I can't believe it!' said Hansie. 'This is the same little guy who bowled to us in the nets before the Test against New Zealand. Remember him, Bob? That action? We didn't think he would make it, did we?'

That was then, this was now. They immediately phoned Bacher with a request to be passed on to the chairman of selectors. They wanted Adams added to the South African squad that had already been named for the first two Tests. Bacher knew what they were asking was unprecedented, but he liked the idea. Three days before the first Test at Centurion Park, the UCBSA gave the selectors permission to add him to the squad if they so wished.

The English press were busy trumpeting the name of Gogga Adams as the answer to a prayer. On 5 January, *The Times* even published an editorial headlined 'Cape Coloured Chinaman', in which it rejoiced in his emergence as a symbol of the new South Africa and a unique new talent in world sport, and said of him: 'Rolled into one set of white flannels is both a match-winner and a demographic leveller.' It had also not escaped their attention that Adams played for the same Cape Town club as Basil D'Oliveira all those years ago.

Peter Pollock and his selection panel were in something of a predicament. They knew that Adams's situation represented a massive gamble that may not only be premature but also very damaging. How could they possibly entertain it? The Test squad had already been selected and, in any event, it included a spin bowler in the experienced Clive Eksteen. What would it do to Eksteen's confidence if another spinner were brought in from the wilderness with only three first-class matches behind him? What effect would it have on an 18-year-old who had had little time to draw breath since making his first-class début at Springs only a fortnight before?

Pollock issued a statement: there were to be no additions to the squad already announced. The English press were amazed. They criticised the South African selectors for missing a golden opportunity.

Ironically, when the final XI was announced for the Centurion Test, there was no place for Eksteen in an all-seam attack. Shaun Pollock would get his first Test match after taking a career-best seven for 33 for Natal against Border two weeks earlier.

HANSIE CRONJÉ HAD been planning carefully for the England series. 'Obviously it was very important for me to do well. Having played at Leicestershire, I knew what we were up against, and I also had a few things to prove after my very poor series in England in 1994.'

Woolmer had also been doing his homework. At the cost of R5 000, he acquired video footage of the previous 12 dismissals of all the England batsmen. The South Africans studied them carefully, noting all the chinks they might exploit. The coach also brought on board a range of expertise that included a medical committee under Professor Tim Noakes, the country's top sports medicine scientist; and Paddy Upton, an exercise specialist who would work closely with the team's regular physiotherapist, Craig Smith. With his eye already sharply focused on a long, hard summer that would be capped by the World Cup, Woolmer knew it was vital that they find ways to reduce the possibility of injuries.

The team was well prepared. Before England's arrival they travelled to Zimbabwe on a short tour to hone their game. After their impressive showings for the South Africa under-24 team in Sri Lanka two months earlier, Hansie's provincial team-mates Nicky Bojé and Gerhardus Liebenberg were rewarded with a call-up. It was the first senior recognition for Bojé, while Liebenberg was given another chance after touring England the previous year without playing an international match. Adrian Kuiper was back in the squad, and Brett Schultz was later added to it as backup for the injured De Villiers. Pat Symcox was also included as the first-choice spin bowler in preference to Eksteen.

The South Africans won all four of their matches by handsome margins, and the solitary Test match at Harare was a personal triumph for Allan Donald, who was now bowling better than ever before off a shortened run-up. His eight for 71 in the second innings was a career-best return – the fifth best by a South African in Test cricket – but his match analysis of 11 for 113 did not surpass his 12 for 139 against India at Port Elizabeth three seasons before. The ace fast bowler was also in good form with the bat. In hitting a Test-best 33, he helped McMillan add 79 runs for the ninth wicket in a total of 346. Big Mac unfortunately ran out of partners in his quest for his second Test match hundred. He was not out on 98 at the end.

Hudson had no problem in finding partners *en route* to 135, his third Test century. Cronjé, out for 5 in the first innings, later hit an undefeated 56 to lead his team to a seven-wicket triumph and their fifth win in as many Tests.

Another encouraging aspect was the fast bowling of Schultz. Playing his first Test after battling with knee injuries for more than two years, his four for 54 was largely responsible for bowling out Zimbabwe for 170 in their first innings.

Zimbabwe was one thing, but England would be another. They had given as good as they got against the West Indies earlier in the year, and the critics agreed that South Africa would have to bowl very well to contain their experienced batsmen at Centurion Park.

Cronjé put them into bat and, at 64 for three, his decision seemed well justified. When they finally reached 381 for nine declared, there was little to alter the abiding view that England's powerful batting would continue to be a source of frustration for the South African bowlers, particularly an attack without a spinner.

It also did not help that Schultz went into the match with a buttock injury that had already restricted his bowling in a Currie Cup match the previous weekend. It began troubling him as early as the first over and furious UCBSA officials criticised everyone involved in his selection, including the player, the team management and the physiotherapist. Bacher was angry that a proper medical diagnosis had not been made before the start of the match, and Schultz was rounded on for agreeing to play while not being 100 per cent fit. What on earth had happened to the specialised back-up team that was supposed to ensure this would not happen?

In the context of the Test match, England's batting ascendancy – in which Hick scored 141 – and the generally disappointing South African bowling effort did not count for much. Heavy rain began falling at mid-afternoon on the second day and continued unabated. Play eventually looked possible only after lunch on the fifth day but, with South Africa about to begin their first innings, the rain started falling again, and the match was abandoned amid terrible disappointment for a ground hosting its first Test.

Dave Richardson at least had the satisfaction of claiming his hundredth dismissal in only his twenty-fourth Test when he caught Mark Ramprakash off Donald. And Pollock could be well pleased with his three wickets on début, impressing the critics with his fast in-swing bowling and the ability to produce a surprisingly vicious bouncer from behind a benign, boyish exterior. His dad, Peter, watched him with interest from the pavilion, disguising the emotions that must come from knowing that your son is now following in your own fast-bowling footsteps. The chairman of selectors had made it clear that his committee was responsible for selecting teams and he, as the convener, did not exert any pressure one way or the other. He was happy that his son had been chosen on merit, and now he was happier still that Shaun had justified his elevation with a top-class start.

There was no doubt that he was the best young fast bowler in the country and that he had the capability of making inroads on the English batsmen. In a Currie Cup game immediately after the Test, he proved as much by taking five wickets in each innings against Eastern Province.

The England team, meanwhile, were busy sharpening their batting in preparation for the second Test at the Wanderers.

At Springbok Park, in a three-day match against Free State, there were centuries from Stewart and Thorpe, as well as 90 from John Crawley and 67 from Dominic Cork. The drawn match also provided the opportunity for another Grey College boy to make his provincial début for a side that now boasted no fewer than seven former pupils from the famous school. The 18-year-old Hendrik Dippenaar drew notice to his fine potential by hitting nine fours and a pulled six off Malcolm in a delightful innings of 66 runs in 46 balls. Cronjé, batting at No 3, hit six fours in his 30 runs.

THE SOUTH AFRICANS made two changes for the Wanderers. Pringle was brought in to replace the injured and out-of-favour Schultz, and Eksteen's spin meant that the vice-captain, Craig Matthews, would sadly have to sit out. In the bitter post-mortems, Eksteen unfortunately shouldered much of the blame for failing to penetrate an obdurate rearguard batting action that saved the match against the odds.

In what England's manager Ray Illingworth described as 'one of the great innings of all time', Atherton held the South Africans at bay for almost 11 hours to record the fourth longest innings by an England batsman, and the longest ever in the fourth innings of a Test.

South Africa had controlled the match from the outset after being invited to bat – particularly when Gary Kirsten finally reached his elusive maiden Test century after having scored seven half-centuries in his previous 16 Tests. But Cronjé was criticised on two counts. Firstly for having allowed his batsmen to leave the field because of fading light that did not appear unplayably bad on the third evening with seven-and-a-half overs remaining and the overall lead already 428. And, secondly, for having allowed his team to bat on for almost the entire first session of the fourth day to allow McMillan to reach the Test century that had been denied him against Zimbabwe.

The lead now was a nominal 479, and the only question was whether England could survive five sessions of play. Cronjé believed he had left himself more than enough time to bowl them out and secure a certain victory, as did the majority of the 30 000 fans when the rampant

McMillan bowled Stewart for 38 and Ramprakash for a duck in the space of three balls to reduce England to 167 for four at stumps on the fourth evening.

Atherton resumed the next morning on 82. The turning point came when he was dropped by Kirsten at short leg on 99. Twice before the England captain had been dismissed on 99 in Test cricket but this time he survived. It was the kind of sharp, in-and-out chance that a close leg-side fielder cannot be blamed for, but it allowed the opener to complete a ninth Test hundred that would eventually reach 185 not out.

When the fifth wicket fell on 232 – Smith out for 44 slashing at Donald – there was still more than four-and-a-half hours' play remaining. It was enough time surely for the South African bowlers to wrap up a longish tail that did not suggest it had the technique or resolve to withstand the mounting pressure.

At this point Atherton was joined by the wicketkeeper Jack Russell, who already had the distinction of making a world record 11 dismissals in the Test match but had once been dropped by England for a perceived lack of batting technique. There were still 284 minutes left, the odds so heavily stacked against England holding out that Martin Johnson, the waggish cricket correspondent of *The Independent,* suggested that Lucifer's cat would have more chance of survival.

But Russell refused to budge. His lanky, unkempt hair sticking out from under his helmet, sunglasses and visor hiding his moustacheoed face, he offered an astonishing range of unorthodox defensive shots from a shuffling, crablike stance almost square on to the bowler. Unflinching under fire in answer to his captain's call to arms, his only blemish came when Pringle spilled a return catch when he had five runs.

Pringle then struck Atherton a hard blow to the jaw, but not a single South African went to his aid. In the press box English cricket writers tut-tutted their disapproval at the total disregard shown by the fielding side for the batsman's plight. After receiving treatment and a new helmet, the England captain buckled down, his face so screwed up with concentration that the acutely perceptive Johnson now suggested it looked like a roadmap.

Together in the trenches, the two batsmen endured, constantly meeting in mid-pitch to egg one another on, and resolutely resisting everything the desperate bowlers could deliver. Of the 235 balls he faced, Russell blocked 221. Eksteen sent down 52 overs for only 76 runs, but he could not engineer the breakthrough. The 15 000 fans who had come to the ground to watch England's demise grew more and more annoyed, often breaking into mindless slow handclapping as the minutes and hours ticked by. Atherton continued to punish any loose delivery but took no risks, while Russell's uncanny vigilance acted as the perfect foil.

With seven minutes remaining, Cronjé finally conceded there was no point in carrying on. After dominating for four days, his team had taken only one wicket on the final day. Russell had batted 277 minutes for his 29 runs, and Atherton's highest Test score of 185 had consumed 10 hours, 43 minutes and 492 balls. Of those 492, only 107 had produced all his runs, 112 of them in boundaries. It was an extraordinary performance that would go down in cricket's rich folklore.

At the press conference afterwards the taciturn England captain showed no signs of fatigue. In fact, he looked perfectly capable of batting another 11 hours if the situation demanded it. The secret of the partnership, he said, was to take it 'ball by ball, hour by hour, session by session'.

Cronjé described Atherton's bloody-minded innings as 'a good knock', an understatement that did not escape the rapt attention of the cricket correspondent of *The Independent.* 'It's a bit like saying that Mozart knocked out the odd catchy tune,' he wrote in the next day's edition.

The fact that the psychological high-ground now belonged to England was later confirmed by Cronjé. 'I was really starting to feel the pressure,' he recalls. It did not abate in the third Test at Durban.

IF THE FROWN on the captain's face were growing deeper, the face of his team was at least growing younger. Into it now came the 20-year-old Kallis. He was selected as an extra batsman and backup seamer at the expense of Eksteen's spin bowling, with scores of 146 and 49 in a recent Currie Cup match against Transvaal suggesting he was a good choice. At the Wanderers, Kirsten's immaculate 110 and Cullinan's dashing 69 had been vital to the top order's stability. With Hudson struggling and Cronjé forced to fill the problematic No 3 berth, there was still a question mark hanging over the batting line-up. This was rudely exposed at Kingsmead where Hansie chose to bat and watched as the innings crumbled from 54 for none to 89 for five.

There had been suggestions that Kallis might at last prove to be the answer at No 3, but Cronjé wasn't going to risk him just yet, so he slotted him between Jonty and Big Mac at No 6. It didn't help. He had scored only one run on début when the twelfth ball he faced, a really good one from the seamer Peter Martin, found the outside edge.

Cronjé was angry, but more with himself than with anyone else. He had got himself out for eight runs while miscuing an irresponsible pull shot into the hands of mid-on. Everything seemed to be falling apart after Hudson had started the innings in rollicking fashion with 36 runs from boundaries in his carefree 45.

But all was not yet lost. Rhodes and McMillan took the score to 141 before they were parted and, in a glorious tenth-wicket stand of 72 in 103 minutes, Pollock batted like a seasoned veteran for 36 not out. Donald, now relishing these rearguard rescues, chipped in with 32 in an unlikely total of 225. Sadly, it was again the inclement weather in the wettest summer in memory that doused the soaring spirits in the South African team. Excellent fast bowling from Donald and the recalled Matthews, allied to breath-taking catching from Hudson, Cullinan and Rhodes, reduced England to 109 for five before the rains came down half an hour into the third day and continued to fall throughout the next two.

With three of the five Tests completed and still no result, Cronjé was palpably battling to ease the mounting stress.

'I'm really feeling the pressure from the media – and I mean the English media!' he told Bertha when he telephoned her from Durban. 'There are 60 or 70 of them touring with the team, and every decision you take, they criticise. They also have about six former Test players on their commentary team, and they always seem to be looking to find fault. I tell you, Bertha, a big part of England's problems has a lot to do with these people. They're always looking to blame someone, and the players have become so scared of losing and of being over-analysed. Gee, if I'm feeling it, I can't imagine what Mike Atherton's going through!'

The South Africans had to make something happen. They dropped Kallis and called up Paul Adams.

IN PORT ELIZABETH before the fourth Test, Hansie drove to the airport to meet Bertha. It was Christmas and the wives and families were coming to join the boys. Bertha's incoming flight from Bloemfontein was delayed so her husband used the opportunity to welcome those team-mates who were arriving from Cape Town. He particularly wanted to meet the new boy and make him feel at home.

Cronjé immediately spotted Big Mac shepherding a young man into the arrivals hall. He was wearing the team's distinctive Nike T-shirt. Aha, Paul Adams. Hansie walked up to him. 'Hi, howzit, welcome to Port Elizabeth! It's really nice to have you here. I hope you have a good time.'

The youngster looked taken aback. 'Oh, thanks very much,' he replied in surprise.

At that very moment Cronjé spotted a familiar face walking through the arrivals gate. It was undoubtedly Paul Adams. The embarrassed skipper realised the mistaken identity. The youngster he had greeted was actually McMillan's stepson, Ryan, who didn't mind one bit that the South African cricket captain had taken the trouble of welcoming him personally to Port Elizabeth.

Adams, meanwhile, was anxious and excited. At 18 years 340 days, he would become the youngest player to represent South Africa in a Test match. That honour had belonged to Arthur Ochse who, in 1889, was 19 years and one day old when he, too, made his début against England at St George's Park. Adams rather hoped the similarities would end there because Osche played only two Test matches in total.

Gogga's rise had been meteoric. In just five first-class matches so far he had taken 32 wickets with his mixture of mystery and mayhem. 'I just laugh!' he chuckled when asked how he reacted to batsmen groping after his tricky deliveries.

In order to protect him from the glare of unexpected fame, the UCBSA formed a tight cordon to shield him from growing media demands and the fans' adulation. This also meant having to change his home telephone number to throw admiring females off his scent. It was very important, said Bacher, that he keep his feet on the ground and remain focused.

The now famous brass band at St George's Park, with its attendant vocal backing, positively outdid itself at this festive time when Gogga was tossed the ball for the first time in his first Test. 'I was very excited and the band kept me going,' he said after a first-day spell of 32-10-73-2. Woolmer was also excited. 'He looks like he's been playing Test cricket for 15 years ... and I hope he does, too!'

Steve Tshwete was also in the ground when Adams came on to bowl. 'It was an absolutely magic moment,' enthused the new minister of sport later that day. 'To me his presence goes far beyond perhaps winning a Test match. In a way it's a message to a nation ... this is the way we must go.'

Adams finished the first innings with figures of three for 75. His victims were Atherton for top score of 72, Thorpe for 27, and Martin for 4, leaving England's 263 well short of South Africa's 428. In the second innings, he had only one success, trapping England's new No 3 Jason Gallian lbw for 28. At this stage England had already opted to play out for a draw, resisting the challenge of scoring 328 runs in 99 overs against a South African team that, in truth, was itself showing signs of negativity. Still, England's ultra-cautious approach seemed partly to confirm Cronjé's opinion that they were too scared to fail lest they be slaughtered by the press. Atherton, in any event, had already become a victim of both the English and South African media, portrayed as a mean-spirited 'Captain Grumpy' who seemed to derive little enjoyment from his cricket. It did not help his cause when it was revealed that he had destroyed a plastic chair in the dressing room after being given out to a disputed catch at the wicket off Adams.

After the match, Cronjé met up again with Kepler Wessels, who had been watching the Test on his home ground. 'He told me that the pressure on England would become too great and that they would eventually fold. The big difference was that while we had been playing ourselves into winning positions at both the Wanderers and St George's Park, England were always battling to save the Tests. I couldn't sense what was going on in their dressing room, but it was true that they were always hanging on for a draw.'

The Boxing Day Test had not been a good one for Cronjé, who failed to get past single figures in both innings, but the captain was still encouraged by some of his team-mates' performances. Kirsten hit two half centuries, Cullinan was out in the 90s for the third time in Tests, Rhodes and McMillan each scored 49, Richardson had delighted his home fans with an innings of 84, and Pollock chipped in with an invaluable 32 in the second innings to help Kirsten turn the tide from a shaky 69 for six to the eventual declaration on 162 for nine.

As for Gogga, his first taste of Test cricket was one he would never forget. Encouraged by his team-mates and the carnival atmosphere in the big Christmas holiday crowd, he was not overawed. Cronjé saw in him a maturity beyond his years, and liked the way he continually tried to work out the batters. 'Give him a bit of time, and he'll win a Test match for us,' Hansie confidently told some of his team-mates.

He did not need to remind them that the Test they had to win was the next one. After four draws in succession it was time to break the deadlock once and for all. It was time for Allan Donald.

'Whenever I need a wicket,' mused Hansie once, 'I would toss the ball to A.D. I don't care what team I'm playing for, as long as he's in it!'

At Newlands on the second day of 1996, the skipper tossed the new ball to his favourite fast bowler. He had to rely heavily on his main bowlers because he had decided to leave out Matthews again and opted for an extra batsman by way of recalling Kallis to play on his home ground. Donald, Pollock, McMillan and Adams had to carry the attack, with support from Kallis and possibly Cronjé himself.

Not for the first or last time, Donald just made it a little easier for his captain. He dismissed Atherton for a duck in the seventh over – before a run had even been scored – and went on to take five for 46. After electing to bat on a pitch that made everyone feel uneasy, England were bowled out for 153 in 69 overs. The only batsman to look anything like a threat was the South African-born Robin Smith. Thrust now into England's problematical No 3 position, he had reached 66 when Adams clean-bowled him. It was a dismissal that raised the rafters of his home ground where, ironically, Gogga had never played before. It had always been his dream to play at Newlands and now he was taking the chance in the best possible way. He was determined to make this a match to remember. So, too, were the batsmen. The bowlers had done their job and it was now up to them to turn the screws...

Kirsten 23, Hudson 0, Cronjé 12, Cullinan 62, Rhodes 16, McMillan 11, Kallis 7, Pollock 4, Donald 3. Cullinan's fourth half-century of the series was the only standout. All the hard work had gone down the tubes and, at 171 for nine, South Africa's lead of 18 was barely an advantage. Richardson was joined by the last man, Adams.

At St George's Park, Gogga had faced five balls in all without scoring a run. In his entire first-class career, he had faced only 16 for a grand total of four runs. He walked to the crease now with the new ball due. It was just after tea on the second day.

Richardson, 18 not out, watched him approach. 'Hey, don't worry, you've played bowlers like this before,' said Swinger reassuringly.

'Oh, no, I haven't!' replied Gogga unblinkingly.

At the bowler's end, Atherton was talking to 'Destroyer' Malcolm, who was clutching the new ball. 'Give him the short-pitched stuff that they give to our tail-enders,' commanded the England captain.

Malcolm had not played at Durban when Pollock and Donald put on 72 runs for the last wicket. In fact, the big fast bowler had not played a part in the series at all since the Wanderers Test a month earlier when he took six wickets. There was bad blood between him and the manager, Illingworth, who had not disguised his belief that Malcolm was unresponsive to coaching and was not entirely fit.

At Newlands, Malcolm was still wicketless when he took the new ball against the little tail-ender. His captain's instructions were clear: 'Blow him away!'

Adams took guard. The first ball went for a quick single but Cork's aimless throw carried for four overthrows. The kid from the Cape Flats had scored a five to open his account in Test cricket. He took a deep breath; there was a hint of a smile.

Malcolm was not listening to his captain. A couple of misdirected half-volleys screamed past wicketkeeper Russell for four leg-byes each. He was not pressuring the young batsman. Adams settled, intent on offering a straight, defensive bat to anything that approached the line of his stumps. The next seven overs brought 31 runs, 26 of them, including the eight leg-byes, from Malcolm's end.

Richardson's plan had been to farm as much of the bowling away from his partner. Now he realised this was not necessary. The kid could bat! Three consecutive balls from offspinner Mike Watkinson went for 4, 2, 1. And when Cork, the team's most successful bowler, advanced down the pitch and glared murderously at the callow youth, Adams responded by giving him a huge wink.

Such cheek! The vibrant Newlands crowd was on its feet, rocking, singing, cheering, yelling, while in the cauldron of the heady, hungover New Year celebrations, Gogga and Swinger were calling the tune, picking their shots, growing the lead stroke by stroke. England, meanwhile, were wilting like men suffering through the morning after the night before. Up in the dressing room, Ray Illingworth was fuming. Richardson moved on to his 50, his seventh in Test cricket, and Adams hit one cracking square drive that raced to the boundary as if struck by a top-order star.

New Year at Newlands has a chemistry of its own, a fusion of time and place that somehow guarantees some form of cricketing explosion. Year after year the expectant crowds flock back, knowing that something unusual is bound to happen under the shadow of the great mountain backdrop. The glorious cameo now playing out before them might well have been beyond even the wildest expectation. The beauty of it was that it lasted long enough – 68 minutes in all – before Adams finally perished to a fine slip catch by Hick off Martin. He had scored 29 runs, including three fours, in just 38 balls. Richardson's two-and-a-half-hour vigil was over. He was 54 not out. Most important, the gallant pair had added 73 runs in 90 balls, the third-best partnership for the tenth wicket by South Africa in a Test. At 244 all out, the lead was now a respectable 91 runs.

In just over an hour, an unlikely partnership had turned the Test. Signs of dejection, so much in evidence in the South African dressing room during the tea interval, had now firmly transposed to the England camp. It soon became apparent that their spirit was broken.

Before the second day's play could end, England would have to bat out seven overs. In the fifth over, Donald struck again. Atherton on 10 edged a sharp lifter into Richardson's gloves, and England's key batsman was gone. The Newlands crowd had got more than even they had bargained for.

The third day, or all that was needed of it, belonged largely to Pollock. Whereas Donald had been the arch-destroyer in the first innings, the ginger-haired 'Polly' now emerged to turn his consistently impressive bowling into real wicket-taking success. When he dismissed the last England batsman on a total of 157, his career-best figures were five for 32. Between them, Donald and Adams shared the other four, and Adams took two catches as well to ensure that the game at Newlands would be nothing less than a 'dream match'.

The one wicket that did not fall to a bowler was Thorpe's. On 59 the left-hander hit a ball from Adams to Hudson at backward square. Hudson whipped it back to the bowler.

Cronjé was central to the controversy that followed. He recalls the incident: 'Gogga's hands were very close to the stumps but I believed the ball hit and Thorpe was clearly out. When the umpire, Dave Orchard, said "Not out", I thought that Paul must have hit the bails off with his hands. I went to him and asked, "Did you hit the bails off?" He said "No!" I then thought, hang on a sec, then this guy's out. So I walked up to Orchard and said – with my hands in my pockets and in a friendly way – "If you're not sure, why don't you use the television?" I mean, the technology was there so why not use it if there was any doubt about Gogga's hands.'

Cronjé deliberately kept his hands in his pocket to resist making the distinctive signal that umpires use to call in the third umpire's television replay. He knew that fielding captains are forbidden from making any outward demonstration that might be construed as dissent. In his view, he was not putting any undue pressure on the umpire; he was merely making a suggestion that might help him.

He was also convinced that Thorpe was out because he could not help but overhear the cries from the hospitality suites that enjoyed the benefit of watching a replay of the incident on their television monitors. 'Out, out!' they were yelling.

Orchard conferred with fellow umpire, Steve Randell, by which time Thorpe was protesting to Cronjé. 'Hang on a bit, he's made his decision!' complained the batsman. Cronjé replied, 'If the technology's there, why not use it?'

The umpires agreed to call for the television replay. It showed that Thorpe was out of his ground, and that the ball, and not Adams's hands, had hit the stumps. He was given out.

Up in the animated press box, the English media were up in arms. 'Mob rule!' they complained. 'Cronjé is clearly out of line.'

'I was slated all right,' remembers Hansie, 'but all I ever wanted was the truth, the right decision.'

By the time England were all out, there were still 35 overs remaining on the third day. South Africa needed 67 runs to win the match, and the series. Kirsten and Hudson did not hang about. Thirteen boundaries raced to the pickets in quick succession, and the required runs were on the board within 16 overs without the loss of a wicket.

As the South Africans celebrated a glorious victory with more than two days to spare, their captain was questioned at length about the Thorpe run-out affair. He was later hauled on to the carpet by the match referee, Clive Lloyd, who fined him half his match fee for appealing for the replay against regulations laid down by the International Cricket Council. Some said it was money well spent because it heightened the need for technology to be utilised properly in the game.

The British tabloid press took another view. On 5 January, the *Daily Mirror* ran the banner headline 'SCUMBOKS' above a cartoon of a springbok in a white floppy hat urinating on cricket's law book. Inside the paper, a double-page spread was emblazoned with the words 'Hansie up if you lot are ... CHEATS!'

The report began: 'South Africa's captain Hansie Cronjé should have been the proudest cricketer on earth today. Instead he stands accused of being a bully-boy after being fined for an outrageous show of bad sportsmanship.'

ON WHAT WAS originally intended to be the fourth day of the fifth Test, 5 January 1996, two unexpected disclosures of some significance were made. Cronjé confided that the team's hangover count was close to zero, and Matthew Engel revealed that South Africa were now the undisputed current world champions of Test cricket. The second was probably more startling, coming as it did from the editor of the *Wisden Cricketers' Almanack,* the most respected record book in world cricket.

Cronjé's admission was in keeping with the professional outlook he had instilled in his clean-cut team. Over an early breakfast the day after the series victory, he reflected, 'Maybe three years ago after a big victory some of the guys struggled a bit the next morning, but these days they are much more professional in their outlook, and use every scrap of their spare time to be with their families.'

Indeed, the South African captain had already calculated that during the next three months he would spend exactly five days with Bertha who, now married for eight months, must have been wondering why golfing widows kick up such a fuss.

Engel, meanwhile, had been doing some calculations of his own. Having already pushed for the establishment of a World Championship of Cricket based on performances in Test series, he felt it wrong that the holders of the World Cup were too easily called the 'world champions'. He rightly argued that performances in a single limited-overs tournament could hardly surpass achievements in the Test arena, and had therefore worked out a simple league system based on points awarded for series won and shared between the nine Test-playing nations over a two- or four-year cycle. According to his formula, one-off Tests also constituted a series.

In Cape Town on the morning after the Test triumph, the editor of *Wisden* needed to find something interesting to write for his weekly column in *The Guardian* (this newspaper's readers are not particularly interested in yet another rehash of yet another miserable England performance), so he set out to calculate Test cricket's league standings from a cutoff date of 1990.

'I fully expected Australia to be the reigning champions,' he explained, 'but, no, I have to admit that it is South Africa who are top of the log. As the record shows during that period, they have beaten India, Sri Lanka, New Zealand, Pakistan, England, Zimbabwe and have shared series with England and twice with Australia.'

On the *Wisden* Plan league, Australia were placed second, followed by the West Indies, Pakistan, India, England and Sri Lanka tied, New Zealand and finally Zimbabwe. This admission must have been hard for an Englishman to make, particularly so soon after such a big drubbing, but the relative standings of South Africa and England were of no surprise whatsoever to anyone who had watched Hansie and the boys outplay Atherton's team for much of the series.

The extent to which England were outperformed was measured by the way they collapsed like a pack of cards inside three days at Newlands, a situation already predicted by Wessels when he chatted to Cronjé in Port Elizabeth. The pressure on England had also increased with the arrival of Adams.

'It was always my dream to captain our first development player in the Test team,' enthused Cronjé, 'but I never imagined it would happen so soon. Before this summer, no one had even heard of him. He has made it entirely on merit and is a great asset, the perfect role model. He reminds me a lot of the golfer Ernie Els: cool-headed, never bothered, always capable of playing his natural game. I must admit I didn't realise he was such a strong character. I think he reminded us how important it is for South Africa to play its own brand of positive cricket.'

In the strict meaning of the word, Adams was not exactly a 'development' player who had come up through the ranks of the under-privileged township cricketers. His route instead had followed the more establishment path through Plumstead Boys' High and the Western Province Cricket Academy. Still, within the proud ethos of Cape coloured cricket, he was most certainly a demographic leveller who, in the unlikely role of batsman, had helped turn a Test series upside down.

One small question remained, and it concerned the No 3 spot. In the view of the critics, Cronjé had done himself no favours by batting in a position where, in his last six innings, he had totalled only 113 runs. 'I decided to bat there because I didn't want to disturb our middle order where guys like Daryll and Jonty have been performing,' he explained. 'Maybe in time Jacques Kallis will be the answer, but I'm not in this side for the sake of Hansie Cronjé. I'm in it for the team. I will always be second to the team's interests.'

THE TEST SERIES against England had cast the spotlight on the respective fast bowling of the two teams. Malcolm had arrived as the 'destroyer', but left under a dark cloud of failure. Illingworth had blamed him squarely for the Newlands defeat and he, in turn, accused the management of unfair treatment. Later the two would harangue each other publicly and be severely reprimanded by the Test and County Cricket Board. Illingworth, the feisty Yorkshireman who had established himself as the supremo of the England team, soon disappeared from the scene altogether, and more than a year went by before Malcolm re-emerged in international cricket.

Donald and Pollock had no such problems. They had been central to South Africa's success, taking 35 wickets between them in the five Tests. Donald's bowling at Newlands won him Man of the Match. His 19 wickets overall brought him Man of the Series.

Cronjé watched him in awe as he received his awards. He remembered the times all those years ago when they had had such fun as boys in Bloemfontein – all elbows and knees and lightning pace, the pretensions at being a batsman, and the long spindly legs pumping the pedals on those daily bicycle rides. He recalled the time after their schooldays when he and Sling had shared a house together, when his friend's puzzling lifestyle included waking at 9 am, immediately downing a litre of Coca-Cola, returning to bed to sleep till lunchtime, and then rising again to consume vast amounts of food. Here now was one of the fittest, leanest and fastest bowlers you could ever wish to see. He just shook his head and marvelled.

ON THE AFTERNOON of 16 January 1996, Hansie Cronjé drove his hired car back to Johannesburg International Airport from Pretoria. It had been a memorable luncheon with President Mandela, and his thoughts lingered on having witnessed the great man's first meeting with Basil D'Oliveira. Yes, thought Hansie, life does come full circle.

He was also on a circular route now, about to board the return flight to Durban to rejoin the boys in their battle with England, needing one more win to clinch the limited-overs series. Fit again, Fanie was back in the side, 'A.D.' and Polly were playing like stars, and young 'Kalahari' Kallis was starting to get among the big runs.

Pollock was the real revelation. On his one-day international début at Newlands a week earlier he had blasted 66 at a run a ball before shooting out England seven runs short of their victory target with figures of four for 34. Four days later he again won the Man of the Match award at the Wanderers when he dismissed Atherton first ball as part of an opening spell of 6-2-8-3. The only match South Africa had not won so far was at Springbok Park, where Snelly's 63 in 65 balls as the recalled pinch-hitter was rather negated by Atherton's 85.

Yet, on the question of batting highlights, nothing could yet touch Gary Kirsten's *tour de force* in the fourth encounter at Centurion Park. Up until this stage Gazza had not been an automatic choice for the limited-overs team. When he did play he was sometimes used only as a stabilising batter in the lower middle-order. He was not particularly pleased with this arrangement and felt he had as much to offer as a regular opener.

At Centurion he was given that chance, and he converted it into the only century of the seven-match series. He and his old mate Hudders hurried the total to 73 in the first 15 overs. Hudson hit 72 in 84 balls and Kirsten reached a career-best 116 in 125 balls. A glorious opening stand of 156 was just what Cronjé needed to regain his batting confidence, and his whirlwind 47 in 46 balls steered his team to a handsome seven-wicket victory.

As for the *Daily Mirror*'s assertion that the South African captain was a cheat, Hansie now made all his accusers eat their words in a situation rich in irony. After a lofted shot to long-on seemed certain to take him to his half-century, Cronjé watched as Thorpe ran adjacent to the boundary rope to get under the steepling ball, took the catch ... but then stepped backwards. Umpire Wilf Diedricks immediately signalled a six. The crowd was on its feet, Thorpe was protesting, and Cronjé was already walking back to the dressing room. Whether or not it was in response to the fieldsman's 'request' was never certain, but Diedricks now decided to ask for the third umpire's ruling from the television replay. It showed that even though Thorpe had taken a step backwards, his foot had not crossed the rope. The catch was good. Diedricks looked around for Cronjé in order to signal his dismissal, but he was too late. The skipper knew that the catch was fair, and he had long since departed. For both Thorpe and Diedricks – ironically the two central characters in Cronjé's two brushes with authority – there was much food for thought.

Back in Durban, the captain rose early on the morning of 17 January, the day he planned to play England out of the series. Victory would put the boys 4–1 up with two to play, and he asked them for one more big effort. That afternoon at Kingsmead, Donald blasted out the top four England batters in a row, and later that night Kallis joined Cronjé in setting a new South African third-wicket record of 118. 'Kalahari' was in such fine form in scoring his first half-century in international cricket that he actually assumed the senior role in the partnership. His innings of 67 came in 107 balls, while Cronjé, who was dropped three times, was happy to play along for 78 in 133. Victory by five wickets. The deed was done.

Gogga Adams, meanwhile, was far from forgotten. He had been hit out of the attack by Hick in his limited-overs début at the start of the series at Newlands, during which two overs went for 18 runs. He did not like all the talk about it being too risky to take him to the forthcoming World Cup in Pakistan. Back in the side now for the sixth match at East London, he was crowned Man of the Match after skittling three batsmen, including Hick, as England disintegrated to 115. The next day, 20 January, was Gogga's birthday and the boys gave him a party, complete with paper hats and balloons. On the big chocolate cake were 19 candles.

Still, there was sadness.

Swinger Richardson, the 36-year-old backbone of the team, had broken his left index finger while standing up to Kallis. He was out of the side and out of the World Cup.

For the final match at St George's Park, 25-year-old Steve Palframan received his senior call-up as the new keeper. It was a good start for him because South Africa won the match and the series 6–1. For his 13 wickets at an average of 16.30, and some lusty batting besides, Pollock was the popular choice as Man of the Series. To have made his international début in the midst of 'Goggamania' might somehow have blurred the reality that Polly, perhaps, was the true find of the season.

BEFORE THE SUMMER was over, Cronjé produced one final masterstroke. It came in the Benson & Hedges Series final at the Wanderers where Transvaal were captained by an old adversary, the former New Zealand skipper Ken Rutherford, who had quit his country to settle in Johannesburg.

Rutherford's team struck a crippling early blow when they dismissed Free State's favourite pinch-hitter Franklyn Stephenson to his seventh ball, only to discover, at their peril, that Cronjé had a new trick up his sleeve. He immediately sent in a second pinch-hitter, Bradley Player, who crashed 83 runs from 50 balls for Free State to amass a 45-over record total of 290 for six.

Player later took three for 36 in his nine overs to clinch a massive 142-run victory. Hansie's boys had done it again – their third successive B&H title was in the bag.

15

For Gazza, Read Legend

O N A SUNDAY AFTERNOON in Karachi, Pakistan's biggest city over-looking the Arabian Sea, the South African players were in their hotel rooms and the tour selectors were in conference. It was 5.15 pm. An hour later they would all assemble for the team meeting at which the next day's playing line-up would be announced and the battle plan discussed.

At 5.45 pm the selection meeting ended. It was now the captain's duty to embark on a mission he hated. The players knew all about it. They waited in their rooms. If the captain knocked, the news would not be good; if he didn't, well, everything was fine. They hated those knocks because it meant they were not on the team sheet. The captain would explain to each individual why he was not playing.

Hansie Cronjé knocked. 'I'm sorry, Fanie...'; he knocked again, 'Sorry, A.D....'

It was 10 March 1996. The next day South Africa would play the West Indies in the World Cup quarter-final. They would do so without the experienced fast bowling duo of Fanie de Villiers and Allan Donald.

After the scheduled team meeting, Cronjé went off alone. His team-mates wondered what had become of him; why he had suddenly become so unsociable. It wasn't like him at all.

'I felt so sorry for Allan and Fanie that I just wanted to be by myself. They were the two hardest calls I've ever had to make.'

SOUTH AFRICA BADLY wanted the World Cup. It looked to its cricketers to complete what it believed was a pre-ordained triple triumph in the space of nine joyous months. Its rugby team had won the Rugby World Cup against the odds in June 1995; its soccer team had just become champions of all-Africa by winning the Cup of Nations; and, amid the incredible fervour that now gripped the Rainbow Nation as it took one

237

major sporting prize after another, came the fervent belief that Hansie and the boys would provide the crowning glory.

The squad that carried the hopes of a nation was: Hansie Cronjé (captain), Craig Matthews (vice-captain), Paul Adams, Daryll Cullinan, Fanie de Villiers, Allan Donald, Andrew Hudson, Jacques Kallis, Gary Kirsten, Brian McMillan, Steve Palframan, Shaun Pollock, Jonty Rhodes and Patrick Symcox.

Based on their burgeoning prowess in limited-overs cricket, and mindful of their country's high expectations, the team set out to deliver the goods. They tackled the task with immense panache and with amazing zeal and confidence. Before leaving for Pakistan the squad spent several days thoroughly preparing themselves at an isolated country resort. They were taken painstakingly through one-day disciplines; they each compiled a three-page document based on psychological exercises; they climbed sand dunes, had team-building sessions, and played golf and tennis. They did everything but practise cricket.

Their match venues, practice facilities and hotel accommodation in Pakistan were all carefully checked out in advance. Woolmer might have lost his first six matches as coach in that country, but he had learnt many lessons from that harsh experience and was determined to use it to the team's advantage. In the limited-overs series against England they had performed with growing confidence and success, upping the tempo of their game, experimenting with combinations and trying out innovative techniques and, under the progressive leadership of Cronjé and Woolmer, they had been given the licence to play with greater freedom without risk of repercussions.

'Don't be afraid to express yourselves,' Hansie reminded them in the days leading up to the World Cup. 'Rather get out playing your natural game than get bogged down trying to play some other way. Just be yourselves, and have fun!'

The sixth World Cup was contested all over the Asian subcontinent. It was an unwieldy arrangement that would become a logistical nightmare with matches scheduled throughout Pakistan, in Sri Lanka and at no fewer than 17 venues across the width and breadth of India.

For their Group B round-robin matches, the South Africans played exclusively in Pakistan. They were in a class of their own. In the space of 20 days they played and won all five of their matches at Rawalpindi, Karachi and Faisalabad.

They bowled out the United Arab Emirates for 152, contained New Zealand to 178, dismissed England for 152, checked the rampant Pakistanis on 242, and dispatched Holland for 168.

In their turn at bat, the boys rewrote the record books. Kirsten's undefeated 188 against the UAE surpassed the previous World Cup high of 181 set by Vivian Richards for the West Indies against Sri Lanka in 1987; and Kirsten and Hudson's opening stand of 186 against Holland erased the previous World Cup record of 182 held by Rick McCosker and Alan Turner of Australia.

Against the UAE at Rawalpindi, Kirsten was padding up when he noticed a bright bandanna in the colours of the South African flag that Cronjé always carried in his kit bag. 'Do you mind if I wear it?' he asked his captain.

'Go for it,' replied Hansie, 'I hope it brings you luck.'

When Kirsten reached his century, he raised his bat to acknowledge the applause and immediately removed his helmet to display the South African flag tied around his head in the form of a *doek*.

Cronjé was batting with him at the time in the midst of a 116-run partnership. 'I was so proud of him. It showed just how much it meant for him to be playing for his country under its new flag at the World Cup. I told him to keep the bandanna.'

Kirsten, in his distinctive headgear and raising his bat to signal another individual milestone, was a sight the world would witness on many other occasions in the months ahead.

At Rawalpindi, the only disappointment about his big innings was that it fell just one run short of Richards's all-time record one-day international score of 189 not out against England at Old Trafford in 1984. Gazza batted in the mistaken belief that he had already broken the record when he went past the great West Indian's World Cup best of 181.

Against the UAE, the South Africans totalled 321 for two – their highest total in limited-overs cricket – but against Holland they went even better. This time Hudson led the way with a 161 in 132 balls in a total of 328 for three.

In the field, the game plan was both simple and effective. The bowlers were required to bowl one side of the wicket and the fielders were expected to catch and stop and return everything that came their way. When the bowling was good, the team ground out its advantage; when it wasn't up to scratch, the fielders took control. *The Hindu* newspaper enthused, 'It is impossible for a shot to pass through the ground or in the air if someone like Jonty Rhodes stands vigil at point. Anything 10 metres from him is a sure stop and, beyond that, a diving stop.'

For sheer consistency and excellence, these superlative displays of out-cricket both amazed and thrilled the cricket fans of the subcontinent.

They had never seen anything like it before. Eight run-outs came from an uncanny knack to hit the stumps with full-blooded throws or well-aimed underam darts. Against Pakistan, Cronjé engineered the turnaround when he ran out the big-hitting Inzamam-ul-Haq; against New Zealand it was Rhodes and Kirsten who were on target to run out Nathan Astle, Adam Parore and Chris Harris; and against England, Symcox and De Villiers threw out Alec Stewart and Phil DeFreitas. All the time, McMillan's close catching on both sides of the wicket was a crucial weapon.

Discipline and dedication were the cornerstones of the effort. Even before the game against lowly Holland, the players practised their skills for four straight hours. From the harsh lesson of 1994, the Dutch would never be underestimated again. They paid dearly for this attention, defeat by 160 runs.

Cronjé gave all the credit to Woolmer for the team's remarkable per-formances in the round-robin section. 'You've got to take your hat off to the man because he turned the whole one-day thing around. At Warwickshire, he and the county's captain, Dermot Reeve, had pretty much got the one-day game down to a T, and now he taught us every-thing he had learned. The players knew exactly what to do and when to do it. We learnt how to upset the spinners and to score more quickly against them. Until then, the spinners had been our downfall, often bowling their 10 overs for 25 runs and taking two or three wickets. Bob taught us where to look to hit, he gave us a lot of options of where to score against certain bowlers; he gave our bowlers more variety and dif-ferent field settings, and he showed them how to bowl in the first 15 overs and how to bowl at the death. My job was to take these skills on to the field and put them into practice. After the game I would discuss with him any areas of concern and he would go away to find the solutions and the answers.'

From his early days as coach, the cerebral Woolmer had equipped himself with a laptop computer which was always at his fingertips. Into this he constantly fed information on both his own players and their opponents, analysing their strengths and weaknesses in different game situations and then plotting strategy for each individual.

Off the field, the players maintained a high level of dignity and were popular wherever they went. They also had the usual fun and games and Hansie again emerged as one of the main pranksters. His worst trick was played on Paddy Upton. The fitness coach was looking for some malaria pills so Hansie came to the rescue and handed him two pills. Unbeknown to Paddy, they were sleeping tablets.

In the public domain, Cronjé led by example, the master of diplomacy and goodwill. After victory over England at Rawalpindi, he addressed a packed post-match press conference. On the table in front of him lay a battery of tape recorders, carefully placed there by reporters who did not want to miss a single word or a quotable quote from the well-liked captain. Midway through the meeting, with questions and answers flying back and forth, Cronjé held up his hand to call a halt. The reporters were puzzled because they had not yet finished their business with him.

Hansie picked up one of the portable tape recorders. 'Whose is this?' he asked. A Pakistani reporter at the back of the room claimed ownership. 'Your tape's come to an end and it's switched itself off. May I turn it over and start it up again for you?'

Once he had performed this thoughtful task on behalf of the grateful newsman, Cronjé invited more questions. When he was done, he made way for the England captain to take his turn at the head of the table.

'Grumpy' Atherton was not in a good mood. He had been dismissed by Pollock for a duck and South Africa's continued domination of England had inflicted defeat by 78 runs. After mumbling some answers, Atherton was asked to speak up. 'No,' he shot back abruptly.

Asghar Ali, a reporter from the Pakistan Press Association, asked a question. His English was only passable and Atherton looked puzzled. 'Try that again,' he said. When Asghar repeated his question, the England captain complained, 'I don't know what you are asking.'

Asghar persisted. Atherton cast his eyes disdainfully to the ceiling and then, looking round the room, commanded, 'Will someone remove this buffoon?'

The Pakistan press corps was up in arms and Asghar was deeply offended. 'I thought he had called me a baboon,' he told *The Daily Telegraph* later. 'I don't think I should have been embarrassed by the England captain like that.'

Atherton apologised the next day but the image of the England team had not been enhanced in Pakistani eyes.

The format for the World Cup was seriously flawed. While it was perfectly acceptable for the UAE, Holland and Kenya to make their débuts in an expanded 12-team competition, the actual structure of the tournament left a lot to be desired. At the 1992 World Cup the round-robin matches had automatically produced four semi-finalists; this time the teams were divided into groups of six for an exhausting series of league matches that would ultimately produce eight quarter-finalists.

It took three weeks of often meaningless round-robin action, during which teams were moved interminably from pillar to post, to bring about the largely predictable elimination of the three newcomers and Zimbabwe for the important knockout stages. It was then that the real tournament began and it was all jammed into 10 days.

Group B was dominated by South Africa, the only country to win all five of their games. In Group A, Sri Lanka were easily the top team at the end of the round robin, but their passage to the quarter-finals was never going to be a problem. The reason for this was that both Australia and West Indies had controversially decided not to play any of their matches scheduled in Sri Lanka. A fortnight before the start of the tournament a terrorist bomb had exploded in Colombo, killing 90 people, and the Aussies and West Indians chose to forfeit their matches rather than go there. Both countries came under fire for this decision, but the Australians were the prime target. They were accused of using the Colombo bomb blast as an excuse for boycotting a country where they believed they would be most unwelcome anyway.

Earlier in the summer the Sri Lankans and Australians had been involved in an acrimonious series in Australia which produced any number of unsavoury incidents. The trouble started with accusations of ball tampering by the Sri Lankans and then escalated when umpires Darrell Hair and Ross Emerson no-balled leading wicket-taker Muttiah Muralitharan for throwing. The Sri Lankans responded by criticising the umpiring, and becoming involved in verbal and even physical brushes with the Australian players; Shane Warne disclosed that he and several of his team-mates had received death threats; and finally the Sri Lankans refused to shake hands with skipper Mark Taylor at the final presentation ceremony. Elsewhere on the subcontinent, the Australians were already an unpopular team because of sensational claims by Warne, Mark Waugh and Tim May that the Pakistan captain Salim Malik had once offered them bribes to fix matches.

The upshot of all this was that Sri Lanka automatically received the match points for the cancelled games against Australia and the West Indies, yet such were the imperfections of the format that both these countries could afford to forgo these points and still make it through to the quarter-finals.

THE ONE VENUE in Pakistan that was not on the South Africans' schedule was the historic garden city of Lahore, home of the Shalimar Gardens, the Jehangir Mausoleum and the Baadshahi Mosque, all of them dating back to the seventeenth century. It was also the site of the Qaddafi Stadium where the World Cup final was due to be played on

17 March. It was to this ground and to that match that the South Africans aspired.

In the meantime, Karachi would be the scene of their quarter-final against the West Indies.

The West Indies were not in good shape. The nadir of their round-robin campaign came when lowly Kenya pulled off the greatest upset in World Cup history, bowling out the former champions for 93 to bag an amazing 73-run victory. The West Indies had looked half a side for most of their league matches. This was not surprising because they were a team riven by tension and in-fighting: captain Richie Richardson and recalcitrant golden-boy Brian Lara had fallen out, their officials were at each other's throats, and fans back home were calling for heads to roll.

The loss to Kenya was their darkest hour, but four days after that humiliation they picked up the pieces to beat Australia by four wickets in their first worthwhile result of the tournament. It was a personal triumph for Richardson who, with the wolves baying for his blood, produced a magnificent innings of 93 not out and immediately announced that he would retire from cricket once the World Cup was over. Lara's innings of 60 was the first time in the tournament that the world's top batsman had passed the half-century mark. Had he suddenly regained his form, or was it just fleeting?

The South Africans were wary of their opponents. Cronjé warned his team-mates, 'They could be very dangerous in this situation. Remember, we're into the knockouts now so we can't afford a single slip-up. Defeat means we're out of it!'

Krish Mackerdhuj and Ali Bacher arrived in Karachi from South Africa to join the touring party at the start of the crucial knockout section. Their hope was that they would follow the team all the way to the final, but Bacher cautioned, 'The West Indies are an unpredictable and brilliant side. They are dangerous when they are wounded.'

Victory for South Africa would also equal the world record of 11 consecutive victories for which the West Indies claimed proud ownership. It would be a big game, there was so much at stake ... why on earth were they not playing their most experienced fast bowlers, and Donald in particular?

'It was a very difficult decision,' remembers Hansie. 'In our previous game at Karachi, the Pakistan batsman had taken on Allan and hit him for 50 runs in eight overs. The conditions there looked better suited to our spin bowlers and Paul Adams seemed like a good option because the West Indies had never seen him. So we decided to play both Gogga and Symmo.'

In the case of De Villiers it was reasoned that he was too short of match practice. He had broken down at the start of the tournament with an ankle injury and had played only one match since then, taking two wickets against England and hitting 13 runs from 11 balls. Still, he was the man for the big occasion, with plenty of guts, determination and character ... and this was a very big occasion.

Lara's half-century against Australia was not a flash in the pan. At the National Stadium in Karachi, he hit 111 in 94 balls. He had started cautiously, picking up only four runs in his first 18 deliveries, but then he cut loose. His 50 came in 45 balls and his 100 in 83. Five of his 16 fours came in one over from Symcox.

The South Africans were strangely jittery. Even Jonty dropped a catch at cover point. The left-hander Shivnarine Chanderpaul had scored 25 when he was dropped by Palframan off Pollock, a 'life' that was to prove very costly when measured against his eventual score of 56 as part of a pivotal second-wicket partnership of 138 with the imperious Lara.

The West Indies' total of 264 for eight was good enough. Fine knocks of 54 by Hudson, 69 by Cullinan and 40 by Cronjé lifted South African hopes, but it was the West Indian spinners, Jimmy Adams and Roger Harper, who wrapped it all up with seven wickets between them. The left-arm Adams dismissed Hudson, Cullinan and Cronjé, while Harper crushed what remained of South Africa's chances when, in the first over of his second spell, he removed Rhodes, McMillan and Palframan. By the time Symcox hammered Harper for two sixes in one over it was too late; South Africa were all out for 245 with three balls remaining, defeat by 19 runs.

There were no second chances; Hansie and the boys were out of the World Cup.

After the match, Woolmer surveyed the dressing room. Never before had he seen such utter dejection. 'The boys were just sitting there, stunned, shattered. It was a heart-breaking scene. Then one by one they stood up, shook hands, said, "Thanks, it's been a great season, well done," and that was that.'

Donald had watched helplessly from the pavilion. He was deeply hurt at being left out of the team and he was particularly sore that Lara, the overseas professional who had replaced him at Warwickshire in 1994, was the victors' hero and the Man of the Match ... and that he had not had a chance to have a crack at him. 'Alan was fantastic,' recalls Hansie. 'Although he was shattered inside, he rallied around at the end, put his arm around me in commiseration and tried his damnedest to lift the spirits of the boys. It's at moments like these that I realise what a great team man he is.

'I was absolutely stunned by what had happened. I couldn't believe that we were out of it. We had been playing our best cricket up until then, everything had gone 100 per cent to plan, and then we had one bad match. It was so terribly disappointing. I felt very sorry for Bob. He had done everything that was expected of him, and more. It wasn't his fault that we didn't win.'

It didn't much matter now, but Hansie could look back on a tournament in which he averaged 55.20 runs per innings and was twice named Man of the Match. Others who had reason for personal satisfaction were Kirsten, with an average of 78.20, Hudson with 68.75 and Cullinan with 63.75. In spite of not playing in the quarter-final, Donald was still the leading wicket-taker with eight scalps at an economical 15.75 runs each.

Later, Woolmer reflected on a campaign that promised so much until the cruel turnaround at Karachi. 'I personally feel we set the standard at the World Cup. There was no question that we were the best team throughout the league section. And then we fell at the quarter-finals. We fell for a variety of reasons. One of them was Brian Lara. Another was the fact that before the game we had our longest period off between matches and we allowed our focus to shift away from the quarter-final. There were stories about Brian McMillan being offered a contract to play for Surrey (which he later turned down in deference to the UCBSA's wishes) and there was speculation that Jonty Rhodes might be included in the hockey team for the Olympic Games in Atlanta. All these things deflected our focus and it somehow reflected in the field when we put down a couple of catches and were not as sharp as usual. Also our batting, which had been so methodical, came unstuck against the spin of Harper and Adams. Gary Kirsten failed for the first time in the tournament when his boot slipped and dislodged a bail, out hit wicket for 3. And, of course, we left out Allan Donald because we thought the wicket would turn in our favour...'

The World Cup campaign also reminded Cronjé how much he missed Dave Richardson. 'It's only when he's not there that you realise how valuable he is in more ways than one. For the captain, he is a great help on the field, giving advice on bowling changes and field settings. We certainly missed his presence on the field. With his experience we might not have made the mistakes we did. Also, Swinger doesn't say much, but when he does you hear him. As a result he has a tendency to put batters off. He did it against me in provincial cricket and it really cheesed me off. When I told him this, he said he was surprised because he didn't think it really worked.

'He's also a fun guy in his own quiet way. I remember once when Meyrick Pringle was reading *Long Walk to Freedom*, Swinger walked past him and said, "I don't want to spoil the book for you, Pring, but you know that he eventually gets out of jail and becomes president." Pringle tossed the book aside in disgust. "Hell, Swinger, now you've ruined the whole story for me!"'

In the aftermath of Karachi, no one was much interested in frivolity. In trying to find reasons for South Africa's defeat, the critics suggested that the team had not paced itself properly by treating each of the league games as if they were the very final itself. They also noted that South Africa's five victories had been achieved so ruthlessly that there had been little chance for the lower-order to get any decent batting practice. The theories abounded, but they did not change the reality.

In the semi-finals, Australia beat the West Indies by five runs after Richie Richardson's men lost both their nerve and their last eight wickets for 37 runs; and Sri Lanka were awarded the result against India when a crowd riot at Calcutta cut short a match that was rapidly slipping away from the home side. On a black day for Indian cricket, sections of the 100 000-strong crowd were so incensed when their team lost seven wickets for 22 runs that they pelted the ground with bottles and set fire to a section of the seating. Match referee Clive Lloyd immediately called the teams off the field, attempted to restart the match 15 minutes later but, sensing further danger, had no hesitation in awarding it on default to Sri Lanka who were going to win anyway. A report in the *Indian Express* said simply, 'It is impossible today to be Indian and not be ashamed.'

As if pre-ordained, the final at Lahore was played between two bitter rivals who had been kept apart controversially in the league section. In what was perceived by the entire subcontinent to be the proper outcome, Sri Lanka, once the whipping boy of international cricket, comfortably beat Australia by seven wickets in a fairy-tale ending to their tournament and a conquest that was acclaimed around the cricketing world. The measure of the Sri Lankan dominance was seen in one over from Warne who was made to look perfectly ordinary in conceding a six-ball sequence of 6, 4, 2, 1, 4, 4. Sri Lanka's battle plan throughout was built on proficient batting spearheaded by their combative opening pair of Sanath Jayasuriya and Romesh Kaluwitharana, who regularly attacked the first 15 overs of the innings like other teams attack the last 15. Jayasuriya was named the Most Valued Player of the Tournament even before the final was played; of his several belligerent innings none surpassed his 82 from 44 balls against England in the quarter-finals.

Cricket writers were disgruntled that Jayasuriya's contract with the Sri Lankan Cricket Board prevented him from talking to the media. Eager to know what he was saying they listened in to the pitch microphones to catch the odd unauthorised statement. What they regularly heard in his conversations with Kaluwitharana was, 'Don't bother, it's gone for four', or often, 'It's okay, that one's a six!' Those phrases summed up perfectly a diminutive, 1.68 metre-tall batsman who apparently didn't much enjoy running between the wickets but chose instead to hit a wide range of boundaries, not by wanton slogging, but with a wide repertoire of classical, orthodox shots.

The sixth World Cup ended as it had started, in a shambles. The opening ceremony in Calcutta a month earlier had been a badly mismanaged and instantly forgettable occasion, and the closing presentations came amid chaotic scenes that were beyond the control of the security personnel. The Sri Lankan players found themselves caught up in a stampede by spectators and when they got back to their dressing room, having been unable to take part in the traditional lap of honour, they discovered that the winner's cheque of £30 000 had been stolen.

STILL STUNG BY disappointment, Hansie and the boys immediately set out on a brand-new adventure. Since 1981, annual triangular tournaments had been staged in the emirate of Sharjah on the Arabian Gulf, at a lovely cricket oval that was literally a green oasis in the middle of the desert. This was the first time that a South African team would be playing there. Their opponents would be Pakistan and India.

The squad for Sharjah showed two changes from the World Cup. Dave Richardson was back from his injury to replace Steve Palframan, and Allan Donald asked to be rested and was replaced by Derek Crookes. If people were expecting the South Africans to go into their shell after their downfall at Karachi, they were badly mistaken. Their performances at Sharjah were best summed up by Woolmer who described the team as 'awesome ... unmatchable' in winning all five games, including the final against India.

The sight of Kirsten whipping off his helmet to reveal his rainbow-hued bandanna became commonplace as he strung together scores of 106, 39 and 115 against India, and 64 and 32 against Pakistan for a batting average of 89. He was named Man of the Series and also took the Best Fielder prize. Cullinan hit a top score of 110 not out against Pakistan for a batting average of 68.00, Hudson hit two half-centuries with a top score of 94 not out against Pakistan – although he was out first ball to Javagal Srinath in both his matches against India – and Cronjé scored 90 before being run out against India.

Matthews won the tournament's Best Bowler award for his consistently tight line and length that brought him six wickets in all and three for 19 against Pakistan; and Vinnige Fanie also bowled splendidly to end as the team's leading wicket-taker with 10 victims.

Symcox at times impressed as the team's pinch-hitter, saving his best for last when he hit 61 in just 49 balls in a 38-run victory over India in the final. Big Mac was also in a mean mood with the bat in the final. He clubbed 37 runs in 25 balls and two of his three sixes were struck right out of the ground.

It was Kirsten, though, who fittingly won the Man of the Match, batting through the innings for 115 not out, his fourth limited-overs century of the season and the fifth of his career. Amazingly, earlier in the season he had not even been considered as a regular one-day opener but the turning point had clearly come three months earlier when his century against England at Centurion Park cemented his position at the top of the order.

Cronjé was overjoyed at the form of his free-scoring opening batsman. 'For a long time Gary had the reputation of being someone who was able to score 40s and 50s and 60s but could not convert them into hundreds. A lot of people kept saying to him, "Gary, when once you score a hundred you're going to get a lot of them," and how true that was. When the hundreds began to roll, we gave him the nickname 'Legend'. He certainly lived up to it.'

IN THE SOUTHERN hemisphere winter of 1996, Shaun Pollock ventured into county cricket for the first time. He had performed well enough at both the World Cup and Sharjah and now he was booked to have a season with Warwickshire. He obviously went there highly recommended by Woolmer, the county's former coach, and by Donald who was also returning to the Warwickshire staff as the bowling coach.

At the same time, John Commins was appointed captain of a strong South Africa A team for a two-month tour of the United Kingdom. It included Crookes, Klusener, Liebenberg, Bojé, Gibbs, Adams, Palframan, Schultz and Kallis.

Polly started sensationally with Warwickshire. In their opening Benson & Hedges Cup one-day match, he became the first bowler in the history of the competition to take four wickets in four balls. He ended with figures of six for 21.

A few weeks later he scored 107 against Northamptonshire – his maiden first-class century – before being bowled by Curtly Ambrose. He also took six wickets in the match and was warned by the umpire for bowling too many bouncers in one over. Warwickshire certainly liked the look of their fiery, red-haired recruit from Natal.

For the South Africa A team, meanwhile, Herschelle Gibbs was on a roll. The outstanding young Cape Town batsman was busy amassing 867 runs in 14 innings for a batting average of 66.69, the top gun of the touring team. He hit five half-centuries and two centuries, and his consistency was mirrored by scores of 57 and 183 against the MCC, 95 and 85 against Nottinghamshire and 58 and 178 against Surrey.

Unfortunately, the team did not play against Warwickshire where Pollock would have been an interesting opponent.

Crookes was also having a good tour, featuring better with the bat than with the ball. He scored three half-centuries and, in successive matches, hit 105 against Glamorgan and an undefeated 155 from 157 balls against Somerset.

Others to score hundreds were the skipper Commins, Liebenberg and Meyrick Pringle, who was flown in as a replacement for the injured Schultz. The growing injury list included Kallis with a stress fracture and Adams with shin splints and a groin problem.

Because of the injuries, a lot of the bowling burden was shouldered by the never-say-die Klusener. As he had shown in Sri Lanka 12 months before, he had the capacity to bowl long spells in difficult conditions as well as to make useful contributions with the bat. In all he bowled 233 overs, took 31 wickets – twice as many as anyone else – and got five for 74 in the first innings against Somerset. In the match against Nottinghamshire he scored 79 to finish with a tidy batting average of just under 35.

By mid-August Pollock had taken his run tally to over 600 – including a career-best 150 not out against Glamorgan at Edgbaston – and had taken 42 wickets in 13 matches when misfortune struck. His already fragile left ankle gave in on him and there was no way he could continue to play. He was forced to return home for immediate surgery.

Gibbs's England tour did not go unrewarded. After many years of threatening to hit the big time, he finally made the transition when he was named as the only new boy in the 14-man South African squad that would make its first visit to Kenya for a four-nations limited-overs tournament in September 1996. The other visiting teams were the World Cup champions Sri Lanka and Pakistan. Injuries had sidelined Pollock, Adams and Kallis, and into the team came Bojé, Crookes and Gibbs.

'I'm very happy for Herschelle,' said Woolmer. 'I've known him since he was 11 and he showed in England how he has matured as a batsman. His big hundred against the MCC was an innings of supreme class. By playing that way he has said, "Here I am. Take notice of me."'

Amid a growing injury list, further misfortune struck in Kenya when the team lost its vice-captain, Craig Matthews, who pulled up lame with a hamstring injury in the first game against Pakistan and had to return home. The boys would miss him because he was such an integral part of the side and was a ready source of useful and sometimes useless information. His nicknames ranged from 'Stats' to 'Trivial Pursuit' because he had an encyclopaedic knowledge of sport.

Lance Klusener was busy touring Zimbabwe with Natal when he answered the SOS to fly to Kenya as Matthews's replacement. Back in January he had been included for the last three one-dayers against England; in his only game at East London, he did not shape and missed selection for the World Cup. In Kenya now, the closest he got to playing was as the twelfth man in the final match.

South Africa's opening game at the Nairobi Gymkhana ground was a crushing triumph over Pakistan. It was also a fabulous match for Cullinan and Rhodes. Both hit their highest scores in limited-overs internationals – Daryll getting 124 in 117 balls and Jonty 121 in 114 – as part of a new world record stand of 232 for the fourth wicket. The best of the Pakistan batsmen was Ijaz Ahmed whose typically dashing 88 in 63 balls was not enough to carry his side to South Africa's impressive total of 321 for eight.

Not so impressive was their score in the next game against Sri Lanka. This was the one the boys had been waiting for – a crack at the World Cup champions – but only Cullinan's 51 stood out in a total of 169. Arjuna Ranatunga also proved that sportsmanship was not dead. When Richardson was given out stumped for a duck, he was called back by the generous Sri Lankan captain who conceded that his 'keeper had dropped the ball. Four wickets by Muttiah Muralitharan – whose suspect bowling action had by now been cleared after an exhaustive investigation involving scientific tests – helped curtail the innings with a full eight overs remaining. This was not the way to beat the Sri Lankans and, when Saneth Jayasuriya picked up on his World Cup form to blaze 45 runs in 30 balls at the top of the innings, the champions looked well set for an easy win. Symcox then produced an excellent spell of tight bowling to remove both openers and, with five wickets tumbling for the addition of only 44 runs, the South Africans got a sniff of victory. In the end it was denied them, but there were eight wickets down when the winning runs were scored.

Donald had arrived in Kenya well rested and raring to go. The first two matches had brought him five wickets and, after the disappointment of Karachi, all the old enthusiasm had returned to the man they called 'White Lightning'.

'I'm so keen to play now I just want to jump out of my shoes out there,' he enthused before stepping out on the Gymkhana ground and taking a new career-best six for 23 against an outclassed Kenya in the next game. Cronjé and Rhodes, with half-centuries each, were also in good shape in a fifth wicket stand of 101, while Kirsten hit top score of 66 in 73 balls. This was just a dress rehearsal for the in-form Gazza who, in a manner now becoming him, hit 118 not out to spearhead South Africa's seven-wicket victory over Pakistan in the final and to take the Man of the Match award yet again.

Pakistan had squeezed into the final by the narrowest of margins on run-rate, beating Sri Lanka in their last pool match after scoring a massive 371. This was largely due to the pyrotechnics of an unknown pinch-hitter named Shahid Afridi, a teenager claiming to be only 16 in his first one-day international, who smashed a world record century off 37 balls with 11 sixes. The Pakistanis had ironically included him as a specialist leg-spin bowler, but they decided to try him out as a pinch-hitter. They naturally asked him to do the job again in the final, but he was caught behind off Donald for 14.

Donald was named Man of the Series for his 14 wickets in four games and South Africa walked off with the winner's cheque of $50 000. It was a good first visit to Kenya, but there was still concern over the injuries. When the team was announced for the coming tour of India, four players were not considered. They were Kallis, Adams, Matthews and Schultz. Klusener retained his place as Matthews's replacement and Kirsten was named as the new vice-captain.

Almost five years had elapsed since South Africa's historic first tour of India and, of that team, Rice, Cook and Yachad had all retired, and Wessels, Peter Kirsten, Kuiper, Snell, Shaw, Eksteen and the coach Procter were no longer in the frame.

16

From Zero to Hero

THE PLAYERS WALKED out of Hyderabad airport at the start of a two-month tour that was to take them on a fretful journey into the unknown. It would tax both body and spirit in ways they had never before experienced. The team bus was waiting for them. It was a dilapidated vehicle that looked like a relic from the Fifties. 'Oh no,' cried Bob Woolmer, 'not again! We had this bus on my last tour of India.' That was with England back in 1976...

There was greater cause for alarm when the driver adopted a side-on seating position so that he could talk to the players while he steered with only one eye on the road. 'Where's Jonty Rhodes, where's Jonty Rhodes?' he asked frantically as he jammed the accelerator flat on the floorboards and the teeming traffic, and a few cows, dodged out of his way.

It was mid-October and the team was in Hyderabad, the southern Indian city known for its fine textiles, to play against the host nation in the opening match of the Titan Cup limited-overs triangular tournament that also featured Australia.

BETWEEN THE TEST match against England at Newlands in the first week of January and the next one against India in the third week of November, Hansie and the boys played 29 one-day internationals. If ever proof was needed of what makes modern-day cricket tick, this statistic would do very nicely. No matter how ill-disposed the purists might feel towards limited-overs cricket, with all its attendant hype and hoopla, there was no doubt that this was the cash cow of the game. It was also an animal that did not adequately provide the players with the kind of all-round preparation they might need for Test match duty. Batting techniques suffered, the bowlers often felt marginalised, and the frenzy of it all placed a heavy burden on both mind and body. At least in the area of fielding it had brought about something of a revolution in the overall standards of the game at large; also, it had spawned a positive, attacking mindset among most players, which spilled over well in the Test arena.

Of those 29 one-dayers, the South Africans won 25. This included their distinguished progress to the quarter-finals of the World Cup in March, by which stage they had won 10 in a row; their triumphant first visit to Sharjah the next month; their victorious trip to Kenya; and now on to the Titan Cup where they beat India at Hyderabad at the start of an extraordinary sequence of victories *en route* to yet another final.

Australia – whose deficiencies showed without the services of the injured Shane Warne and Craig McDermott – lost all three of their matches against the South Africans, and India suffered the same fate on the two other occasions they played South Africa in the pool matches.

The final would be between South Africa and India at Bombay's Wankhede Stadium. On a poor one-day wicket, Hansie and the boys lost their way...

WHAT WILL MODERN-DAY cricket make of the subcontinent? Its spectators are knowledgeable yet often given to odd behaviour, the food is totally foreign to the Western palate (note to visitors: don't eat the pork, it's probably off; don't eat the beef, it's probably water buffalo; don't eat the mutton, it's probably goat), and accommodation often less than bearable. At Rajkot, the hotel not only ran out of toilet paper for the three days the team stayed there but also was unable to dispense a decent meal. The players subsisted on a diet that consisted mainly of toast and jam.

Having beaten India by five wickets there in the pool section of the Titan Cup, the boys were pleased to be out of the place. To do so, however, was far from simple and further underlined the nightmares of travelling in those parts. The problem now was that their next engagement was against the Aussies at Guwahati on 1 November. There was no direct flight. In order to accomplish their tortuous journey, the team left Rajkot at 11 am on 30 October, arriving in Bombay just after midday. There they remained in transit until 4.30 pm before catching a flight to Calcutta. Having arrived there at 7 pm, they then set off on a 45-minute drive to a hotel for an overnight stay. At 5 am the next day, they were awoken from their fitful slumbers to catch their flight to Guwahati. They arrived there at 7.20 am, boarded another bus and finally reached their destination at 8.15 am on 31 October. The trip had taken almost 22 hours and, with no chance of preparation in unfamiliar conditions, they were required to play Australia the next day. Given these crazy arrangements, it was hard to imagine how a team could be expected to maintain a zest for the game, let alone a high level of performance. Yet the boys duly thrashed the Aussies by eight wickets.

It had also become apparent that scorers were a problem. When the boys played Australia at Bombay, the scorers mixed up Kirsten and Hudson, crediting Gazza with the four runs that would have taken Hudders to 53 and his seventeenth international half-century. Glancing at the scoreboard, Hudson saw he was on 49. Eager now to score a quick single, he succeeded only in getting out. 'We tried to get a message out to him to tell him that he was already past 50,' said Woolmer, 'but it was too late.'

As for Guwahati, in the eastern zone of that vast country, Kirsten best summed it up. 'It was the first time I had ever been into the central business district of a town and seen more animals than human beings on the street.'

Gazza also made the mistake of leaving his bedroom window open one night while he went downstairs to prepare yet another 'dinner' of toast and jam. When he returned, thousands of flying insects had moved in. It took Donald's size-11 boot to sort them out. The walls were not a pretty sight afterwards.

Ah, India. There is an inherent danger in touring those parts and, quite apart from the understandable complaints of the bowlers, there is a shocking lack of appreciation that good one-day cricket demands good batting wickets. Most of the pitches are, at best, over-prepared and bereft of a blade of grass. While this does nothing to aid the seam-bowlers, these slow tracts of dirt and dust also do very little for batsmen who like to play their shots. The one for the Titan Cup final at Bombay was a one-innings wonder.

Sachin Tendulkar won the toss and batted, as well he might; the South Africans were set a victory target of 221 on a track that deteriorated into a slow, low horror that was pitted with holes. One by one they fell victim to it, most of the recognised batsmen driving at balls that didn't come on to the bat and sending them high into willing Indian hands. It was left to Richardson and Symcox, the two old men of the party, to attempt a rescue act. From 96 for seven, they valiantly took the score to 184 for eight, largely employing a back-foot technique to help them prosper in their 88-run stand. Still, it was an arduous task, and a slow one at that, and when the time came to chase up the scoring tempo, they too came unstuck. Richardson was out for 43 and Symcox followed him a run later for 46; the team was all out with more than two overs to spare.

'One of the hazards of playing in the intense heat is wet and slippery gloves,' explained Cronjé later. 'You've hardly played a shot and your gloves are wet. It's not all that surprising that guys get out trying to hit over the top. The bat tends to slip a fraction and you don't make proper contact.'

On one occasion during his heroic innings, Symmo lost hold of his bat altogether and it took off like an unguided missile. By the end of his knock he had changed gloves six times. Swinger lost his cool with Craig Smith, exchanging heated words with him out in the middle when the physiotherapist refused to give him more salt tablets to ease his cramps.

Cronjé attributed South Africa's defeat in the final to his having lost the toss, a common enough complaint in India where the ball generally goes through the top alarmingly early in the course of a match. 'I'm irritated, I don't like losing,' he told the travelling media contingent afterwards. Even though the team had won six matches out of seven, he was concerned that fans back home would be critical. 'People are more likely to remember our defeats at the World Cup and here than our victories at Sharjah and Nairobi.'

Brian McMillan had missed the match through injury, but Hansie refused to use this as an excuse. 'We took the field with our best available side and that should have been good enough.'

Still, 25 wins from 29 starts was by no means a bad record (at a comparative stage in world cricket, most of the other top teams enjoyed no better than about a 50 per cent success rate). It was churlish of critics to suggest that, as 'proven' at the World Cup and Titan Cup, the South Africans were not up to it when the chips were down. It was far better to consider that, since the World Cup, the team had reached three finals in limited-overs tournaments in foreign lands and had won two of them. The only matches they lost during this period were against the West Indies in the World Cup quarter-final, against Sri Lanka in Kenya (oddly, the only time they played the World Cup holders during an exceedingly busy year), once against England in the seven-match series at the start of the year, and now against India. In the Coopers & Lybrand world one-day rankings, South Africa was far and away the top team of 1996.

It seemed a pity, though, that teams were ultimately judged on their performances in one-off finals, because for sheer consistency Hansie's boys had no equal. On an individual level, Donald was named Man of the Series for the second successive tournament. He had made adjustments to his run-up and action in England in the winter months, his away-swinger was working again and his yorker was a deadly weapon.

After his unhappy World Cup, 'White Lightning' was now performing as well as at any time in the past.

Kirsten was also riding the crest of the wave. The new vice-captain had become the proud holder of three international records. Apart from his World Cup record score of 188, he had also broken Tendulkar's record of five one-day centuries in a single year and had surpassed fellow left-hander Brian Lara's high-water mark of 1 349 runs in a calendar year. In 1993, the West Indian compiled his runs in 30 innings with four centuries and seven fifties for an average of 49.96. By the third week of October 1996, Kirsten had reached 1 352 runs from 24 innings with six centuries and four fifties for an average of 67.60.

'What's the use of becoming swollen-headed?' said Gazza shortly after breaking the record against India at Jaipur. 'Cricket's such a funny game that one day you're on top and the next you could be at the bottom of the barrel.' In his next innings two days later, he was dismissed for one against Australia at Faridabad...

For those who had the privilege of watching his older brother Peter in his prime, Gary's run-glut was seen as a logical extension of the great Kirsten dynasty. Gary himself seemed surprised at his achievements but Peter always had great faith in his ability. He was instrumental, along with the Western Province coach Duncan Fletcher, in helping his kid brother develop his batting technique by making simple adjustments to his bottom hand grip. Now Gary was flourishing in the interests of the team amid their aggressive new game plan, his goal to score a run a ball through the opening 15 overs, always aiming to anchor the innings and bat right through. In achieving this on a regular basis, the runs just flowed. Back home, Peter would merely smile that crooked little smile of his. He had been denied the opportunity of playing international cricket at a younger age, yet was still good enough to score a maiden Test century against England at the age of 39. It was reassuring for him to know that Gary was now performing the kind of batting feats that he might have aspired to had he had the chance all those years ago. 'He's scoring all my runs!' he chided as he watched with admiration from afar the deeds of a brother almost 13 years his junior.

THE SEEMINGLY INTERMINABLE stream of one-dayers behind them, Hansie and the boys now reset their sails for the longer and far more important voyage of their first Test series in India. During the fortnight that followed the Titan Cup final, they played a couple of three-day warm-up matches in Cochin and Baroda. Neither proved particularly useful from the point of view of giving the regular Test batsmen enough opportunity to hone their skills for a five-day contest.

Against a President's XI at Baroda, tail-ender Salil Ankola completely missed the first three balls bowled at him by Symcox. This was too much for Symmo to ignore without a word of encouragement. 'Hey, do you want me to put bells on it?' the big fellow asked. The next three balls were dispatched for 6, 4, 6.

Two of the better performances came from Gibbs, who hit a fluent 74 against the President's XI spinners, and Klusener, who took an impressive haul of 14 wickets in the two outings. But neither of them was down to play in the opening Test. Fanie de Villiers's return to the camp for the second warm-up match at Baroda was, in fact, a far more significant development. He had left for South Africa immediately after the Titan Cup final, hurrying home for a week's compassionate leave to be at the side of his wife, Judy, who had undergone abdominal surgery. Now he was back in harness, but not before he had made a perfunctory detour. During a 15-hour wait in Bombay for a connecting flight to Baroda, the adventurous tourist went off in search of a cemetery that was known to house the graves of South African prisoners of war who had been interned in India during the Anglo-Boer war. 'The graves were gone,' lamented Fanie, 'but there's a monument there now.'

Questions were being asked about the team's state of preparedness. Although Fanie had immediately slipped back into his stride with an impressive match return of nine for 83 at Baroda, a mood of apprehension clung to the regular batsmen. All were way short on first-class outings and none had had a decent run at Cochin or Baroda. The stark reality was that the top seven Test batters had not played more than three first-class matches in almost 11 months; Kirsten's undefeated 76 for Western Province against Natal way back in January was the highest score of the lot. This was hardly the way to ready a team for the rigours of five-day cricket. No one could doubt the monumental task that awaited them: India had not lost a Test series at home for 10 seasons and were further buoyed by their recent victory over Australia by seven wickets at Delhi.

And so to Ahmedabad...

Of the three Test match venues that lay in wait, the South Africans expected the pitch at the Sardar Patel Stadium there to be the most difficult. Also, the Indian selectors gave them more than a hint of what to expect when they included four spin-bowlers in their squad. Still, the visitors continued to debate their options, heightened by the impending arrival of Paul Adams following his long injury lay-off. The initial view was that, in the finest traditions of post-isolation South Africa, Cronjé would rely on a four-pronged pace attack, giving Klusener his first cap, with the selection of only one spinner in Symcox. Apart from Adams, two more spin-bowlers, Crookes and Bojé, were waiting impatiently in the wings. Which way to go?

Woolmer viewed the issue with characteristic circumspection. The son of a British insurance executive who had played representative cricket for Uttar Pradesh in the Ranji Trophy, he was born in India and lived there till the age of seven. Just as India was in his blood, so too was cricket; he tells how, shortly after his birth in May 1948, his father had placed a bat and a ball in one corner of his cot in their home in Kanpur, saying, 'Son, I hope this will be your life.' He also recalls practice sessions with his dad in the nets of the Tollygunge and Calcutta Cricket Clubs; and how, under Tony Greig in 1976, he was a member of an England team that achieved a rare Test series victory in India.

Woolmer knew that the Sardar Patel pitch would probably start to turn on day one. The tour selectors – himself, Cronjé, Kirsten, Richardson and Peter Pollock – finally decided to play both Symcox and Adams. Symmo had been bowling aggressively in the nets, but Adams had only just arrived and had no more than six hours to acclimatise. To suggest, as one South African television commentator did, that Bojé was hard done by was, at best, misleading. After all, Adams was the incumbent in the Test team and both Bojé and Crookes had gone to India as members of the original one-day squad.

One of the priorities was to get Adams fit in time for the Test matches and here he was now, a bouncy fellow who was more than happy to be thrown in at the deep end again. As was the case on his début against England, and still a teenager now, he seemed content to cede all nervous reactions to those ageing critics who apparently harboured doubts in their pallid hearts.

At around this time, Cronjé was approached by an Indian journalist. 'He asked me whether I thought the team could now be considered a multi-racial one because of the inclusion of three coloured players in Adams, Gibbs ... and myself. I replied that, yes, I was very happy!'

The two-spinner strategy was a departure from the now almost obligatory South African emphasis on seam and swing, but conditions made this imperative. It was clear that the pitch would turn square on day one. The Indians opted to play three of their slow bowlers – the deadly accurate wrist-spinner Anil Kumble, the left-arm Sunil Joshi, and the leg-spinner Narendra Hirwani. What would the South Africans make of them on this turner? A lot would depend on the toss. Tendulkar won it. He didn't want to bat on this dust bowl in the fourth innings. But that was only the start of South Africa's problems.

Cronjé remembers it well. 'You hear all those bad things about playing cricket in India, then you go there and experience them for yourself. I was told by former Test cricketers like Ravi Shastri and Kapil Dev that Ahmedabad was not fit for international cricket. They weren't kidding. The pitch was a disgrace, there were no proper practice facilities, and the change rooms were filthy and smelly. The crowd, too, gave us problems. Apart from being unco-operative, they put some of our players in very real danger. Also, according to Test match regulations, the outfield should be mowed before start of play each day. This was never done. And, on top of all that, the hotel was not up to international standards.'

When the tour was over, the UCBSA's Krish Mackerdhuj would inform the Indian Board of Control that South Africa would not accept Ahmedabad as a Test match venue on future visits to that country. It was the highest form of condemnation and was surely justified.

On the eve of the Test, the boys needed no reminding that the toughest of assignments had now dawned, yet, far from showing signs of anxiety, the opening day of the match found them in high spirits. They were to be joined that day by their wives, girlfriends and loved ones who were given a 50 per cent subsidy from the UCBSA to join the tour for the next two weeks. Hansie was thrilled to be reunited with Bertha, Hudders with Tracey, Gazza with Debbie Cassidy, Daryll with Virginia, Jonty with Kate, Big Mac with Denise, Swinger with Jenny, Zulu with Isabel Potgieter, Herschelle with Gwynneth, Derek with Gail, Symmo with Liz, A.D. with Tina – and Fanie with his brother Nelis. Those who remained 'single' for the time being at least were Gogga, Nicky and the coach.

What exactly was in store for the now expanded South African touring party could not be predicted; there was no way of knowing about the impending drama, danger and defeat, neither the acts of heroism, the memorable milestones, nor the final, ironic twist of fate that were all destined to take place in the days to follow. There would also come the moment, unprecedented in South African cricket history, when Cronjé would take his team off the field in the face of ugly behaviour from a section of the volatile crowd. It happened on the third afternoon.

Fielding at long leg, Adams was hit a sharp blow in the back by a flying object. Almost immediately, he was struck again. Then Donald and De Villiers also became targets. Sensing that something was amiss, Cronjé walked down to long leg where he retrieved a handful of rocks and jagged pieces of concrete in the area of the attack. He had no hesitation. Grim-faced, he signalled to his team-mates to follow him. They left the field.

In a tense and anxious dressing room, the match referee John Reid told the team management, 'If I am assured the players will be safe, then we go back on. If not, we all go home.' Reid, a former New Zealand skipper, was known as a tough character who brooked no nonsense. After a 10-minute break, during which khaki-clad security men were mobilised in the concrete stands, Reid told the players it was safe to continue. Cronjé, who was commended for his initial action, then had the further good sense to take the inexperienced Adams away from the trouble spot and post the street-smart Symcox at long leg. The good-natured Symmo waved to the spectators in a gesture that effectively broke the tension; later a woman in the crowd was seen holding a placard containing a single word: 'Sorry'.

The Indian high commissioner, Gopalkrishna Gandhi, deplored the unruly actions of the crowd. 'The throwing of stones by hooligans on South African fielders is a disgraceful event, besmirching India's cricket culture and hospitality. On behalf of the millions of cricket lovers in India, I deplore this abhorrent action and express the sincerest regrets.'

Out on the field of play, there was no place for regrets, apologies or excuses. This was Test match cricket at its most uncompromising. In the treacherous batting conditions of Ahmedabad, not to mention the vagaries of the umpiring, scoring runs was a relative thing. It was something that seemed to escape some observers when South Africa had India on 215 for eight at the close of the first day. They seemed to think that South Africa already had the Test in the bag, forgetting of course that the first judgement can only be made once both teams have had a turn at bat.

Having dismissed the home side for 223 early on the second morning, South Africa suddenly found themselves staring down the barrel on 119 for seven in reply. While it was true that both Cronjé and Cullinan had been the victims of shocking lbw decisions from the Indian umpire, S.K. Bansal – Cronjé was given out for one when a ball from Hirwani pitched outside the leg stump, and Cullinan was done for a fine 43 when he stretched so far down the pitch to Joshi as to make the decision beyond comprehension – there was no arguing with the scoreboard. It read 119 for seven as clear as day when De Villiers joined Symcox. 'Every run counts now, Fanie!' were Woolmer's parting words.

Fanie had been there before and he remembered Adelaide. At the crease now were two of the finest rearguard fighters any captain could ever wish to have. They knew what they were up against. When Symcox was eventually trapped by Joshi for 32 while attempting the cut – one lbw decision that no one could argue with and a 'nominated' shot that was far too risky – the total had climbed to 182 for eight. 'Ag, you know Symmo,' said Fanie afterwards, 'he talks a good game and has got all these theories. Just before he got out he told me he was going to cut Joshi. I told him he was mad. My approach? It was sort of defend, defend, defend, sweep ... then leave, leave, leave, sweep ... then defend again.'

In this way, De Villiers was undefeated on 40 at 202 for eight at stumps on the second day. What had earlier loomed as a big first innings deficit was now, thanks largely to Symmo and Fanie and a willing No 10 in Donald, almost back to parity.

AFTER THE DAY's play Cronjé called the entire touring party on to the field, the team, the reserves, the support crew. He put his unhappy dismissal behind him and he only looked ahead. 'It's been a rough day and we've got to put it behind us. We're back in the match, we can't afford to lose our focus. What we need now is more guts and character and determination.'

Fanie was far from finished. On the third morning he advanced his score to an undefeated 67 – his highest in Test cricket – while he and Donald added 60 runs for the ninth wicket. At 244 all out, South Africa enjoyed a 21-run lead that had once seemed impossible. What's more, India quickly lost both openers, Manjrekar and Mongia, to Donald's splendid bowling before the deficit had been knocked off, and they then plunged to 91 for five.

From tea to tea on days two and three, South Africa had turned the match upside down. Having been 104 runs in arrears with only three first innings wickets intact, 24 hours later they had restricted India to an overall lead of just 70 runs with five second-innings wickets in hand. Still, it was far from over...

Just as South Africa had looked to the unlikely batting duo of Symmo and Fanie to pull them around, the Indians now found their saviours in Test débutant V.V.S. Laxman and the No 9 Kumble. By stumps on the third day, Laxman had scored 50 and his partner 22 in an unbroken eighth-wicket stand of 48. At 172 for seven, India now led by 151 runs. The view from the outset was that anything over 150 might be too steep a target. This was not a criticism of South Africa's batsmen because it was unlikely that any Test team could have achieved such a goal in the fourth innings under these circumstances. The pitch had become a nightmare.

Driving back to the hotel in the team bus that evening, Cronjé still found something to lighten the burden that was beginning to weigh heavily on his shoulders. 'Derek Crookes and I looked out of the window and there we saw a man, a woman and two children riding on one bicycle alongside us. The man then realised who we were and, fixing his eyes on us, he steered the bike straight into a passing cow.'

The start of the fateful fourth day belonged to Adams. Those who still questioned the wisdom of playing him in this match, particularly after only one wicket in the first innings, could only watch in admiration as he rattled through the last three wickets in the opening 20 minutes. His lbw dismissal of Laxman for 51 was a small work of art. Having lulled the watchful young batsman into shouldering arms to three successive googlies leaving the bat, he then fizzed back the chinaman to trap him stone dead. The stark reality now was that India, all out for 190, were inviting South Africa to score exactly 170 runs for victory. It was, in cricket's modern vernacular, a Big Ask; and, what's more, Rhodes had been off the field since mid-afternoon on the previous day with a hamstring injury that was serious enough for Hansie to reshuffle the batting order. Could the South Africans do it? Javagal Srinath thought not.

With the fourth and fifth balls of his opening over, the fast bowler removed both Hudson and Cullinan before a run had been scored; in the space of another over, he dismissed Richardson and Rhodes; with the fourth and fifth balls of his twelfth over, he claimed the final two wickets of Donald and Adams.

'Srinath on Fire' proclaimed one hastily scribbled poster in a delirious crowd, and that he most certainly was. Bowling immaculate line and length, he proceeded to bowl faster than any Indian in recent memory. He further confounded the batsmen by taking full advantage of the wiles of the awful pitch and, to make matters worse, he produced treacherous reverse swing. From 96 for four, the South Africans disintegrated to 105 all out, the last six wickets falling for only nine runs in 25 balls. It was the boys' first defeat in 11 Tests.

In 11 overs and five balls, Srinath produced career-best figures of six for 21 in his twenty-second Test; and, unhappily for the South Africans, the fitful finger of umpire Bansal played its part yet again in debatable lbw decisions against Hudson and Rhodes. Jonty had bravely come to the crease at 96 for five, Kirsten in tow as his runner, and was rapped first ball on the pad by a big in-ducker that looked to be missing leg stump by a foot. He was given out.

Amid the horrendous shambles, the heroes of the first innings recovery, Symcox and De Villiers, came and went within the space of five deliveries without adding to the score. Their undoing came at the hands of Kumble, the spinner who was expected to be the most dangerous of the Indian bowlers. That this honour should fall to Srinath was quite ironic; indeed, on a pitch that would always favour the spinners, the most successful bowlers on both sides were the fast men, Srinath and Donald.

Of all the South African batsmen, only Cronjé could come to grips with the Indian quickie. Each time a new batting partner arrived amid the procession, the skipper would implore him to watch the ball carefully as it left Srinath's hand, the darkened side being the clue to the arrival of another reverse swinger. It seemed, however, that only Hansie could unravel this mystery. In effectively carrying his bat – he had arrived in the cauldron at 0 for two – he produced a resolute captain's innings that lasted almost three hours and left him undefeated on 48 at the end against almighty odds. The only other batsmen to get into double figures were Kirsten on 20 and an aggressive McMillan on 17. There were six ducks.

Cronjé's face told the story in graphic detail. It was as if his dark countenance had been set in granite, his expressive, angry eyes providing the window to the turmoil inside. Apart from the atrocious conditions, the sub-standard umpiring and the poorly behaved crowd, the greatest frustration for him was that his team, having survived so many setbacks throughout the match, had seen defeat arrive so cruelly, so swiftly, so completely. For just over three days, the boys had played with a hunger that suggested they were capable of going all the way to victory. Their positive attitude had been mirrored by Symmo the previous day when he claimed there was always someone on hand to pull them out of a crisis. The breadth of the ultimate crisis was therefore quite stunning.

Cronjé was angry and roundly criticised the conditions they had to play in. 'If we want to pick ourselves up and win the series, it will take a superhuman effort.'

Woolmer was equally outspoken. 'I don't think there is a side in the world who would have beaten India under the conditions we had to endure. If we had prepared a wicket like that during my time at Warwickshire, we would have been docked 25 points for malpractice. No Test side in the world would have been able to cope with those conditions. The bottom line is that we lost the Test because we didn't bat well enough ... yet this side has performed really well for two years and we don't want to make massive changes simply because we've been dismembered by conditions.'

There were still some high points. The Test had been an exciting contest throughout, if not exactly a proper contest between bat and ball. There was Rhodes's fielding in the first innings when his sensational diving catch at mid-wicket to dismiss Tendulkar and his direct hit on the stumps to run out Azharuddin were central to South Africa's early ascendancy; there was the batting of Symcox and De Villiers and later Cronjé; there was Donald's seven wickets in the match, even though he was hampered by a badly bruised heel in the second innings. For India, victory again, Srinath knee-deep in adulation, shoulder-high in triumph.

Kirsten's twenty-ninth birthday happened to fall on the final day of the match. The birthday present he wanted most was victory in the Test. That night the boys and their partners gave Gazza a birthday party at the Trident Hotel, a much plusher establishment than their own, where the media contingent was staying. When Hansie and Bertha returned to their hotel later, a reporter from a Johannesburg radio station phoned to ask, among other things, if he was watching the live telecast of the 1996 Miss World pageant which was taking place amid much controversy in Bangalore that night. 'No,' replied Hansie, thoroughly dejected at the day's events but still not without humour, 'I've got Miss World in my room with me!' The radio reporter, no doubt unaware that the wives had joined the tour, was taken aback. Who knows what he might have written had he been a reporter from Britain's *Daily Mirror*?

In their hotel room, Hansie and Bertha were actually watching a rerun of *The Sound of Music*, an old movie that just about epitomised the lack of modernity in never-to-be-forgotten Ahmedabad.

BACK HOME, MEANWHILE, a relatively new name was commanding attention. Adam Bacher, the young Transvaal opener, was on a roll. In the night series league he had hit three scores in excess of 135, including a magnificent 137 earlier in the season against a full-strength Free State attack that included a pulverised Donald, as well as two half-centuries. Little over two weeks after his twenty-third birthday, and a week before the Ahmedabad Test, he went up a gear to score a double-century and a century in the same four-day match against Griqualand West. His 210 and 112 not out on a slow pitch at Kimberley made him the first cricketer to score a double-century and a century in a first-class match in South Africa.

On the same ground the previous season, he had given notice of his talent when he scored a century for South Africa A against England. He might have been Ali Bacher's nephew but he was clearly his own man; in his range of shot selection it was also just possible that he would become a more accomplished top-order batsman than his illustrious uncle. Those who knew him also spoke in awe of his fine temperament and his habit of taking cold showers to keep the adrenalin pumping during breaks of play. There was a view, and not for the first time, that Hudson's place in the national side was under threat.

IN CRICKET, WOUNDS often heal quickly. The disappointments of the first Test were soon forgotten as the boys arrived in Calcutta a day earlier than scheduled. In the City of Joy the frowns of the previous week were soon replaced by smiles as they checked in to the fine Oberoi Grand. At Eden Gardens, one of the world's truly great cricket grounds, the practice facilities were found to be excellent. An inspection of the pitch a day before the start of the second Test also made everyone happier. If Ahmedabad was an unfriendly dustbowl, Eden Gardens looked quite the opposite. It was hard and pacy, a much friendlier venue in more ways than one.

Hansie was convinced the pitch would provide a much fairer contest and that the conditions would favour his fast strike-bowlers. The Indians had similar thoughts, a situation that created a series of ironies in the warring camps which were to have sensational repercussions in the days ahead. The South Africans decided to omit 32-year-old De Villiers and include 25-year-old Klusener for his first Test; the Indians thought long and hard about dropping Venkatesh Prasad, the young paceman who had achieved little at Ahmedabad but, at the eleventh hour, they changed their plan and gave him another run.

Both selections were to have a huge impact on the game but, in the meantime, Fanie had the difficult task of coming to terms with having been dropped again. The ebullient cricketer had pulled his weight quite admirably in a beaten cause at Ahmedabad and was relishing the idea of having a better crack at the bowling whip in Calcutta's more conducive conditions. It was a ground that he particularly loved and, when the captain knocked on his door at 5.45 pm on the eve of the Test, his heart sank.

The downcast Fanie listened as Cronjé explained that the attack needed more strike power with the new ball, and that the pacy Klusener, with his slingshot action, was reckoned to be the better bet to complement Donald. Fanie was not the type to begrudge a younger player a big opportunity, but it was clear from his demeanour that he was burning up inside. Woolmer also attempted to explain the selection to the media. 'Fanie swings the ball but is just lacking that little bit at the moment. We feel that Lance might take wickets in conjunction with Allan. The two of them together will be a slightly harder proposition for the Indians.'

It was obvious that the South Africans were looking to the more aggressive Klusener to get the ball up around the batsmen's ribs.

In another change to the team that did duty at Ahmedabad, Gibbs was awarded his first cap in place of Rhodes. Jonty's hamstring injury was much worse than earlier diagnosed and was serious enough to put him out of action for the rest of the tour. To cover for Rhodes's absence, the selectors flew in John Commins who had averaged 25 in his three Tests against New Zealand and Pakistan. Commins was in good form. He had returned to Western Province from Boland to take up the post of captain of his original province and the previous week had scored 148 not out in victory against Boland. He was named twelfth man at Calcutta.

Gibbs had already made strong claims for a Test batting berth, but his athletic fielding was a big plus in his favour and an indication that the youngsters were now closing the gap on Rhodes in the specialist fielding department. 'Herschelle brings to the field what we lack without Jonty,' said Woolmer. 'It's important to have someone who throws himself around at cover point.'

As for the injured Rhodes, even greater disappointment lay in store for him when the first Test of the return series was played on his home ground in Durban, but that was still a long way away.

Galvanised by the knowledge that India had not lost a Test match at Eden Gardens since the 1983/84 season, Cronjé made the perfect start by winning a rare toss. Perhaps enthused by this lucky break, Hudson prospered in his twenty-seventh Test. By his own admission, he was feeling the pressure when he took his guard that morning, the rave reviews from home about Adam Bacher's purple patch not having escaped his attention.

Hudson acknowledged that his Test form had been unconvincing and that doubts were beginning to creep in. Indeed, the night before the match he had spent some time wondering about his future as a Test batsman after a serious chat with Woolmer. He might also have pondered on the rotten luck that had dogged his career, a man so often the victim of a freakish dismissal or an umpiring aberration.

Suddenly, that late November morning, his luck changed. As if in compensation for the two poor lbw decisions against him in the previous Test, he was now given lives on 0 and 4 – later he was caught at slip off a no-ball from Prasad – en route to his fourth century in Test cricket and his first against India. It could not have come at a better time, nor at a more significant venue. It was, after all, on this ground five years earlier that Hudson had made his international début in the first match upon South Africa's return to the international fold. On that occasion he lasted three balls of the opening over before being dismissed for a duck by Kapil Dev. Now, in this 'almost mystical' place, he was acknowledging a century that followed those he had already scored in Barbados, South Africa and Zimbabwe.

Hudson took 223 minutes to reach his century, whereupon he informed his partner that he was planning on going nowhere until Kirsten had also reached his. Just 22 minutes later, it was Gazza's turn. Hudson promptly hugged his partner to celebrate what Kirsten later characterised as the personal highlight of his tour. Expanding on this, he added, 'Sir Garfield Sobers once said that your Test education isn't complete until you have played a Test at Eden Gardens. It's mind boggling ... 90 000-odd people inside the stadium and 20 000 outside listening on radios and waiting to catch a glimpse of their heroes at the end of the day.'

Gazza was playing his twenty-second Test, and, in spite of his consistent batting form, this was only his second hundred. It might have taken him longer than Hudders to reach the three-figure mark but the truth is that he enjoyed less of the strike. In terms of balls received, Hudson had needed 181 to Kirsten's 164. In the two hours between lunch and tea, the gallant pair of openers amassed 138 runs, advancing the total from 98 without loss at the first interval to 236 without loss at the second. It is never advisable to make hasty predictions in cricket, but at this point on the first day of the Test match the feeling was that South Africa could hardly lose it. The question, of course, was whether they could win it.

Two balls after tea, Kirsten got an inside edge on to his stumps, bowled by Srinath for 102. The opening stand of 236 was the highest for any wicket by South Africa since its readmission and the highest opening stand on this ground in 28 Test matches. The new No 3 batsman, Gibbs, had been waiting for four hours with his pads on, but he could not have wished for a better platform from which to launch his Test career. Hudson, moreover, was now in full cry and the pair advanced the score by 60 runs before Hudders was bowled off the inside edge by Prasad. He had scored 146.

In the dressing room that evening the South Africans could be well pleased with themselves. The not-out batsmen were Gibbs and Cullinan on 28 and 29, and 339 runs had been scored in the day for the loss of two wickets. Little did they know that it was merely the calm before the carnage...

The second day got underway sedately enough, the first hour claiming only the wicket of Gibbs for 31. In the hour between mid-morning drinks and lunch, four more wickets crashed for the addition of 33 runs. Central to the demolition job were the Indian pacemen, Srinath and Prasad, who bowled unchanged throughout the pre-lunch session, with

Prasad continuing after the interval to take five wickets for 41 runs in 16 overs. South Africa lost their last eight wickets for just 89 runs with Richardson hanging in manfully to finish undefeated on 36. Prasad, the bowler who almost didn't play, finished with figures of six for 104.

Still, the South African total was 428, hardly something to sneeze at, but the Indian openers, Nayan Mongia and Rahul Dravid, seemed unimpressed. They raced to 68 in the first 17 overs before it all changed with startling suddenness. The first wicket fell on 68, the second on 71, the third on 77, the fourth on 114 and the fifth and sixth on 119. This amazing sequence of hasty departures was the result of renewed bowling determination and exceptional fielding, notably from Hudson who held a blistering slip catch to get rid of Dravid, and from Gibbs who, in justifying the pre-match words of his coach, did a pretty good imitation of Jonty Rhodes in throwing down the stumps of Mongia and running down those of Sunil Joshi.

At the end of a gripping day, India were struggling on 152 for six and, to make matters worse, Mohammed Azharuddin was battling with illness and had retired hurt on 6 after being struck on the left elbow by McMillan. In all, 241 runs had been scored in the day for the loss of 14 wickets. The pitch was slow and contained no demons, a fact that would become obvious the next morning.

The Indians were up against it on 161 for seven early on the third day, when Azharuddin put the elbow injury and his illness behind him and rejoined the action. Two hours later, he had completed the fourth-fastest Test century of all time, racing to 100 in just 74 balls. All the South African bowlers were mauled in the process, but none more so than poor Klusener who, on his début, was bludgeoned for four consecutive fours while conceding 75 runs in 14 overs by bowling too short.

When the brilliant 'Azhar' was eventually caught and bowled by Adams, he had scored 109 in 78 balls – his fourth Test century at Eden Gardens and his fifteenth in all – and he and Kumble had shared a run-a-ball stand of 161, breaking an Indian eighth-wicket record that had stood since 1965. Kumble scored 88, his highest score in 29 Tests, before Gibbs's pinpoint throw from the outfield ran him out.

When the innings closed on 329, South Africa's lead had been whittled down to 99 runs. It was a good enough platform and Kirsten and Cullinan used it to perfection. In a glorious display of batsmanship, Kirsten became the first South African since Alan Melville and Bruce Mitchell in the series against England in 1947 to score a century in each innings of a Test. When he was run out for a career-high 133, he and Cullinan had put on 212 for the second wicket; and when the declaration came on 367 for three, Cullinan had batted for almost six hours for an undefeated 153, also his highest score in Test cricket. He had languished in the 90s for an hour before reaching his second Test hundred; his 102 against Sri Lanka had come in only his fourth match and his second 'ton' came now in his twenty-first.

The Test match had already produced five centuries; what would India do in their second innings? They needed 467 runs to win and David Hookes, the former Australian batsman who was on the television commentary team, suggested, 'If they get those runs, they'll have more records than Michael Jackson!'

There were those who believed that Klusener would never recover from his mauling by Azharuddin – some even suggested that his Test career might end after only one match – but the rugged Zulu was made of sterner stuff, even if he did carry a tatty little teddy bear in his kit bag as a good luck charm.

With Donald unable to take the field (his damaged heel was playing up again) the new boy knew that the fast bowling burden would fall heavily on him. He had tried in vain to bomb out the batsmen in the first innings, so now he resolved to bowl line and length and wait for things to happen. Happen they did; almost single-handedly he bowled out India for 137 inside 54 overs.

His eight for 64 was the best return by a South African on début and the third best ever after Hugh Tayfield's nine for 113 against England in 1956/57 and 'Goofy' Lawrence's eight for 53 against New Zealand in 1961/62.

Azharuddin was always going to be India's big hope. After his brilliant century in the first innings, the flamboyant shot-maker went to his fifty in 54 balls with a crashing four off Klusener. The next ball he was gone, a big flashing drive taking the outside edge into the safe hands of McMillan. Big Mac was an inspiration, bowling unchanged with Klusener and playing a far more important role than his one wicket suggested. At slip he was also peerless, taking three catches off Zulu's bowling. Symcox took the remaining wicket and an important one at that: Tendulkar out for two. It was all over half an hour before lunch on the final day, victory to South Africa by 329 runs.

When a beaming Klusener left the field, he was immediately engulfed in a dual embrace by Donald and De Villiers. He was now one of the boys, a fully fledged member of the brotherhood of fast bowlers.

He could hardly believe what had happened to him or, as someone put it, 'from zero to hero in your first Test match'. Besieged by the media for interviews, he confided, 'It's a very close-knit team and all the guys are there for anyone who does well. They make everyone feel part of the team, but it's easier to feel part of it if you've contributed on the field.'

At Durban Boys' High, he had been an opening batsman who didn't bowl. After an undistinguished schools career, which did not include Natal Schools honours, he was first spotted while turning his hand to fast bowling on the country districts circuit. It was here that he was recommended to Graham Ford at Natal and before long he was bowling in tandem with the great Malcolm Marshall who was completing his playing days with the province. His senior provincial début at Kingsmead on New Year's Day of 1994 came just one day before 'Fanie's Test' at the Sydney Cricket Ground.

BEFORE THE THIRD Test match at Kanpur, Ali Bacher invited Klusener to join him in his hotel room for a chat. The former Springbok captain was more than a little surprised at the lad's rapid rise in the game. His report cards from Clive Rice at the national cricket academy suggested that, as a promising fast bowler, Klusener was still a yard short on pace to be a real factor at the highest level. Bacher, however, did not detect any such deficiency when he watched him bowl at Calcutta, a hugely determined bowler who was prepared to bend his back and unleash a really quick delivery. The UCBSA official was intrigued and he invited Klusener to talk a bit about his game. Zulu explained that he had spent long periods in the gym before the England A tour in an effort to build his strength and his pace. Bacher saw the hunger in his eyes. It reminded him a bit of Rice as a youngster. Not surprisingly, Klusener gave a lot of credit to Rice for helping him develop at the academy.

Cronjé was also full of admiration for his new team-mate. 'He's all heart,' he said. 'He is always prepared to run in for his captain, even if it's against the wind or not at the favourable end.'

Zulu refused to allow the success to go to his head. 'There's a long way to go,' he cautioned. 'There will be expectations that will be hard to live up to. I must learn to be consistent.'

The other Test débutant, Gibbs, was also beginning to flourish quite spectacularly. His first Test at Eden Gardens had brought scores of 31 and 9, but in the next match against India A at Nagpur he opened the batting and hit 200 not out in the first innings and 171 in the second to join Bacher in that rare group of one-game-treble centurions. No one was really surprised at the 22-year-old's big appetite for runs; his previous best first-class scores of 183, 178 and 152 not out suggested that a double-century was the logical progression. To underline his precocious talent, he hit a six to reach his 100 in the first innings. 'It augurs well for our future,' said Cronjé. 'I think Herschelle and his generation will be a lot better than us. When we started out, we were basically all newcomers who had to learn from scratch. Today we are an established side so the younger players can blend in with the more experienced players.'

Commins batted at No 3 at Nagpur, scored a quickfire 22 and then pulled out of the match through injury. It was obvious he would not play again on tour so he was given permission to return home. The story went that he was paid R100 as his share of the win bonuses but, because of his premature departure, he had to pay back five days' tour allowance and ended up with the grand total of R28. The story did not add that his one-off tour salary amounted to some R18 000 for one brief appearance.

At Nagpur, Big Mac got in some good batting practice for the coming Test with an innings of 130 and Klusener showed he was not only a destructive fast bowler by smashing 102 not out off 80 balls.

IT TOOK THE boys 20 hours to travel from Nagpur to Kanpur for the third Test. On the map it looked to be a straightforward trip, but it turned out to be yet another circuitous excursion that left them very little time to prepare. In the meantime, a local newspaper reported that the Indian coach Madan Lal had made a special trip to the Green Park ground several days earlier to talk with stadium officials. Since then the pitch had hardly been rolled. Lal denied he had been involved in the making of a pitch that looked under-prepared and liable to deteriorate. Green Park was not noted for its results. Of its 16 Test matches, 11 had ended in draws.

Donald's injury allowed De Villiers to return to the team for the deciding match of the series. He took the new ball with Klusener but neither prospered. Gibbs was down to bat again at No 3, yet he failed in both innings. He was not alone. Cronjé's fifty in the second innings was the highest by any South African in the match. The boys were bundled out for 177 in the first innings and, when set a victory target of 461 in a possible five sessions, they were shot out for 180 just after lunch on the final day.

While the Indian bowlers did well to share the wickets, it was again the giant batsmanship of Azharuddin that rode roughshod over the South Africans. He had been dismissed by Adams for five runs in the first innings – part of the little spinner's career-best return of six for 55 – but he took complete control in his second turn at bat, smashing 106 runs in boundaries in his imperious 163 not out. It was his bold intervention that allowed the Indians to prosper from 192 for five to 400 for seven and, when the Man of the Match and Man of the Series awards were handed out, there was only one candidate.

Adams's superb bowling in the first innings was now, sadly, only a distant memory. It was he who was instrumental in India losing their last seven wickets for just 52 runs to be bowled out for 237; and so excited was the engaging youngster at all this that he performed an amazingly acrobatic head-over-heels flip each time he took a wicket. No one had ever before seen such antics in the deadly serious business of Test cricket, but the uninhibited Gogga knew nothing of such niceties as he brought yet another breath of fresh air to the staid, tradition-bound game. The fun-loving Cronjé had himself suggested that Gogga perform the stunt out in the middle after watching him doing his tricks, amid much hilarity, at the pre-Test net practice. The purists did not like it one bit and later, in a quite ridiculous debate, South African officials advised the 'frog in a blender' to stop it because they feared he might do himself a grievous injury if he continued to express his jubilation in this way.

In the South African dressing room now, there was no such jubilation. The boys had been trounced by 280 runs and had lost their first series.

THE FINAL GAME of the Indian tour brought even more unhappiness. Half the touring party was ill, the rest were fatigued and homesick, and at Bombay the crowd erupted again.

The occasion was a benefit match for the former Indian player Mohinder Amarnath. It was classified as an official limited-overs international in spite of the South Africans' protestations. It was the last thing they needed at the end of a long and crippling tour. Cronjé was particularly unhappy. He had calculated that his hundredth appearance in official limited-overs internationals would take place on the return tour in South Africa at his beloved Springbok Park. He was always under the impression that the Amarnath match would be an unofficial one that would not change his number of appearances, but the Indian Cricket Board prevailed upon the UCBSA to agree to change its status to official for reasons relating to sponsorships and television coverage. The benefit game would bring up Hansie's hundredth a long way from home and in the worst possible way.

All hell broke loose when the crowd favourite Azharuddin was given out to a bat-pad catch by Kirsten off Crookes. On the big screen it became patently clear that the ball had looped off the pad and was nowhere near the bat. The crowd watched the replay and then went wild. Adams, who had been hit by pieces of concrete during the Ahmedabad Test, was now pelted with plastic bottles and bags filled with water. Cronjé immediately took his team off the field once again. He was adamant he would not return because that was the promise he had made at Ahmedabad. 'If it ever happens again,' he had said during the first Test stoppage, 'we will not go back.'

Officials pleaded with the South African captain. If he didn't take his team back, Amarnath's benefit would suffer. Hansie had no option. After an 18-minute interruption, he led his bedraggled side back. With so many players ill and injured, the South Africans had been forced to play all four spin-bowlers with Kirsten keeping wicket.

De Villiers, who should have been in bed, could manage only five overs and Adams and Symcox conceded 34 runs between them in their last two overs. Tendulkar was given three lives *en route* to 114 in a total of 267 for six. An ailing Cullinan did well to score 42, Cronjé scored 10 and the innings closed on 193.

At no stage did any official bother to mention that the South African captain was playing his hundredth game. No official even shook his hand.

THE TEAM RETURNED home amid the first signs of crisis in their ranks. South Africa had endured 10 series or one-off Tests without signs of cracking, yet their crushing defeat at Kanpur had broken the spell. The captain was also facing a personal battle. His fifty in the last innings at Kanpur was his first half-century in eight Test matches and, in six innings in India, he had totalled just 152 runs.

'It was a disappointment that we only batted well in Calcutta where conditions were favourable. I would have liked to see us apply ourselves on bad pitches and save a game. You learn from that and then you can do it again.'

Part of the problem was surely the loss of form of McMillan and Richardson who, unlike previous series, did not rise to any great heights. Swinger's batting average for the three Tests was 14.00 and Big Mac's a paltry 12.00. Donald's heel injury was also a problem, but Klusener's emergence was a positive sign and Adams was now taking on the form of a genuine strike-bowler. His five Tests so far had brought him 22 wickets, and he was the leading wicket-taker in India with 14 scalps.

ADAM BACHER'S CLAIM for a place in the squad was now impossible to ignore. A week before the announcement of the team for the opening two Tests of the home series against India, the run-hungry opening batsman scored yet another century for Transvaal, this time against an Eastern Province team captained by Kepler Wessels at the Wanderers. His captain, Ken Rutherford, assured him during the match that a century would secure his place in the South African team. 'I'll stand by that,' promised the former New Zealand skipper.

When Mackerdhuj announced the new squad on television later that week, 23-year-old Adam Bacher was a popular newcomer. Like many other cricket lovers, he stayed up late with his girlfriend Haley to hear Mackerdhuj's live broadcast. He must have been half expecting it because everyone else was expecting it, but when his name was read out he couldn't believe his good fortune. Congratulatory messages immediately began pouring in and his telephone did not stop ringing. It was probably the first and last time that his telephone was busier than his uncle's.

Like Ali, Adam was educated at King Edward VII School, a constant source of sporting talent. He made his first-class début for Transvaal B against Natal B at Kingsmead in November of 1993 – the day after South Africa lost to India in the semi-final of the Hero Cup. His scores were 18 and 3 in that three-day game and, in the one-dayer that followed against the same opponents, he was out for 1. He was given another chance for Transvaal B in their next match against Border B in East London and was out for a duck and 2. It was not a good start to his provincial career and he was immediately dropped. So what was the reason for his incredible success since then? Hard work, for sure, and also the fact that he was not the first player, nor the last, to find his way into the Test team through Clive Rice's cricket academy.

Amid the happiness there was heart-break. Jonty Rhodes was dropped and so too was Fanie de Villiers; two of the great stalwarts of post-isolation South African cricket were no longer there. Rhodes's plight was perhaps the greater because he had lost his place in India through injury and now, fit again, he could not regain it. In effect, he was overlooked in favour of Gibbs, and Fanie had to make way for the fit-again Pollock. Also, of the four spin-bowlers who toured India, three of them, Symcox, Crookes and Bojé, were dropped from a squad that included only Adams.

The trials and tribulations of the India tour were soon forgotten. From the outset it became apparent that Indian teams simply do not prosper abroad, a fact borne out by an away record of only one Test victory during their last 10 years of touring. On a hard and bouncy track at Kingsmead, the South Africans went into the first Test without a spinner, opting for an attack of Donald, Pollock, Klusener and McMillan. It worked wonders against batsmen who, grown used to the dead wickets back home, could not come to terms with the rising ball.

The match was over in three days and South Africa won by 328 runs. India were skittled for 100 in the first innings and 66 in the second, an all-time low for any team against South Africa. Azharuddin was dismissed for scores of 15 and 8.

Donald started the rot in the first over of the second innings when he took two wickets in successive balls to end with an incredible four for 14 in 11 overs and nine for 54 in the match. Pollock also signalled his return with five wickets in the match for just 43 runs.

Bacher's first Test had been a good one as the new No 3, the eighth batsman to be tried in this position since 1991. He had scores of 25 and 55 – a rare half-century by a South African No 3 – and with Hudson he put on 62 in the first innings and 111 in the second, going about his business with an excellent temperament and a solid technique. Hudson, almost axed from the team at Calcutta, was named Man of the Match for his knocks of 80 and 52.

'We've won this match, now we must start again,' Hansie told the boys afterwards. It was his eighth win as captain, one more than the record held by Jack Cheetham. Now he just needed to score some runs again. At Kingsmead, he had got 15 and 17.

Gibbs would have wanted nothing more than to play on his home ground of Newlands in the second Test but, sadly, he was dropped. With Bacher installed at No 3, he had batted at No 6 at Kingsmead and had gone out for a duck and 25.

Into the side now came Adams to provide the spin variation. He ended with five wickets in the match.

Even on a Newlands pitch that approximated to the one at Eden Gardens, it was the South African batsmen who finally dominated. A record aggregate crowd of 75 000 packed the Cape Town ground to watch a feast of runs that was characterised by five centuries over the New Year weekend of 1997.

At close of the first day South Africa were 280 for four. They also enjoyed their fair share of luck. After failing in both innings in the first Test, Kirsten was dropped on 0 and 10 before scoring 103, his fourth Test century. Again he found a willing partner in Cullinan who hit 77 and shared a record stand of 114 with Gazza for the third wicket. Hudson was out for 16 and Bacher for 25. That night Woolmer said, 'It would be nice to see something in excess of 400 on the board.' South Africa returned the next day to total 529 for seven declared.

In only his fourth Test, the remarkable Klusener hit three successive boundaries off Srinath to move from 90 to 102 not out in 100 balls, while McMillan, on his home ground, batted almost six hours for 103 not out for South Africa to complete the rare feat of three centuries in the same Test innings. The last time that happened was at Old Trafford in 1955 from the trio of Jackie McGlew, Paul Winslow and Johnny

Waite. Also, the unbroken eighth-wicket stand of 147 between Big Mac and Zulu broke a record that had stood since 1902. It was heady stuff, but there was more in store.

A capacity crowd of more than 18 000 watched as India hit rock bottom at 58 for five when Tendulkar was joined by Azharuddin, the old captain joining the new one. What followed was a partnership that will go down in Test cricket folklore. It yielded 222 runs in under three hours, a pulsating scoring rate of more than five runs to the over. It was stupendous stuff. President Mandela pitched up at lunchtime and for the hour after the interval the two Indian stars were in a class of their own. In the 14 overs bowled during that period they added 105 runs after Azharuddin had started the fun by pumping Klusener for three successive fours. In his third showstopper of the season against South Africa, Azhar again cast all caution to the wind as he lashed out lustily and often through the air. The South Africans seemed so overwhelmed by these pyrotechnics that they dropped several catches along the way and no bowler was spared. Klusener, on yet another rollercoaster ride, was thrashed for 60 runs in six overs and Donald went for 50 in seven.

Azharuddin's seventeenth Test century was scored in 96 balls. Tendulkar reached his eleventh hundred in 138. A partnership of glorious contrasting styles was characterised by Azhar hitting everything with absolute disdain before he was finally run out; and Tendulkar batting with grace and style before falling to an astonishing one-handed catch by Bacher on the square leg boundary. The Indian captain stood for a moment in sheer disbelief at the fielder's incredible effort, then he pulled a wry face and made his way back to the dressing room. At least his team had saved the follow-on but they still trailed by 170 runs on the first innings.

India struck back immediately, removing both Kirsten and Bacher for ducks in quick succession; but half-centuries from Hudson, Cullinan and McMillan, and an undefeated 40 from Pollock allowed Cronjé to declare on 256 for six.

The victory target was now an unrealistic 427, but India might still save the match if either Tendulkar or Azharuddin could play another big innings. Alas, they departed within nine balls of each other for scores of 9 and 2 and the innings predictably fell away to 144 all out. A great triumph for South Africa was also marked by a happy milestone for their faithful wicketkeeper. It came when Richardson got his first stumping in Test cricket.

With a record of over 100 catches already to his name, Swinger had been wondering for a long time whether a stumping would ever come his way. The magic moment finally arrived when Venkatesh Prasad was stranded after trying to hit Adams out of the ground. Gogga romped down the pitch to embrace his beaming pal; he had always promised Richardson that one day he would make it happen. At the age of 37 in his thirty-third Test, Swinger had finally become the complete wicket-keeper.

South Africa's 282-run victory meant the series was already won with one match left to play. Time to relax? Apparently not. On the eve of the Wanderers Test, Woolmer told cricket writers, 'We made a New Year's resolution as a team to try to become more consistent. We have to maximise our batting, maximise our bowling and maximise our fielding if we want to achieve our aim.'

Cronjé agreed with the coach but he gave the official line a slightly different emphasis, leaning more heavily towards the batting. 'Our bowlers have been consistent over the last five or six years, but I think from a batting point of view we should be looking to score bigger totals more regularly.' Everyone knew that Hansie was actually focusing on his own below-par batting, yet Woolmer immediately came to his rescue. 'I'm as concerned as Hansie about his lack of form. These things happen in cricket. Every now and again he shows glimpses of his true form and then unfortunately gets out. His runs are obviously important to the team but as a captain, a motivator and a leader he probably starts each game on 60 not out anyway.'

The night before the Test got underway, the UCBSA hosted a dinner in the Wanderers Long Room for the two teams. The guest speaker was the great Indian batsman Sunil Gavaskar, the first Test cricketer to score over 10 000 runs and, like Kirsten, a batsman who had once hit two centuries in a Test at Eden Gardens. In his speech that night, he said, 'During their recent tour of India, in the way they conducted themselves off the field with their outgoing and courteous demeanour, their constant willingness to mingle with the people and sign autographs without a word of complaint, Hansie Cronjé and his boys did more for the cause of South Africa than any politician or diplomat could ever do.'

The next day Cronjé would equal the South African record of 18 Test captaincies set by Herby Taylor in the Twenties. Also, his nine Test victories as captain were more than any of his predecessors.

AT NEWLANDS, GIBBS had been left out to accommodate Adams, and now there was speculation that an extra batter would be added to the team for the Wanderers. Gibbs was twelfth man at Newlands, but Kallis was in the frame after recent knocks of 94 and 79 for Western Province against Eastern Province.

What of Jonty? He was back playing for Natal and, on the eve of the announcement of the Test team, he scored a wonderful unbeaten 156 against Free State. Peter Pollock and his selectors took note of all this, but they still decided to stick with the same side that had triumphed in Cape Town.

Woolmer expressed great faith in Adams as the youngster prepared to play at the Wanderers for the first time in his career. 'He's only 20 years old, he's taken 27 wickets in six Test matches and I think he has an unbelievable future. He takes wickets with full tosses and long hops. He's a strike-bowler, a strike-spinner, and I think he'll be one of the greatest wrist-spinners of all time.'

At the Wanderers, Gogga bagged another four wickets in a drawn Test that India claimed as a moral victory. That South Africa survived was due largely to the intervention of rain at a critical stage on the final day and to the gutsy batting of Cullinan and Klusener.

The rain came at an oddly fortuitous time. At midday, with South Africa reeling on 76 for five in pursuit of 356, the biggest roar that was heard all day from the pensive crowd greeted a deafening thunderclap over the stadium. The heavens immediately opened and the players left the field. Even when the rain let up, umpires Cyril Mitchley, who was officiating in a record fifteenth Test for a South African, and Peter Willey declined to take the teams back because they considered conditions too dangerous for play. The Indian dressing room was in uproar. 'As far as I am concerned, this Test is India's,' fumed their manager, Sunil Dev. Three hours later, play resumed. South Africa still had 45 overs to survive.

Pollock and Richardson were soon out and, at 95 for seven, Klusener joined Cullinan. Together they put on a match-saving 127 – a record eighth-wicket stand in a Test at the Wanderers – with Cullinan showing incredible determination and character in scoring 122 not out, and Klusener also demonstrating great resilience in his 49. Donald then stuck around long enough to see off 16 balls without scoring to hold out on 228 for eight when stumps were drawn.

Cullinan's innings – his third Test century – had lasted for four hours and 20 minutes which, in the circumstances of a match that was fast slipping away from his team, was probably his most valuable innings yet. Hansie had earlier been run out for 6 by Cullinan, but he was so pleased with Daryll now that it was impossible not to forgive him.

The Indians could be well satisfied with their effort. They showed immense pride to come off two successive defeats and dominate a match in which the weather gods dealt them a cruel hand.

In their first innings of 410, there was none better than their No 3 batsman, Rahul Dravid, who scored his maiden Test century in six-and-a-half hours and was eventually dismissed by Cronjé after scoring 148 in nine hours of remarkable concentration and endurance. He found a willing partner in the entertaining left-hander Saurav Ganguly who scored 73 in their partnership of 145. Azharuddin began by blazing four boundaries but, in a duel that had been raging all summer, Klusener rejoiced by dismissing the dangerman for 18.

Dravid and Ganguly were by no means finished. Together again in the second innings, they put together another century partnership before Adams claimed both their wickets, Ganguly 60 and Dravid 81.

South Africa's first innings of 321 was due largely to Pollock. In hitting a Test-best 79, he went past his father's career-best of 75 not out scored against Australia at Newlands 30 years earlier. Peter Pollock watched proudly from the pavilion as his son reached the milestone. Ali Bacher also watched his nephew Adam scoring 13 and 23 on his home ground; on both occasions he was dismissed without offering a shot.

Cronjé's 43 in the first innings had given him some hope, but his happiest moments came with the ball when he dismissed his opposite number, Tendulkar, cheaply in both innings. Donald's six wickets in the match confirmed his fitness and form; to his burgeoning collection of awards was now added the Man of the Series accolade for his 20 wickets in the three Tests.

Amidst all the drama at the Wanderers came news of some significance from Port Elizabeth. Natal were playing there against Eastern Province and Jonty was in the thick of things again. This time he scored 108 and with Errol Stewart put together a third-wicket partnership of 235 to break a Natal record that had stood for 60 years. Rhodes's intention to re-establish his credentials were inescapable; and, what's more, his absence during the three Test matches had strangely coincided with a notable slump in the South African fielding effort.

THE SEEMINGLY INTERMINABLE cricket season still had a long way to run. A triangular one-day series against India and Zimbabwe would be followed by the main event – a home series against the menacing Australians.

For the triangular series, South Africa recalled Symcox and Kallis … and Jonty Rhodes.

A day after the squad was announced, Big Mac cried off with an ankle injury. He was replaced by Matthews who had been out in the cold for the past three months.

Rhodes wasted no time. In the opening game against India at Springbok Park he claimed Man of the Match for an unbeaten 57 in only 39 balls. On the occasion of his one-hundred-and-first limited-overs international on his home ground, Hansie joined Jonty in an unbroken match-winning partnership of 102 and was undefeated on 44. 'It was great to have him back again,' beamed the captain, 'you just can't keep a good man down!'

Against Zimbabwe at Centurion Park, the boys almost came unstuck after losing their first three wickets for seven runs, but a record 123-run stand featuring Cronjé's 87 not out and Cullinan's 73 carried them to an unlikely win. Matthews's return was tragically short-lived. After bowling one ball at Centurion, he broke down again with injury and was back on the sidelines, his international season over.

His place in the squad was awarded to Rudi Bryson, the in-form Northern Transvaal and former Eastern Province fast bowler who got the first of his three matches in a five-wicket victory over Zimbabwe at Newlands. Two catches went astray in his opening three overs, and for his solitary wicket of the series, he bowled Andy Waller with a delivery timed at 141 kilometres per hour.

At the Wanderers against Zimbabwe, it was Cronjé and Pollock who came to the rescue when things looked bleak. Back on his favourite cricket ground, Hansie hit 70 not out to claim the Man of the Match, and Polly, rekindling his Test match form, was out for 75.

In his first appearance of the season, Kallis claimed Man of the Match for his 79 at Port Elizabeth; a day later he hit 52 not out at East London and Kirsten scored 82 for the boys to continue their victory roll.

In the final at Kingsmead against India, Hansie lost the toss for the thirteenth time in 14 matches. Donald also lost his cool when Tendulkar and Dravid hit him for sixes in successive overs. In a tight, tense and rain-interrupted game, India fell 17 runs short of a reduced target after Kirsten's 51, Kallis's 49 and Rhodes's 41 had laid the foundation of South Africa's 278 for eight.

Cronjé was a happy man again. He was acclaimed Man of the Series, his boys had won seven limited-overs games in a row, and they had dispelled the notion that they were chokers when the chips were down. The latest victory had taken his record to 20 out of 23 since the World Cup defeat at Karachi and, since taking over from Wessels, he had now led South Africa to 43 wins in 57 starts.

Yes, the Aussies could come...

17

Search for the Hero

A T THE SYDNEY Cricket Ground, Mark Taylor tossed the ball to
Shane Warne. It was shortly before lunch on the final day of the
second Test and the West Indies' batsmen Carl Hooper and Shivnarine
Chanderpaul were growing in confidence. Their unbroken stand for the
fourth wicket stood on 117 and their team was on target for the 340 runs
needed for a victory that would level the series at one match each.
Warne had bowled earlier that morning but could make no inroads
against the 21-year-old Chanderpaul, a resolute, no-frills left-hander
who was 18 when he first played Test cricket. In the first innings, Warne
had dismissed him for 48 but the little Guyanan was now on 71 and
looking good.

Warne inspected the ring finger on his right hand, his famous,
heavily insured spinning finger. Then he squeezed the ball tightly
against it and rhythmically began his effortless, measured run-up. One,
two, three, four, five … rip! The leg break fizzed out of his hand, aimed
at a spot well outside the left-hander's off-stump. Chanderpaul made to
cut. He figured the ball would turn just right for him to send it racing to
the boundary backward of point. It pitched into the rough and spat
back venomously. The West Indian's bat was at the apex of the backlift.
Desperately, he tried to bring it down in time to close the gate.

It was too late. The leg break turned a full metre out of the worn
patch, scorched across the hapless batsman and knocked back his leg
stump. Up in the press box, the Aussie journalists were vividly
reminded of Mike Gatting's dismissal back in 1993. Had they just witnessed the second Ball from Hell?

From 152 for three, West Indies were bowled out for 215 and
Australia had won by 124 runs. It was a victory that skipper Taylor
credited to the ball that castled Chanderpaul, the leg break that told him
that Shane Warne was back in action. He ended with four wickets in the

innings and seven in the match. It was 3 December 1996. Two days earlier, South Africa had levelled the Test series at Eden Gardens.

In the preceding weeks and months, all the talk in Australian cricket circles had revolved around the wellbeing of their demon spinner. Back in May he had undergone delicate surgery to repair the torn ligaments in his spinning finger and was forced to miss a tour to Sri Lanka and India.

The initial prognosis after the operation was not good. There were fears he would never be the same bowler again and at one point he even admitted to thoughts of retirement.

By the start of the first Test against the West Indies at Brisbane in late November, Warne had played only two first-class matches in preparation. Even he did not know for sure whether he was ready for the big time again. In order to prepare himself psychologically, he ordered a compilation video tape of his best wicket-taking deliveries. He watched it over and over again, not through vanity but because he wanted to remind himself of what he was capable of doing. His fellow Australians were praying he would be all right.

In his 44 Tests so far, he had already taken 207 wickets, including no fewer than 10 'fifors'. To beat the West Indies they would surely need him to be firing again.

At the Gabba, he did little to allay the fears. His two wickets in each innings were not bad going – Australia, after all, had won the match by 123 runs – but most critics, including former skipper Allan Border, believed that the characteristic swerve, dip and rip of his deliveries had not been in evidence. By the time he came to Sydney for the second Test he was still undergoing daily treatment. The finger had to be iced and massaged each day and at night placed in a brace. He was also receiving ongoing physiotherapy on his right shoulder. The Sydney Test was the turning point.

He had been scared to give the ball a good rip but, mindful of the growing threat of the Hooper–Chanderpaul partnership, he knew he had to do it. As Chanderpaul departed so Warne's confidence came flooding back.

By the end of the five-match series his wicket tally was 22 and Australia had triumphed by three victories to two. Warne was back in business. The next stop would be South Africa.

'THE MYTHICAL WORLD CHAMPIONSHIP' was the way the newspapers and sponsors billed it. The players claimed it was just another Test series. One way or the other it was the Big One. Matthew Engel had done his calculations. Australia were the world's top team and South Africa were in second place. They were about to cross swords in a three-match series.

At one point during the summer of 1996/97, the two teams shared joint top spot with the West Indies on Engel's Wisden World Test Championship log. Then Hansie and the boys lost in India and Taylor's Aussies beat the West Indies. South Africa's subsequent home series win over the Indians gave them the edge over the West Indies ... but not over the Australians.

The newspapers loved it. No matter how hard the players tried to downplay the magnitude of the contest, journalists were happy to tell their readers that this three-match series would decide the Championship of the World. What's more, a lot of good, honest and sober folk were convinced that the South Africans were about to take over the mantle. And why not? They were playing at home, they had just beaten India by a handsome margin, the pitch at Ahmedabad was a distant memory and, in previous contests, they had shown themselves to be the equals at least of the Australians.

On the eve of the tour, Mike Procter, now back in the fold as a member of Peter Pollock's national selection panel, was asked how he felt the Test series would turn out.

Three years earlier he was the coach when South Africa under Kepler Wessels shared the honours with Border's Aussies in home and away series.

'I think we'll beat Australia for two reasons,' he ventured. 'The first is the quality of our fast bowling. I think we have the best fast bowlers in the world. And I also think that in Hansie Cronjé we have the best captain in the world.'

In also tipping South Africa, Jackie McGlew cited the captain's prowess. 'It is my humble opinion that Hansie Cronjé has blossomed into Test cricket's most astute captain. Whatever he does, he sets a sparkling example. In terms of inspiration, he is the genuine article.'

McGlew was very proud of Hansie. As the convener of the national schools selection committee back in 1987, he had chosen the Grey College boy as SA Schools captain. Since then he had watched his progress with growing admiration.

Cronjé was determined to keep his feet on the ground. He knew the Aussies well and he knew how tough they would be. Twin brothers Steve and Mark Waugh were among the world's top batsmen; tall paceman Glenn McGrath was named Man of the Series against the West Indies for his 26 wickets; vice-captain Ian Healy had scored a wicketkeeper's record 161 not out against the West Indies at Brisbane; Matthew Hayden had hit his maiden Test century in the recent fourth

Test at Adelaide; Greg Blewett boasted centuries in his first two Test matches against England; and the super-fit middle-order batsman Michael Bevan had suddenly emerged as a bowling spearhead whose sensational 10-wicket haul with his left-arm wrist spin at Adelaide had earned the Aussies an unassailable 3–1 series lead over the West Indies.

There were other young players, too, who could well pose a threat, among them the impressive top-order batsman Matthew Elliott and the fast bowler Jason Gillespie. And, of course, there was Warne. He was already on record as saying that he would like to bowl to Daryll Cullinan for a living.

If there was one question hanging over the Australians, it concerned their skipper. Although Taylor was acknowledged as one of the finest leaders in the international arena, his batting slump was causing growing concern. Fifteen Test innings had now passed without even a half-century.

The South African captain, too, had not been enjoying the best of batting form in five-day cricket, but he was faced with a far more daunting prospect as he approached the first Test at the Wanderers. It concerned the key figure of Brian McMillan who was out with an ankle injury; the man who had topped the batting averages with a formidable 98.66 in the recent series against India would have to miss his first home Test.

Jonty Rhodes was back to replace him at No 6, but the balance that Big Mac brought to the side through his excellent bowling would be sorely missed. In order to compensate for this, the selectors dropped an unlucky Adam Bacher and called up Jacques Kallis. He would bat at No 3 – the ninth player now to be used in this role – and be the backup bowler to Donald, Pollock, Klusener and Adams.

Cronjé elected to bat on a Wanderers pitch that showed signs of some grass and moisture under the surface. It was a good enough decision at the time, but McGrath soon had everyone wondering if it was the right one after all. In a wonderfully controlled opening spell, he removed Hudson for a four-ball 0, Kallis for 6 and Kirsten – dropped on 3 by Taylor off Gillespie – for 9. The big fast bowler's opening spell read 10-4-10-3 and after lunch he got Cullinan, too, for 27.

Cronjé had come to the crease in the pre-lunch session with his side in early trouble.

This was surely a time for guts, determination and character and, despite what the critics might be saying about his form, he was not going to give it away. It took him 33 balls to get off the mark and, as wickets continued to fall, he stuck gamely to his task. His best support came from Pollock who struck eight fours in a carefree 35 before he was dismissed by Bevan. Warne, meanwhile, was getting little assistance from the pitch in his fiftieth Test match. He had to wait until after tea for his first wicket when Mark Waugh held a stinging catch at short extra cover to remove Cronjé for 76. The skipper had batted stoically for three hours, but at 195 for eight the Aussies were still firmly in the driving seat.

For the opening day of the so-called 'World Championship' only 8 000 people had pitched up. If that was a surprising statistic, it was nothing like the 101 minutes that followed before close of play.

During that period the total advanced by 107 runs as Richardson, Donald and Adams, Nos 9, 10 and 11, seized the initiative in glorious fashion.

First Richardson and Donald put on 58 runs for the ninth wicket in 57 minutes; then Swinger and Gogga added 49 runs for the last wicket in 44 minutes of absolute mayhem. Richardson smashed 10 fours, and a six off Warne, in his undefeated 72, A.D. stroked four boundaries in his 21 and Adams, in his first meeting with the mighty Aussies, simply took the mickey out of them. The spiteful McGrath gave him a first-ball bouncer which hit him on the helmet, but Gogga recovered well enough to stick his tongue out later at the snarling bowler and pull a face at him.

In a near repeat of their match-winning partnership against England at Newlands the previous season, old man Swinger took the kid aside to give him some fatherly help and advice. 'When he was hit on the head, I straightened his helmet for him, satisfied myself that he was all right and told him to keep his eye on the ball and not just swing at everything. It was like playing with my little boy in the backyard at home.'

Adams was in the mood for some fun. Facing Warne for the first time, he played a perfect reverse sweep which even had Ian 'Bowled Shaney!' Healy in stitches behind the stumps. Warne was clearly not amused, but Adams endured for 33 deliveries before he was trapped leg before wicket by the leg-spinner for 15.

Fittingly, Richardson was unbeaten at the end. He had once been a top-order batsman but had slipped gradually down the order to accommodate the growing band of young all-rounders. At No 9 now, he had done another wonderful job for his captain.

After the top-order shambles, a total of 302 looked respectable enough, but no one could say how good it was until Australia had had their turn at bat.

They began their innings on the second morning. When bad light and rain ended play for the day seven minutes after tea, they were 191 for four. At close of play on the third day, Sunday, they were 479 for four.

AFTER SATURDAY'S RAIN, the Sunday of the Test match came in bright and sunny. A fair, but still disappointing crowd of some 15 000 was in the ground for what they hoped would be an exciting contest. At 191 for four there was still a chance of South Africa taking a first innings lead. At the crease were the overnight batsmen, Steve Waugh on 14 and Blewett on 3.

In their last Test innings against the West Indies at Perth a month earlier, both had been dismissed for ducks. Blewett, in fact, had been bowled first ball and Waugh had faced only six deliveries. A quick breakthrough now and Hansie and the boys would be on their way.

At lunch, Waugh had 48 and Blewett 46. The total now read 284 for four and the crowd was growing fidgety. After the interval, the batsmen walked out to resume the innings but, before the first ball could be bowled, Waugh sank to the ground suffering from cramps in both legs. There was a long delay while salt tablets and massage were administered before he hobbled painfully into the crease and continued. At tea, Waugh's score was 93 and Blewett had advanced his to 103, his third century in Test cricket and 12 runs short of his highest against England.

Australia were now 378 for four and the crowd, both absorbed and anguished, was still waiting for the breakthrough.

At stumps, Waugh had rolled on to 137, his twelfth century, and Blewett had prospered to 156; the total was now 479 for four. The crowd was stunned into silence. For the twelfth time in Test-match history – and the first time against South Africa – two men had batted throughout an entire day's play. Ironically, the last two batsmen to achieve this feat – Mark Taylor and Geoff Marsh against England at Trent Bridge in 1989 – were at the Wanderers. Marsh was now the team coach and Taylor the captain.

Also watching the cricket that Sunday was Conrad Hunte, the great former West Indian batsman who had batted through a whole day when Gary Sobers made his then world record 365 not out against Pakistan at Jamaica almost 40 years before. Hunte was now living in South Africa where he was a playing an inspirational role in the UCBSA's development programme.

Hunte and Sobers had added 357 runs in a day, Taylor and Marsh 310, and Waugh and Blewett 288. This might have been even higher had it not been for the number of runs that the South Africans cut off in the field. It was to their credit that they did not once hang their heads throughout a day of fruitless endeavour, a day when the ball beat the bat on fewer than 10 occasions. Donald and his fellow fast bowlers were made to look ordinary and it was left to Adams, in his eighth Test match, to emerge as the one bowler who looked capable of breaking through. It was a day when Gogga would know the true meaning of Test cricket and, as he trundled down over after over, he learnt some very valuable lessons.

Blewett, too, was learning fast at the knee of the ruthless Waugh. The 25-year-old stroke-playing batsman had scored a 99 against the West Indies at Adelaide five weeks earlier and now, whenever he looked in danger of losing concentration, his 31-year-old partner would walk down the pitch and give him words of advice.

'Don't take any risks and we'll grind them until they disintegrate,' was the constant message.

There was no better batsman in the world to exploit the situation. Waugh's powers of concentration were legendary and his ability to play every ball on its merits and eliminate high-risk shots was his strong suit. Six of his previous 11 Test centuries had reached scores of between 150 and 200 and on only five of those 11 occasions had he been dismissed.

He was the archetypal Australian cricketer, tough as nails and fiercely loyal to the cause; where other team-mates would easily go into the field wearing white floppy hats, he insisted on wearing the trademark baggy green cap that signified the immense pride he felt in playing for his country.

With Australia now 177 runs ahead and six wickets still in hand, the overnight debate raged over the Wanderers pitch. It was supposed to aid the South African pace bowlers but it had played right into the hands of the Aussie batsmen. Some officials were downright angry; this was hardly the way to set up a home series.

The new head groundsman, Andy Atkinson, whose previous boasts were that he had metamorphosed formerly dead wickets at Edgbaston in Birmingham and Newlands in Cape Town, predicted before the match that the pitch would provide an 'even contest between bat and ball'.

At this stage, the dominance of the bat was the only feature and there was no doubting that South Africa should have scored more than they did in the first innings. Amid the hue and cry, Transvaal officials protested that the pitch had been deteriorating for a long time and needed to be relaid. It had also been over-used in the winter months for a series of matches involving the Academy team and had not had enough time to recuperate.

The fourth day began much as the third had ended. Waugh and Blewett took their monumental stand to 385 – the highest by any team against South Africa – when Waugh gave Kallis his first Test wicket, caught by Richardson for 160. He had batted for eight hours and 24 minutes and still looked disappointed at getting out. The pair had been together from 2.42 pm on Saturday until 12.14 pm on Monday. It was the twelfth-biggest partnership in Test cricket and fell just 20 runs short of the 50-year-old world record fifth-wicket stand that Don Bradman and Sid Barnes set against England at Sydney.

At lunch on the fourth day, the total had climbed to 574 for five with Blewett not out 213. Still the innings continued until, 14 overs after the interval, Taylor finally called a halt on 628 for eight, the highest total in a match between the two countries. Blewett's 214 was the highest score in a Test at the Wanderers, beating Mike Atherton's 185 the previous season, and he took eight hours and 41 minutes to make it. In his previous Test innings at Perth he had been at the crease for only eight minutes when Curtly Ambrose rearranged his stumps.

South Africa trailed by a massive 326 runs when they began their second innings with one-and-a-half sessions remaining on the fourth day. As early as the tenth over Taylor tossed the ball to Warne. The leg-spinner had spent the luncheon interval in the nets where his personal bowling coach, Terry Jenner, helped him iron out a few problems with his action. More confident now, he bowled Kirsten for 8 and had his old adversary Cullinan, on the eve of his thirtieth birthday, caught by Healy for a duck.

Steve Waugh, meanwhile, was apparently not content with his earlier batting heroics. He scored a direct hit from a full 30 metres to run out Hudson for 31 and then, with only his third delivery, he induced Cronjé to chase a ball wide of his pads into the hands of Healy. Hansie was furious with himself. He had batted an hour for his 22 runs and now he was out to a shot that he knew was a hangover from too much limited-overs cricket. At close of play his team was 99 for four. The nightmare was not yet finished.

The next morning South Africa lost its last six wickets for 31 runs to the devastating spin-bowling of Warne and Bevan. Warne started the rot when he trapped Rhodes for 8 and knocked back Kallis's leg stump for a gutsy 39; then Bevan finished it off spectacularly by taking the last four wickets in the space of 12 balls while only three runs were added. It was all over before lunchtime. A pitch that had initially helped the Australian batsmen had now become a paradise for their spinners. Each took six wickets in the match.

Defeat by an innings and 196 runs was the biggest hiding for South Africa since readmission, the highly touted Wanderers showdown had been watched by fewer spectators than the previous month's Test against India, and a crestfallen Cronjé admitted that his team would have to improve 100 per cent if they hoped to get back into the series.

In announcing the crushing defeat, *The Star* headlined its report 'Taylor's Aussies are on another planet'. Johannesburg's major daily might have added that, for all the good of their home wicket, Hansie and the boys might have been better off playing on Mars.

There were no excuses from the South Africans. Hansie was gracious in defeat, acknowledging that the Australians had performed 'on another plane', while Woolmer mused, 'We just weren't there, something just wasn't right, an intangible thing ... it was like all the boys were trying, but nothing was happening here.'

To the growing chorus of criticism that now engulfed the team was added a new voice. Kepler Wessels was contacted by the Cape newspaper *Die Burger* for his comments. He told them that questions had to be raised about the team's leadership. 'Somebody must take the lead on the pitch,' he said, implying that control of the game plan might have been exercised elsewhere. Asked by the reporter if Cronjé's leadership was adequate, the former captain replied, 'Did it look like it?' What the team needed, he added, was 'big-hearted players' like Brian McMillan to withstand the pressure.

The good news at a pretty bleak time was that Big Mac had recovered from his ankle problem and was ready for the second Test at St George's Park.

TWENTY YEARS SEPARATED the ages of South Africa's current No 3 batsman and the man who, during the isolation years, was rated as one of the finest No 3s in the world. On the weekend between the first and second Tests, both Jacques Kallis and Peter Kirsten would grab the spotlight for very different reasons.

Playing for Western Province against Natal in a four-day match at Newlands, Kallis scored 138 and Herschelle Gibbs 163 not out in a record third-wicket partnership of 257. The big crowd cheered. At the same time in East London, the 41-year-old Kirsten was leading Border against the Australians. He was dismissed for 2 and the Aussies joined the 500 spectators in applauding him all the way back to the dressing room. It was his last innings in first-class cricket. In a career spanning 24 seasons, he had played 567 first-class matches and scored 22 635 runs. The brave little battler had finally quit.

IN PORT ELIZABETH, Ali Bacher took yet another call on his ever-present cell phone. This one was from President Mandela's personal assistant.

'Hey,' she said, 'we're disappointed.'

'I'm sorry, why's that?' he replied in alarm.

'We can't get through to Hansie. The president badly wants to talk with him.'

'Give me a few minutes, then please try again!'

In a flash Bacher was off to find his captain with an order to stand by his phone. It soon rang.

'Hello, this is Hansie Cronjé.'

'Hello, Hansie, I am calling to wish you and your team every success for the Test match...'

The next day it would start. The St George's Park pitch looked totally out of character. For a track that was traditionally a brown, batting wicket this one was unusually green. If this was the plan to blunt the menace of the Australian batsmen, what would it do for their less experienced counterparts?

Even though the South African selectors had opted for an extra batsman at the expense of Klusener, they had taken the radical step of dropping two of their most experienced players in Rhodes and Hudson. Hudders could feel a little aggrieved.

He had scored a century and three half-centuries in his seven Tests of the summer and, in the second innings at the Wanderers, he had stroked a fluent 31 before being run out. With 1 920 runs in 32 Tests, he was still his country's highest run-scorer since readmission. Cronjé's 1 906 from 34 Tests was the next best.

'I seem to have walked a tightrope throughout my career but still managed to keep a foot in,' recalls Hudson. 'My confidence does take a knock when I am dropped because I have an immense belief that I am good enough to play at this level.'

For Jonty – after just one Test back for scores of 22 and 8 – it was another big blow.

Reflecting on the axing of the two great stalwarts, Woolmer said, 'It's sad for me that I couldn't keep them in the side because, after all, that's my job.'

Gibbs was named as Jonty's middle-order replacement, Bacher was selected as Kirsten's new opening partner, and Kallis was retained in the No 3 slot.

On the wall of the South African dressing room, Woolmer had affixed a placard. It read, 'Search for the hero inside yourself.'

Taylor took one look at the pitch. He had no hesitation in asking South Africa to bat. His pacemen, McGrath and Gillespie, would relish the conditions. Kirsten out for 0, Kallis out for 0, Bacher 11, Cronjé 0 ... at 22 for four the boys were in dire straits on a wicket that elicited big bounce and lateral movement. It did not get much better. Cullinan was bowled by Gillespie for 34, Gibbs was bowled by Gillespie for 31 and Pollock was trapped lbw by Gillespie for 0. At 95 for seven, South Africa was staring defeat in the face.

The search for heroes was now critical. Gillespie had already taken his first 'fifor' in only his fourth Test and McGrath, battling with an ankle injury, had taken the other two wickets.

Big Mac and Swinger had been there before. They were together for the first time that dreadful rain-swept night in Sydney in March 1992 when the scoreboard suddenly flashed 'South Africa need 22 runs from 1 ball' and now, almost five years later to the day, they were there again. There was no threat from the weather, but there was a big threat from 'Dizzy' Gillespie and McGrath, from Shane Warne and a spiteful pitch.

For heroes, read McMillan and Richardson. Both were given lives, McMillan on 19 and Richardson on 25, but they rode their luck in a great show of guts, determination and character for almost two hours to add 85 gilt-edged runs for the eighth wicket. Warne eventually removed both of them, Richardson for 47 and McMillan for 55, but South Africa's all-out total on a treacherous, under-prepared wicket now stood at a respectable 209.

Wessels's contention that the South Africans were suffering from lack of leadership and steel was badly exposed on the second day. With superb discipline from the bowlers and fielders and strong leadership from their captain, the boys bowled out the Aussies for a paltry 108, their second-lowest total in Tests between the two countries.

A six-man attack shared the wickets – Pollock limped from the field with a torn hamstring after only two overs but he had already removed the openers Hayden and Taylor – and Donald's solitary wicket was scant reward for exceptionally straight, fast bowling in which he conceded only 18 runs in 23 overs. Cronjé's bowling was also exemplary and at one stage his figures read 10-6-7-2 after the important dismissals of Mark Waugh and Healy.

The skipper was also responsible for starting the collapse when he succeeded in parting Elliott and Steve Waugh as they were just beginning to get into their stride. His wonderful stop in the covers and quick return put the batsmen in two minds and resulted in Elliott being run out for 23 after a two-hour stay. Steve Waugh was out two runs later for 8 when Swinger obliged with the catch off his old mate Big Mac.

There was enough time left on the second afternoon for Kirsten and Bacher to produce South Africa's best start of the series. Buoyed by the 101-run first-innings lead, they set off confidently to rattle up 50 runs inside the first 15 overs, a scoring rate that was in sharp contrast to the Aussies' miserly one-and-a-half runs an over throughout their innings. At stumps, with 30 overs bowled, the new opening pair had taken the total to 83 without loss to give their side an overall lead of 184 runs with all the second-innings wickets intact. For the first time in seven days of Test cricket there were smiles in the South African dressing room.

AT THE START of the fateful third day, the music was playing. The team's backroom boys had put together a compilation audio tape that featured each player's favourite song. It was all inspirational stuff aimed at getting them into the right mood for the fray ... from Bryan Adams's 'Everything I Do, I Do It for You' to Pavarotti's rendition of 'Nessun Dorma', a piece favoured by Cullinan.

From 83 without loss, they collapsed to 168 all out. The trouble started early. Kirsten had added two runs to his overnight 41 when he played back instead of forward to Gillespie and was bowled. Bacher on 49 was eager to reach his second half-century in Test cricket but he became over-zealous. He hit the ball to mid-wicket and set off for the run. Kallis responded but Blewett was quicker. He cut off the ball brilliantly, turned sharply and scored a direct hit. Kallis out for 2. One run and three balls later, Bacher hooked at Gillespie and succeeded only in top-edging the ball into the hands of McGrath at fine leg. Out for 49. Apart from Cronjé's knock of 27 – during which he overtook the absent Hudson as the team's highest Test run-scorer – and Pollock's 17, no one else got into double figures.

After the glorious fight back of the previous day, this was purgatory. To make matters worse, umpire Srinivas Vekatraghavan, a former Indian spin-bowler, left a lot to be desired. On several occasions he failed to call no-balls, two of which resulted in the dismissals of Cullinan for 2 and Gibbs for 7.

It was also the day when Warne had the last laugh, which was to back-fire on him. He doubled over in mirth and directed great hoots of mocking laughter down the pitch in the direction of Adams who, in trying another elaborate reverse sweep, simply shovelled a dolly to Taylor at slip.

For his childish behaviour Warne was rounded on by sections of the Australian and South African media. It was even suggested that he should be fined under the Code of Conduct. Still, there were those who said that if Adams wanted to play the clown he should expect to be treated as one. What was no laughing matter was the fact that, in effect, South Africa had lost all 10 wickets for only 85 runs and squandered a golden opportunity to play the Aussies out of the match.

The third day was only half complete when the Australians began their second innings. They needed 270 runs to win, South Africa were without the injured Pollock, and McMillan was complaining of a bruised heel. By close of play, they had reached 145 for three with the Waugh brothers at the crease.

At the team meeting that night, a thoroughly disenchanted Cullinan drew attention to the inconsistent batting. Failure was following failure and he wanted to know what they were going to do about it. 'I want the six batters to stay,' said Woolmer, 'the rest can go.'

The six remained. Kirsten and Bacher, Kallis and Cullinan, Cronjé and Gibbs. Between them, they now had a grand total of 102 Tests compared to the 255 of their counterparts; the Waugh brothers alone had played 140 between them. The great chasm that separated the teams in terms of experience was all well and good, but what were the batsmen going to do about collapses that, in their most horrendous dimensions, were there for all to see: from 90 for three to 130 all out at the Wanderers and from 83 without loss to 168 all out at St George's Park? 'Back to basics,' advised Woolmer. 'Concentrate, bat through sessions, don't take risks, occupy the crease, set goals, be patient, build partnerships and, for heaven's sake, don't worry about your places in the side.' His words rang out; then all the batters had their say. They so badly wanted to do well.

The batsmen had had their chance. It was now up to the bowlers. Search for the hero ... remember guts, determination and character.

AUSTRALIA BEGAN THE day needing 125 runs with seven wickets in hand. The previous afternoon Taylor had been dismissed by McMillan for 13, Hayden was run out by Cronjé for 14 and Elliott was caught and bowled by Adams for 44. Now the Waugh twins walked out to resume the innings. This time it was Mark Waugh who took charge. In what he described as the best century he had scored in the circumstances, he batted for five-and-a-half hours to hit 116 for his eleventh Test hundred. Brother Steve was caught by Cronjé off Kallis for 18, Blewett was bowled by Adams for 7 and Mark was eventually bowled by Kallis after putting on 66 runs with Bevan for the sixth wicket. It was now 258 for six, just 12 runs needed, and an easy victory loomed.

Immediately, Bevan was caught by Cullinan off Cronjé for 24. It was now 258 for seven. Then Warne came and went, trapped lbw by Kallis for 3. It was 265 for eight. Healy was the only recognised batsman left. Five runs were still needed and South Africa's tail was up.

Amid unbearable tension Cronjé grasped the ball and bowled to Healy. A mighty swing caught the ball in the meat of the bat. Up it went in the direction of square leg, ever higher now, over the fence ... a six!

The beaming batsman turned on his heel in the direction of the dressing room and raised both arms in the air. Victory by two wickets, the series was theirs, and South Africa had been beaten at home for the first time since readmission. Taylor called it the greatest Test match he had played in.

Ali Bacher paid his customary visit to the dressing rooms, congratulating the victor, commiserating with the vanquished. The South African players sat in silence. The atmosphere was like a morgue. Cronjé blamed himself. The Healy six was playing backwards and forwards through his mind like a programmed video tape, a recurring nightmare.

HANSIE AND THE BOYS left Port Elizabeth immediately and went straight to Johannesburg to prepare for the third Test at Centurion Park later that week. The mood of gloom in the country dogged their footsteps, yet Woolmer was adamant that they would not allow it to affect them.

'The team ethic is such that it might be hurt but it won't be destroyed,' he said. 'We can pontificate about systems and batting orders until the cows come home, but the only thing we need right now is to take fire.'

The coach refused to be cowed by people suggesting that South Africa now faced the awful prospect of losing all three Tests, a miserable distinction that belonged to the South African team against England as far back as 1912. He told an enquiring sports journalist, 'If we lose 3–0, that is the reality, it's not the fear.'

Ali Bacher was soon in contact again. He wanted Woolmer and Cronjé to know that they weren't under any pressure from the Board. No one's job was on the line. There was no cause for panic. Woolmer appreciated the sentiment but doubted the reality. 'If a team continues to lose, heads normally roll,' he mused privately. 'I know what it's all about. I mean, I took this job because it's the ultimate pressure.'

Bacher remained philosophical. 'The mood of depression around the country is astonishing,' he confided, 'but it proves something very positive. It proves how much the nation cares for our cricket team.'

In the team, there was a feeling of irritation brought on by the easily forgotten fact that Australia had been bowled out for 108 in their first innings at St George's Park. Also, had the South Africans scored just 30 more runs in their second innings, the series would probably have been level when it arrived at Centurion Park.

There were those who said that Hudson and Rhodes would have made a difference, but they were still out in the cold. Of the defeated team, Gibbs and Adams were dropped and Klusener and Symcox recalled. At the age of 36, and after nine appearances abroad, Symmo would at last be playing his first Test match on home soil.

Also back into the team came Brett Schultz, named to replace the injured Pollock for his eighth Test and the first since his controversial breakdown on the first morning of the first match against England at Centurion the previous season.

His career had been dogged by recurring problems, but he had used the domestic season with his new team, Western Province, to shake off a reputation for being prone to injury. It was said that he carried too much weight, but he had been working hard on his fitness and was now down below the 100 kg which was reckoned to be just about right. It was no wonder the boys called him 'Bear'.

Schultz had made it easier for the selectors by capturing 36 first-class wickets in the domestic season, but his recall to the Test squad came as a pleasant surprise to him. 'My target this season was just to stay on the field!' he enthused.

In spite of Woolmer's protestations, the South Africans did indeed pontificate about the batting order and other permutations. The medical view was that McMillan's heel injury was not that serious but that he might not be able to bowl until later in the match. When the team was announced on the morning of the Test, Big Mac was pushed up the order to fill the No 3 batting slot – his previous experience in this position was against New Zealand at the Wanderers in November of 1994 – with Kallis returning to the middle-order.

The Centurion Park groundsman, Hilbert Smith, admitted there was a little more grass than usual on the pitch – 'it's only there to bind it together for five days' – and when Cronjé won the toss he sent the Aussies in to bat on a wicket that was still slightly damp. It would not have pleased the skipper when Donald and Schultz then proceeded to waste the new ball with some strangely wayward bowling that included several wides and no-balls. Perhaps they were trying too hard, but they just could not put it in the slot.

Schultz finally got it right with the second ball of the eighth over when he squeezed one between bat and pad to dismiss Hayden for 10. More than an hour later, Elliott top-edged an attempted hook off Donald and Schultz, not renowned for his fielding, took a fine running catch at long leg, only just keeping his feet in the playing area. 'I always knew I had a chance against Elliott,' said Donald that evening, 'because he's an obsessive hooker.' He had played the same shot at St George's Park but on that occasion the catch was put down by Adams.

At lunch, with Australia 64 for two, Cronjé chided his bowlers for their early inconsistency. 'Come on, guys, we need more discipline. Let's get stuck in!' When they returned for the middle session there was an immediate improvement in their line and length.

Donald quickly clean-bowled Mark Waugh for 5 with a thunderbolt and Klusener claimed the battling Taylor for 38 after an innings that lasted more than three hours.

Still, when tea was taken on 146 for four, there were fears creeping in that Cronjé might have made the wrong decision. Steve Waugh and Blewett were now beginning to dominate amid the lingering memories of their epic partnership at the Wanderers. Soon after the interval the 50-run partnership came up and 45 minutes after the break it was moving comfortably into the 70s...

Symcox, as always, was enjoying himself immensely, appealing for everything, sharing countless theories with anyone who would listen, and offering all sorts of dubious advice to the batsmen. Back into the attack now, he got a ball to kick and Blewett was out, caught at the wicket, for 37. The breakthrough had come at 4.22 pm, the partnership split on 80, and Australia were 190 for five.

Less than three overs later it was 197 for six, Steve Waugh unluckily given out on 67 by English umpire Mervyn Kitchen to a legside catch by Richardson which seemed to flick the pad. Schultz did not share the great batsman's anguish. He whooped with delight and pulled an ugly face. He was in his element.

Healy was soon in the thick of it, the object of a series of demonstrative appeals from Schultz. Healy was lucky not to be caught by Richardson and, in between, he survived two heated shouts for leg before wicket. This prompted Schultz to stick three fingers in the air, a gesture he later denied was any sign of disrespect to Kitchen but rather his way of telling Healy that it was a case of third time lucky.

The story is told of Schultz once beating the bat with four successive deliveries aimed outside the off-stump. His team-mates suggested he bowl the next ball at the stumps. 'What for?' he snarled. 'He'll probably miss a straight one, too!'

Inspired by the combative antics of Schultz and Symcox, the boys were now exerting real pressure. In the space of four deliveries the Bear trapped both Bevan and Warne, who was booed to and from the wicket by a crowd that was still upset at the way he had ridiculed Gogga Adams at Port Elizabeth.

Klusener and Donald then picked up the last two wickets in double-quick time with Healy becoming A.D.'s one-hundred-and-fiftieth Test victim, an illustrious milestone passed only by one other South African, Hugh Tayfield, many years before.

From 197 for five, Australia were all out for 227 with one ball remaining in the day. There was much for Hansie and the boys to reflect on. They had woken that morning to read, if they dared, Wessels's ongoing criticism of them. In a newspaper interview, he claimed South Africa's Test cricket had fallen completely flat, a fact hardly borne out by that day's play.

The ex-captain was also adamant that Cullinan should be promoted to No 3, McMillan to No 4 and that Cronjé was no longer worthy of the No 5 slot. He was not yet finished. As the second morning of the Test match dawned, Wessels again featured prominently in print. In a highly critical column in the *Saturday Star,* he lambasted Bacher for sacrificing both his own and Kallis's wickets in attempting to reach his fifty at St George's Park the previous week; he was critical of the selectors; and he felt it was 'most disturbing that Hansie Cronjé had said in his post-match comments (at Port Elizabeth) that he wasn't destroyed by the loss'.

Wessels should have known that Cronjé was not the type of leader to admit to feeling 'destroyed' and that he was now working on plans for a major revival at Centurion Park. His decision to field first had clearly paid off; now it was up to the batsmen to show some guts, determination and character.

In the view of Peter Roebuck, the former Somerset county captain and celebrated cricket journalist, Schultz and Symcox had already changed the mood in the South African team. In a delightful column in the *Sunday Times*, he wrote, 'South Africa had been playing mineral water cricket. Schultz was in the bar roaring with laughter; Symcox was playing a piano and singing lustily and to hell with misadventure. Inhibitions were removed by this pair.'

Symcox might have taken only one wicket but it was a crucial one to break a menacing stand; as for Schultz, 4 for 52 in 20 overs went a long way to re-establishing his credentials and he happily told reporters, 'My motto is that I never give up.'

Would the mood continue? Could the South African batters disprove Wessels's theory that they were lacking backbone?

At close of play on the second day, South Africa were 240 for three, a lead of 13 runs with seven wickets in hand. Adam Bacher, much maligned by the old captain, was 94 not out and had batted throughout the day, the very picture of a young man playing for his side. Kirsten was out for 16, giving Healy his three-hundredth Test dismissal behind the stumps; Cullinan was bowled for 47, but by McGrath, not Warne; and McMillan's 55 was the first time in 28 Tests that a South African No 3 had scored a half-century in the first innings. The last time this had happened was when Cronjé reached 71 at Melbourne in 1993.

Still, for all the significance of that achievement, it was Bacher and not McMillan who was the centre of attention when the media gathered around him at day's end. Had he read Wessels's comments about him in the morning newspaper? No, he had not. Had he thought about his score at any time during his 269-ball vigil? Again, no. 'I didn't think about numbers today and I won't tomorrow either. Six more runs might mean batting for another session.'

The one sadness was that Ali Bacher was not there to watch his nephew bat. The UCBSA official, recently appointed as chairman of the International Cricket Council's new development committee, had left the previous day to attend a series of meetings in Malaysia. 'Maybe he should go away more often!' joked Adam.

In his 12 Tests in the Sixties, Ali's highest score was 73. It was now up to his 23-year-old nephew, fresh-faced, boyish and very single-minded, to give a famous family their first Test match century.

The next morning, the Sunday of the Test, he faced a further 55 balls while advancing his score from 94 to 96. Sadly, he then failed to move his feet properly and was trapped in front by a superbly accurate McGrath. If Wessels thought that Bacher had been selfish at St George's Park, he could have had no case now. 'I guess I could have tried to push my score along,' explained Adam, 'but we had lost another couple of wickets and I thought to myself that we could find ourselves in trouble if I did anything foolish. I told myself to be patient and let it come. Of course, I was really disappointed when I got out short of the hundred.'

The day so far had claimed the night watchman Symcox for 16, Kallis for 2 and Bacher for 96. The scoreboard read 262 for six. Immediately it became 262 for seven when, in the same over as Bacher's dismissal, McGrath bowled Richardson for 47. The previous Sunday at Port Elizabeth, Bacher's demise had precipitated the horrific batting collapse. Now, amid the pedestrian scoring rate, it was difficult to dispel thoughts of another bloody Sunday.

Cronjé would not hear of it. He hit an undefeated 79 in 111 balls with his last 74 runs coming off 81 deliveries. A six off McGrath sailed over point and, with the help of an equally belligerent 30 from Klusener, 68 runs were added in 15 overs.

South Africa's first innings lead of 157 was to prove decisive. Inspired by their captain's innings, the bowlers responded magnificently. Donald in particular was in top form, ripping into the batsmen to take five for 36 for his eighth Test 'fifor' and his first against Australia.

The Aussies' disenchantment was best mirrored by Healy who was given out for 12 in almost identical fashion to Steve Waugh in the first innings. For voicing dissension at his unlucky dismissal and then hurling his bat at the top of the dressing room steps, he was handed a two-match suspension by match referee Raman Subba Row. Australia were all out for 185 – of which the Waugh brothers together contributed 102 – and South Africa knocked off the 29 runs needed for victory for the cheap loss of both openers.

The series might have been lost, but at least the boys and their coach had won back some pride in the face of the mounting criticism. This included Eddie Barlow's opinion that English coaching was stifling the creation of a distinctive South African style of play and that South Africans should be brought in to do the job.

Of all the criticism from former players, however, Wessels's outpourings had hurt the team the most. While the players accepted that much of what he had written was true, they would have preferred him to make his views heard in the privacy of the dressing room rather than in public. Cronjé was a great admirer of his former captain – at one stage he had hero-worshipped him – and he felt badly let down. But there was more to it than just the criticism. As part of his coming benefit season, Hansie planned to host a special dinner in Bloemfontein during the off-season for former Test captains. Wessels, naturally, had received an invitation … but he turned it down.

IN A SEASON of astonishing twists and turns, the shocks were far from over. Three days before the first Test at the Wanderers, Gary Kirsten was named with Allan Donald as South Africa's joint Cricketers of the Year. A month later he was dropped from the team for the seven-match series of limited-overs internationals. Just 12 months earlier he had been South Africa's top gun at the World Cup and Sharjah, averaging over 80 in the two tournaments and emerging as one of the world's outstanding, record-breaking one-day batsmen. Now, after scoring only 82 runs in six Test innings for an average of under 14, he was reckoned to be suffering from fatigue and mental burnout.

'It's a shock and it hurts,' wrote Kirsten in his weekly column for the *Cape Times*. 'Even when things were going brilliantly for me, I always reminded people that one has to remain humble in this game because it has a habit of biting you when you least expect it. Still, you can only play yourself back into form … you can't take a pill.'

Kirsten could also point out that, in the nine Tests of the summer of 1996/97, his aggregate of 541 runs was second only to Cullinan's 683. Cold statistics, however, did not mean a thing right now. The selectors felt he was in need of a rest and his departure would leave the iron man Cronjé as the only player to retain his place in the side for every match in two successive seasons. For all the talk about his lack of form going into the Aussie Test series, the South African captain had come out of it as the team's leading run-scorer with 204 for a top average of 51.

Bacher's average of 40.25 in his two Tests against the Australians meant that Hudson would still not get a look in, but Jonty was back because one-day cricket was not the same without him. Among others called-up to a 14-man squad were Gibbs, Rudi Bryson and Derek Crookes, while Kirsten's top-order slot was awarded to the only new-comer Louis Koen. The Eastern Province batsman's elevation was not unexpected. For the past two seasons he had been the leading run-scorer in domestic cricket and earlier in the season had hit 105 for South Africa A in a one-dayer against India at Pietermaritzburg. Koen was now one of the boys, but he was not exactly a youngster. The Port Elizabeth policeman turned 30 shortly after his selection.

Fanie de Villiers was sorely disappointed. Earlier in the season he had suffered a freak injury when he cut the fingers of his bowling hand in a lawnmower accident, but he was playing again for Northern Transvaal and had openly expressed the hope of an international recall. It was not to be. Of the squad that Cronjé had first led as the caretaker captain in Australia three seasons before, nine players were no longer there – De Villiers, Hudson, Gary and Peter Kirsten, Dave Callaghan, Craig Matthews, Dave Rundle, Richard Snell and Errol Stewart.

The closest De Villiers came to the action was when he parachuted on to the field at a packed Wanderers stadium during the dinner break of the fifth day/night match – part of a fund-raising drive to help deaf children. Fanie's little daughter suffered from this affliction but had happily been helped by an expensive and intricate operation. The big-hearted fast bowler wanted other kids to benefit. He was that kind of guy.

The in-form Koen was surprisingly left out of the team for the opening one-dayer at East London – a six-wicket victory for South Africa that extended their limited-overs wins to 35 in their last 41 starts – but he finally got his big chance two days later on his home ground at St George's Park. It was the moment he had been dreaming of for so many years and the local morning newspaper was right behind him. 'Koen's chance to show he's a belter,' it proclaimed. He was out first ball, caught at slip. 'It kicked on me at the last minute,' he said later. 'That's the way it goes, that's cricket for you.'

With Mark Waugh hitting his tenth one-day century at the scene of his marvellous Test match hundred, and brother Steve adding a run-a-ball 50, the Aussies were able to square things up at one victory apiece. Their one-day record was now an unimpressive seven wins in 20 starts since their loss to Sri Lanka in the World Cup final, but the current series looked to be heading for a ding-dong battle.

At jam-packed Newlands, South Africa went into a 2–1 lead thanks mainly to Rhodes's glorious knock of 83 not out in 76 balls, but in the next match on his home ground of Kingsmead he was out for 1. It was left to Pollock, his fellow-Natalian, to steal the show with his four for 33 and 41 not out. In the end his efforts were not enough and the Aussies drew level again at two wins each.

On a cold April night at the Wanderers, the boys watched breathlessly as Fanie performed his pinpoint parachute descent … and then they slumped to 31 for three in pursuit of 259. Half-centuries by Cullinan and Kallis later restored the balance and, going into the last over, 14 runs were needed for victory with Cronjé on strike and looking good. Healy, who had taken over the Australian captaincy from the injured and out-of-form Taylor, tossed the ball to Warne. Where any other team would call on their best seam bowler to take care of the vital final over, Australia were content to award it to their ace spinner. Unperturbed by the baying and booing crowd, the man South Africans love to hate conceded only six runs off the last six balls. The Aussies were back in the lead at 3–2 with two matches remaining.

TWO DAYS LATER, at 10 o'clock on a Thursday morning, Hansie Cronjé decided to go back to bed for an hour. He was suffering from an acute case of laryngitis and was on medication. His 40 not out at the Wanderers had been scored in biting cold and it had taken its toll. Had Hansie been a schoolboy that Thursday morning, his mother would have sent a sick note to his teacher. Instead, a man in charge of his country's cricket fortunes took himself off to class. The examination would be severe. His team were trailing 3–2 against the rampant Australians and he knew they had to win this sixth match to stay alive. The seventh and last would be Bloemfontein and he owed it to them to bring the decider. He wanted the schoolboys in the scoreboard to feel the thrill and excitement that he had once experienced.

At noon on that Thursday, and still feeling fatigued after his nap, Cronjé left for Centurion Park where the sixth day/night game would soon begin. He won the toss, promoted himself to his old No 3 slot in the batting order and hit 80 runs in 81 balls. There had been fewer better innings from the South African captain.

That cold autumn's night at Centurion Park the braai fires threw a blanket of smoke across the excited oval while, out in the middle, it was steam that rose from the sweat-drenched bodies of the toiling players. There was no lack of guts, determination and character from Hansie and the boys as they powered themselves to 284 for seven with Cronjé run out for 80 and Cullinan nabbed by Warne for 89.

Then, in a rude departure from the script for the wildly expectant crowd, Michael Bevan and Steve Waugh bludgeoned a record 189-run partnership for the fourth wicket. Heavy dew added to the South Africans' woes as the wet ball went out of shape and slipped maddeningly out of the fingers of the bowlers and fielders.

The floodlighting at Centurion was also not good – a handicap the Aussie batsmen had to overcome – but the wet ball and the slippery field combined to be a far more difficult burden for the fielding team to carry. This was not to take anything away from a batting performance that was as good as anything seen on this ground; Bevan, in fact, might never score a better century than his 103 in 95 balls. It was the highest winning score for a team batting second in a limited-overs international in South Africa. The Australians had again turned the tables.

TWO DAYS LATER, Cronjé got out of bed early. In his beloved Bloemfontein, he was about to lead his boys on to his home ground in quest of nothing more rewarding than a 3–4 consolation prize.

Klusener opened the batting and hit 92 from 118 balls, Cronjé scored 69 from 63, Cullinan 57 from 39 – his fourth half-century of the series – and South Africa's total of 310 for six was the first time they had passed 300 in a one-day game against Australia.

One of Cronjé's three massive sixes powered into the packed crowd on Springbok Park's grass embankment. It hit a six-year-old boy in the chest and broke his breastbone. Little Corné van Zyl was rushed to hospital. His parents Esté and Corrie were at his side. Corrie van Zyl had played enough cricket matches with Hansie Cronjé to know how hard he could hit the ball.

The next day young Corné was in high spirits again. The son of the Free State coach proudly showed his friends his X-rays. He would always know how hard Hansie could hit a six.

The South African players, meanwhile, were again reminded how well Steve Waugh could stroke a cricket ball. At Bloemfontein, he was awarded his country's captaincy for the first time – for such a proud Aussie there could no greater honour – and in typical fashion he lashed 91 runs from 79 balls. His team-mates, however, had little to offer and they were bowled out for 201. They didn't much care. They had beaten South Africa at home in both the Test and limited-overs series.

The World Championship was over.

Epilogue

Full Circle

THE FINE LINE between success and failure was no better illustrated than in the summer of 1996/97. During the course of the season, both South Africa and Australia played nine Test matches. The Aussies won five and lost four and South Africa won four, lost four and drew one. That's how close it was in the overall context, but the big difference, of course, was that Australia won two Test series and South Africa lost two. Cricket takes no prisoners.

There was much to reflect on as the players went their separate ways. Hansie Cronjé took up an offer to play briefly in Ireland; Jacques Kallis accepted a contract to play for Middlesex; Allan Donald was back again at Warwickshire as their principal fast bowler; and Lance Klusener went to Madras to attend Dennis Lillee's famous school for fast bowlers.

At the Clontarf Cricket Club in Dublin, Hansie helped Ireland make cricket history by beating a top English county for the first time. On his début for his adopted country, he hit an undefeated 94 and took three wickets for 38 against an outclassed Middlesex team that included Mike Gatting.

Cronjé had come a long way all right. He had once bet Kepler Wessels that he would better the old captain's 18 wickets in one-day internationals. His tally was now 69. In 36 Test matches he had scored 2 012 runs and had taken 17 wickets. He had also become one of the most astute captains in the game, and South Africa's most successful.

Kallis was maturing fast. Three half-centuries in the limited-overs series against Australia were followed by another on his one-day début for Middlesex. Then, in the space of three first-class matches in the 1997

County Championship, he hit 121 against Northamptonshire and 96 against Glamorgan. More was to follow. A match-winning century and four wickets against Gloucestershire carried Middlesex into the NatWest Trophy semi-finals.

Donald was also back in business. After a five-week layoff because of a back injury, he took a stunning five for 8 to send Surrey crashing from 87 for one to 144 all out. He was white lightning for sure, but the man who had bagged 155 wickets in his 33 Test matches and 147 in 67 one-day internationals was now thinking about his future. 'If I make it that far,' said A.D., 'I'll give serious thought about retiring from international cricket after the World Cup in 1999.' His dream was still to break Hugh Tayfield's South African record of 170 Test wickets.

The United Cricket Board, meanwhile, released details of its new contracts. Andrew Hudson and Jonty Rhodes were downgraded to B Category players and Shaun Pollock — Man of the Series in the one-dayers against Australia — joined the A Category. Fanie de Villiers and Craig Matthews were given short-term retainers that would expire in December 1997 if they had not proved themselves again by then. The irrepressible Fanie was as determined as always to play international cricket again. He set out in the winter months on a rigorous workout programme that he promised would make him a fitter and stronger bowler than ever before.

Peter Pollock and his national selectors named the Test squad for the tour to Pakistan. Rhodes was back in place of Herschelle Gibbs who was thought likely to join the tour at a later stage for the one-dayers. Kallis, Klusener, Adam Bacher and Brett Schultz were all included ... and so too was the evergreen Pat Symcox. As for Paul Adams, with 35 wickets in just nine Test matches, well, he was an automatic choice. So, too, was Brian McMillan whose Test career batting average of 42.55 was the best of all the boys. He would go as a specialist batsman rather than an all-rounder and would probably be awarded the No 3 batting berth.

AT MADRAS IN 1997, Pakistani opener Saeed Anwar hit 194 in a one-day international against India to break Viv Richards's world-record 189 not out. Mohammad Azharuddin was dropped from the Indian team because of poor form. Sachin Tendulkar warned him that he would have to start making runs more consistently if he hoped to get back again. After the 1997 off-season, and without proving the form that his captain wanted, Azhar was a surprise choice for India's tour of Sri Lanka. He immediately scored successive centuries in both Tests, but the great Indian batsman was still upstaged. In the first match, Sanath Jayasuriya scored 340 — the fourth-highest Test score after Brian

Lara's 375, Gary Sobers's 365 not out and Len Hutton's 364 – and shared a world record stand of 576 with Roshan Mahanama in a mammoth total of 952. In the second match, Jayasuriya was dismissed on 199. The left-handed Sri Lankan opener proved once and for all that he was not just a one-day wonder who had averaged two runs a ball at the 1996 World Cup.

Back home, Dave Rundle retired from first-class cricket after 14 seasons, Derek Crookes switched provinces from Natal to Transvaal, Rudi Steyn left Natal for Northerns[†] and Eddie Barlow accepted a new coaching position with Griqualand West. Louis Vorster had returned home to Potchefstroom after a long time away and was now the North West province's top batsman. He finished the 1996/97 season with a limited-overs batting average of 98.00.

Graham Ford was appointed director of Natal's cricket academy. In his place as the new Natal coach came Frans Cronjé.

Hansie's benefit season got underway in July 1997 with his dinner for former captains in Bloemfontein. Jackie McGlew was ill and could not attend. He sent a glowing tribute. Kepler Wessels was notably absent. He turned down the invitation for 'business reasons'.

THE CRITICS CONTINUED to call for the head of Mark Taylor but he retained the captaincy for Australia's Ashes tour of England. In the first Test at Edgbaston, he hit a century. It had taken him 18 months and 22 Test innings to get past 50.

Mike Atherton received the OBE shortly before becoming England's longest-serving Test captain against Australia in the second Test at Lord's. In his forty-second match as captain, he was dismissed for 1 by Glenn McGrath whose eight for 38 was a new record for an Ashes series. England were all out for 77, their lowest score at Lord's this century. In the third Test at Old Trafford, Shane Warne took nine wickets in a big victory to overtake Richie Benaud's 248 wickets and become the most prolific leg-spinner in Test match history. In the same match, Steve Waugh became the first batsman in 50 years to score two centuries in an Ashes Test. For the second year in a row he was named the Coopers & Lybrand International Cricketer of the Year.

The English critics rounded on Atherton when Australia retained the Ashes in convincing style for a record fifth successive time. The England captain said he had no intention of quitting.

Matthew Engel released his latest Wisden Test Championship rankings. Australia were placed first, West Indies second, South Africa

[†] formerly Northern Transvaal

third, India fourth and Pakistan fifth. Ali Bacher released the itinerary for the tour of Australia in the summer ahead. He called it 'the ultimate challenge'.

In Birmingham, to help Warwickshire qualify for the NatWest Trophy final, Donald took five Sussex wickets . He then hurried off to London where he and Tina caught the evening flight to Johannesburg. The following night, 15 August, dressed in his distinctive green and gold striped Protea blazer, he received a gold-class Presidential Sports Award at a glittering banquet in Pretoria. When all the award-winners posed for a group photograph, President Mandela called A.D. from the back row and invited him to sit next to him in the front. Mandela threw his arm around the proud cricketer.

The gold-class award is the highest honour that can be bestowed on a South African sportsman or woman. Generally, it is awarded to current stars, but this time the President insisted that some heroes of yesteryear also be honoured. Among them was Basil D'Oliveira. He was unable to make the trip from Warwickshire but, in a taped video interview screened at the gala event, he told Mandela, 'I am with you in spirit.'

IN THE EARLY spring of 1997, Ewie Cronjé paid his customary daily visit to the University Oval in Bloemfontein. He wanted to make sure that everything was in place for the season that was about to unfold.

The University Oval was Ewie's first love; even the emergence of Springbok Park down the road could not steal his heart away. There would be some gripping cricket matches on the Oval in the summer ahead, and the old cricketer wanted it to be in immaculate condition for those special days and for those special young men with so much to prove. The people would turn up to watch because they had grown to love this great game, and at Springbok Park there would always be more than the 9 000 spectators he had once dreamed of. He chuckled quietly now as he imagined himself running round the ground without his clothes.

Alone with his thoughts, he walked across the Oval and on to the square where he stood for a while, gazing into space. He thought of a time just 10 years before when two young men, W.J. Cronjé and J.N. Rhodes, had strode proudly on to this ground to open the innings on the biggest day of their young lives. He could still see them now, anxious and determined, taking their guard, while the wild, young fast bowler, A.A. Donald, carefully measured out his run.

He thought of them now, far away in another country, men and not boys on another important mission, carrying the hopes and fears of

South African cricket on their ample shoulders. 'Remember,' he thought, 'guts, determination and character!'

Then he turned slowly and shook his head; just 10 years ago ... and it felt like a lifetime.

Bibliography

Arlott, John: *John Arlott's Book of Cricketers* (Sphere Books, London 1982)

Bryden, Colin: *The Return of the Prodigal* (Jonathan Ball, Johannesburg 1992)

Cook, Jimmy, with Cleary, Frederick: *The Jimmy Cook Story* (Pelham Books, Johannesburg 1993)

Crowley, Brian: *Cricket Exiles* (Don Nelson, Cape Town 1983)

D'Oliveira, Basil: *Time to Declare* (Macmillan, London 1980)

Graveney, Tom: *The Heart of Cricket* (Arthur Barker Ltd, London 1983)

Griffiths, Edward: *Kepler, The Biography* (Pelham Books, Johannesburg 1994)

Harte, Chris, and Hadfield, Warwick: *Cricket Rebels* (QB Books, Sydney 1985)

Lamb, Allan: *My Autobiography* (Collins Willow, London 1996)

Woolmer, Bob: *Bob Woolmer, Pirate and Rebel?* (Arthur Barker Ltd, London 1984)